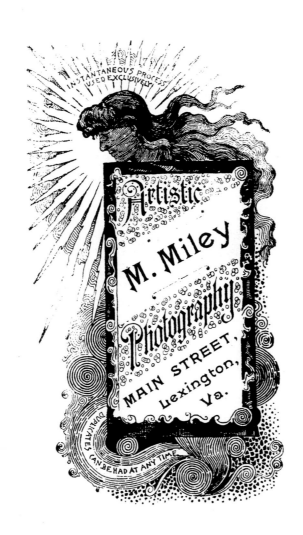

INSTANTANEOUS PROCESS USED EXCLUSIVELY.

Artistic

M. Miley

Photography

MAIN STREET, Lexington, Va.

DUPLICATES CAN BE HAD AT ANY TIME

Rockbridge County Artists & Artisans

BARBARA CRAWFORD

ROYSTER LYLE, JR.

Sponsored by Southern Virginia College

UNIVERSITY PRESS OF VIRGINIA

CHARLOTTESVILLE AND LONDON

For Katie and Mario

UNIVERSITY PRESS OF VIRGINIA
Copyright © 1995 Barbara Crawford and Royster Lyle, Jr.
First published 1995

LIBRARY OF CONGRESS CATALOGING-IN-PUBLICATION DATA
Crawford, Barbara.
Rockbridge County artists & artisans / Barbara Crawford, Royster Lyle, Jr.
p.   cm.
Includes bibliographical references and index.
ISBN 0-8139-1638-0
1. Decorative arts—Virginia—Rockbridge County. I. Lyle,
Royster, 1933-   . II. Title.
NK835.V82R633   1995
680′.9755′852—dc20   95-18877
                                                                        CIP

Printed in the United States of America

PRODUCED BY ARCHETYPE PRESS, INC., WASHINGTON, D.C.
Project Director: Diane Maddex
Managing Editor: Gretchen Smith Mui
Editor: Cynthia Ware
Editorial Assistant: Kristi Flis
Indexer: Teresa Purvis Barry
Art Director: Marc Alain Meadows

Page 1: MICHAEL MILEY ADVERTISEMENT. *Known as "General Lee's photographer,"
Miley had a prolific career in Lexington from 1866 to 1918.* Frontispiece: HOUSE
MOUNTAIN, *by John Johnson, 1871. An Ohioan, Johnson painted Rockbridge County's
second most famous natural landmark—after Natural Bridge—during a visit. The
painting now hangs in the Governor's Mansion. Oil on canvas, 31 x 55 inches.* Pages
6–7: PEACEABLE KINGDOM OF THE BRANCH, *by Edward Hicks, c. 1825–30. Hicks, a
Quaker minister from Pennsylvania, produced more than sixty variations on this
biblical theme. A half dozen of them show Rockbridge County's Natural Bridge. Here,
William Penn appears below the arch, negotiating his historic peace treaty. Oil on
canvas, 32¼ x 37¾ inches.*

Contents

THE PEACEABLE KING

lamb & the leopard shall

The wolf also shall dwell with the

together; and a little ch

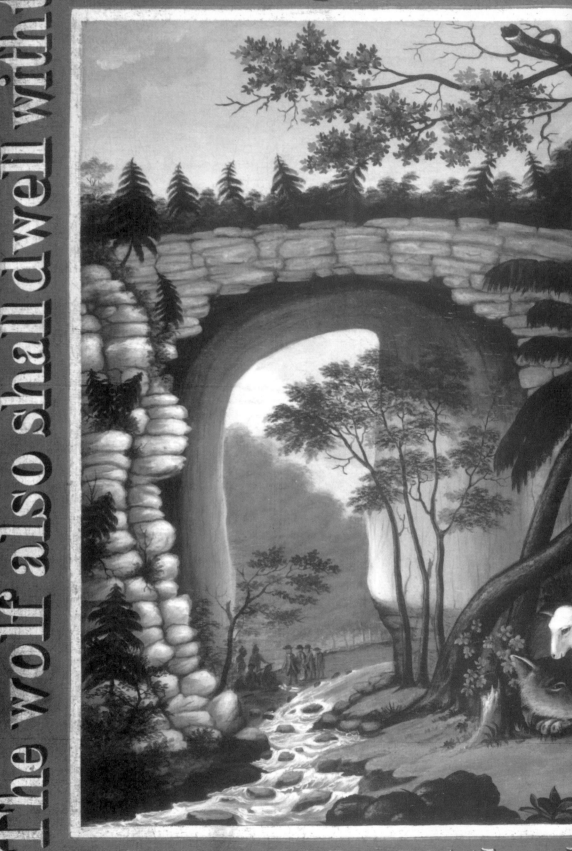

OM OF THE BRANCH.

e down with the kid; & the calf & the young lion & the fatling

ld shall lead them.

Foreword

This scene is worth a voyage across the Atlantic.

—THOMAS JEFFERSON, NOTES ON THE STATE OF VIRGINIA, 1785

In *Notes on the State of Virginia* Jefferson describes the confluence of the "Patowmac" and Shenandoah Rivers, just before they pass through "the Blue ridge of mountains" at Harpers Ferry, West Virginia. It is "one of the most stupendous scenes in nature," he writes, elaborately describing a view of it from "a very high point of land." As he tells the "Foreigner of Distinction" to whom these notes are addressed, it merits an arduous trip over the seas, "Yet here, as in the neighborhood of the natural bridge, are people who have passed their lives within half a dozen miles, and have never been to survey these monuments of a war between rivers and mountains, which must have shaken the earth itself to its center."

Leaving aside the snobbishness of such a remark, was it true? Certainly it is human nature to take for granted anything that is too accessible, and a form of local chauvinism might even take the opposite position, that that which distinguished foreigners would travel oceans to see cannot compare with other wonders familiar to the local inhabitants. At the time Jefferson began to write these notes, 1781, the lives of the first European settlers of the Great Valley of Virginia, predominantly Scotch-Irish and German, were far from settled. The Valley had only begun to be peopled with Europeans in the previous fifty years. Those who had lived there since 1750, the year in which this study of artists and artisans in Rockbridge County, Virginia, begins, had survived the guerrilla raids and counterraids that formed the local action in the Seven

Years' War (approximately 1756–63), the fears brought about in 1763 by Pontiac's war (about which Francis Parkman wrote, "The country was filled with the wildest dismay. The people of Virginia betook themselves to their forts for refuge"), and of course the American Revolution itself, in which the Scotch-Irish proved especially valuable fighters. Even if the Valley had remained as peaceful as it was before 1750 (and would be again from the end of the Revolution until the Civil War), the ordinary people within and beyond Jefferson's six-mile limit of Natural Bridge would not have had his freedom to wander about and speculate on ancient geological forces. They would have been establishing their homes, farms, businesses, towns, churches, and schools with an industriousness and amplitude of talent at which we can only wonder, and out of a nothingness that is unimaginable to the contemporary mind.

In *The Scotch-Irish: A Social History* (1961), James G. Leyburn writes, "The deficiencies of this people in aesthetics were, as critics of the young Republic saw them, representative of American deficiencies in general. . . . In the earliest days of settlement there was no time for the artistic, even if the motive had been present. . . . Not only were there no Scotch-Irish artists; there was little even that could be called folk art, if the term implies work that has the extra touch of originality and verve that transforms a useful object into a pleasant bit of handicraft." Rockbridge and Augusta Counties claim to be the most heavily populated by Scotch-Irish of any in the country, Leyburn writes. In this assiduous study of artists and artisans in Rockbridge, and to some extent in nearby Augusta, from 1750 to 1900, Barbara Crawford and Royster Lyle, Jr., undermine Leyburn's assertions. The sheer volume and variety of fine arts and home crafts, from painting and photography to quilt- and furniture-making, suggest a people more dedicated to beauty than the pinched reputation of the Scotch-Irish would suggest.

Why would this be? Although Leyburn argues that no motive was present in the everyday struggle of their lives, he lays the framework for a motive elsewhere in his book, in a chapter entitled "Frontier Society," where he describes the evolution of the class system among the Ulster citizens who settled the Great Valley. As with other European settlers in America, the Scotch-Irish held at first to a European system of class, in which one was, for the most part, born to the class in which one would remain. But particularly with the Scotch-Irish, who were an especially peripatetic people, these distinctions of birth began to break down quickly, and accomplishments became the standard. Leyburn lists a number of practical ways of establishing oneself in the social order: by having cleared a field of stumps, for instance, or possessing a cabin "most ambitiously laid out and most neatly constructed." Leyburn says that "an almost absolute clue to status" was whether the women of a house were required to work in the fields or not. Thus he walks right up to the edge of the accomplishments documented in this book. As society became more civilized, the standards by which people distinguished themselves from their neighbors became more civilized, too. Furniture would go beyond the utilitarian; those women freed of field work would create ever more elaborate and distinctive quilts; the neatly constructed cabin would become the decorated house. The successful farmer's well-educated son would take up the painter's brush. So there was no shortage of motive.

But was Rockbridge County especially rich in artists and artisans? That is a question beyond the scope of Crawford and Lyle's study. The breadth of their book suggests that it was, but how many other counties can claim an artistic history this carefully documented? My guess is that it was richer than most, in part because it continues to be richer than most. But why would this be so? I can't help thinking of those people to whom Jefferson alludes, who were impervious to the world-famous natural wonder in their neighborhood—perhaps because all of Rockbridge County, to the present day, is rich in natural beauty, from Goshen Pass down the Maury River as it meanders through it, and from House Mountain to the Blue Ridge. Does natural beauty inspire a love of beauty in those who live with it each day? Or are those with an artistic sensibility drawn to it in Rockbridge County just as they are in Taos or Venice, Provincetown or Provence?

ROBERT SPENCER WILSON
LITERARY EDITOR, CIVILIZATION MAGAZINE

Preface

Augusta, the largest County perhaps in Virginia, is almost wholly settled by [Presbyterians] ... tho they are Dissenters, they have as much Religion as renders them good Subjects, and entitles them to an extensive Toleration. They are Products of their Land and their Manufactures are different from those of the Virginians, they strengthen the colony in its weakest Parts, and furnish us with those Necessaries and Accommodations which our eternal Piddlings about the Sovereign Weed Tobacco hinders us from providing in sufficient Plenty.

—Virginia Gazette (Williamsburg), March 5, 1752

Contemporary historians are increasingly showing that an awareness of the habits and objects of everyday life is as important to the understanding of our past as the recording of political events and military battles. In the past few years a number of area studies have examined artists and artisans and their "manufactures" of everyday life produced in the eighteenth and nineteenth centuries. Because of the role and influence of the Museum of Early Southern Decorative Arts (MESDA), Colonial Williamsburg, and several other institutions, a good portion of these studies pertains to the South.

The idea for this book goes back several decades, when a number of local residents began to suspect that the early artistic heritage of Virginia's Rockbridge County (once part of Augusta County) was especially rich and that the story of its artists and artisans and their products deserved recording before the documentation and the artifacts were lost.

Of special concern was the accelerated speed at which locally produced furniture, paintings, pottery, long rifles, and quilts were leaving the county. Until about twenty years ago, at family auctions at county houses up one of the mountain hollows almost every-

thing was bought by members of the immediate or extended family or by the neighbors down the road. These days, however, when there is a sale for an old county family, the vans along the road belong to dealers from Pennsylvania to South Carolina. Furniture and other household items that have been in these houses for four or five generations are leaving for good.

This scattering of cultural artifacts is not limited to Rockbridge by any means, but the unique history and geography of the county make these potential losses even more regrettable than usual, or so it seemed to us. John Bivins, Jr., in *The Furniture of Coastal North Carolina, 1700–1820,* laments that so "much early North Carolina furniture has been purchased by out-of-state antique dealers, especially in the 1930s and 1940s. . . . " But he takes heart that some "treasures still remain for the student to locate and record [to] provide ample reason for research to continue."

With the encouragement of many colleagues in Rockbridge and friends elsewhere, we decided to document and catalogue what we could find before it was too late. Our goal was to present this information in a publication as a first step in understanding the work of eighteenth- and nineteenth-century artists and artisans who were born and reared in Rockbridge County or who came here to practice their artistry for a short period because of the special attraction of the area. Our survey has produced a mountain of new material on what was painted, sculpted, woven, cast, thrown, molded, and constructed in the county over a 150-year span, 1750 to 1900, all of it available to other researchers interested in the

House Mountain, *opposite, by Michael Miley, c. 1885. The Lexington photographer found endless inspiration in the*

Rockbridge countryside. His view also captured the Maury River and the railroad tracks to Buena Vista. Glass negative, 7½ x 9½ inches.

history of the county and the Valley. *Rockbridge County Artists and Artisans* is only a beginning in understanding the creative legacy of the long list of creative people who were active in Rockbridge County from the mid-eighteenth century and throughout the nineteenth century. But the first step has been taken.

During the 1970s a number of local activities brought attention to architecture and the decorative arts in Lexington and Rockbridge County. Research by the staff of the Stonewall Jackson House during its restoration shed new light on the nature of household furnishings in mid-nineteenth-century Lexington. The publication of *The Architecture of Historic Lexington* in 1977 brought attention to the town's architectural heritage. Pamela H. Simpson, professor of art history at Washington and Lee University, produced a series of exhibitions on the decorative arts in Lexington beginning in January 1977 with a show at Washington and Lee, American Sculpture in Lexington. This was followed by exhibitions on Architectural Drawings in Lexington, 1779–1926, which opened January 1978, and Michael Miley, American Photographer and Pioneer in Color, which was held in the winter of 1980. These shows were followed by an exhibition of paintings and engravings of Natural Bridge entitled So Beautiful An Arch: Images of the Natural Bridge: 1787–1890. This show brought to Lexington the Frederic Edwin Church painting of Natural Bridge (see page 17), as well as Edward Hicks's *Peaceable Kingdom* (see pages 6–7) from the Reynolda House collection in Winston-Salem. This last exhibition included some forty-four images of Natural Bridge—engravings, drawings, and paintings. Professor Simpson's pioneering efforts were of inestimable value to our study and this book.

Our first effort was to see what was available to be studied. Field representatives of MESDA had spent some months in the Rockbridge area in the early 1980s, and their research and photographs were made available to us. MESDA's files were invaluable, as were the help and encouragement from MESDA's staff as we began to develop a direction for the project. An early objective was to build on the MESDA field work and its extensive database of artisans. MESDA's period of collecting stops at about the 1820s. We wanted to document the midcentury period particularly, as well as the post–Civil War period.

We already had a general idea of what we were getting into and what we might find. For instance, we were already familiar with the "Junkin sideboard" at the Jackson House, which bore the name "Lexington" and the signature "James Barrett" on the bottom of one of the drawers. We had seen several tall case clocks with "Jacob Bear, Lexington, Va." painted on the dials, but we knew nothing of Barrett or Bear. We also knew of several pieces of furniture that had descended in the families of county cabinetmakers John W. Miley and Gardner Paxton Hutton; and we had found one stoneware crock stamped "Rockbridge." We had talked to

friends who were earnest collectors and who had already developed opinions on what we might find if we carried through on such a study. The prevailing view was that we were not going to find any "fine furniture" or any highly decorated items that could be attributed to Rockbridge.

We appealed to the Virginia Foundation for the Humanities and Public Policy in Charlottesville to fund a countywide survey project to be called "A Search for Early Rockbridge County Artisans: A New Awareness of Local Material Culture." The project would be sponsored by Southern Virginia College and would involve—we hoped—many people throughout the area whose interests we had already identified. Essential to the Virginia Foundation–sponsored projects are public programs. Working with the foundation and other local groups, as well as with an advisory group of specialists, a program of public meetings and research was outlined.

The first public program took place in October 1984, at the R. E. Lee Episcopal Church, with approximately one hundred twenty persons attending. Speakers included Laura Stearns of the Southern Virginia faculty, who gave a description of the eighteenth-century settlement in the Rockbridge-Augusta area; Barbara Luck, curator of the Abby Aldrich Rockefeller Folk Art Museum, who spoke on new research on textiles in the Valley; H. E. Comstock, Winchester writer and collector, on furniture in the Valley; and Ann McCleary, folklorist and architectural historian, on Augusta County folk painting. Many of those attending this first program brought items that were known or suspected to have been made locally, such as quilts, chairs, pottery, and paintings. The visiting lecturers discussed the various articles with those attending. A card was made on each item and a snapshot taken for the record. Afterwards, the items that appeared to be of importance to the project were further examined, researched, and better photographs made.

During the second public meeting in March 1985, an all-day gathering held at Southern Virginia's Chandler Hall, more time was allotted for discussion. The first talk was by William G. Moore, director of the Greensboro Historical Museum, who spoke on folk art pieces in his museum's collection. He was followed by John McDaniel, professor of archeology at Washington and Lee, who discussed artifacts (some suspected of being locally made) found at the Liberty Hall dig and other several recent excavations in the Lexington area; Linda Hyatt, a Rockbridge writer, on the works of John Joseph Hileman, a local nineteenth-century marble cutter and tombstone maker; Wallace C. Gusler, curator of furniture and firearms at Colonial Williamsburg, on pre-Revolutionary long rifles in Augusta County (including part of Rockbridge); Pamela H. Simpson, professor of art history at Washington and Lee, on architectural details and decoration in Rockbridge houses; and Sue H. Stephenson, a Lynchburg writer, on basketry of the Appalachian Mountains. Artifacts brought by participants were placed on tables in front of the room so that the visiting speakers could discuss the objects during their talks. The items were examined by the lecturers, and comments were made to the audience. All who participated in the two meetings were pleasantly surprised at the enthusiasm of those who attended and the interest in learning more about locally made pieces.

These two meetings were followed by a Quilt Day held at the Lexington Presbyterian Church in July 1985. Invitations were issued in the newspaper and otherwise "to bring your quilt to the church and have it photographed" and discussed by several local experts.

As a result of these several meetings and the attendant publicity, we received many requests from county residents who wanted to learn more about their own furniture, paintings, and other items that might have been produced locally. By invitation, we began visiting households in the county—and we found an even stronger interest in and involvement with local artifacts and a real pride in what was made here. On several occasions, when we were invited to county houses to look at furniture, crocks, quilts, and such items, the parents or grandparents collected up the children and made them follow us around the house as we examined things, looking for local stylistic features of the furniture or possible signatures. We were often asked to explain to the children why a table or clock was "important."

During the several years following our two public meetings, we were asked to give slide talks to more than sixty professional, historical, fraternal, and civic organizations in Rockbridge and the surrounding counties. This was another key to our finding furniture and other items needed for our survey. Early on we established a policy that we would keep all of our findings of household belongings in strictest confidence.

While we were searching for objects around the county, we were also examining the obvious available historical sources. For instance, every Lexington newspaper published in the nineteenth century was read carefully, and any mention of craftsmanship was recorded. Every estate inventory in Rockbridge County's will books from 1778 to 1850 was copied and the key items entered into our database, as were the vital statistics of the artisans from the county's censuses, marriage records, and birth and death registers. Early county censuses list only heads of households and give some indication of the ages of family members and other occupants of the residence. Beginning in 1850 the censuses give occupations, as well as locations in the county, together with places of birth (the state, if other than Virginia, or the foreign county). This was especially helpful, because if we suspected a county resident

of being, for example, a cabinetmaker in 1820–30 or 1840, the 1850 census generally confirmed this.

We were also fortunate to find journals of two Lexington blacksmiths in the 1790s, John Walker and Adolphus Weir; a chairmaker, Samuel Runkle Smith; and two cabinetmakers, Andrew Wallace Varner and Milton H. Key, all of whom were active before the Civil War. We also found a plow manufacturer's journal from the 1870s.

Our field work in the county was both frustrating and rewarding, as would be expected. We were not surprised that only a few pieces of furniture were signed. John Bivins reported that in his study of *The Furniture in Coastal North Carolina,* he found fewer than twenty signed or labeled pieces among the hundreds that he examined.

We were fortunate that the Lexington cabinetmaker John Smith signed his name inside two tall case clocks and in one chest. One of these clocks was found in Charlotte, North Carolina, one in Roanoke, and a chest in Michigan. Another chest by the Lexington cabinetmaker James Barrett was located in Richmond. We spent many hours looking under tables, desks, and chairs hoping to find the names of local artisans, such as Mathew Kahle, Andrew Varner, Milton Key, Samuel Smith, and others but with little luck. We did find two early Windsor chairs that had "A. Shields" branded on the bottom of the seats, but we could not find an A. Shields who was a local chairmaker. Shields, it turns out, was the owner of Eagle Tavern, an active establishment on Lexington's Main Street in the 1790s, and Shields must have marked his barroom chairs for what would seem to be obvious reasons.

Other pieces that we examined bore signatures. The clockmaker Thomas Whiteside engraved his name on the brass dial of one of his tall case clocks, which we found in Austin, Texas, after a long paper trail. And we found several long rifles by William Zollman and John Clemmer, who engraved their names on the tops of the barrels.

After we had photographed, measured, and catalogued hundreds of objects, both in Rockbridge and elsewhere, we had to decide which groups of artifacts should be published. We settled on those categories that are generally considered decorative arts—weaving, quilting, and other textiles; furniture; tall case clocks; rifles; ironwork; and pottery—and the fine arts, including painting, sculpture and photography. We omitted stonemasons, carpenters, and several dozen other crafts that were included in the survey and divided the book's scope into seven key chapters. Silversmiths are mentioned in both the chapters on clocks and rifles.

Four hundred artisans who were active in the county and in the fields covered in the book are described in the final chapter. Their profiles document a creative legacy begun more than two hundred fifty years ago—one that continues to enrich us all today.

Rockbridge County Artists & Artisans

NATURAL BRIDGE, *page 17, by Frederic Edwin Church, 1852. One of the Hudson River School painters and a student of Thomas Cole, Church was by midcentury America's best-known landscape painter. In 1851 he visited Virginia and completed this view of the bridge the following year. Oil on canvas, 28 x 23 inches.*

FAIRFIELD, *right, by Bessie Anderson Patton, c. 1900. This large landscape, one of several painted by Anderson that remain in the family, shows Fairfield in the late nineteenth century. According to family tradition, Patton took up painting as a "feminine art," as did many of the young ladies of the day. Oil on canvas, 30 x 55 inches.*

CANAL ALONG THE JAMES, *above,*
by William Matthew Prior, c. 1845.
Various modes of transportation
are depicted on the James River,
which runs through the southern
part of Rockbridge County. Oil on
canvas, 20¼ x 27⅛ inches.

SEAL OF VIRGINIA, *opposite, by*
Lewis P. Clover, Jr., 1853. The
Episcopal minister painted this
emblem for the Virginia Military
Institute Society of Cadets.
Oil on canvas, 24½ x 29½ inches.

GEORGE WASHINGTON, *right, by Mathew Kahle, 1842–44. This carved statue was created for the octagonal cupola at Washington College. Painted poplar, 98 inches.*

GENERAL THOMAS JONATHAN ("STONEWALL") JACKSON, *far right, by Edward Virginius Valentine, 1888–91. This memorial statue marks Jackson's grave in Lexington. Bronze, 96 inches.*

ROBERT E. LEE, *bottom, by Valentine, 1875. Considered Valentine's masterpiece, this recumbent statue depicts Lee in his military uniform asleep on his camp bed. Marble, 100½ inches.*

VIRGINIA MOURNING HER DEAD, *opposite, by Moses Ezekiel, 1869– 1903. The plaster model was not cast until 1900. Bronze, 84 inches.*

REID-WHITE HOUSE, *above,*
by Samuel McDowell Reid, 1821.
Reid, a Lexington lawyer and
landowner, prepared the designs
for his classical-style house on
Lee Avenue. Ink and watercolor
on paper, 10½ x 14 inches.

CORNER SHELF, *opposite, by*
Charles P. Augustus Brady,
1875–1900. Brady carved a basket-
weave pattern on the surfaces,
as well as figurative scenes on the
door panels and legs. Walnut,
76½ x 39½ x 27½ inches.

JACKSON HOUSE KITCHEN, *opposite. While living in Lexington, from 1851 to 1861, and teaching at Virginia Military Institute, Stonewall Jackson purchased the only house he would ever own. The 1978–79 restoration and furnishing of the house was based primarily on Jackson's probate inventory. Today the collection includes numerous pieces that were locally made and similar to those listed.*

ROCKBRIDGE STONEWARE, *bottom, c. 1830–60. Jugs and jars were often enhanced with incised designs or brushed cobalt. 10¼ x 7¼ inches, 15¼ x 9½ inches, 12 x 7 inches, and 15 x 8¾ inches.*

ROCKBRIDGE JUG, *right, attributed to John Morgan, Bustleburg-Firebaugh pottery, c. 1830–50. This one-gallon, ovoid jug is stamped "Rockbridge" and decorated with a brushed cobalt floral motif. 12 x 7 inches.*

TIN PIE SAFE, *details, top and above. Attributed to Mathew Kahle, this pie safe from the McDowell family depicts George Washington on the front doors. Panels on both sides give the family name and date. Pine, 84 x 40 inches.*

BIRTH RECORD, *opposite, by Martha A. Conner, 1883. Conner, of Collierstown, signed and dated this birth record for Jenetta Bell Goodbar and Mary Grace Goodbar. Watercolor and ink on paper, 13½ x 19½ inches.*

ROCKBRIDGE COUNTY ARTISTS & ARTISANS / IN PHOTOGRAPHS

NEEDLEWORK PICTURE, *top,*
by Mary Abney, c. 1802. This piece
depicts Palemon and Lavinia, a
romanticized version of the Old
Testament story of Boaz and Ruth.
A similar piece is shown on page 75.
17 x 15¾ inches.

SAMPLER, *bottom,* by Martha
("Patsy") Moore, 1804. Moore
(1791–1851) inscribed this sampler
"Patsy Moore worked this in the 14th
year of her age 1804." She included
the names of her parents and eight
siblings. 11 x 11 inches.

CRAZY QUILT THROW, *opposite,* by
Blanche Gilkerson Wright, 1890.
The late-nineteenth-century "crazy
quilt" was a popular Victorian piece,
most often used a parlor "throw."
Traditionally it was constructed of
scraps with sentimental associations—wedding dresses, baby clothes,
award ribbons—and finished with
elaborate embroidery that decorated
and secured the patches. Crazy quilts
represented a variety of fabrics, from
silks and velvets to wools and plaids,
and a range of skills. Descended
in the family. Mixed fabrics, 65½ x
91½ inches.

Lexington the County Seat of Rockbridge County, ten mile from the natural bridge, the —Vhouse mountain is in Side of the town, and washington College, and A military School. Cadets. Lexington is one of the most beautiful seats in virginia, A pleasant appearance.

The Residence of David Laird, seven mile from Lexington On the banks of the north fork of James river, and A chain of the Blue Ridge, John Miller Carpenter is worken here 1849.

Introduction

This day John McDowell of Orange County in Virginia have agreed with Benjamin Borden of the same place that he . . . would go now with his family and his father and his Brothers and make four Settlements in the said Bordens land . . . and that he . . . would cut a good Road for Horses loaded with common Luggage and blaze the Trees all the way plain. . . .

—BENJAMIN BORDEN, SEPTEMBER 19, 1737[1]

In 1716 Alexander Spotswood, then governor of Virginia, rode out to the wildernesses of the western part of his state to explore "the Great Valley of Virginia," as it soon came to be called, although it is more widely known today as the Shenandoah Valley. Shielded by the Blue Ridge Mountains on the east and the Alleghenies on the west, the Valley spreads southward the long distance from Winchester in Frederick County to Fincastle in Botetourt. Occasionally the mountains stretch and turn, encroaching on the plain, but never very far and always slowly and gradually. Arms of the Shenandoah and Potomac Rivers in the north, and those of the James and its various branches in the south, flow quietly along low, curving banks, leaving the land well watered.

Attracted by the valley's fertile soil and by the inducements of Virginia's governors, settlers began arriving in the 1730s. To encourage the population of part of the area that was to become Rockbridge County, Governor William Gooch gave Benjamin

Borden a half million acres with the stipulation that one hundred families would have to settle within the tract before he could receive title. The grant required a settler to build a log cabin to establish a claim. By 1738 there were almost ninety-two cabins, built mainly by Presbyterian Scotch-Irish who had migrated from Pennsylvania, bypassing the German settlements in the northern part of the Valley, in Shenandoah and Rockingham Counties. Many of the settlers had arrived from Northern Ireland earlier and were continuing their search for better conditions after spending a generation or so in Pennsylvania. Many followed friends or kin.

The settlers in the Rockbridge area quickly established churches and schools. They also built mills and introduced a variety of industries, often grounding them, no doubt, on commercial principles they had known in Ulster. In any case, skilled artisans made an early appearance in the area. Migration into the Valley increased greatly in the last quarter of the century. With extensive wagon transportation, which had been developed in the 1760s to support a thriving hemp industry, and improved trade routes, the upper area was set for rapid and successful economic growth. Historian Laura Stearns notes that these early settlers were "arriving in such impressive numbers within so short a time, and having no competition or influence from any permanently entrenched neighbors, [they] carved a frontier society singularly stamped with Scotch-Irish manners, morals, and beliefs."[2]

LEXINGTON, THE COUNTY SEAT OF ROCKBRIDGE COUNTY *and* THE RESIDENCE OF DAVID LAIRD, *opposite, by Lewis Miller, c. 1853. During a visit to Rockbridge County, probably in 1853, Miller made detailed sketches of*

Lexington and the house of David Laird. Miller's notes indicate that his brother John Miller (1790– 1866), who was a carpenter, worked at Laird's house in 1849. Watercolor and ink, 12½ x 7⁹⁄₁₆.

33

As the population of the Valley grew, so did the need for closer and more conveniently located county seats. Petitions from the residents of what is now the Rockbridge area complained about the distance they had to travel to go to court in Fincastle or Staunton, the seats, respectively, of Botetourt and Augusta Counties. (Each of these towns is located more than thirty miles from Lexington.) The state legislature answered the problem by introducing legislation in October 1777 to form a new county, carved from the southern part of Augusta and the northern part of Botetourt. At the time both counties counted their lands all the way west to the Mississippi River, although they had little knowledge, let alone control, of those vast regions.

The new county was called Rockbridge after a landmark that was famous not only in Virginia but also throughout America and Europe. The "Rocky Bridge" of Virginia ranked, along with Niagara Falls of New York, as one of the two natural wonders of the New World. Visits to both sites were often undertaken with the air of religious pilgrimages. Thomas Jefferson, who acquired the bridge by patent from George III in 1774, describes it in his 1785 *Notes on the State of Virginia* as the "most sublime of nature's work" and noted that it was "impossible for the emotions, arising from the sublime, to be felt beyond what they are here . . ."[3] The extent to which the bridge had entered the national consciousness is indicated by the fact that in 1851 Herman Melville could assume his reference to it in *Moby Dick* would be understood. More vivid testimony is in the iconic power of his allusion, as he compares the arching body of the whale to the bridge's negative space: " . . . [and] Moby Dick moved on, still withholding from sight the full terrors of his submerged trunk, entirely hiding the wretched hideousness of his jaw. But soon the fore part of him slowly rose from the water; for an instant his whole marbleized body formed a high arch, like Virginia's Natural Bridge, and warningly waving his bannered flukes in the air, the grand god revealed himself, sounded, and went out of sight."[4]

Despite the landmark's remoteness, or perhaps because of it, many made pilgrimages to the bridge, artists and writers among them. The earliest known images of the bridge were produced by the French Baron de Turpin, who visited Virginia in 1782 with the Marquis de Chastellux. De Turpin was followed by other European and American artists such as Frederic Church, John Johnson, and Edward Beyer.[5]

The site selected for the new county seat, Lexington, was not the well-established community surrounding the Timber Ridge Church but farmland belonging to Isaac Campbell several miles to the southwest. The ten acres that Campbell donated offered the benefit of several strong springs. It would also place the county seat on the Great Wagon Road where it forded the North (later Maury) River. This road served the major trade and migration route from the north to the south and the west. In naming the town the legislature chose to commemorate the battle for independence that took place three years earlier at Lexington, Massachusetts. The legislature stipulated the size of the town— 1,300 feet long and 900 feet wide. Surveyor James McDowell named some of its streets—Jefferson, Washington, Henry, and Nelson—after Virginians who had played a role in the Revolution. The attention to history remains apparent. More than 85 of the town's 120 street names refer to local people or events.[6]

In 1790, little more than a decade after Lexington's founding, an Englishman, Thomas Chapman, described the village as having "about fifty houses, most of which are built of logs and boards."[7] The wooden structures were soon joined by those of brick and stone. A brick courthouse had already been completed in 1786. It was followed a few years later by the large and impressive brick residence of William Alexander, which survives today. At the edge of town, on Mulberry Hill, rose a three-story stone structure that served as the classroom and dormitory for Liberty Hall Academy. In 1796 the school changed its name to Washington Academy in honor of its most famous benefactor, George Washington. Also in 1796 fire destroyed Lexington's "elegant brick courthouse," its "two principal taverns," and as many as sixty houses along with their furnishings. According to one report the property saved was "inconsiderable, and many of the unfortunate sufferers [were] reduced to a state really pitiable."[8] Historians can be grateful that the court records survived, even while they regret the loss of so much material culture. After the fire, much of the town was rebuilt in brick and stone.

The eighteenth- and early-nineteenth-century inhabitants, known as Presbyterian "Dissenters," were "Ulstermen [whose] loyalty was to the culture and traditions they had known in Ulster. They hoped to recreate familiar patterns in the wilderness, including strong patriarchal families, [and] adherence without question to Presbyterian discipline."[9] At first they built mainly log houses. Before the formation of Lexington and the county, most of the significant buildings were churches, and with no towns as focal points, these took their names from the physical features of their various areas—Timber Ridge, Falling Springs. The earliest of those that survive, Timber Ridge (1755), served many of the area's prominent settlers—the Houstons, Davidsons, Paxtons, Mackeys, and Whitesides. Most of these families built substantial homes of stone or brick.

Nineteenth-century Rockbridge continued to grow and prosper. In addition to agricultural and industrial activities, Lexington saw the establishment of the Ann Smith Female Academy in 1808, the expansion of Washington College (which later became Washington and Lee University), and the formation of a state arsenal that was to evolve into the Virginia Military Institute, opening its doors to cadets in 1839. New transportation routes brought an increase in trade and travel. John Jordan built roads that connected Lexington with both the east and west. Rockbridge was also connected to the east by the bateau canal system, later by the North River Canal system, and eventually by the railroad. By 1827, according to William Darby's *Universal Gazetteer,* Lexington had "about 120 houses, many of them handsomely built of brick, a court-house, jail, and Presbyterian and Methodist houses of worship; the pop. is 766, and the town is improving."[10] The other county communities, Brownsburg, Fairfield, and Springfield, were experiencing similar growth. The building industry boomed in the 1820s and again in the 1850s, when many of the county's large and significant houses were built.

Throughout the first half of the century the Scotch-Irish heritage was dominant in Rockbridge. James G. Leyburn put it this way in *The Scotch-Irish: A Social History* (1962): "Two counties in the Valley of Virginia, Augusta and Rockbridge, claim to be the most Scotch-Irish counties in the present United States. It is said that they have more Presbyterians within their borders than the members of all other denominations together."[11] John S. Wise, who came to Lexington as a cadet in the 1860s, paints a vivid picture of the "tribe of Presbyterians" in his *End of an Era:*

Their impress was upon everything in the place. The blue limestone streets looked hard. The red brick houses, with severe stone trimmings and plain white pillars and finishing, were still and formal. The grim portals of the Presbyterian church looked cold as a dog's nose. The cedar hedges in the yards, trimmed hard and close along straight brick pathways, were as unsentimental as mathematics.[12]

It has long been the view that the Scotch-Irish were not as creative or as artistic as their German neighbors to the north. Most scholars, including Leyburn, supported the view. The objects surveyed for this study suggest another view of the county. But although eighteenth- and nineteenth-century Rockbridge was predominantly Scotch-Irish, outside influences and contacts were numerous. The artistic outlook was, in fact, diversified. As early as the eighteenth century various European cultures were mingling in Rockbridge. This was as true for the craftsmen as for the population at large. For example, an examination of shop ledgers shows that there was a blending of the two principal ethnic groups—Germans and Scotch-Irish—in artisan partnerships as in marriage. And while Washington College was Presbyterian, Virginia Military Institute was predominantly Episcopalian. The patronage of these institutions had an impact on local production, since local craftsmen supplied the schools' needs for everyday items. Throughout the nineteenth century VMI tended to commission work of nationally known artists and architects,

whereas Washington and Lee exercised its preference for local talent. The dichotomy here between rural and urban, amateur and professional, is reflected in other examples of artistic and artisanal production from the county.

The two schools also brought to Lexington its two most famous nineteenth-century residents. Thomas Jonathan ("Stonewall") Jackson joined the VMI faculty in 1851 and married and established a home in Lexington. Robert E. Lee arrived after the war, bringing his family with him. Fully committed to rebuilding Washington College, he was ready and eager to assume the role of its president. Lexington is the final resting place for both men and for their families. Artists of the postwar period made pilgrimages to Lexington to make portraits of Lee, much as artists had come a generation earlier to record their experiences of Natural Bridge. Portraits and statues of Lee and Jackson are public memorials to the two generals and form a significant part of the county's artistic heritage.

Among the old families of the county one finds no special interest in aspects of its history and landscape that have national significance: that this is the birthplace of Sam Houston, that the young Cyrus McCormick had his blacksmith shop here, that residences of Lee and Jackson are to be seen here, beautifully restored, and that one of the Seven Wonders of the Natural World is a part of the local landscape. Residents do not talk much about these things; their preoccupation, rather, is with the physical character of their valley—the mountains, the rivers and the creeks— and with animal lore and the lore of migration and settlement. There is passion here, as elsewhere, for politics, but the things that truly unite and distinguish the people are the Ruritan clubs, the volunteer fire departments, and the church congregations. Longtime residents, in other words, maintain a nineteenth-century outlook and set of values. This is evident in all aspects of their culture, from the conventions of conversation, the same conventions that inform their narratives, to the various forms of their ritualized gatherings.

These ways are becoming more difficult to preserve. The growth of modern industries is beginning to accelerate. Two interstates have replaced the early transportation routes, and scenic blight has begun to encroach. The area has begun to attract a new migration, bringing people in such numbers that they must inevitably destroy the very things that attracted them. If the historian bemoans the prospect of loss, the native senses it as genuine anxiety. Meanwhile, county, town, and the academic institutions remain relatively small. Among most people the conventions are still observed, and the social and religious institutions continue to thrive. Latecomer as it is to modernity, the county has had time to muster strength for the effort to preserve its identity. In its small way this book is intended as a contribution to the effort.

I'm thinking of thee!

When the wild winds are howling, now distant, now nigh,
and the Storm-King is growling, and clouds veil the Sky;
when the tempest is foaming, O'er Ocean and Sea,
my thoughts are not roaming — I'm thinking of thee!

When the mild, gentle Showers distil from the Sky,
and the bright blooming flowers delight the glad eye;
when the Zephyrs are playing So blandly and free,
my thoughts are not Straying — i'm thinking of thee!

When the beams of Aurora are flooding the earth,
with morn's radiant glory and day's jovial mirth;
when the gay birds are Singing, in innocent glee,
As their clear tones are ringing, i'm thinking of thee!

When day's fading Sky — light wanes Slow from the west,
and the Shadows of twilight Steal Soft o'er its breast;
when luna is Shimmering O'er land and o'er Sea —
while the bright Stars are glim'ring i'm thinking of thee!

A mid gay festive pleasure, where mirth leads the Song,
there my heart has no treasure — thou'rt not in the throng
but forgetting the present, its wild merry glee,
my communings are pleasant — i'm thinking of thee!

A ridge of rocks at Buffalo creek or river, in Rockbridge-Co.
September 20 — 1849 "

Fine Arts

With an inexpensive engraving, an ornament or two, a hammer and a box of tacks, she could furnish a room artistically.

—ELIZABETH PRESTON ALLEN, *The Life and Letters of Margaret Junkin Preston* (1903)

My statue of "Virginia Mourning Her Dead" I have kept in plaster all these years—the mail-clad female figure is seated mourning upon a piece of breastwork and her foot rests upon a broken cannon overgrown with ivy, and she holds a reversed lance in her hands. This statue in bronze . . . I would consider the most appropriate ideal representation of what it is proposed to do. The hackneyed shafts and bronze soldiers that have so often been erected have little or nothing to do with such an object as ours and mean nothing.

—MOSES EZEKIEL TO THE BOARD OF VISITORS, VIRGINIA MILITARY INSTITUTE, 1893

Despite its predominantly Presbyterian and Scotch-Irish heritage, Rockbridge County encouraged and supported artistic endeavors and was receptive to urban styles and influences. Both well-known and anonymous artists who lived in the county or had strong ties to it produced the traditional range of images, from landscapes and scenes of daily life to portraits memorializing family members and friends, from decorative embellishments of houses, businesses, and institutions to civic art, such as monumental works commemorating heroes and historic events.

BUFFALO CREEK, *opposite, by Lewis Miller, 1847, one of several Rockbridge scenes in the visiting artist's sketchbook. 9¾ x 7¾ inches.*

JULIET LYLE, *right, by E. Deane, 1807. Lyle (1749–1820) was the daughter of James Lyle (c. 1754–93) of Timber Ridge, clerk of the district court. This miniature, signed "Deane 1807," was probably painted in Richmond by an E. Deane who advertised his services in the* Richmond Enquirer.

ARTISTIC INTERESTS

Rockbridge County residents who did not have the resources to travel would have had access to few original works of art. In 1840 a pair of paintings, *Adam and Eve* and *The Temptation and the Expulsion,* by J. G. Gale, were exhibited in Lexington. Admission was 25 cents a ticket or 50 cents for a "season ticket."[1] In nineteenth-century Rockbridge, as in other nonurban areas of the time, reproductions in the form of inexpensive prints were the images most people would have known. They were popularized not only by their availability and modest price but also by such advocates as Andrew Jackson Downing, who advised:

There are few persons living in cottages who can afford to indulge a taste for pictures. But there are, nevertheless, many in this country, who can afford engravings . . . to decorate at least one room in the house. Nothing gives an air of greater refinement to a cottage than good prints or engravings hung upon its parlor walls. In selecting these, avoid the trashy, colored show-prints of the ordinary kind, and choose engravings or lithographs, after pictures of celebrity by ancient or modern masters.[2]

Probate inventories suggest that in the late eighteenth and early nineteenth centuries few county residents had much more than a

SPLATTERWORK, *by Elizabeth Green (Mrs. George) Ayres, before 1900. Splatterwork, a decorative technique popular in the late nineteenth century, was created by arranging pressed leaves and flowers on paper and then splattering the background evenly with watercolor or ink. Descended in a Collierstown area family. 22 x 28 inches.*

map hanging on their walls. By midcentury there are occasional references to pictures. These were probably inexpensive prints, as indicated by their low valuation. For example, in 1850 Henry Firebaugh had eight pictures worth $1.50, and in 1860 John Curry had "five pictures in parlor" valued at 50 cents.[3] A wealthy person such as John F. Caruthers, a Washington College trustee and an early member of the Virginia Military Institute's Board of Visitors, had only "two picture frames" valued at 75 cents, and these were in a bedchamber, while the rest of the house was furnished with luxury items such as a piano ($100.00), a mahogany music case ($10.00), a gilt-frame mirror ($12.00), and an extensive collection of silver.[4]

The most atypical inventory belonged to John Blair Lyle, who owned a bookstore in Lexington. Lyle, a bachelor, lived in the back of his Main Street store. His 1859 probate lists items necessary to furnish a bedchamber in addition to two mirrors, one oil painting ($50.00), fourteen "lithographs," and two "prints" ($18.00). The total value of his furnishings was a little more than $32.00. The painting and prints together were worth twice as much as the furnishings. The lithographs included *Gov. McDowell, The Nun, Lady Jane Grey, General Washington, Jolly Flat Boatman,* and *Sir Walter Raleigh.*[5]

Many of these prints were probably acquired through his membership in the American Art Union. The union, of which Lyle was honorary secretary in 1849, offered, for an annual membership fee of $5.00, to "improve the public taste upon the subject of paintings." Members received an engraving "well worth the annual contribution" and an opportunity to purchase a painting from a collection gathered and exhibited by the union in New York City.[6] An 1849 announcement in the *Lexington Gazette* for the Union lists the engravings offered that year: *Signing the Death Warrant of Lady Jane Grey* and *Illustrations of Rip Van Winkle.*[7] The *Gazette* urged, "Surely the encouragement of the fine arts is well deserving the small amount which is risked by each member" and gave the assurance that secretary Lyle would gladly refund any subscriptions of unsatisfied customers.

The following year two notices appeared for the Cosmopolitan Art Association. The second one, in November, reported that the association was in its second year and that its goal was the "diffusion of Literature and Art." Lexington merchant R. I. White was the local agent. In 1855 the call for membership offered subscribers a bust, with a choice of subjects: *The Wood Nymph, Henry Clay, Daniel Webster, George Washington,* or *Apollo and Diana.* Samuel D. Baker, tailor and merchant, was secretary for Lexington. In 1859 then-secretary Dr. John W. Paine solicited subscriptions for which members received the engraving *Shakespeare and His Friends.*[8]

In addition to the titles offered by the association, midcentury Lexington enjoyed the services of Washington, D.C., artist Casimir Bohn. Bohn produced sketches of Lexington and the

PAIR OF DOGS, *c. 1850. Drawings and paintings of domestic subjects—baskets of flowers or fruits and family pets—were favorite illustrations for decorating homes. Collected locally. Painting on cotton velvet, 13½ x 9½ inches.*

schools during a visit in 1856. Soliciting subscriptions for the lithograph, Bohn used his illustrations of Washington and of the University of Virginia as examples of his skills. He returned the next summer and established a shop in the Lexington Hotel, where he sold a colored lithograph of the town for $5.00. The *Lexington Gazette* reported that "while there are some defects in the sketch, it is quite a fair representation of what it purports to be and gives us a very just idea of the appearance of our village. It is a handsome picture, well executed, and exhibits many marks of unmistakable taste and skill." The following year Bohn produced lithographs of Washington College, Virginia Military Institute, and Natural Bridge and reportedly "splendid lithographs of Henry A. Wise, James Buchanan, John C. Breckinridge, Millard Filmore [sic] etc. . . . "[9]

In Rockbridge County as elsewhere, young women who were educated traditionally were taught drawing and painting, at home as well as at "female academies." At Lexington's Anne Smith Academy, organized in 1807 and incorporated in 1808 as the first incorporated school for girls in Virginia, students received instruction in "ornamental work," which included drawing, painting, and embroidery, in addition to reading, arithmetic, grammar, and geography.[10] VMI drawing instructor Thomas Hoomes Williamson taught "Drawing and Painting, including sketching from Nature" in 1843.[11] When the Commoran Institute advertised the opening of its "Female School" in Collierstown, the curriculum included courses in "Drawing, Linear and Crayon, $3.00," and "Embroidery (various kinds), $10.00."[12] Such drawing, painting and embroidery may have decorated county homes.

Visiting artists offered their services as instructors or portraitists. One of the earliest documented, Samuel Anness, a miniaturist and engraver, came to Lexington from Philadelphia in 1819 and advertised in the paper "Miniature likenesses, taken for Two Dollars and upwards. Also done on reasonable terms by Samuel Anness. Specimens can be seen at the News-Letter office."[13] That year Nathaniel F. Lovejoy advertised "paintings of all descriptions" in Augusta and Rockbridge.[14] George A. Young visited in 1847, announcing his "new and beautiful system of monochromatic painting" to the ladies and gentlemen of Lexington. In fifteen lessons, based on a few "general principles," Young offered instruction in painting from "Nature, as accurately and with nearly as great facility as he himself can do."[15] In 1850 and again in 1851 S.A.F. Sherrard advertised that she painted "portraits and landscape sketches."[16] In 1857 Susan J. Slagle, from Lynchburg, offered drawing and painting classes.[17]

While no work by any of these artists has been documented it is assumed that they found employment during their stay. Mrs. Sherrard's repeat visit might indicate her success the previous year. Portraits of individuals from other parts of the Valley by the miniaturist Francis Rabineau, who was in Lynchburg in 1804, and French portraitist Charles Balthazar Julien Fevret de Saint-Memin, who was in Richmond in 1807, serve as examples of what would have been available to early-nineteenth-century Valley residents. Many local portraits were probably created by these traveling artists in urban areas such as Richmond, Washington, or Lynchburg during a visit by the sitter. Most portraits studied, from the first half of the century, were unsigned and have not been attributed to a particular artist. Whether they are the works of traveling artists or those in urban areas, they represent the clients' artistic preferences and their economic resources.

Two examples suggest that residents of nineteenth-century Rockbridge valued the artistic attainments of others in their community. Margaret ("Maggie") Junkin came to Lexington from Pennsylvania in 1848 when her father, the Reverend George Junkin, assumed the presidency of Washington College. Local ladies were much taken with Maggie's "acquaintance with libraries, pictures, etc." and were charmed by the way in which she shared her knowledge. After Maggie married VMI professor Major John T. L. Preston in 1857, her home was considered "beautiful, tasteful, comfortable, and even elegant." It was believed that "with an inexpensive engraving, an ornament or two, a hammer and a box of tacks, she could furnish a room artistically."[18]

Lewis P. Clover, Jr., came to Lexington in 1852 as rector of Grace Episcopal Church. Clover was the son of a New York merchant who owned a framing gallery and dealt in artists' supplies. Lewis P. Clover, Sr., owned one of the earliest known images of Natural Bridge by a professional American painter, Jacob Ward, which he loaned to an American Academy of Fine Arts exhibition in 1835. He also sponsored the publication of an aquatint by William James Bennett based on Ward's painting. Lewis Clover, Jr., who was a young man at the time, was probably familiar with Ward's and Bennett's work. Before his ordination Clover had studied with Asher Brown Durand and had been elected an associate member of the National Academy of Design. His engravings of paintings by Dutch, Flemish, and Italian masters appeared in the U.S. edition of John Burnet's *Practical Hints on Composition in Painting*, a standard for English artists published in a less expensive version in Philadelphia in 1853.[19]

Soon after arriving in Lexington, Clover was commissioned by the VMI Society of Cadets, a literary and debating society, to paint the Virginia coat of arms, probably for its meeting hall in one of the two end towers of the newly completed barracks.[20] Clover's painting shows Virginia as Liberty, dressed as a Greek goddess, sword in one hand, pole topped with a liberty cap in the other, and the fallen British monarch, King George, at her feet. The painting incorporates elements of the school's diploma, designed in 1842 by James Smellie, a New York engraver, as well as those in a 1796 engraving by Edward Savage. The Savage image was the source of inspiration for many interpretations of the subject. Its background includes the British fleet leaving Boston Harbor, while the VMI diploma depicts Natural Bridge. Clover's painting includes local landmark House Mountain in addition to the VMI barracks and the Corps of Cadets.[21]

The *Lexington Gazette* described the painting as "executed in the finest style of the art" and stated that it "reflects great credit on the worthy gentleman and excellent artist. The production of this admirable painting clearly shows that Mr. Clover wields the pencil and the brush with a Master's hand."[22]

ERASMUS STRIBLING (1784–1852), *opposite top, by Francis Rabineau, c. 1802–4. Stribling, from Staunton, probably had his portrait produced by miniaturist Rabineau while the* artist *was in Richmond in 1802 or in Lynchburg in 1804. Watercolor on ivory, 2³⁄₁₆ x 2 inches.*

LEWIS P. CLOVER, JR., *opposite bottom. This photograph shows the New York–trained artist turned minister, who was a resident of Lexington in the early 1850s.*

MARGARET JUNKIN PRESTON, *above, by William D. Washington, 1868. This portrait was the frontispiece for Elizabeth Preston Allen's 1903 biography of Preston. Oil, 22 x 27 inches.*

LANDSCAPE, *by Michael Miley, late 1800s. This photograph of a Rockbridge County farm was printed from the original glass plate.*

IMAGES OF ROCKBRIDGE

Artists living in the county produced images of locations that were important because of their local familiarity or significance. The work of a frequent visitor, Pennsylvania painter and carpenter Lewis Miller, offers a visual frame of reference that places Rockbridge and Lexington in the context of similar places and emphasizes ties between the Germanic communities of Pennsylvania and the Valley of Virginia. Miller's freehand sketches are graphic records of all aspects of daily life. In addition to household and farm chores and community activities, he illustrated and described events of historical importance such as the assassination of Lincoln in 1865 and the 1870 death of General Lee in Lexington.

Born Ludwig Miller of German ancestry in York, Pennsylvania, "Loui," as he was known, executed more than two thousand sketches and watercolor views of his travels along the East Coast of the United States and in Europe. The illustrations are often accompanied by English, German, or Latin text and reflect his literary and classical education under his father, a schoolmaster at the German Lutheran Parochial School in York.[23] Miller's earliest drawings date from 1812 and the Virginia scenes from 1846–71. The Rockbridge scenes resulted from frequent trips to visit his nephew, Charles A. Miller, a student at Washington College in

LEWIS MILLER, *above, self-portrait, c. 1820. Ink and watercolor on laid paper, approximately 9⅞ x 7⅝ inches.*

EAST LEXINGTON, *below, c. 1850. This painting shows Jordan's Point (now VMI Island). Oil on board, 16½ x 11½ inches.*

BESSIE ANDERSON PATTON, *above, late 1800s. A resident of Fairfield, Patton (1870–1942) painted a number of landscapes of Rockbridge County.*

Lexington, and his brother Joseph, who lived south of Rockbridge in Christiansburg. Another brother, John, a carpenter like Loui, visited Rockbridge and worked for David Laird in 1849. Lewis, a bachelor, moved to Christiansburg around 1879 to live with a niece and died there in 1882.[24]

Miller's earliest image of Rockbridge County is a sketch of *High Rock on Buffalo Creek.* Illustrations of Natural Bridge date from 1849, 1853, and 1867; other drawings include *Lexington, the County Seat of Rockbridge County* and *The Residence of David Laird* (c. 1853). In 1867 he drew *Lexington Military School* and *The Residence of Mr. Schener,* in addition to the *Natural Bridge Hotel.*

By the mid-1840s most major eastern towns supported a daguerreotypist, and Lexington also appears to have offered a flourishing market for the new French invention. During the 1840s more than a half dozen photographers, including T. H. Smily, J. D. Pickard, Charles F. Hamilton, R. Platt, William Yarnell, and B. F. Haight visited Lexington and advertised their services. In the next decade R. J. Rankin, N. S. Tanner, Samuel Humphreys, and Samuel G. Pettigrew were in operation. Pettigrew, who operated a long and successful business, is best known for his 1857 portrait of VMI professor Thomas Jonathan (later "Stonewall") Jackson.

Photographic portraits were popular not only because of their reasonable cost but also because of their accuracy as likenesses. During the Civil War the small, easily carried images were treasured reminders of loved ones for both soldiers and their families. After the Civil War inexpensive images of Stonewall Jackson and Robert E. Lee, as well as other heroes, were widely distributed. Just as Mathew Brady came to be known as "Mr. Lincoln's cameraman," in Lexington Michael Miley established his reputation as "Lee's photographer." Miley is credited with producing the first successful colored photographic prints in the United States. His importance, however, is not only in his contribution to the development of American photography but in the remarkable body of work he created during his years in Lexington.

A native of Rockingham County, Miley moved to the Fairfield area of Rockbridge as a youth. He served in the Stonewall Brigade during the war and afterward worked with Staunton photographer John H. Burdett. From Burdett he probably learned the wet-plate or collodion process. This process allowed the photographer to create permanent negatives on glass plates from which an unlimited number of paper prints could be made.[25] Miley later worked with Lynchburg tintypist Andrew Plecker and probably introduced him to the wet-plate process. It was at this time, in 1866, that the well-known photograph of General Lee on his horse, Traveller, was made.[26]

Later that year Miley established himself in Lexington and formed a partnership with John Clinton Boude. Boude, listed as

MICHAEL MILEY, *photograph by Suddards and Fennemore, Philadelphia, c. 1876. Miley* *documented the people, landscapes, and activities of Rockbridge for more than fifty years. 3⅝ x 2¼.*

a cabinetmaker in the 1860 census, appears to have been a business partner. The arrangement allowed Miley to operate a studio in the Hopkins Building on the corner of Main and Nelson Streets.[27] The studio, known as the Stonewall Art Gallery, became "one of the sights of Lexington. Here portraits of General Robert E. Lee and his family, to the third generation; of President Jefferson Davis, John C. Breckenridge, General Beauregard, Jubal Early, Commodore Maury, John Randolph Tucker, of all the professors in the University and Institute faculties . . . and many other notable men and women. All of these pictures were from sittings and a large portion were lifesize."[28]

Information about Miley comes mostly from a 1941 interview with his son and business successor, Henry.[29] He remembered that the photograph of "General Lee on Traveller was the most salable photograph that Father made of him from direct life." The 1866 photograph, which depicted Lee in uniform for the first time since the end of the war, was taken in the garden behind the president's house on the Washington College campus.[30] Although Andrew Plecker, Miley's partner, has traditionally been given credit

MAJOR THOMAS JONATHAN ("STONEWALL") JACKSON, *right, by Samuel G. Pettigrew, 1857. A Lexington daguerreotypist, Pettigrew produced this image of Jackson while he was a professor at Virginia Military Institute and living in Lexington. Ambrotype, 3¾ x 3¼ inches.*

LEXINGTON MILITARY SCHOOL, *bottom left, by Lewis Miller, 1867. The drawing of Virginia Military Institute is inscribed "Lexington Military School. / for Cadets of— the State of Virginia / all the Publick Buildings are in Ruin / was dun in the late war, by the united States, / military." Watercolor and ink, 6¹¹⁄₁₆ x 7¾ inches.*

GENERAL THOMAS JONATHAN ("STONEWALL") JACKSON, *opposite and bottom right, by Moses Ezekiel, 1912. The sculptor was an 1866 graduate of VMI and produced two works for the school, the Jackson memorial shown here and* Virginia Mourning Her Dead. *Bronze, 86 inches.*

for another famous image of Lee, according to Henry Miley the photograph was the work of his father. Henry remembered:

One of the first pictures of General Lee, after he came to Lexington, was made by my father at Rockbridge Baths. He and Plecker went there in a van—a boxcar wagon in which they would travel from place to place and stay as long as business was good. . . . Father took two pictures of General Lee at Rockbridge Baths—one on his horse and one standing beside it. These pictures were small photographs made on a wet plate and were about 3½ inches by 4 inches. Plecker had these pictures enlarged and worked up, but General Lee did not look natural. Father laughed about Plecker claiming to have made these pictures, but as he was working for Plecker, the negatives belonged to Plecker, but Father made the sittings himself.[31]

Miley created a number of portraits of Lee over the next few years, including one called "the last portrait," done in 1870, the year Lee died.

Miley's long and successful career was based on more than the popularity of the Lee photographs. In addition to making portraits of faculty and students, Miley was responsible for photographing the annual academic, athletic, and social events at Washington and Lee University and Virginia Military Institute. He approached his work with both an artist's eye and a scientific interest. In addition to making studio images, Miley transported a large-view camera and necessary equipment around the countryside in hopes of a picture. According to his son, Miley would "always look out for any special picture. He would get the carriage ready in a hurry if he saw that there was going to be a pretty cloud effect and rush down to the bend in the North River before the cloud would leave. He wouldn't waste any time getting set up, either."[32]

Late in the century Miley began experimenting with color, using carbon printing. When Henry joined the business in 1895, he took over much of the daily operations, allowing his father time to continue his experiments. After many years of trials the father and son team perfected their color technique and in 1902 received a patent for the process. Three years later they received the Medal of Merit from the Franklin Institute. Although other photographers had experimented with similar methods, the wording of the award stated, "The novelty of the Miley process appears to be in the method of developing the prints and transferring them after development, to their final support."[33]

ROBERT E. LEE IN HIS STUDY AT WASHINGTON COLLEGE, *above, by Adalbert Johann Volk, 1870. Volk painted Lee after traveling to Lexington. Oil on canvas, 17 x 20½ inches.*

ROBERT E. LEE, *detail, left, by Edward Virginius Valentine, 1875. Valentine's sculpture, considered to be his masterpiece, depicts Lee asleep on his camp bed dressed in military uniform. Marble, 100½ inches long.*

LEE ON TRAVELLER, *opposite, by Michael Miley, 1866. Miley photographed Lee often during his last years in Lexington.*

A NATIONAL
ICON

George Washington, Stonewall Jackson, Robert E. Lee—one would expect any community with such figures as these to boast its share of commemorative and public sculpture. When in 1844 Mathew Kahle's wooden statue of George Washington was installed atop Center Hall at Washington College, it became an icon not only for the college and the town but also for the county. Today it stands as probably the best-known example of "folk" carving in the Valley.

Kahle, a Lexington cabinetmaker born in Pennsylvania, had a long and productive career in Lexington, and the statue reflects his involvement in the life of the community. He was highly respected in the community and was a member of the Franklin Society (a local literary and debating society), a stockholder in the North River Navigation Company, and an active participant in the county agricultural fair.[34] Kahle's extensive business relationship with both Washington College and VMI, ranging from carpentry and cabinetmaking work to serving as VMI hospital steward during the Civil War, is well documented in the schools' records.[35]

A carved mantel in the Hopkins House, Lexington, completed in 1844, is attributed to Kahle. With its simple outline and quick gesture, it could easily have been produced with common cabinetmaker's tools, and its vase and flower motif are common in Germanic folk art and similar to decoration used on tombstones in Pennsylvania.

Kahle's statue, installed in May 1844, was the culmination of an extensive remodeling program, begun in 1841–42, to harmonize Center Hall with the current Greek Revival style. The thirty-foot-high cupola, modeled after the octagonal Tower of the Winds in Athens, was added at this time. Topped with Kahle's statue of Washington draped in a toga, it contributes to the architectural theme and created, in the eye of a contemporary observer, a "beautiful Grecian temple."[36] The statue is carved in poplar, painted white to simulate marble.

The trustees' minutes indicate that the statue was the cooperative effort of Kahle and VMI professor Col. T. H. Williamson. They report that the statue was "finally made by a combination of the genius of Col. Williamson of the Virginia Military Institute and Mathew Kahle, a cabinet maker of Lexington."[37] Williamson, a professor of engineering and architecture, established the first architecture class at VMI and wrote his own text for the course. In it he praised the beauty and simplicity of Greek architecture as "superior to all that has been designed or executed since."[38] Williamson is also credited with the design of Lee Chapel, completed in 1867.[39]

George Washington, *opposite and top, by Mathew Kahle, 1842–44. Kahle's statue of the first president combined elements found in Houdon's marble depiction of Washington (above) as well as Rush's wooden version (above right). Painted poplar, 98 inches.*

George Washington, *above left, Jean Antoine Houdon, 1785. Houdon's marble statue at the Virginia State Capitol was reproduced in bronze in 1853 and installed on the VMI campus. Marble, life size.*

George Washington, *above right, by William Rush, 1814. Rush's work, particularly this carved and painted wooden image of Washington, may have been familiar to Mathew Kahle, who was also from Pennsylvania. Painted pine, 73 inches.*

J. D. Morrison, a local resident and an 1854 graduate of Washington College, remembered Kahle working on the statue in 1842, starting with a "huge white pine log fresh from the forest of the Blue Ridge." Morrison also wrote that "the only action of the college authorities I can find on the subject is a single sentence in the proceedings of the board of trustees at a meeting February 22, 1842."[40] William Henry Ruffner, president of Washington College, reported that the statue was "ordered" in 1844.[41] But the 1844 records, dated March 13, record a recommendation that "the board approve the suggestion of the building committee that a wooden statue of Washington be placed on the cupola . . .";[42] and the statue was installed on Saturday, May 25, a little more than two months later.[43] It is not certain why, if Kahle started the statue in 1842, the year in which the renovation of Center Hall was completed, it was not installed until two years later, although in December 1843 Kahle advertised that he had been "under the weather for sometime" but was now prepared to meet the needs of his customers. He also asked his debtors to be patient and offered to make furniture to cover his debts.[44] The lack of advertisements by Kahle for several months before December suggests a lengthy illness and possibly the reason for the delay in the completion and installation of the statue.

Trustees' records show that the statue was paid for by subscription rather than by the college, and Morrison later noted that Kahle was "poorly paid" when he learned that compensation was less than $100. Morrison wondered if the Greek artist "Phidias himself could have done better with nothing but a pine log and a broad-axe, a foot adze and a draw-knife and a few chisels and gouges to work with." Morrison also noted that Kahle had a reputation of being a "remarkable, skillful and ingenious worker in wood." In Kahle's shop, he wrote, were "some portraits and other pictures and some medallions. I take it that these and his native skill was all that he had to guide him in the work. It is a wonder he succeeded so well."[45]

When the work was installed the *Lexington Gazette* praised it as a "well executed work of art" and described Kahle as a "kind of 'universal genius'": "Whatever he turns his hand to, from the statue of the Father of his country, down to a cradle for some new-born American he does 'with all his might,' and in a way this is hard to beat. Mr. Kahle is one of our most ingenious and enterprizing mechanics, and deserves the encouragement and patronage of a liberal community."[46] The *Valley Star* reported another view:

It does great credit to the artist and is a handsome ornament to the College. To our unpracticed eye, it looks well. [But] it is true—some critics think—that the Father of his country should have been honored with at least a hat, and others, that the dress should have been that 'same old' continental uniform.[47]

Although any of several statues of Washington that incorporate classical references may have influenced Kahle and Williamson, the two most similar to Kahle's work are one by William Rush in Philadelphia and one by Jean Antoine Houdon in Richmond. Kahle might have seen both works on one of his buying trips for his cabinetmaking business, which were reported in the local newspaper. In 1839 he announced his return from Richmond with a new shipment of mahogany and the "latest styles." Two years later he noted that "having lately returned from a visit to the North . . . he had laid in a much larger stock than usual."[48]

Kahle's statue shows Washington in a pose most like that of Houdon's work, in the Rotunda of the Virginia State Capitol. Houdon's marble statue of Washington, commissioned by the Virginia General Assembly in 1785, is in the tradition of classical European sculpture. Washington's left hand rests on the ancient Roman symbol of authority, the fasces, and he is hatless.

Kahle's work also shares characteristics with William Rush's wooden statue of Washington. Rush, son of a ship's carpenter and apprenticed as a wood carver, became one of America's first native-born sculptors. His 1815 statue, like Kahle's, depicts Washington in modern costume draped with a "flowing Grecian mantle." Other classical elements are the scroll in his left hand and a column.[49] The statue was first exhibited at the Pennsylvania Academy of Fine Arts in 1815 and again in 1821–24.[50]

The Franklin Society library records show that several times before 1842 Kahle checked out Jarred Sparke's *Life of Washington*. Sparke's publication illustrates Washington in American military dress, while Kahle's image has the uniform draped in Roman attire. Kahle's statue carries a sword in one hand and in the other a scroll, pairing the attributes of military and civil authority, a popular concept in depictions of Washington, who was compared to the Roman citizen-soldier Cincinnatus. The statue combines the classical European tradition with the American sculptural tradition rooted in carved ships' figureheads.

Kahle's statue remained the town's only public sculpture for more than a decade and must have been a source of pride for him, Washington College, and the community. In 1853 the Virginia General Assembly commissioned Richmond artist William James Hubard to produce bronze copies of Houdon's marble statue of Washington in the state capitol. One of the six completed copies was installed on the VMI campus.[51] Elaborate dedication arrangements included an address by Governor Henry A. Wise that lasted more than two hours. No account exists of a similar event for the installation or dedication of Kahle's statue. Local tradition holds that the statue was transported from Kahle's shop to the school in a wheelbarrow. Kahle's statue remained atop Washington Hall for almost 150 years, until 1990, when it was removed for restoration.[52] Today the original is housed in the Washington and Lee University library, and a bronze replica stands in its place.

MEMORIALS TO HEROES

Post–Civil War Lexington became home to painter William D. Washington. Washington, a native of Clarke County, Virginia, is best known for his painting *The Burial of Latane,* popularized through several engravings and distributed by *Southern Magazine.*[53] Washington studied painting at the Düsseldorf Academy in Germany and in 1855 returned to America to open a studio in Washington, D.C., where he was one of the founders and first officers of the Washington Art Association.[54]

In 1868 Washington began a series of portraits of Virginia Military Institute alumni and professors killed in the war. The paintings, designed to hang in VMI's Corcoran Gallery of Pictures, were paid for by contributions from institute alumni and friends.[55] Washington completed seven signed and dated portraits between July and December of 1868 and probably finished another eight before the institute's board meeting the next July. At that meeting the board approved the establishment of a chair of fine arts and the appointment of Washington to that position. Once in Lexington Washington continued the series of portraits in addition to producing a number of landscapes and genre paintings. While his military portraits are straightforward and somber, his landscapes show the influence of the German Romantics with whom he studied.

In December 1869 VMI developed another plan to memorialize those who lost their lives in the war as well as those who had made commitments to rebuilding the institute's ruined campus. Washington prepared a sketch, *General Smith Addressing the Faculty in Regard to Restoration of the Institute, 1865,* but was never able to complete the painting. Lengthy debate over which persons to include delayed the work, and Washington died the following winter. In 1931 artist Benjamin West Clinedinst, VMI class of 1880, completed a painting based on Washington's sketch.[56]

Of all the Civil War figures associated with Lexington, Robert E. Lee was the most powerful symbol of the "lost cause" as well as of the noble qualities of the southern gentleman. Many painters, photographers, and sculptors created images of Lee. A few traveled to Lexington to work directly from life. One of the portraits that resulted is of particular interest here because it serves as his memorial. In May 1870 Lee, while in Richmond for a medical examination, visited the studio of Edward Virginius Valentine. Valentine, according to his account of the visit, "spoke of how [his own] fortunes had changed since the war, possibly with the expectation of hearing some very sympathetic words from him; but to my surprise he simply remarked that 'an artist ought not to have too much money.' I am sure that he had at that moment

GENERAL SMITH ADDRESSING THE FACULTY IN REGARD TO RESTORATION OF THE INSTITUTE, 1865, *by William D. Washington, 1869. Ink on paper, 11 x 17 inches.*

CLIFFS ON NORTH RIVER, *by* *William D. Washington,* *c. 1869–70. The artist produced* *a number of portraits and land-* *scapes while he was in Lexington* *but is best known for his* *painting* The Burial of Latané. *Oil on canvas, 16 x 21½ inches.*

no conception of my purse, for in less than ten days after this conversation I had to borrow from a relative the necessary funds to go to Lexington to model the bust which I have mentioned."[57]

In Lexington Valentine worked in space that the general found for him in a vacant store "under the hotel on Main St."[58] Almost immediately after Lee's death in October of that year, the Lee Memorial Association was formed and commissioned Valentine to create a memorial of the general. The finished sculpture, now in the Lee Memorial Chapel at Washington and Lee, arrived in Lexington five years later, and even then it had to remain in storage for eight more years until a mausoleum addition to the college chapel was completed.[59] Valentine's sculpture, which uses the bust he modeled as the head for a full-length portrait in marble, is considered to be his masterpiece. In the tradition of tomb sculpture it depicts Lee asleep on his camp bed and dressed in military uniform.

Valentine first studied anatomy at the Medical College of Virginia and then drawing with William James Hubard. From 1859 to 1865 he studied in London, Paris, Italy, and Berlin and then returned to Richmond, where he opened a studio. An article by Margaret Junkin Preston in an 1880 publication of *American Art Review* commented on his return. She wrote: "At times we are dis-

posed to think that he has made a great mistake in not changing his studio to one of our large Northern cities, where the art spirit, art taste, and the ability to purchase works of art exist as they cannot anywhere now in the impoverished South. Asking for bread, as our people do, how can Valentine offer them a stone! But his strong love for his ancestral soil holds him in Richmond, and hence he has not attained that national renown to which his remarkable merits entitle him."[60] In addition to the memorial for Lee, Valentine was commissioned in 1888 to create a memorial statue to mark the grave of Stonewall Jackson in Lexington. The bronze statue was dedicated in 1891.

Another Richmond sculptor, Moses Ezekiel, entered VMI as a cadet in 1862. There he studied "shade, shadow, and perspective" in Colonel Williamson's classes. When General Jackson's body was returned to Lexington in 1863 Ezekiel stood as honor guard over the former professor, and in 1864 he fought with his classmates in the Battle of New Market. After the war, in the fall of 1865, Ezekiel and the other cadets returned to Lexington to complete their studies. During those early days after the war, Lee visited the returning cadets and questioned them about their plans for the future. Because his family's business had been ruined in the burning of Richmond, Ezekiel despaired of an artistic career and contemplated a more practical vocation. In his biography, *Memoirs from the Baths of Diocletian,* Ezekiel reconstructed the conversation, beginning with Lee's question:

"I have often heard about your talent for painting and sculpture. Don't you think you will follow art as a profession?" That idea, I told him, I had given up entirely, much as it pained me to do so, but I saw no earthly prospect of my ever being able to go to Europe and devote myself, as I had once hoped, to art. General Lee said, "I hope you will be an artist as it seems to me you are cut out for one. But whatever you do try to prove to the world that if we did not succeed in our struggle, we were not worthy of success. And do earn a reputation in whatever profession you undertake. For myself," he said, "I have buried the past with my sword, and I never expect to refer to it again."[61]

Like Valentine, Ezekiel studied anatomy at the Medical College of Virginia. In 1869 he left to study at the Royal Academy in Berlin, later moving to Rome, where he remained the rest of his life. His artistic accomplishments brought him recognition in Europe, including knighthoods from both the Italian and German governments. While in Berlin, Ezekiel created a plaster model for a sculpture, *Virginia Mourning Her Dead.* The sculpture was to be a personal statement created as a memorial to his fellow cadets who had died in the Battle of New Market. In 1893 a campaign was launched to raise funds to erect a memorial to the New Market cadets on the VMI Parade Ground, near their graves. Ezekiel wrote from Italy:

As orderly sergeant of Company C. Virginia Military Institute, I feel it almost a duty to write and say that if you intend putting up a memorial to my fallen comrades in the battle, I hope to be the means of rendering my tribute to their memory in the work of my hands in my own art. My statue of "Virginia Mourning Her Dead" I have kept in plaster all these years—the mail-clad female figure is seated mourning upon a piece of breastwork and her foot rests upon a broken cannon overgrown with ivy, and she holds a reversed lance in her hands. This statue in bronze (if placed on the parade ground) I would consider the most appropriate ideal representation of what it is proposed to do. The hackneyed shafts and bronze soldiers that have so often been erected have little or nothing to do with such an object as ours and mean nothing.[62]

In 1903 a bronze sculpture from the model was unveiled in Lexington. On that day Ezekiel cabled from Italy, "I am with you, and . . . mindful of the past and faithful, I send congratulations."[63]

Ezekiel also completed in 1912 a statue of Stonewall Jackson depicting the general on the morning of his fatal wounding, which stands at the entrance to the VMI barracks. But of *Virginia Mourning Her Dead* he wrote in his memoirs that it was "one of the most sacred duties in my life to remodel my bronze statue of *Virginia Mourning Her Dead,* to be placed . . . overlooking the graves of my dead comrades, so that their memory may go on in imperishable bronze, sounding their heroism and Virginia's memory down through all ages and forever."[64]

The Rockbridge County artists included in this study produced works that ranged from the local and familiar, such as silhouettes of family members and representations of their homes, to ambitious paintings in the grand tradition, presenting images that have contributed to the national consciousness: a military hero, a battle scene, a famous landmark, or a political and moral allegory. These works are integral to the complex and fertile artistic environment that is explored in the following chapters.

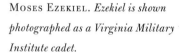

MOSES EZEKIEL. *Ezekiel is shown photographed as a Virginia Military Institute cadet.*

VIRGINIA MOURNING HER DEAD, *by Moses Ezekiel, 1869–1903. Bronze, 84 inches.*

Textiles

In the country life of America there are many moments when a young woman can have recourse to nothing but her needle for employment. In a dull company and in dull weather for instance . . . the needle is then a valuable resource. Besides without knowing to use it herself, how can the mistress of a family direct the works of her servants?

— THOMAS JEFFERSON TO HIS DAUGHTER MARTHA, 1787[1]

The commercial production of fibers for transportation to a regional market was important in America's economic development. Domestic preparation of fibers and production of fabrics for household and farm needs were universal in eighteenth-century America. In Rockbridge County the domestic production of linen and wool existed alongside a thriving commercial hemp industry in the Valley.

Prerevolutionary Augusta County shipped so many wagonloads of domestic fabric to the lowland plantations that it was thought that it alone "produced enough osnaburgs [cloth] to supply the entire population of the state."[2] When the colonies were cut off from English goods during the American Revolution, the need for home production of textiles became urgent, and the Valley was better prepared than most other areas to meet it. Augusta and Rockbridge, along with other Valley counties, played a vital role in the production of fibers and textiles for both northern and eastern markets, a trend that continued into the early decades of the nineteenth century. In the 1812 "Digest of Manufactures," *American State Papers, Finance,* Virginia was reported as producing the largest yardage of goods "made in families" (9,605,000 yards) of any state, with New York second (9,050,000) and Pennsylvania third (6,400,000).[3] The same census reports no commercial textile manufacturing in Virginia.

Colonial Governor William Gooch noted as early as 1739 that "our new inhabitants on the other side of the mountains make very good linen which they sell up and down the country."[4] In the 1760s

WHITEWORK BEDCOVER, *opposite, by Verlinda Alexander Porter (1793–1846), 1815. In cross-stitch across the top are initials of family members' names, the maker's name and the date July 4, 1815. Cotton embroidery on cotton, 101 x 88¾ inches.*

MAKING CLOTHES FOR THE BOYS IN THE ARMY, *right, by Frederick Volk, 1861–63. This sketch illustrates stages of domestic textile production that were common in the eighteenth and nineteenth centuries. Etching on paper, 6⅜ x 5⅞ inches.*

FLAX SCUTCHING BEE, *by Linton Park, c. 1860. Flax preparation required separating the seeds from the stem with the rippling comb, crushing the stalks with a flax brake, and then "scutching" to soften and separate the fibers further. The final phase was pulling the fibers through a hatchel. This work was often accomplished at a gathering called a "scutching" or "scotching" bee. Oil on bed ticking, 31¼ x 50¼ inches.*

hemp replaced flax as the major fiber crop in the Valley.[5] But improved wagon transportation was needed to get it to market. Valley hemp production became so important that during the Revolutionary War the state began to assume responsibility for its transportation. It also established ropewalks and cloth factories in the Alexandria, Richmond, and Winchester areas, and a sailcloth factory in Staunton, all of which used Valley hemp.[6] According to Oren Morton's *History of Rockbridge County, Virginia* (1920), in 1785, Rockbridge residents were allowed to pay their taxes with the crop.[7] While much of the hemp produced was exported, significant amounts remained in the county and were converted to fabric for home use alongside wool and flax. The hemp "not sent to market," according to Morton, was "made into sacking, or into a hard, strong cloth of a greenish hue that slowly turned to a white."[8]

Some of the textile goods used in the county could have come from any of the five retail merchants documented between 1786 and 1790 or the sixteen that had been issued licenses by 1800.[9] Yet

the bulk of fabric needed in the home—clothing, sheeting, blanketing, sacking, and floor covering—was produced locally. Domestic textile production was traditionally a self-sufficient activity. All aspects of the process—growing the fiber crop, cleaning and preparing the yarn, dyeing, and weaving fabric—could be performed in the home.

Estate inventories for the last quarter of the eighteenth century indicate both domestic and commercial aspects of textile production. Of the 174 Rockbridge County inventories recorded between 1778 and 1800, over half (57 percent) listed equipment for yarn and fabric production. Out of this group, 80 listings included yarn preparation equipment: spinning wheels (a total of 148), cards, and hackles. The descriptions for spinning wheels indicate their types: "large," "big," or "great" (23), wool (20), "small" or "little" (8), flax (8), quill (7), lint (4), cotton (2), linen (1). Wool required a larger spinning wheel than other yarns, and the "large" wheels noted were probably for its use. It appears, then, that the largest number of

Ireland and emigrated to America around 1770.[14] Although Robinson was a successful weaver, his local reputation was that of a keen horse trader. He died in 1824, leaving a considerable legacy to Washington College.

Estate inventories also provide evidence that several people in addition to John Robinson produced fabric commercially in Rockbridge before 1800. Inventories for James McKees (1778), George Weir (1781), James Gilmore (1783), and Robert Guthery (1789) contain listings of equipment and supplies related to yarn and fabric production that indicate either extensive domestic activity or commercial manufacturing. James Gilmore's household, for example, had two looms, four reeds, several sets of loom gear, two "check reels," four little wheels, two big wheels, a quill wheel, and sundry weaving utensils.[15]

Early inventories reflect other aspects of fiber processing with numerous references to hemp and flax in various stages of preparation. To obtain the fiber the flax stems were soaked in water for various lengths of time. The process, known as retting, allowed the breakdown of the woody tissue and dissolved the gum substances binding the fibers. Afterward the stems were beaten and scraped to further remove unwanted materials and leave only the fibers. At this stage the product could be used to weave coarse materials—sail or tent cloth or osnaburg—or put through a final combing (hackling) to produce a finer fiber.[16] Hugh Weir, in 1779, had 160 pounds of hemp; James Gilmore, in 1783, 8 bushels of hemp seed and a "quantity of hemp laying to water"; George Salling, in 1788, "a quantity of hemp in a barrack" and 769 pounds of "merchantable hemp"; and Alexander McClure, in 1790, a "quantity of unbroak hemp." Robert Guthery, in 1789, had 150 pounds of "clean flax" in addition to "undrest flax," while Sarah Beggs had "flax in the meadow" and "flax in the shop."[17] Henry Miller had "unwatered flax" and "flax watered" in addition to "28 pounds of hackled flax."[18] These carefully detailed listings indicate the importance of textile production in the community. Inventory references to fabrics give descriptions that are equally varied and detailed, from descriptions of fabric suitable for clothing or sheeting to rough or coarse fabric for sacking or bagging. Some of the varieties listed included the following:

> 7 yards country made thick cloth
>
> 30 yards blanketing
>
> 13 yards and three quarters of eight hundred linen
>
> 21 yards of seven hundred linen
>
> 20 yards of thick cloth
>
> 13 yards tow linen
>
> 13 yards of ten hundred linen
>
> 34 yards cotton cloth
>
> 2 yards blue broad cloth.[19]

spinning wheels in use were for the preparation of wool yarn. The descriptions of other wheels listed are simply "wheel" or "spinning wheel" or, for several, the additional characteristic "old."[10] Of the equipment needed for fabric production, the estate inventories specified a total of 55 looms in 51 listings. The combined figures show that a number of households had the means to prepare yarn but not the equipment necessary to turn it into fabric. Because several also had looms but no spinning equipment, households probably exchanged goods or services.[11] It is also likely that the county was visited by professional itinerant weavers and that many Augusta County weavers may have been employed.[12]

Between 1770 and 1774 more than ten thousand Irish linen weavers emigrated to America and brought with them the skills and equipment necessary for the production of textiles.[13] Many of these settled in Augusta and contributed to the Augusta and later Rockbridge textile tradition. The best documented is John ("Jocky") Robinson, who was apprenticed to the weaving trade in

COMMERCIAL MILLS

Mills aided the textile industry in the county, simplifying the process of production with a variety of services: washing, carding, dyeing, and fulling, the last a process of cleaning and pressing woolen goods to produce a fabric more compact in structure and softer in texture. The earliest documented mill, a fulling mill, was built by Solen Hays on Moffett's Creek (northern Rockbridge, then Augusta) between 1747 and 1749.[20] In 1751 the *Augusta County Order Book* indicates plans for a "road from Hays fulling mill to Timber Ridge meeting house."[21] By 1810, according to the *Census of Manufactures,* Rockbridge had two carding machines and three fulling mills and produced 34,801 yards of flaxen, 10,557 of woolen, and 13,500 of cotton goods, for a total valuation of $30,492.[22]

Andrew and George Hays, who were probably related to Solen Hays, were involved in the textile trade in 1782, when their probate listed "12 yards of Linen Seven Hun[dred] to W. Hays, 15 yards seven Hundred linen from Hugh Wilson," and "6 yards tow linen."[23] The 1791 probate for Alex Searight indicates his involvement in the fulling business when it lists "one set press plate, . . . and shers [sic] and other tools belonging to the . . . fuller business."[24] In 1806 Gideon Mercer advertised fulling and dyeing, the latter in "all colors, both common and fashionable. . . . Cloth will be received at

ADVERTISEMENT, *1856. Robert H. and John W. Brown purchased the Rockbridge Woolen Factory in 1856, changed its name to Monmouth Woolen Factory, and operated it until the 1880s.*

Mr. Garber's tavern, in Staunton, on the last Thursday in every month, and delivered the last Friday month following. . . ."[25]

While Mercer dyed finished cloth, Robert Sloss advertised, in 1803, that he would dye yarn:

DYING [SIC] & STAMPING

THE subscriber begs leave to inform the Citizens of Rockbridge County, and the public in general, that he has commenced

BLUE DYING & STAMP

-ing, at Mr. JAMES LONG's, two miles from Lexington, on the road leading to Alexander Fulton's Mill, where he will Dye Wool, Cotton and Linen Yarn, deep blue, at the customary price in this part of the Country, and half Blue in Proportion.—Those who may please to favor him with their custom, may leave their Yarn at Mr. William Hillis's in Lexington, they writing their name, and the necessary direction on a piece of paper, and stitch it to their respective hanks or bunches; at which place he will attend to receive and return it when finished. He also, has a perfect cure for the TOOTH ACHE. He hopes by assiduous attention to his business, to merit the patronage of a generous public.

ROBERT SLOSS

P.S. I will attend in Lexington, on Saturdays and at the different Courts throughout the year for the purpose of receiving Yarn to be dyed.
R.S.[26]

Mills provided other services that hastened production and provided more consistent quality. Carding, a simple process of straightening and aligning the yarns in preparation for spinning, was the most labor-intensive aspect and often involved all willing hands. Wool was carded with a pair of flat, rectangular boards covered on one side with rows of fine hooked wires set in leather. As the boards were drawn in opposite directions, the fibers were combed straight and dirt was removed. Wool comb plates produced similar results. The water-powered carding machine, not uncommon by the end of the first decade of the nineteenth century, greatly reduced the time necessary for preparation of yarns. The earliest activity in the county is that of James Mitchell, who advertised in 1819 the beginning of his carding machine operation on Buffalo River.[27] In 1838 Thomas Cross announced that he would build carding machines.[28] Thomas was probably related to and working with John A. Cross, who in 1844 advertised a fulling and dyeing operation aided by an "excellent northern workman."[29] Reeds, devices that separated the warp threads and kept them evenly aligned during weaving, were produced by documented reedmaker John Bernard in 1850.[30]

Other early textile artisans have been documented. John Spence advertised in 1803 concerning a runaway apprentice to the "Weaving business."[31] Also, John Erhardt was indentured as a woolwright and spinning-wheel maker to James Lackey in 1787.[32]

In the 1820 *Census of Manufactures* James Lackey was listed as a woolwright and spinning-wheel maker.

One of the best documentations of textile production from this period and in this part of the state is that at Thomas Jefferson's Monticello. Although Jefferson's operation was probably more extensive than most of those in Rockbridge, it employed typical methods. In 1812 Jefferson reported:

... my household manufactures are just getting into operation on the scale of a Carding machine costing 60 dollars only, which may be worked by a girl of 12 years old, a Spinning machine, which may be had for 10 Dollars, carrying 6 spindles for wool, to be worked by a girl also, another which can be made for 25 Dollars, carrying 12 spindles for cotton, and a loom, with a flying shuttle, weaving its 20 yards a day. I need 2000 yards of linen, cotton and woolen yearly, to clothe my family, which this machinery costing 125 Dollars only, and worked by two women and two girls will more than furnish.[33]

The level of early-nineteenth-century production was certainly a consequence of needs, but it was also the result of the county's program to encourage and support local manufacture. In 1808, at a meeting held at the courthouse "for the purpose of encouraging domestic manufactures," Thomas Lewis Preston, a Lexington lawyer, presented resolutions to restrict exchange with "foreign" markets and to develop local sources.[34] He recommended that a committee be appointed to formulate plans for the development of manufacturing in the county. These plans were to be presented at the next meeting, as part of the Fourth of July celebration, where the "citizens present ... will appear dressed as far as possible in domestic manufactures."[35]

Efforts to encourage and develop county manufacturing continued throughout the century. In 1834 the Rockbridge Manufacturing Company was chartered "to build on North River ... a mill for cotton, woolen, and hemp goods."[36] During the 1850s the subject took on broader significance: economic growth would not only benefit the community but also advance the cause of establishing economic independence.

An 1849 article proposing the establishment of a new woolen mill at Jordan's Point in East Lexington stressed the economic benefits. Not only would the mill create sixty new jobs; it would also increase the incentive of county farmers to raise sheep. The author found it a "matter of surprise that Virginia Wool should be sent to Massachusetts to be manufactured into cloth and the very same article sent back here and sold to us for our consumption, when we ought to be able to manufacture it as cheap as they can."[37] The next month editors of the paper supported the campaign when they reported on the success of a Winchester factory. They suggested that Lexington with "her fine water power may speedly [sic] go and do likewise."[38] Another editorial, in 1851, proposed that the true secret to wealth and prosperity was local in-

dustry and recommended "voluntary rather than legislated prohibition of Southern trade with the North."[39]

In addition to encouraging local manufacturing, several newspaper articles promoted silk cultivation, urging Americans "who have at heart the good of their country" to participate in this industry so as to "render themselves independent of foreign nations." Raising silkworms was touted as an "easy and profitable employment of the aged, the infirm, the sickly, the weak, and the lame," one that should be considered by overseers, directors, and managers of the "Poor Houses of the United States."[40] The Rockbridge Agricultural Society also supported silk culture by offering premiums for spun silk and silk cocoons at its fairs.[41]

The Rockbridge Woolen Mills in Brownsburg demonstrates a succession of owners and services during the mid-nineteenth century. The predecessor of the Rockbridge Woolen Mills may have been a mill operated by Samuel Patterson. In 1854 John L. Coleman announced acquisition of the "Rockbridge Woolen Factory" and that, in addition to spinning yarn and fulling, dyeing, and dressing "country cloth," the mill kept on hand a variety of fabrics. The following year Coleman, apparently responding to public demand, announced, "At the solicitation of many farmers and iron masters we shall keep constantly on hand a large assortment of ready-made clothing"[42] (probably goods from northern suppliers). The next May he announced the sale of the factory to settle a chancery suit. The sale, to take place on May 24, included twelve or sixteen acres of land

on which are situated the Factory, which is a large Stone Building, a large frame CLOTH HOUSE, A WOOL HOUSE, THREE GOOD DWELLING HOUSES, and necessary out houses. The property is in good condition, and has all the Machinery, Fixtures, etc. necessary to its successful operation in the manufacture of WOOLEN CLOTH, YARNS, etc. It is situated on Whistle Creek, which furnishes it a good supply of water power—about 2½ miles from Lexington and 3 miles from the terminus of the North River Canal. This is the only Factory of the kind in the County of Rockbridge, and the Woolen Factory nearest to it is 36 miles distant. The surrounding county produces abundant supplies of wool and is an excellent market for the Manufactured Product.[43]

The factory was purchased in 1856 by Robert H. Brown and John W. Brown.[44] The business, now called Monmouth Woolen Factory, seemed to do well. Just a year later, in 1857, the Browns announced, "After many calls by our friends to get spinning done, we have agreed to set apart the month of July next, to spin for those friends and customers who want yarn, with the express understanding that we will not obligate ourselves to give each one the yarn of their own wool but will come as near it as the nature of the case will allow. We want to buy all the Wool, Lard, etc. for our Factory we can get, for which we will give fair prices."[45]

OVERSHOT COVERLET, *below,* by Elizabeth Elvira Blair, c. 1850. This coverlet was made on the Rockbridge County farm of Blair (1817–91), who married William Reynolds in 1858. Descended in the Reynolds family. Red and green wool, 86 x 76 inches.

COUNTERPANE, *right,* 1814. This whitework has fringe on three sides and is marked "William M. Lusk 1814." Lusk (1787–1861) married Martha Moore (1791–1851) in 1814. Descended in the family. Cotton, 101 x 84 inches.

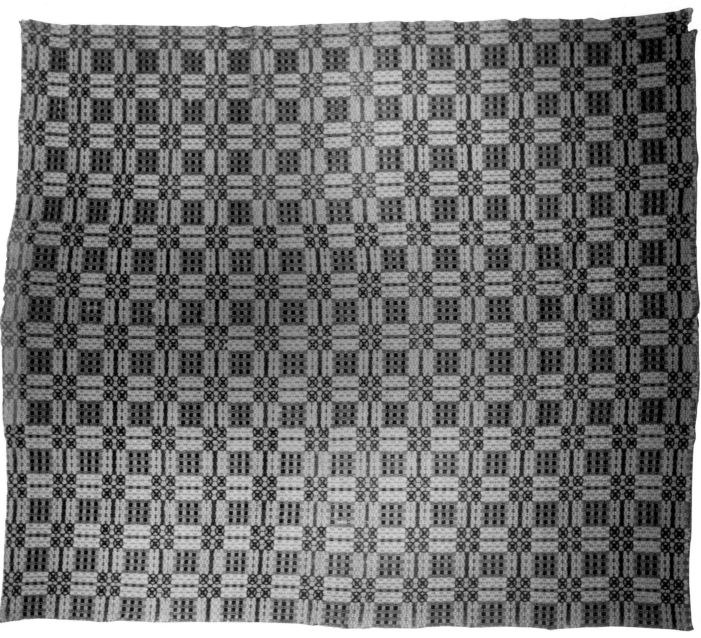

BEDCOVERS

One important aspect of commercial and domestic textile production was the creation of bedcoverings. Woven bedcovers from the latter part of the eighteenth and from most of the nineteenth century are of two types: counterpanes and coverlets. Although most bedcoverings listed in eighteenth-century county inventories are referred to as "bedstead and coverings" or "bed and clothes," there are specific listings of coverlets and counterpanes in addition to quilts. Listings for woven bedcovers throughout the nineteenth century contain a wider variety of descriptions and reflect a greater diversity of styles. Counterpanes are heavy white, dimity, old, new, and yarn. Other descriptive variations are woolen spreads, cast-up white bedspreads, knotted white bedspreads, flannel bedspreads, and linsey comforts. John McConkey's 1813 listing indicates the high valuation bedcoverings often received:

1 bed quilt	$7.00
3 coverlids	30.00
5 coverlids	35.00
1 stand of bed curtains	20.00 [46]

The common counterpane, popular around 1800 to 1820, was most often woven in cotton, with decoration created in the weaving process. Loops of cotton fibers were raised to create geometric patterns, dates, and initials on a plain cloth background. Home-woven counterpanes were often simple in design and created out of two separate widths of fabric, since most domestic looms were narrow. Those created by professional weavers were often woven full width, had more complicated designs, and often were dated and numbered by the weaver. [47]

Other woven coverlets made in the county were the work of either domestic weavers or professionals such as Christopher Baker, John Robinson, or John Spence. In 1806 Baker advertised that he "continues to weave Coverlids, at his home on Buffaloe Creek.— His price is for weaving a double coverlid twelve shillings, and six for a single one." [48] John Spence advertised for an "eloped" apprentice in 1803. [49]

The most universal and simplest coverlet, the overshot, was created on the common four-harness loom with a natural-colored linen warp and dyed wool weft. [50] The term *overshot* is derived from the effect achieved when the colored warp was allowed to float, unwoven, over a small section of plain-weave linen background, creating a simple geometric decoration. Varying the arrangement and color of the yarns could produce an infinite variety of pattern combinations.

The geometric decoration of a double-weave coverlet was also a result of the weaving process. It differs in that the process created two layers of warp, producing a mirror image of the front on the back with the colors reversed. This type of fabric could be produced on the four-harness loom, but the more elaborate arrangement of six or eight harnesses provided the weaver with more patterns. The flat geometric patterns are similar to those of overshot weaving but do not have the long "floats" of warp thread typical of the latter.

A mechanical attachment for the loom, developed by the Frenchman Joseph Jacquard, was introduced to American weavers in the early 1820s. The Jacquard loom allowed weavers to produce complicated naturalistic designs with elaborate borders. The border design allowed space in the corners where the weaver created his or her name and date or that of the owner. Most Jacquard weavers were professionals, and many originated in the German communities of Pennsylvania. Although no professional Jacquard weavers were documented as living in Rockbridge County, several pieces have survived that could have been locally produced.

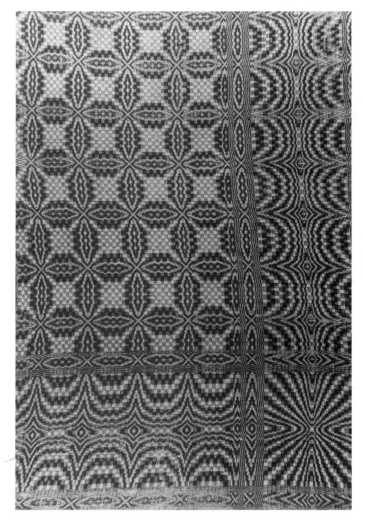

OVERSHOT COVERLET, *fragment, c. 1830. Blue and white wool and linen, 106 inches wide.*

DOUBLE-WEAVE JACQUARD
COVERLET, *right, c. 1850. Blue
and white wool.*

DOUBLE-WEAVE COVERLET,
*bottom left, 1800–1850.
Red and blue wool with white
cotton warp.*

DOUBLE-WEAVE JACQUARD
COVERLET, *fragment, bottom
right, 1825–50. Red and white
wool.*

DOUBLE-WEAVE COVERLET
WITH PINE TREE PATTERN,
*opposite, 1825–50. Blue wool on
white cotton warp, 62½ x 62½
inches.*

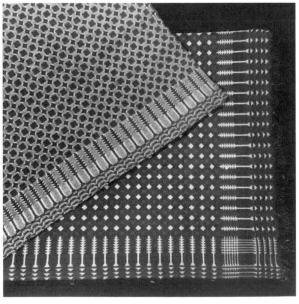

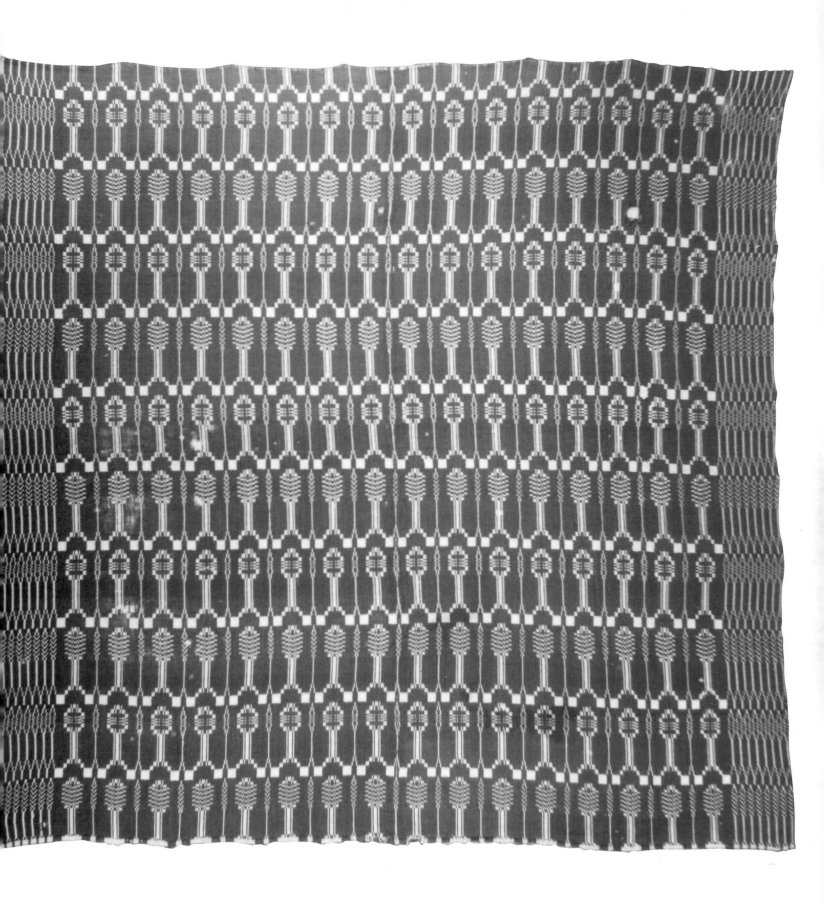

NEEDLEWORK

While textile production had both domestic and commercial aspects, needlework, whether utilitarian or decorative, was a domestic art. Women were expected to be adept at needlework, from plain sewing for everyday clothes, making and marking names and initials, to piecing, quilting, and fancywork found on samplers and embroidered pieces. In Rockbridge as elsewhere, these occupations were an important part of women's lives.

Quilts, both pieced and appliquéed, have survived in greater number than any other type of textile and represent the diversity of their makers' skills and talents. Constructed of three layers,

and often of wool, quilts provide warmth; because of their decorative quality they also served as bedcoverings. Their survival indicates not only their sturdiness but also appreciation for their decorative quality and their sentimental value. More is known about quilts and their makers than any other product from the area. For many women the quilt was more than a utilitarian object: it came to represent stages in their lives and those of their families. "It took me more than twenty years, nearly twenty-five, I reckon," runs a reminiscence from *Anonymous Was a Woman*. "My whole life is in that quilt.... All my joys and all my sorrows are stitched into those little pieces."[51] No doubt Rockbridge

WHITEWORK COVERLET, detail, top, by Rebecca McNut McCorkle, 1789. The border of grape clusters and vines twines into a heart motif. Descended in the family. Cotton, 91 x 96 inches.

WHITEWORK FURNITURE COVER, left, by Nancy Christian Welsh, probably early nineteenth century. Linen embroidery on linen ground, 26 x 26 inches.

WHITEWORK TABLE COVER, opposite, by Nancy Christian Welsh, 1818. Cotton twill embroidered with a vase of flowers and decorative border, 28 x 44 inches.

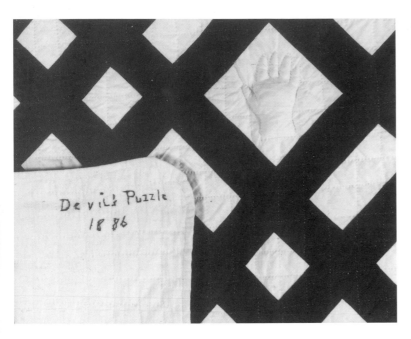

DEVIL'S PUZZLE QUILT, *detail, above, 1886. Three center squares feature children's hands in stuffed work on this quilt of blue appliqué on white background from Buena Vista. Cotton, 81½ x 80 inches.*

PRICKLY PEAR QUILT, *opposite, top left, Sarah Hayslett, 1882. This pieced quilt is signed on the back "Willanah Stuart Alphin, Presented by her Grandmother, Sarah Hayslett, Sept. 28, 1882." Cotton, 79 x 90 inches.*

EIGHT-POINT STAR QUILT, *opposite, top right. The design of this patchwork quilt is a variation on the Sunburst pattern. Descended in the family of the Reverend Samuel Houston (1758–1834), minister of High Bridge Presbyterian Church. Cotton.*

POINT STAR QUILT, *opposite, bottom left, Blanche Gilkerson Wright, 1890. This quilt is signed and dated by the maker. Descended in the family. Cotton, 94 x 108 inches.*

COURTHOUSE STEPS QUILT, *opposite, bottom right, 1850–75. The maker incorporated a large number of cotton fabrics—plaid strips, solids, and prints—as well as a wide variety of colors in this courthouse steps pattern, a variation of the log cabin pattern. Cotton.*

quilts had the same kind of personal significance to their makers.

The earliest documented county textile is a whitework coverlet from the Collierstown area. Whitework, a popular late-eighteenth-century form of needlework, employs both quilting and trapunto (stuffed work). Because the stitches were typically small and precise and the designs intricate, works like this demonstrate both design sense and craftsmanship. Most quilts documented were created in the nineteenth century. They represent a broad range of styles and designs, although no particular pattern is unique to the area. They also demonstrate a wide range of skills, from simple to fine.[52]

One of the earliest domestic tasks of a young girl was to create a sampler using a variety of stitches to form letters and numbers. The sampler would later serve as a reference of those stitches; when family names and birth dates were stitched into the piece, it became a genealogical record. As the sewer's skills grew, the sampler took on more decorative elements and was often enhanced with religious and moral sentiments, pictorial designs, and decorative borders. Catharine E. Beecher, in her *Treatise on Domestic Economy* (1843), recommended that "every young girl should be taught to do the following kinds of stitch, with propriety. Over-stitch, hemming, running, felling, stitching, back-stitch and run, button-stitch, chain-stitch, whipping, darning, gathering and cross-stitch."[53]

Fancywork was also taught to students attending female academies. Lexington's Ann Smith Academy, which was organized in 1807 and incorporated in 1808, was the oldest incorporated school for girls in Virginia.[54] In addition to the regular classes taught—reading, arithmetic, grammar, and geography—the students were given instruction in "ornamental work," which included painting and embroidery.[55] One surviving example from the academy is probably not unlike others produced in the area. It can be assumed that the style of the samplers varied somewhat over the years as the students responded to current styles as well as to their teachers' instructions. Captain Thomas H. Williamson, engineering and architecture professor at Virginia Military Institute, taught drawing at the academy in the 1840s and could have influenced the design aspects of the students' needlework.[56]

One pair of needlework pictures, made about 1802, represents the sharing of techniques and styles. The pieces were produced by two Augusta County women—Drusilla De La Fayette Tate and Mary ("Polly") Abney. Abney married Robert Kenney and, according to family history, had Rockbridge connections. Drusilla married, probably around 1815, Dr. John Davidson Ewing (1788–1877) and moved to Rockbridge, where Ewing, a Presbyterian minister, taught at Washington College. The works incorporate similar verses, stitches, and materials and were probably created under the same tutelage. It would not have been uncommon for the women to share motifs and techniques.

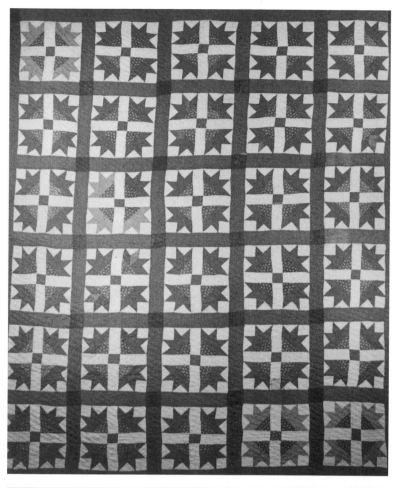

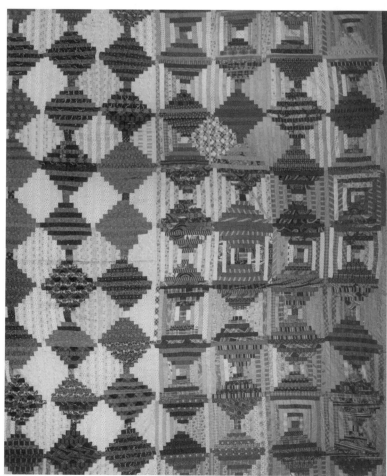

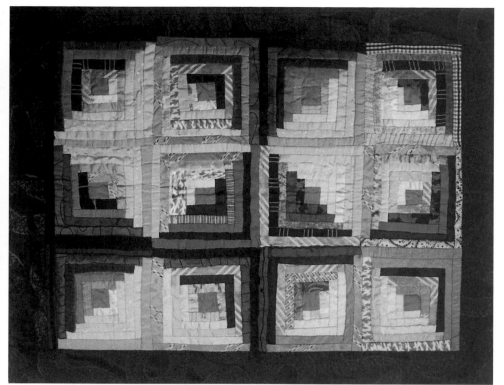

Log Cabin Crib Quilt, *top left, 1850–75. This quilt is pieced in a variety of fabrics. 25 x 20 inches.*

Windmill Blades Quilt, *detail, top right, late 1800s. The design of this pieced quilt is a variation of the log cabin pattern. Silk.*

Tulip Appliqué Quilt, *left, by Sarah Mildred Willson, 1850–75. Willson (b. 1834) of Collierstown married Lafayette Sehorn in 1865. Descended in the family. Cotton, 101 x 91 inches.*

Patchwork Throw, *opposite, 1850–75. This throw is pieced and backed but not quilted. Cotton, 69 x 80 inches.*

Bedcover, *detail, top left, 1850–1900, from the Buena Vista area. Floral cotton appliqué without quilting, 89 x 89 inches.*

Appliqué Throw, *top right, by Jane Eliza McCown Firebaugh, late 1800s. Firebaugh (1833–97) was from the Fredericksburg community near Rockbridge Baths. Descended in the family. Pieced wool and cotton, 74 x 78 inches.*

Patchwork Throw, *right, 1850–75. This throw is a variation of the log cabin pattern in mixed fabric pieces. Mixed fabrics.*

Patchwork and Appliqué Crazy Quilt, *opposite, by Ada Booze Pettigrew, c. 1885. Descended in the family. Mixed fabrics, 62½ x 76½ inches.*

SAMPLER, *right, 1819. This piece is marked "Female Academy Lexington March th 28 1819." Silk on linen, 16⅛ x 17½ inches.*

NEEDLEWORK PICTURE, *bottom, by one of the women in the Charlton family, c. 1795. It shows the three Marys at Christ's tomb. Descended in the family. Needlework on silk enhanced with silver wire and watercolor, 19½ x 25⅛ inches.*

PALEMON AND LAVINIA

Then throw that shameful pittance from thy hand | Express'd the sacred triumph of his soul
But ill applied to such a rugged task. | Nor waited he reply, won by the charms
This field, the master, all my law, are thine. | Of goodness irresistible, and all
Hear ceas'd the youth, yet still his speaking eyes | In sweet disorder lost—She blush'd consent.

DRUSILLA DE LA FAYETTE TATE   1802

NEEDLEWORK PICTURE, *by*
Drusilla De La Fayette Tate, c. 1802.
Tate's version of the Palemon
and Lavinia story is similar to Mary
Abney's, shown on page 31. Silk on
silk and linen with paint, padding,
mica, and sequins, 16¾ x 17½ inches.

THE ROCKBRIDGE AGRICULTURAL SOCIETY

The weaving, quilting, and decorative needlework produced in Rockbridge County represent more than the domestic necessities of the community. A variety of records stands as testimony to the pride felt by the community in both domestic and professional textile producers of the area. This community pride is not unusual for the early decades of the nineteenth century. What is of significance is that the county continued domestic textile production long after commercial, machine-produced goods became readily available.

Pride in local products was often a focus of the Rockbridge Agricultural Society, formed in 1827 to "facilitate improvements in agricultural and rural economy" and to encourage the "progress, prosperity and operations of good husbandry and domestic manufacture." From its beginning the society offered premiums for certain items of both "husbandry and domestic manufacture."[57] Although there was a lengthy list of items of domestic manufacture to be judged at the society's first exhibition in 1828, only Emily Houston and Joseph Steele were reported as winners. The categories to be judged—linen cloth for sheeting, table linen, figured table linen, flannel, casinet or woolen jeans, blankets, and carpeting—are indicators of the variety of goods being produced in the county at that time.[58] A listing in the *Lexington Gazette* in 1836 is typical of those for several decades. That year the society offered prizes for livestock, grain, fruits, and vegetables and for the following textiles:

For the best piece of flannel not less than one yard wide and containing at least 15 yards. All wool—

For the best pair of blankets all wool, not less than 2 yards wide and 2¼ yards long, with or without a seam—

For the best piece of carpeting not less than 1 yard wide containing not less than 20 yards, all wool—

For the best and handsomest article of men's summer clothing, not less than 10 yards wide—

For the best piece of Table Linen not less than 10 yards—

For the largest quantity of Coocoons produced by one family—

For the best 2 dozen skeins of sewing silk—[59]

Activities of the Ladies Fair and the Ladies Sewing Society of the Presbyterian church drew the Agricultural Society's attention. The society praised the enthusiasm and devotion of the women with characteristic rhetoric, even quoting from the book of Exodus: " . . . all he women that were wise-hearted did spin with their hands, and brought that which they had spun, both of blue, and of purple, and of scarlet, and of fine linen: for the purpose of suitably ornamenting the sanctuary of the Lord, down to the present moment when the ladies of Lexington are engaged in a somewhat similar exercise."[60]

The "similar exercise" the women were engaged in was to raise money for "some object connected with the interest of the Presbyterian Church." Their efforts that year, 1842, produced $450 for the church.[61]

Often an article extolled the virtues of "industrious, unselfish, benevolent women" in reporting on the products created for the fair: "Upon six tables were tastefully arranged the numerous and elegant products of female skill and industry. There were embroidered slippers, reticules, pincushions, caps, for ladies and children, baskets, etc. . . . All were executed with the taste and elegance which uniformly characterize every work of woman's hands."[62] Pride in locally produced items was again demonstrated in 1843 when the society passed a resolution that the officers and members of the society appear at the next anniversary meeting "clothed in domestic manufacture."[63]

Throughout decades of change that included the devastation of the Civil War, there was a persistent adherence to traditions. As late as 1883 the Rockbridge Agricultural Society was still offering awards for textiles similar to those given fifty years earlier and for similar levels of production. In a period of largely mechanized textile production, we find individuals still producing sheeting and carpeting in ten- and twenty-yard amounts.[64]

Another indication of textile production after the Civil War is an 1871 advertisement by Robert H. Brown of the Monmouth Wool Factory, in which he states that he will "spin all your WOOL this season, from the 15th of June to the 15th of Sept. The wool to be delivered clean and in good order. I will furnish the oil, card and spin for 20 to 25 cents per lb., to be paid in wool or cash before it is taken away." He concludes the advertisement with

"No more long Credit,
and then not pay.
'Pay and be paid.'
is my motto
and yarn my currency."[65]

SAMPLER, *by Cynthia Cloyd, 1802.*

Embroidery on linen, 19⅛ x 14⅞ inches.

Furniture

On May 12, 1858, Thomas Jonathan ("Stonewall") Jackson purchased a crib and hair mattress for his new daughter from the local cabinetmaker Milton H. Key. Jackson returned two weeks later to buy "1 fine cloth coffin and box." His child, Mary Graham, had died the day before.[1]

—Edwin L. Dooley, Jr., "Lexington Ledgers: A Source for Social History," Rockbridge Historical Society Proceedings 10 (1980–89)

Late-eighteenth-century and early-nineteenth-century cabinetmakers arrived in newly formed Rockbridge County from the same northern Virginia and southern Pennsylvania areas as most other Valley settlers. In addition to their skills they brought the traditions they had inherited, and, as they moved south through the Valley, they may also have adopted construction techniques and design characteristics from various ethnic groups that had settled in different areas. Throughout the eighteenth century Rockbridge County remained predominantly Scotch-Irish, but other ethnic groups, including Germans in Shenandoah, Rockingham, and Augusta Counties, contributed to its cabinetmaking tradition.

Locally produced eighteenth-century pieces such as a communion table made by Samuel Lyle, from the Timber Ridge Presbyterian Church, and a wainscot chair reflect European furniture traditions. The table, the earliest dated piece of Rockbridge furniture examined in this survey, is a simplified version of the

DESK AND BOOKCASE, *opposite, with glazed doors, molded cornice, fluted quarter columns, and ogee bracket feet. It once belonged to Judge Trice Patton of Fairfield. Descended in the family. Walnut, 84¾ x 44½ x 23⅜ inches.*

COMMUNION TABLE, *right, by Samuel Lyle, 1756, with chamfered legs, a box stretcher base, and a three-board top with rosehead nails. Walnut, 30½ x 45 x 28 inches.*

WAINSCOT CHAIR, *top left, eighteenth century, featuring the mortise-and-tenon technique typical of panel construction. Walnut, 44 x 23½ inches.*

FEDERAL-STYLE TABLE, *top right, 1800–1850, an example of the one-drawer, tapered-leg stand. This table, from predominantly German Rockingham County, is enhanced with a vine inlay typical of that area of the Valley. Walnut, 28½ x 21³⁄₁₆ x 20½ inches.*

FEDERAL-STYLE TABLE, *opposite, 1800–1850, an undecorated example of the one-drawer stand. Descended in the Pendleton-Gadsden family of Lexington. Cherry, 30⅞ x 26⅛ x 21½ inches.*

William and Mary style and relates to medieval refectory tables. Lyle, a carpenter born in Ulster and one of the early trustees of Liberty Hall Academy, presented the table to the church in 1756. His uncle, Daniel Lyle, had completed the church's stonework the year before. The wainscot armchair also displays older European characteristics. A chair of this type would have been an important piece of furniture in seventeenth-century colonial homes.

Immigrant craftsmen like Lyle were probably trained in rural areas of England, Scotland, Ireland, and Germany. By the end of the eighteenth century at least a generation separated most Americans from their European backgrounds. During the second half of the eighteenth century local cabinetmakers revised and redefined the forms and styles of their European heritage, and the differences between American and European furniture styles became more pronounced. Helen Comstock, in writing about American furniture, notes that its "consistent simplicity" is one of the qualities that set it

Early buildings and surviving documents indicate that
many prominent craftsmen in Lexington were aware of current architectural trends. Entrepreneurs John Jordan, Benjamin Darst,
and Samuel McDowell Reid constructed several important early-
nineteenth-century buildings. Jordan, who did some of the brickwork for Thomas Jefferson's Monticello, is credited with introducing the classical style to Lexington. Jordan and his partner,
Darst, were responsible for many of the county's early classical
buildings, including Center Hall (1824) at Washington and Lee
College and Jordan's own residence, Stono (1818). Just as they
influenced architectural trends in the county, they probably also
influenced furniture styles. Carpenters often worked as both
builders and furniture makers, a combination of trades that was
common in rural areas.

A number of late-eighteenth- and early-nineteenth-century
county residences, with their fine proportions and interior details,
serve as examples of the Federal and neoclassical styles. The latter, especially in the version associated with Scottish architect
Robert Adam and imported to this country, emphasized the inte-
gration of architecture and furniture to achieve a total, unified design. Although most of these houses have passed out of the original families and do not contain their original furnishings, it can be
assumed that the owners demanded a level of quality and style in
their furnishings that was consistent with the architecture. Tall
case clocks produced between 1790 and 1819 by clockmaker
Thomas Whiteside and cabinetmaker John Smith (see chapter 5)
or a sideboard marked "Made by James Barrett, Lexington, Sept
24th 1803" are appropriate examples for these homes.

The first phase of the neoclassical style in American furniture,
the Empire period, covers a wide range of work. Early works, like
those of New York cabinetmaker Duncan Phyfe, represent superb
design executed by a master craftsman. But the introduction of the
steam-powered band saw prompted the decline of the style. The
"pillar and scroll" version of the Empire style gained popularity
through John Hall's 1840 publication *The Cabinet Makers' Assistant*. The first design book for cabinetmakers published in the
United States, his work illustrates furniture designed using C and
S scroll elements, which could be produced in various combinations by the scroll saw. Hall emphasized that his designs were intended to be labor saving and economical to produce. The result,
massive forms emphasizing outline instead of detail, replaced the
earlier delicate style. The pillars and scrolls were most often executed in an inexpensive local wood covered with richly grained
imported veneers.

apart.[3] Many of the pieces studied differ little from the "plain style"
pieces found throughout the United States in the nineteenth century.

Artisans who responded to the demand for popular and fashionable pieces were aided by pattern books, such as those of the
English cabinetmakers Thomas Chippendale, George Hepplewhite, and Thomas Sheraton in the eighteenth century and later
by the designs of the American architect John Hall. Pieces produced in the late eighteenth and the nineteenth centuries by
Rockbridge County furniture makers were simplified interpretations of styles popular in urban centers elsewhere. Rockbridge's
Scotch-Irish Presbyterian preference for simplicity is evident
when compared with work by northern Germanic neighbors.
Charles F. Hummel, in his book about Long Island craftsmen,
distinguishes between traditional and fashionable, rather than
city and country. In nineteenth-century Lexington, cabinetmakers were still producing traditional as well as fashionable goods.[4]

ROSETTES AND LEAF MANTEL
CARVINGS, *top, left and right,*
c. 1820. Carved oval paterae with
rosettes and leaf pattern in the
neoclassical style were featured on
a mantel from a house in the
Brownsburg area.

LEAF AND SUNBURST MANTEL
CARVINGS, *above, left and right,*
c. 1810–20. This neoclassical
mantel, with its carved acanthus
leaf and sunburst oval paterae,
is from Mulberry Grove, a
late-eighteenth-century house
located between Fairfield and
Brownsburg.

MANTEL CARVINGS, *top, left and right, c. 1820. Several mantels with ornamental carvings similar to this pine example are found in brick houses in the Brownsburg area.*

FLOWER MANTEL CARVINGS, *bottom, left and right, c. 1844. Simply carved decorations, including a hand and a vase of flowers, from the Hopkins house in Lexington may be the work of Mathew Kahle.*

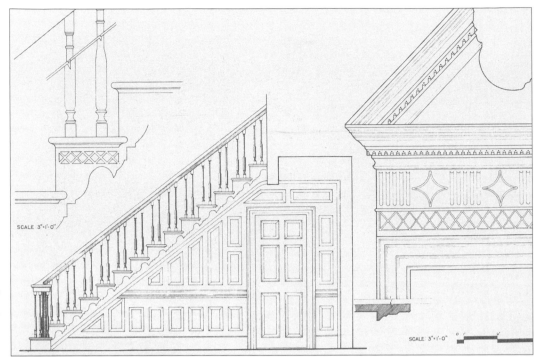

THORN HILL, *right and below, 1793. Built outside Lexington by Colonel John Bowyer, Thorn Hill represents the late Georgian style in its paneled stairhall, broken pediment overdoors, wainscoting, and dentil cornices.*

STAIR BANISTER, *bottom, c. 1818. Stono, John Jordan's house in Lexington, reflects Jeffersonian classicism in many details. This walnut banister terminating in a carved dog's head resembles the carving on an armchair thought to have belonged to Thomas Jefferson.*

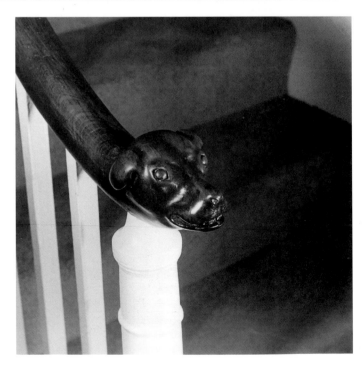

Many local artisans produced pieces in the late Empire style, and a preference for it persisted for several decades. Two examples, a table and a bench, illustrate interpretations of the style. The table, from Lexington, is the more skillfully executed, with veneered surfaces and graceful scrolls. The bench, probably the work of a rural cabinetmaker or carpenter from the Brownsburg area, is simple in construction, and instead of having expensive veneering its surface is painted to resemble highly figured wood grain.

The Gothic style was popularized in America through the work of Andrew Jackson Downing, who declared its virtues in *The Architecture of Country Houses* (1850). Downing's belief that the Gothic was a "simple and chaste" style must have appealed to many Lexingtonians.[5] Several Downing-style cottages can be found in Lexington and the county. The Presbyterian Manse (1848) and The Gables (1850) on Jefferson Street are variations of Downing designs published in the magazine *The Horticulturist* in 1846. The Pendleton-Coles house (1866), on the Virginia Military Institute parade ground, demonstrates continued preference for the style.

Downing also provided drawings and advice for Gothic furnishings. In *Country Houses* he suggested a "hat and cloak stand in a very simple modification of the Gothic style for the entrance hall. . . ." His drawing could be "made by any carpenter." It could be made of "pine, stained," but "for a superior house, it should be made of oak or walnut."[6] It is not surprising to find local cabinetmakers producing a number of pieces in this popular style. Milton Key's ledger refers to a "Gothic Bedstead" that sold for $35.00 in 1857, the highest price for any recorded that year.

The two local schools, Virginia Military Institute and Washington College, were major patrons of local artisans and often

specified the design of the product. One of the earliest accounts of a relationship between a school and local craftsmen dates from 1785, when Liberty Hall Academy records mention the engagement of one John Willson to "procure plank to make convenient seats and tables for the academy" and the employment of "workmen to make the same."[7] These items were probably used in the newly completed structure at Mulberry Hill. That building, which was probably frame, burned in 1790 and was replaced in 1793 by a three-story stone building built by the Rockingham County stonemason William Cravens. In January 1803 this building burned, leaving only the stone walls standing.[8] After the fire at Mulberry Hill the trustees acquired property on the western edge of Lexington and began construction of several buildings— Graham and Union Halls and a steward's house.[9] That year the academy contracted with John Chandler for the carpentry work on the building.[10] The following year Chandler was paid for making panel doors, a circular window, pediments, benches, and more than a hundred feet of hat rack. That same year he billed the academy $8.33 for "making 1 table and 4 benches for Stewards dining room." In addition to Chandler the trustees also hired cabinetmaker William Henry McClung to construct furniture for the new Federal style structures. In December 1803 the trustees paid McClung 10 pounds ⅚ (many records of the time still stated monetary amounts in pounds) for nine square tables, two bedsteads with "turned post" and five "plain" bedsteads. During the first half of 1804 McClung also provided the trustees with six beds and three tables for a total of $19.50.[11]

Washington College maintained a long tradition of employing local cabinetmakers to supply its furniture.[12] A number of midcentury accounts in the trustees records describes the type

BENCH, *top, 1825–50. This bench with painted graining is from the Brownsburg area. Poplar, 31½ x 76¾ x 19 inches.*

TABLE, *bottom, 1830–50. This veneered table with Lexington provenance typifies many mid-century pieces found in the area. Walnut, 28 x 24¼ x 18¼ inches.*

of tables produced locally in addition to the purchases recorded in the Milton Key and Andrew Varner ledgers. For example, in January 1835, James Rockwood billed the school $10.00 for a "Large walnut table with 2 drawers and 6 legs."[13] In 1867, early in his term as president of Washington College, Robert E. Lee hired Varner to make "ten dining room tables for the Washington College Hotel, of the size and patterns of the attached drawing, of good seasoned black walnut, to be made of the best and most durable manner; five to be finished on the 5th day of December & five done on the 1st day of January 1868, all to be oiled."[14]

Lee's association with Varner had begun in 1865 when the general first came to Lexington. Mrs. Lee and the children arrived later, and, as their son recalled:

The house was in good order—thanks to the ladies of Lexington—but rather bare of furniture except my mother's rooms. Mrs. Elizabeth Cocke had completely furnished them, and her loving thoughtfullness had not forgotten the smallest detail. Mrs Margaret J. Preston, the talented and well-known poetess, had drawn the designs for the furniture, and a one-armed Confederate soldier had made it all.[15]

The "one-armed Confederate soldier" referred to was Andrew Varner, and Mrs. Cocke was his customer. On the day before the Lee family arrived Varner, according to his ledgers, billed Mrs. Cocke for

1 Beaureaw	55.00
1 wardrobe	38.00
1 bedstead	24.00
1 washstand	28.00
1 oval table	16.00
1 workstand	12.00
1 small table	8.00
2 chairs	5.00

The *Lexington Gazette* took great pride in announcing the furnishing of the president's house and praised Varner:

"HONOR TO WHOM HONOR"

Some of the handsomest furniture in the President's House, on College Hill, (and alluded to in another connection,) was manufactured by Mr. A. W. Varner, of Lexington. In style and finish it will compare favorably with any imported furniture we have seen. We can see no sufficient reason for

SIDEBOARD, *by James Barrett, 1803. Barrett, an Amherst County cabinetmaker, may have made this piece for Andrew Reid of Lexington. It is signed and dated: "Made by James Barrett, Lexington, Sept. 24, 1803." Mahogany and mahogany veneer with walnut, poplar, and pine, 38 x 77 x 29¼ inches.*

sending our money to Northern cities for articles that can be made in as good, if not in better style, at home. All that our mechanics need is home encouragement, to develop both skill and enterprise. Let us keep our capital in circulation amongst our own people as far as possible.[16]

Lee must have been pleased with Varner's work because he returned the same month and purchased several tables from the shop. In January 1869 he bought a large bookcase ($40.00) and two towel racks ($8.00). One existing piece reported to have belonged to Lee has turned legs similar to those of other pieces attributed to Varner's shop.[17]

In 1848 VMI Superintendent Francis H. Smith engaged the architect A. J. Davis to design the new barracks for the institute. In addition to the barracks, Davis also designed the superintendent's quarters, two faculty residences, the mess hall, and the porter's lodge, all in the Gothic Revival style. In May 1851, during

construction of the barracks, Davis noted in his daybook that he had sent VMI's General Smith drawings for furniture—cases for clothes and books, a rostrum, desk, chairs, pedestals, and a "square plain Gothic table."[18] No furniture designed by Davis for VMI has been located, but the designs may have resembled pieces he designed earlier for Lyndhurst, a Gothic castle on the Hudson River, near Tarrytown, New York. A wheel-back chair (c. 1841) designed by Davis for Lyndhurst was inspired by Gothic rose windows. An unusual set of chairs made by Charles P. Augustus Brady bears many similarities to the Davis chairs. Brady, whose family lived in Rockbridge, was a VMI engineering graduate. He returned to the family home at Buffalo Forge and spent more than a quarter of a century creating a unique group of carved furniture pieces. As a cadet Brady might have seen pieces at VMI similar to the Lyndhurst chairs and used them as inspiration for his.

VMI records indicate, however, that the school relied largely on local makers for much of the nineteenth century. In addition to the items mentioned in the Varner and Key ledgers, the institute made frequent purchases from Mathew Kahle, Samuel Smith, and Leonard S. Palmer. Not all of these were furniture; purchases from Kahle's shop included drumsticks, gun racks, and tent floors. In 1851 the south section of the new barracks was completed. One of the new professors was Major Thomas J. ("Stonewall") Jackson, who had just moved to Lexington. That fall Palmer produced thirty book stands ($4.00 each) and thirty work stands ($20.00 each) for the barracks. On another occasion Palmer supplied the school with twenty-three cadet tables ($57.00), two large walnut dining tables ($18.00), two cupboards ($24.00), one walnut china press ($15.00), one writing desk ($3.00), and a bookcase for an office ($6.00).[19] A number of pieces in the VMI collection are from this period and are probably from one or more of the Lexington shops.

MATERIALS AND TOOLS

The eighteenth- and nineteenth-century cabinetmakers of Rockbridge County used mostly local woods: walnut, cherry, pine, and poplar.[20] An estate inventory for cabinetmaker John Smith made in November 1819 lists walnut, poplar, and cherry plank in addition to poplar scantling.[21] Later probate inventories indicate native woods still in use, in addition to imported mahogany. A typical example, for Milton Key, dated June 26, 1860, included the following:

5,500 feet walnut plank at $2.00	$110.00
180 feet ½ walnut plank at $1.25	2.25
600 feet walnut scantling at 2.75	16.50
144 feet poplar " " at 1.50	2.16
2084 feet poplar plank at 1.50	31.26
100 feet ½ inch poplar plank at 1.25	1.25
150 feet 1¼ inch pine plank at 1.75	2.62½
1 lot of timber for table legs	5.00
122 pieces Mahogany venering at 12¢	14.64
120 pieces Mahogany venering at 10¢	12.00
65 pieces Mahogany venering at 10¢	6.50
58 pieces Mahogany venering at 10¢	5.80
60 pieces Mahogany venering at 16¢	9.60
Lot of Mahogany mouldings	2.50
Lot of scrapes of veneering	1.00
6 pieces walnut veneering at 12 cts	.72
21 pieces of walnut veneering at 10¢	2.10
26 pieces of walnut veneering at 10¢	2.60

Ledgers for local merchants show that Lexington furniture makers were able to purchase the hardware for their pieces locally. For example, Leonard S. Palmer, who in 1844 opened a business in the "Frame Shop in the rear of the Court House," purchased one folding two foot rule, one press lock, three wardrobe locks, three dozen till locks, and one dozen wardrobe hooks from the Lexington firm of Wilson and Barclay.[22] In 1849 he purchased, from J. H. Myers Hardware, one till lock, one turning chisel, one-fourth gross escutcheons, twelve gross plate screws, one cutting knife, two chest locks and six pounds of nails.

Probate inventories for craftsmen, which often list tools, make it possible to reconstruct the contents of a nineteenth-century cabinetmaker's shop. The inventory for the Lexington cabinetmaker Thomas G. Chittum, who died at the age of fifty in 1857, lists the following items:

1 morticing machine	2.00
lot of Chisels, gimblet, files, drawing knife	5.00
3 hand saws, tenant saw & square	5.00
3 setts of planes	12.00
1 work bench	5.00
1 lot of beading plane	10.00
1 turning lathe and chisel	30.00
1 lot of Varnish, Alchohol, turpentine and oil	12.00
3 Augers	.75
1 ½ gross Bed screws	4.50
1 lot chair cane	.50
lot of Shelac	.75
2 paint buckets and brushes	.25
lot of glue and sundrie in box	1.00
1 Hammer and bracebit & bitts	5.25
lot of chair rungs	.75
4 unfinished Bedsteads	8.00
Patterns belonging to Shop	2.00
1 lot unfinished furniture	2.50
1 lot table legs (3 setts)	1.50

VMI COMMANDANT'S DESK, *opposite, by Andrew Varner or Milton Key, 1875–1900. Original inscriptions over the pigeonholes remain. Walnut, 60½ x 30¾ x 54.*

JOHN MILEY SIGN, *right. A Kerrs Creek cabinetmaker, Miley was the brother of the photographer Michael Miley.*

Estate settlement records give both the prices the items sold for and the names of the purchasers. In many cases a fellow artisan or coworker purchased the tools, materials, or equipment of his deceased colleague. At the 1874 estate sale of Andrew Elliot the following cabinetmakers and carpenters made purchases: Charles M. Koones (one set planes, one axe, one hammer, one turning lathe, one lot lumber, and fifty pairs of table stuff), Samuel Holden (one glue stove, one box of nails and one lot tools), Amos Senseney (one carving tool and one lot tools), R.H.Bayliss (one tape line, four bedposts, and one lot lumber), and Jacob Grindstead (one spoke shave and brush, and one lot patterns).[23]

LEDGERS AND SHOP ACTIVITY

Our information about nineteenth-century Rockbridge County furniture comes not only from the works themselves but also from written documents. Account books for the nineteenth-century chairmaker Samuel Runkle Smith and the cabinetmakers Milton Key and Andrew Varner provide a valuable record of the nature of goods produced and sold, the names of customers and employees, the volume of activity, and relationships among businesses.[24]

The earliest ledger belongs to Smith, who seems to have had a long, successful career in Lexington. Smith grew up in Augusta County and, according to family tradition, was apprenticed to a Staunton chairmaker named Kurtz. Family records also indicate that Smith later went to Baltimore to "perfect himself in his business." He worked in York, Pennsylvania, before coming to Lexington.[25]

The ledger for John Ruff, a Lexington hatmaker, indicates that Smith might have been in Lexington as early as 1808 and possibly working with the cabinetmaker William Henry McClung. By 1811 Smith appears to have been a partner in Smith and Terry Chairmakers, also noted in Ruff's ledger, which shows that both purchased "fine hats" at $5.25 each. In 1812 Ruff's ledger credits Smith and Terry for one child's armchair ($1.50), turning three dozen banisters and three newel posts ($2.62½), and one dozen gilded and one dozen red chairs.[26]

In 1813 Smith purchased a lot on Randolph Street from his future father-in-law, Jacob Fuller, and in 1819 a lot and house on Main Street from Jacob Caruthers.[27] That same year he advertised for sale "a large number of chairs, of all descriptions."[28] In 1824 he announced a partnership with Mathew Kahle for the purpose of "chair and cabinetmaking." This notice advertised that they were prepared to make a variety of chair forms: "Cane bottom

Grecian Lounge, Cane and Rush Bottom Chairs, Wood Bottom Fancy and Plain ditto," in addition to "sign and other painting."[29] That year the firm offered to buy a "thousand feet curled maple plank."[30] In 1828 Smith indentured an apprentice. The young man, William G. Hall, was to be taught the "art or mystery of a windsor chairmaker in all its various branches, also to read and write well, and common arithmetic including the single rule of three [i.e., algebraic proportion]."[31] Knowing the single rule of three was a skill necessary in determining the size and placement of chair parts.

vmi treasurer's records documenting a business relationship with Smith show that in a thirteen-year period, from 1840 to 1853, he provided the institute with more than five hundred chairs or stools. None of these items was entered in either shop ledger.[32] Although no signed pieces by Smith have been found, a pair of rod-back Windsor chairs in the Rockbridge Historical Society collection is attributed to him. An 1855 cadet drawing of a room in the barracks illustrates two similar chairs. Given the manner in which the cadets are sitting it is not surprising that Smith provided the institute with so many chairs in addition to making annual repairs.

Two ledgers for Smith's shop survive. The first, for 1831–47, records mostly lumber and plank received and workers employed.

WINDSOR SIDE CHAIRS, *top, by Samuel Smith, c. 1825–50. The chairs, made from a variety of woods, retain traces of the original green paint. 33½ x 17½ x 16 inches.*

SAMUEL SMITH, *opposite left. This photograph shows the Lexington chairmaker, who was an early partner of Mathew Kahle and active from 1819 to 1860.*

vmi BARRACKS, *opposite right, by Cadet James H. Waddell, 1855. This drawing shows cadets lounging in chairs similar to those attributed to Samuel Smith.*

George McMannus, Ely H. Parent, Jacob Parent, Samuel Shelly, Joseph Bell, and James Milton produced a variety of chairs and chair parts for the shop. While working in the shop several of these men boarded with Smith and possibly elsewhere in town. In 1834 McMannus is credited with "plaining and bending bows," "framing 5 doz. Mortis back Chairs," and framing rocking chairs, "1 doz. slat back chairs," and one settee. Ely Parent did turning, framing, and painting in 1835 and again in 1837. Shelly provided similar services in 1836 and 1837. Bell, who boarded with Smith from December 1840 to March 1841, was responsible for various turning jobs, including "3203 peaces rod stretcher—$32.03." Jacob Parent, who "commenced turning" in February 1844, produced 1,400 legs and 675 "common elbows" that month. In March he turned 1,600 stretchers, 2,885 legs, and "fancy stuff"— Stump elbows, Cane elbows, and Fancy stretchers." In two months Parent alone produced enough stretchers to complete more than a thousand chairs.

THE ANDREW VARNER FAMILY, *c. 1900. Pictured here are the Lexington cabinetmaker and his* *wife (front row, center) and various members of his family. Varner was active 1850–85.*

The second ledger, from 1827 to 1859, overlaps the first and also records sales made and goods received. The bulk of activity recorded is from 1836 through the late 1840s, of which the years 1840–45 were the most productive. During that six-year period the greatest number of chairs—a total of 1,059—was sold. Almost half of these, 499, were Smith's "common chair," which sold for $14.00 per dozen. Smith also sold 194 "slat back gilt" chairs that ranged from $24.00 to $30.00 per dozen and could be had with "plain front legs" or "fashionable sweep seats" at $40.00 a dozen. He also sold 114 gilt chairs, most often at $20.00 a dozen. His rocking chairs were "common" ($1.50), "slat gilt" ($2.50), and "high back Boston" ($5.00). Other descriptions from this period include "flower back chairs" (six for $8.00) and "landscaped cane chairs" ($40.00 per dozen). Also sold were "broad-backed," "scroll-back gilt," and "flat-top" chairs, in addition to "gilt slat back settees." Entries from the 1830s include "Mortis back gilt chairs" (six for $12.00), "cane gilt settee" ($20.00), and "Grecian" chairs ($50.00 per dozen).

An advertisement for Smith in 1836 reflects the activity recorded in the ledger. In addition to "fancy windsor chairs" he also advertised that he could make "cane chairs of every kind,

WARDROBE, *left, attributed to the shop of Andrew Varner, c. 1850. This piece has a mitered cornice and turned feet similar to those of the cupboard on page 94. Walnut, 94½ x 52½ x 22½ inches.*

VARNER ADVERTISEMENT, *below. This advertisement appeared in the* Lexington Gazette *in 1865.*

"Home from the Wars!"
A. W. VARNER,
CABINET-MAKER
—AND—
UNDERTAKER,
Main Street, LEXINGTON, VIRGINIA.

THE undersigned takes this method of respectfully informing his friends and the public generally that after an absence of more than four years he has returned to Lexington, and will continue to carry on the CABINET MAKING AND UNDERTAKING BUSINESS at the Old Stand of M. H. KEY. The best workmen are constantly employed, and every order will be met in the most prompt and satisfactory manner.

He keeps constantly on hand and makes to order all kinds of

Furniture and Chairs.

He holds himself ready at all hours to make COFFINS from Common to the Finest, and will carry them in a neat Hearse to any part of the county or State.

☞ COUNTRY PRODUCE and LUMBER will always be taken in exchange for work. Give me a call. Terms reasonable.
ANDREW W. VARNER.
July 26, 1865.

Grecian and Slat Back Cane Settees" and could "repaint and ornament every kind of work in this line of business."[33] In 1838 Smith announced that he was prepared to make to order "cain [sic] bottom, fancy windsor, large easy rocking, writing and common chair sitting chair and settees."[34] Smith's newspaper advertisements continue through 1858 and indicate an active business. Yet it is the last couple of pages in the second ledger that reveal the most about changes in Smith's and others' business activities. Those pages record Smith's payments to "Habliston and Brother" from 1853 to 1856 for chairs, cottage bedsteads, and sofas, all shipped on packet boats on the canal to Lexington. Smith had probably replaced his own goods with factory-produced pieces.

The ledgers of Andrew Varner and Milton Key provide a unique opportunity to study two cabinetmakers working in the

CORNER CUPBOARD, *attributed to the shop of Andrew Varner, c. 1850. This was originally owned by William Nelson Pendleton, rector of Grace Episcopal Church, Lexington, from 1853 to 1883, and is penciled on the back "W. N. Pendleton, D. D. Pendleton, R. P. Pendleton, S. P. Pendleton." Walnut, 90 x 47½ x 20 inches.*

same community during the same decade. The ledger kept by Varner, covering the period 1860–64, reflects the impact of the Civil War on his business, and by extension on others in Lexington. Furniture production was the dominant activity in his shop before the Civil War, judging from the entries for 1860 and early 1861, supplanted by coffin making and furniture repair during the war.

The ledger indicates that Varner employed a number of people to do a variety of work. Cabinetmaker Amos Senseney, who had worked earlier for Milton Key, produced a typical variety of pieces: tables, writing desks, bureaus, china presses, sideboards, chairs, toilet tables, candle stands, center tables, and a "serpentine bureau." Senseney also turned table legs, bedposts, newel post, and sabots[35] and filled custom orders; in April 1862 he turned ten hat blocks for Jacob Ruff, a successful Lexington hat manufacturer. While many of the younger men left Lexington for service in the Confederate army, Andrew D. L. Elliot, who was twenty-nine years old in 1861, worked for Varner throughout the war years. Elliot, like Senseney, produced a number of furniture forms for the shop in addition to making coffins, caning chairs, and varnishing. On one occasion, in 1861, Elliot was responsible for "tinning 2 [food] safes." It appears that another cabinetmaker produced the safes and Elliot installed the tin panels, a practice common in the shop.

In 1860 and 1861 William Charlton, listed as a painter in the 1860 census and one of a large Lexington family of painters, performed a variety of jobs for Varner that indicate types of finishes used in the shop. He received payment for "painting wardrobe," "Graining press," and "Varnishing at Institute." Another Varner employee, Frederick Kurtz, listed himself as a turner in the 1860 census. His work included turning table legs, bedposts, towel rollers, washstand legs, bedpost caps, knobs, roller pins, lounges, cribs, rammer heads (for VMI), trunnel post (oak and plain), and a pair of rosettes. In the 1860 census the sixty-one-year-old Kurtz listed a fifteen-year-old turning apprentice, Iverson Root, who turned bed pins by the hundreds for Varner. Root appeared again in the 1870 census, not as a turner but as a carpenter.

Other employees listed in Varner's ledger—John Boude, James Larew, Francis M. Edwards, and Thomas Forsythe—did the rest of the work for the shop. All employees, no matter what their areas of specialization, also performed more mundane tasks, such as hanging blinds, upholstering chairs, hauling coffins, and cutting bed slats. Payment entries for pieces sold reflect the variety of furniture forms common to the area, yet Varner's most unusual customer was Virginia Military Institute. VMI purchased rammer heads, "cartridge heads for small cannon," mallets, sabots, book stands, pointers, stools, and rulers, in addition to furniture for the barracks and faculty residences.

The ledger provides information not only about Varner's business but also about the lives of residents in the community. In October 1861 Varner charged Stonewall Jackson $2.00 for making a coffin, probably for Jackson's servant, Amy, who died while Jackson was at war.[36] Two years later, on May 10, 1863, Jackson, by then a general, was wounded at Chancellorsville and died three days later. His body went first to Richmond, where it lay in state at the capitol. On May 14 it arrived in Lexington for burial in the Lexington Presbyterian Church cemetery. Varner provided the box and managed the funeral the following day. On May 20 he billed the general's widow $7.00 for "funeral expenses."

Thirteen months later, on June 12, 1864, the forces of General David Hunter occupied Lexington and burned several buildings at VMI. Hunter remained in Lexington until June 14. The next day Varner entered in his ledger: "by making coffin for Yankee soldier—$50.00" He later billed the Corporation of Lexington for the coffin and the city in turn requested payment from Confederate Army headquarters in Richmond.

Milton Key's ledger for 1857–60 lists descriptions and prices for furniture that differ little from those in Varner's ledger. Key and Varner employed many of the same people, who probably worked in their own shops as subcontractors to the various shops in town. Thus the pieces probably varied little in style. On occasion Key returned or refused inferior work. He paid James Knick for 100 "good" table legs and rejected "240 Table legs inferior." One wonders if the inferior legs were later sold to another Lexington shop.

Tabulation of shop sales for the three and a half years indicate the volume of Key's business. In addition to sofas, safes, and coffins he sold

250 tables	127 washstands
207 chairs	80 wardrobes and china presses
200 beds	36 dressing bureaus
160 coffins	34 bookcases and showcases
136 stools	34 utility tables, desk, and secretaries

Key, like many other Lexington craftsmen, was versatile in his production to accommodate a custom market, as reflected in the variety of items produced by the shop. The Rockbridge County Bank purchased seventeen and a half feet of counter ($70.00), four desks ($24.00), and "1 case pidgeon hole" ($6.00). Robert Gillock, a Lexington printer, ordered a type case ($5.00); Lyle Wilson, a merchant, purchased a showcase ($16.00); and Washington College's Graham Society ordered one "book case and case and columns" ($15.00). William Jordan and Company, owners of Alum Springs, in the northern end of Rockbridge County, purchased twenty-four tables and six dozen stools in June 1857, possibly for use at the resort. A few months later the company purchased "2 sets ten pins, $2.50."

Some of the entries in Key's ledger indicating types of pieces and woods follow:

1 Center Table	5.00
1 extension dining table	15.00
8 tea tables (veneer)	24.00
1 cherry table	3.50
1 Dining Table	10.00
1 Secretary	35.00
1 Fine Wardrobe	25.00
1 mahogany bedstead	45.00
1 mahogany center table	45.00

Key's clientele, like Varner's, included some of the better known citizens of Lexington. Archibald Alexander, Jacob Bear, Samuel McDowell Reid, and John T. L. Preston were regular customers, while Stonewall Jackson made a few purchases. In addition to the crib, and later the coffin, for his new daughter, Jackson acquired several items for his new house on Washington Street: a washstand, towel rack, book rack, and candle stand. He also paid Key for "putting up window cornish" and "raising head board." The last two entries were made in May 1859, at the time of a visit from his sister Laura. The Lexington lawyer Elisha Franklin Paxton (later a general) began to build an Italianate villa on South Main Street in 1857 and purchased newel posts and banisters from Key. The next year the house, known today as Silverwood, was completed, and Paxton returned to Key's shop to purchase furniture. The largest single purchase recorded in Key's ledger was made by Joseph Maddox in June 1859 for a total of $1,599.80. It included the following items:

1 set parlor furniture, 24 pieces	$600.00
1 dining furniture, 14 pieces	175.00
1 set chamber furniture, 8 pieces	375.00
2 wardrobes	120.00
2 washstands	30.00
8 chairs	32.00
1 sideboard	60.00
14 8lb hair mattress	88.80
2 shuck mattress	12.00

The entry for Milton Key in the 1860 *Census of Manufactures* shows the value of his investment, his inventory, and his annual output. (In May of that year Key died, and the census lists his wife, Rebecca, as owner of the "Cabinet Business.")

TOTAL INVESTED	$1,500	
Materials	75,000 ft. lumber	750
	2 barrels varnish	160
	Hardware	200
	Miscellaneous	150
Employed	2 hands	

Annual products	50 wardrobes	650
	40 bureaus	1,200
	50 bedsteads	500
	60 coffins	1,200

The cabinetmaking business, like other trades, was a close-knit community, with relationships often resulting in the sharing of styles, ideas, and tools among the different shops. After Key died in 1860, Varner completed work for the Key estate and sold Key's furniture in his shop on Main Street. Rebecca Key was Varner's sister, and the Varner ledger records her receiving credit for the furniture sold.

According to the 1860 *Census of Manufactures,* Rockbridge County then ranked second in the state, along with Campbell County, in the number of individuals (six) who owned furniture-making businesses. Washington County was first with seven. Rockbridge County ranked fourth, behind Washington, Campbell, and Rockingham Counties, in the amount of capital invested, the number of workers employed, and the annual value of goods produced.

Several factors contributed to the decline of furniture making in Rockbridge County after the Civil War. These included the casualties during the war itself, the growth of mechanization, and the increased availability of factory-made goods. Even before the war, with the completion of the James River and Kanawha Canal from Lynchburg and a plank toll road down the Valley in the early 1850s, goods could easily be transported from these centers. By the late 1850s VMI frequently acquired items from establishments in Richmond, Philadelphia, and Boston. Many residents also made purchases from large urban centers that were providing popular, factory-produced furniture. Local newspapers reflect this growing trend with advertisements for firms in Richmond and Lynchburg, in addition to northern establishments. An 1869 shipment for furniture maker Charles Koones, who opened his Lexington business after the war, included various factory-made pieces: chair bottoms, chair backs, chairs, bed railings, and bedsteads.[37] In 1871 he advertised "arrival direct from manufacturers of parlor furniture, marble top and extension tables."[38]

Yet in spite of the availability of factory-made furniture, the public maintained a preference for well-constructed, simple, locally made items into the late 1880s. Andrew Varner must have hoped to appeal to this taste when he returned from service in the Confederate Army. The heading of his 1865 advertisement in the *Lexington Gazette* is simple and direct, characteristic of his own work and that of his fellow artisans:

"HOME FROM THE WARS!"

A.W. Varner

Cabinet-maker and Undertaker

ROCKBRIDGE
FURNITURE TYPES

The furniture items included in the following survey were selected for a variety of reasons. A few were signed by documented makers. However, signed pieces are rare: of the hundreds photographed for this study, scarcely more than a dozen were signed. Most nineteenth-century works studied were the product of furniture shops and the result of the work of several artisans, and it was not uncommon for a craftsman to produce work for more than one shop. Thus a number of works are included because they can be attributed to an individual, a shop, or the area on the basis of design and construction characteristics. A large number of pieces have descended in the families of the original owners.

The types of furniture owned and used in the county can be documented in a variety of sources—shop ledgers such as those discussed earlier, newspaper advertisements, and estate inventories. The discussions accompanying the surveys are based, for the most part, on an analysis of probate inventories. While these listings are invaluable sources of information they must be read with caution. They present the expected and not uncommon problems of reading any early documents—illegible handwriting, grouped and incomplete listings, varied and inconsistent use of descriptive terms. Also, the researcher is at the mercy of the enumerator's judgment and prejudices in interpreting entries such as "the wooden works of one New Wagon thought not to be well done" and "one old worthless negro wench" valued at "nothing."[39] Thus it is often difficult to relate existing pieces to the listings in inventories.

Few inventory listings contain information about the placement of furniture in a room or the type of room in which it was used. The examples we do have provide invaluable insight into a room's use and its furnishings. For example, Samuel Steel's 1808 probate includes a bedstead and furniture in the "little room," a bedstead, bed, and furniture in the "big room" and a bedstead, bed, and furniture in a corner by the chimney.[40] The 1817 inventory for William Skeen, who owned five slaves, listed "negro furniture in the kitchen" valued at $15.00.[41] The most revealing inventory listing, for John F. Caruthers in 1840, included an extensive, room-by-room description of furniture. In it Caruthers's possessions were grouped as "Parlor Furniture," "back room upstairs, "Front room upstairs," "Chamber furniture," "Dining room," and "Passage."[42] One well-researched probate belonged to Stonewall Jackson and was an invaluable tool during the restoration of his Lexington residence.

Local histories often provide information where both probate records and surviving examples are scarce. The first *Rockbridge County Will Book*, covering the period 1778–95, lists relatively little furniture, as one would expect in a new county, and few eighteenth-century pieces have survived. The construction and "furnishing" of an early Valley cabin are described, however, in Samuel Kercheval's 1833 *History of the Valley of Virginia:*

The roof and the floor were often finished on the same day of the "raising" and a third day was commonly spent by a few carpenters in leveling off the floor, making a clapboard door and a table. This last was made of a split slab, and supported by four round legs set in auger holes; some three-legged stools were made in the same manner. Some pins, stuck in the logs at the back of the house, supported some clayboards which served for shelves for the table furniture. A single fork, placed with its lower end in a hole in the floor, and the upper end fastened to a joist, served for a bedstead, by placing a pole in the fork, with its outer end through another crack. From the front pole, through a crack between the logs of the end of the house, the boards were put on which formed the bottom of the bed.[43]

It is often impossible to date a piece by style alone given the persistence of certain older styles. Once a style gained acceptance, it changed little, either because of a basic conservatism or because it had proved acceptable and change was unnecessary. For example, in 1860 Andrew Varner paid one of his workers to construct a "Serpentine front sideboard," a form presumably out of style by that date.

WORK TABLE, *c. 1850. This table with a four-board scrub top and red-painted base is marked in paint on the bottom "W. T. Shields/Gore O. Alexander/Lexington." Yellow pine, 30 x 44½ x 40¾ inches.*

CUPBOARDS, PRESSES, SAFES, AND WARDROBES

The use of large storage pieces— cupboards, presses, safes, and wardrobes—has been documented throughout the history of Rockbridge County. The earliest form documented was the cupboard. This piece evolved from earlier "cup and boards," a simple board shelf or plate rack attached to the wall. Early county probates (1778–1800) describe cupboards as "common," "square," "large," "small," "old," and "kitchen."

These were probably freestanding pieces; built-in cupboards existed but were not included in estate inventories. A number of late-eighteenth-century Georgian or neoclassical Rockbridge houses retain original interior architectural details, including built-in cupboards, both flat and corner, which reflect the style of the house. Almost all built-in cupboards documented were found in the more formal rooms—the parlor and dining room—and could have been the work of itinerant carpenter-joiners. Listings of cupboard furniture (china and so forth) with no reference to a cupboard or press may indicate the use of a built-in cupboard or shelves. For example, the extensive 1821 probate inventory of John F. Caruthers includes several dozen dishes, serving pieces, tumblers, and glasses but does not mention any type of storage furniture.[44]

Freestanding cupboards with high valuations were probably used in these same rooms and, with their displays of china, would have been important focal points.[45] One author has described the corner cupboard as the piece of furniture that best symbolized "Georgian graciousness."[46] By the second decade of the nineteenth century more than half of the probates recorded included cupboards. Descriptive variations include "corner," "small corner," and a "cherry tree cupboard with glass doors."[47]

The dresser, a form brought from the British Isles, also evolved from the earlier cupboard and plate rack. Simple pieces such as the open dresser or kitchen press were often used as storage units in the kitchen area. Few such pieces were documented in this survey; only one "kitchen dresser" was recorded for the second decade of the nineteenth century. Between 1778 and 1800 only three listings included any form of "press," and two of these were given as "clothes press."

CORNER CUPBOARD, c. 1825–50. The cavetto cornice molding, single glazed door, paneled lower doors, and bracket feet of this freestanding cupboard are typical of early-nineteenth-century Valley pieces. Descended in a family with Kerrs Creek connections. Walnut, 74 x 39 x 20 inches.

In the early nineteenth century the glazed-front cupboard or dresser came into use in both the kitchen and the dining room. This storage piece became popular in the Valley of Virginia as well as in the German communities of Pennsylvania and Upper Canada.[48] Often constructed in two sections, it is sometimes referred to as a china press. These pieces were also used to store books and were noted as libraries or book presses. Matthew Bryan's 1854 probate, for example, included "1 press and bookcase $20.00" and "lott Books suposed 135 volumns $50.00."[49] The term *cupboard* continued to appear throughout nineteenth-century probates, many times with modest valuation, from $1.00 to $3.00.

Several artisans of early-nineteenth-century Rockbridge County may have produced cupboards and presses. Cabinetmaker John Smith's 1819 estate inventory listed "1 China Press $30.00," one of the highest valuations for a cupboard from that period.[50] If Smith made his own press, it probably shared stylistic and construction characteristics with his clock cases. Another cabinetmaker, John McClain, is noted in the 1820 *Census of Manufactures* as producing cupboards, in addition to tables and bureaus, using walnut, pine, and poplar plank, although no pieces have been documented as produced in McClain's shop.

Cupboards and china presses are the most common furniture forms documented in this category in the mid-nineteenth century. These pieces are almost always constructed of walnut with glazed, six-pane doors, turned legs, and a sharply mitered cornice. The drawers are either double or single and have turned knobs. This same mitered cornice is often found on punched-tin food safes common in kitchens. An 1855 drawing of a room in the Virginia Military Institute barracks depicts a large storage piece, possibly a wardrobe, with the same flaring mitered cornice.

Milton Key's ledger for 1857–60 indicates that in a three-year period he sold a total of eighty wardrobes and china presses. Key's "safes" sold for $12.00, while the china presses ranged from $12.00 to $18.00. There was a wider range—$5.00 to $20.00—for wardrobes, described as "walnut," "poplar," and "small." The 1860 *Census of Manufactures* reported that Key and Kahle each sold fifty

BLIND-DOOR CORNER
CUPBOARD, 1825–50. *Descended in a Kerrs Creek area family. Walnut, 78 x 50½ x 24 inches.*

wardrobes that year. Kahle's averaged $8.00 and Key's $13.00. Leonard S. Palmer, a Lexington cabinetmaker, was also producing wardrobes; his 1856 estate inventory included cupboards, locks, and wardrobe hooks.[51] Varner's ledger is similar to Key's except that he sold more furniture to VMI. In addition to other items, Varner billed the laboratory department for two "large" presses at $18.00 each. These were probably used for book or specimen storage. Today these pieces—cupboards, presses, safes, and wardrobes—make up a large part of the furniture documented in Rockbridge County.

CHINA PRESS, *c. 1850s. This press has eight-pane, glazed double doors, turned feet, and cavetto cornice molding. Descended in a Lexington area family. Walnut, 87 x 44 x 18¾ inches.*

HANGING CORNER CUPBOARD, *right, c. 1850. Descended in the Pendleton-Gadsden family, Lexington. Walnut, 28 x 17¼ x 11 inches.*

FOOD SAFE AND PANEL, *left and above. This food safe with a plant design punched in tin and traces of original paint has a mitered cornice typical of many* pieces found in Rockbridge County. *Descended in the Alexander-Firebaugh family. Pine, 86½ x 42 x 18 inches.*

CUPBOARD, *above, 1825–50.*
This cupboard has a shaped,
three-sided splashboard over a
single struck-beaded drawer, two
paneled doors, and turned feet.
Cherry, 51 x 52 x 19½ inches.

WARDROBE, *right, c. 1850.*
This large, veneered wardrobe
features a flaring, mitered cornice.
Descended in the Pendleton-
Gadsden family of Lexington.
Walnut with veneer, 94½ x 48 x
19½ inches.

GLAZED PRESS, *opposite, by*
Garner P. Hutton, 1870. This
press was made for Calvin Goodbar
(1844–1920) the year he was
married. Walnut, 76 x 43½ x 19½
inches.

DESKS, SECRETARIES, AND BOOKCASES

The organization of this group of pieces is a reflection of the terms found in county estate inventories. Most of the few eighteenth-century listings were for pieces that had a combined function—desk and cupboard, desk and bookcase, bureau and bookcase—in addition to simple desks. Between 1778 and 1825 a total of 421 probate inventories was recorded, and only 62 of these included desks, bookcases, or secretaries. During the early decades of the nineteenth century pieces in this category appeared more frequently and under a wider variety of descriptive terms, including, in addition to those already noted, "writing desk," "desk of drawers," and "bookcase with drawers."

The earliest reference to a secretary occurs in the 1819 probate of the Lexington cabinetmaker John Smith, which lists "one unfinished secretary $14.00." Smith also had one bookcase, valued at $8. Hugh Willson, in 1809, had "1 desk & bookcase of cherry—$45.00" and "1 desk & bookcase of walnut—$15.00."[52] A number of pieces documented could have been the work of Smith's shop or of any of several other artisans known to have worked in the county.

Desks and bookcases usually received high valuations. On occasion the piece and contents were given one price. For example, Samuel Wilson's 1808 probate lists a desk, bookcase, and books for a total of $40.00.[53] A number of inventories for individuals included extensive listings of books but no record of bookcase or secretary. Several mid-nineteenth-century probates indicate that the cupboard was used to store books. Storage units referred to as libraries included the books. Shop ledgers for both Milton Key and Andrew Varner record the production and sale of bookcases, secretaries, and desks. In 1857 Key's bookcases ranged from $18 to $40, and a secretary cost $35. Desks sold for $1.50 to $16.00, most at $5.00 and $6.00. Key's 1860 probate listing included two unfinished desks, one valued at $5.00 and the other at $7.00.

Varner's entries, which are similar, include a bookcase and writing desk for $30.00, a writing desk for $12.00, and a book stand for $4.50. Varner also provided furniture for the Virginia Military Institute as well as smaller enterprises. In 1860 Louisa Bull, who was apparently furnishing a schoolroom, purchased four writing desks for $14.00 and five benches for $10.50, in addition to a book stand and blackboard. That year Francis Edwards was apparently doing the same when he purchased six writing desks for $15.00 and another six for $18.00.

DESK AND BOOKCASE. *This slant-lid desk over four graduated drawers, from Brownsburg, has ogee feet and blind paneled doors. Walnut, 86 x 41 x 20½ inches.*

DESK AND BOOKCASE, *early 1800s. A light wood inlay embellishes the drawers and bookcase cornice. Descended in a Fairfield family. Cherry and cherry veneer, 88¾ x 43¼ x 21 inches.*

SHOPKEEPER'S DESK, *top left, c. 1850. Simple pieces such as this desk, found in Buena Vista and typical of the mid-nineteenth century, would have been common store items. Walnut, 44 x 35 x 25½ inches.*

SLANT-FRONT DESK, *right top and bottom, 1800–1825. This desk with French feet originally belonged to Matthew White (1786–1864), who emigrated to America from Ireland in 1802, farmed near Brownsburg, and later lived in Lexington. Cherry, 44½ x 41½ x 21¾ inches.*

DESK, *opposite. This desk was used at the Virginia Military Institute hospital. Walnut, 55½ x 56½ x 30¼ inches.*

SLIDING TOP CHEST, *left, early 1800s. A Chippendale-inspired bracket base enhances the simple design. Mixed woods (primarily walnut), 17 x 25 x 18 inches.*

DOUGH CHEST, *opposite top, late 1800s. The style of this Augusta County chest would have been reflected in Rockbridge County pieces. Yellow pine with oak top, 29½ x 44⅞ x 18 inches.*

TWO-DRAWER CHEST, *opposite bottom, early 1800s. This red chest from Greenville reflects the Pennsylvania German vernacular style and is typical of late-eighteenth- and early-nineteenth-century chests found throughout the Valley. Poplar, 28½ x 50½ x 22⅞ inches.*

CHESTS, CHESTS OF DRAWERS, AND BUREAUS

Rockbridge County estate inventories for 1778–1800 reflect the evolution of the chest form. Early listings refer to "chest" or "chist" with the descriptors "large," "small," "old," "meal," and "dough," in addition to various wood types. In the sparse interiors of early houses these pieces were important items. An early type of chest with a hinged top served as a storage unit and, when needed, as a seat or low table. Such pieces, whose simplicity was indicated by their modest valuation, were probably constructed by simple joining and given little decoration, such as painting or graining. Documented Rockbridge County chests are often plainer that those of neighboring Augusta and Shenandoah Counties.

By the end of the eighteenth century we find the entry "chist with drawers." These pieces were probably simple hinged-top chests with one or two drawers added below. This form was soon superseded by the chest of drawers we know today, often referred to as "case of drawers" and "drawers casse."

The next phase of evolution was the addition of drawers continuing to the top and the elimination of the hinged top section. The stacking of drawers, resulting in new vertical proportions, was made possible by the use of dovetail construction. Two local examples represent the continuation of the type of high chest of drawers typical of provincial Pennsylvania. Local cabinetmakers may also have been influenced by the work of the firm Martin and Fry of Winchester, which produced examples featuring ogee bracket feet and reeded quarter columns. Several known Rockbridge County makers who worked in the early decades of the nineteenth century—John McClain, John Smith, Thomas Hopkins, and James Barrett—probably produced similar pieces.

County estate inventories also provide information about the variations of the form, type of wood, valuation of pieces, and frequency of appearance. Walnut was the most frequently noted wood, with poplar second. An example in cherry—"1 large cherry tree case of drawers"—was listed for Polly Ramsey in 1795.

In the first decades of the nineteenth century the term *bureau* becomes common, most often referring to a piece containing four drawers and used for clothing storage. "Cherry" and "walnut" were frequently used in conjunction with "bureau." By midcentury the Empire style, with pillar and scroll or paw feet and split, turned columns became popular. The Lexington cabinetmakers Milton Key, Andrew Varner, and Mathew Kahle probably produced bureaus in this style. The 1860 *Census of Manufactures* listed Key's bureaus at an average price of $30.00 and Kahle's at $20.00. Both reported producing forty to fifty of these a year.

High Chest of Drawers
with Vine and Vase Inlay,
*opposite, 1800–1825. Descended
in a Lexington family. Walnut,
58¼ x 47½ x 23⅛ inches.*

High Chest of Drawers,
*top left, early 1800s. This piece
once belonged to Zachariah
Johnston of Rockbridge County,
whose home, Stone House (1794),
is on the western edge of Lexington.
Descended in the family. Walnut,
72½ x 42½ x 25½ inches.*

High Chest of Drawers,
*top right, 1800–1825. This chest
of drawers, from Kerrs Creek,
features open dovetailing on the
ends and pegged base and cornice
moldings. Primarily cherry,
65 x 42 x 24½ inches.*

FOUR-DRAWER BUREAU, *top,
early 1800s. This piece features
French feet and simple string
inlay frequently found in Rockbridge County. Descended in a
Fairfield family. Walnut, 36 x
40 x 20⅝ inches.*

CHEST WITH GRADUATED
DRAWERS, *bottom, 1825–50. The
influence of the Sheraton style
can be seen in the slender, turned
feet, flush drasers, and turned
pulls. Descended in the Pendleton-
Gadsden family, Lexington.
Cherry, 46 x 42½ x 20½ inches.*

BUREAU WITH MIRROR,
*by John Rusk, 1868. This bureau
is marked "John Rusk Cabinetmaker at Mrs Firebaugh's Mill &
Shop June 1, 1868." Descended in
the Alexander-Firebaugh family.
Walnut, 77 x 43 x 22½ inches.*

Most early residential structures in the county were one-room log cabins or log houses of two or four rooms. Rooms were usually multipurpose; a single space might be used for food preparation, eating, and sleeping. None of the eighteenth-century county inventories studied is itemized by room, making it difficult to determine the type of room in which a table was used. Most descriptive variations note age and size ("old," "new," "large," "small," "square") and use ("kitchen," "tea," or "dressing" for a table). Woods are often noted (walnut, pine, poplar, and one "pine painted" table).

Carpenters and joiners as well as cabinetmakers may have produced these early pieces. Eighteenth-century county artisans such as Thomas Taylor, Valentine Dudden, and Matthew Donald all owned the tools and equipment necessary to produce simple furniture items.[54] Samuel Lyle, who built the communion table for Timber Ridge Presbyterian Church shown at the beginning of this chapter, owned "5 molding planes, 2 chisels" in 1797. Similarly, George Kelly, perhaps a carpenter or cabinet-

DRAWING OF TABLE, *top. The table was signed "Walker" and was found in the Hopkins house (c. 1840), Lexington. Pencil drawing, 4½ x 5 inches.*

DROPLEAF TABLE WITH SIMPLIFIED CABRIOLE LEG, *right, early 1800s. Descended in an early-nineteenth-century Fairfield family. Walnut with oak and poplar, 29¼ x 17¼ x 38 inches (29¼ x 35 x 30 inches extended).*

maker, received $70.00 in 1780 for making a table for the clerk of the new county court.[55]

Some of the pieces recorded probably represented simple variations of the refectory table used in rural kitchens in the British Isles during the eighteenth and nineteenth centuries. These long, rectangular tables, called stretcher tables, were an important furnishing in colonial American households. Inventories frequently include listings for "falling leaf" tables. Several variations are illustrated. By the turn of the century estate listings indicate a wider variety of table forms in use. The 1806 listing for Christian Varner, who operated the Eagle Tavern in Lexington, included one dining table, two square walnut tables, and one tea table.[56] Thomas Land in 1810 owned one oval cherry table, one square dining table, and one backgammon table.[57] Each owned other tables described as types of wood or finish rather than form: poplar, painted poplar, pine, walnut.

A "dining" table first appears in the 1797 probate listing for Samuel Lyle. After the turn of the century, when the dining room as a separate room became more common, the term appears more frequently. With its increased popularity came the development of pieces such as the sideboard. Sideboards with cellarettes, or cabinets for wine and liquor, were introduced about 1785 and soon became essential in dining rooms of fine homes.

Most of the tables documented from the first part of the nineteenth century were rural interpretations of Hepplewhite and Sheraton designs of the Federal period. In the inventories studied from this period most dining tables were given a valuation of $2.00 to $5.00. Inventories at midcentury indicate a variety of forms and woods in descriptions such as "mahogany leaf table," card table, "dining table," "half round table," and "mahogany dining table." Mahogany pieces always received higher valuations than those in other woods.

In addition to the table forms mentioned, listings include candle stands, washstands, toilet tables, tea tables, center tables, and writing tables. All of the candle stands listed before 1840 carried considerable valuation ($2.00 to $3.00), while after that date they were usually listed as less than a dollar, reflecting a new fashion for center tables, which began to appear in listings after the 1850s.

Ledgers for the Milton Key and Andrew Varner shops record table forms that correspond to those in estate listings: dining, end, side, tea, center, writing, and toilet tables. This study found a group of tables characterized by a simply turned leg style associated with Varner's work.

DROPLEAF TABLE, *top, 1825–50. Collected in the Lexington area. Walnut, 29½ x 42½ x 38 inches (extended).*

DROPLEAF DINING TABLE, *bottom, attributed to the shop of Andrew Varner, c. 1850. Walnut and veneer, 28¾ x 58¼ x 48¾ inches.*

WORK TABLE, *top, 1800–1850. This utilitarian table has a single drawer and carved feet. Walnut, 28¼ x 39¼ x 26 inches.*

DINING TABLE, *bottom, by Mathew Kahle, c. 1850. This extension table originally belonged to the Pendleton-Gadsden family of Lexington. Walnut, 29¼ x 44 inches.*

WORK TABLE, *top, c. 1850. This table has a one-board top, square, tapered legs, and traces of green paint. Pine, 33¼ x 56½ x 20⅜ inches.*

SCRUB-TOP WORK TABLE, *bottom, c. 1850. This table has a four-board scrub top and a red-painted base. Yellow pine, 30 x 44½ x 40¾ inches.*

ONE-DRAWER TABLE, *opposite top left, attributed to Andrew Varner, c. 1850. Descended in a Kerrs Creek family. Walnut, 28½ x 20 x 18 inches.*

TWO-DRAWER TABLE, *opposite top right, attributed to Andrew Varner, c. 1850. Descended in a Kerrs Creek family. Walnut, 28 x 21 x 21 inches.*

ONE-DRAWER TABLE, *opposite bottom left, attributed to the Andrew Varner shop, c. 1850. This piece, with curved upper stiles, was originally owned by the Gadsden family, Lexington. Walnut, 29 x 30 x 19 inches.*

TWO-DRAWER SEWING TABLE, *opposite bottom right. This table was originally owned by the Pendleton-Gadsden family, Lexington. Walnut, 28¾ x 23¼ x 19¾ inches.*

WASHSTAND, *top left, c. 1850. This piece features a curved splashboard, turned legs, arrow feet, and the original varnish. Walnut, 34 x 26¾ x 19 inches.*

CANDLE STAND, *top right, early 1800s. From the Fairfield area. Walnut, 27½ x 20⅛ x 19⅞ inches.*

DRESSER STAND, *left, c. 1850. This two-drawer stand has turned legs. Descended in a Rockbridge County family. Walnut, 28 x 18 x 18 inches.*

BEDSTEADS

Few bedsteads were photographed for this study because of the limited number that has survived, but probate references to bedsteads—the wooden frame that supported the "bed" and "bed clothes"—reveal the number in use, the types, and the range of appraised valuations of pieces in eighteenth- and nineteenth-century households. Less than half of the probates recorded in the first *Rockbridge County Will Book,* covering the period 1778–96, list bedsteads. During the first quarter of the nineteenth century the frequency of appearances increases, as does the number of bedsteads per household.

The combined listing, characteristic of this period, of bedstead and clothing, or bedstead, bed, and furniture, makes it impossible to determine the valuation of the bed clothes and the bed frame separately. While a bedstead would often receive a modest appraisal—$0.50, $1.00, $4.00—the addition of a feather bed would always increase the valuation significantly. Judith Moody's two feather beds were appraised at $30.00 in 1827, and in 1825 Michael Kirkpatrick had four bedsteads, beds, and clothing, listed at $123.00.[58] During the first quarter of the nineteenth century most households owned one or two bedsteads, and often only one received a high valuation. An exception is the 1825 probate for Joseph Treavy, which lists nine beds and their furniture for a total value of $320.50.[59]

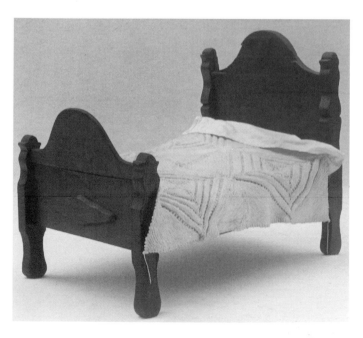

Although probate listings gave brief and simple entries to most furniture, George Wier's 1781 probate contains unusually descriptive entries for bedsteads: an ash bedstead with a "feather bed and furniture of blue stripped tick" valued at 10 pounds, a walnut bedstead with "feather bed and yellow stripped tick furniture and childs bed" at 11 pounds, a "short post walnut bedstead" with "broad blue stripped tick furniture and an underbed" at 12 pounds, and another walnut bedstead with "corse linen furniture" plus a child's bed for 3 pounds 10.[60] Robert Moore's 1783 appraisal includes "one bedstead with turned rounds," "one bedstead with turned post," and "one bedstead with square post."[61]

In the first *Rockbridge County Will Book* bedsteads are described as "small," "short," "high post," "walnut," "walnut short post," "ash," and "painted." Listings include children's beds, trundle bedsteads (bedsteads on wheels), and "underbeds." At the turn of the century these descriptions continue to appear, in addition to "acorn," "common and old," "boys," "childs," and "negroes." Poplar and mahogany were listed as woods and "yellow," "painted," and "stained" as finishes. By midcentury the terms "lounge," "turned," and "cottage" appear. In 1854 Thomas Dryden had a total of seven bedsteads, three described as "round top," one of which was walnut. Another three were listed as "acorn," one as walnut, and one as maple.[62]

Throughout the nineteenth century bedsteads were often listed as "with cord" or "without cord," referring to the hemp rope strung as a support for the mattress, or "bed." The "bed" could be made of a variety of materials, including feather, hair, and straw. The bedstead could be "dressed" with clothes, curtains, or canopy.

The most common bedstead form documented from the midcentury was the popular cottage bed, which belongs to the Elizabethan Revival (c. 1850), one of the many substyles of the Victorian period and closely related to the Gothic Revival. Although mass-produced parts were available from urban sources, local cabinetmakers continued to produce them throughout the mid-nineteenth century. The spool turnings could be produced easily and cheaply on a turning lathe and were an inexpensive alternative to the more elaborate detailing of the Gothic Revival style. The same turned members were also used on towel racks, tables, and hall stands. Andrew Jackson Downing's *Architecture of Country Houses* even suggests that "elaborate bed-room furniture in the Gothic style is seldom seen in country houses in the United States. More simple sets of cottage furniture, in an Elizabethan or mixed style, are preferred, as cheaper and more appropriate."[63]

Andrew Varner's ledger for the 1860s records the sale of "cottage bedsteads" ranging from $10.00 to $12.00, while a plain bedstead sold for $5.00. Varner's shop also produced a "Jenny Lind bedstead," a type of cottage bedstead, for $36.00. Milton Key's 1860 probate indicates a similar inventory.

SENILITY OR INVALID'S CRADLE, *right. This adult cradle was used by Mary Moore Brown (1776–1824), who as a child in Tazewell County, Virginia, lost her family in an Indian massacre and spent some years as a captive of the Shawnee Indians in Ohio. After her rescue she married the Reverend Samuel Brown and settled in Brownsburg. Haunted by her experiences, she is said to have found relief from her insomnia in this cradle. Walnut and poplar, 6 feet long.*

CHILD'S BED WITH SHAPED HEADBOARD, *top, c. 1850. Walnut, 40 x 21½ inches.*

COTTAGE-STYLE DAYBED, *left, late 1800s. This piece, with its scroll arm and sausage-style turnings, is a country interpretation of the Empire style . Walnut, 74 x 26½ inches.*

DOLL'S BED, *opposite, late 1800s. This handcarved doll's bed is evocative of the Renaisance Revival style. Walnut, 16½ x 10¾ x 13¾ inches.*

CHAIRS, BENCHES, AND SETTEES

Eighteenth-century households possessed few chairs; simple benches or stools were more common. The earliest account relating to seating production is a 1780 court order that allowed Samuel Wallace 12 pounds for "2 days making benches for the use of the county."[64] In the first *Rockbridge County Will Book* (1778–95) 40 inventories (from a total of 132) listed 324 chairs. Descriptive terms include "frame," "walnut," and "white oak bottom." Probates in the second *Will Book* (1796–1806) list Windsor and split-bottom chairs, side chairs, armchairs, and rocking chairs, walnut being the only wood listed. Out of fifty-six listings, thirty-one of these had a total of 214 chairs. One entry, dated June 1799, mentions "one chair joiners work." [65] By the middle of the nineteenth century many households owned chairs in sets of six or twelve. John F. Caruthers listed more than fifty chairs on his 1840 probate inventory.

Estate inventories indicate that by the early nineteenth century the Windsor chair was the most common type of seating in Rockbridge County homes.[66] This popularity may account for the large number of these chairs that survive. The earliest record of Windsor chairmaking in Rockbridge County is an 1801 advertisement by William Keys and James Dixon, who announced that they have commenced "WINDSOR CHAIR MAKING, on Main Street next door to Mr. Samuel Harkins, HATTER. All persons who favor them with their custom, may expect good work, executed in the newest and neatest manner."[67]

Dixon's 1820 probate inventory listed "1 set chairmakers tools including turning lathe."[68] Windsors listed in inventories are described as "armed," "square backed," "armed square back," "round back," or "common." They are also noted as being of maple or mahogany, although this probably refers to a painted finish instead of the wood type. Because their construction characteristics made it necessary to combine hard and soft woods, Windsors were usually

painted, generally green (the color most frequently listed) or black. Chairs described simply as yellow or red were also often noted, and these also could have been Windsors. The second most common type of seating listed in estate inventories is the split-bottom chair.

Throughout the nineteenth century chairs are described by function as well as form: sewing chairs, venting chairs, writing chairs, high chairs for children, short chairs, office chairs, and parlor chairs. These chairs are often described as "old," "fine," "new," "ornamented," or "common," as well as by color—green, black, red, or yellow.

Although a few artisans such as Samuel Smith advertised themselves as chairmakers, cabinetmakers such as Milton Key and Andrew Varner also produced chairs, as is clear from their ledgers. In addition, many of the chairs studied could have been produced by a carpenter, wheelwright, or house joiner using simple tools and local materials.

SIDE CHAIR, *opposite left, late 1700s. This chair belonged to Zachariah Johnston, whose 1801 probate listed six walnut chairs. Walnut, 37¾ x 7 inches.*

WILLIAM AND MARY–STYLE ARMCHAIR, *opposite center, late 1700s. Walnut, 45 x 22 inches.*

NATURAL BRIDGE CHAIR, *opposite right, 1825–50. A painting of Natural Bridge decorates this "fancy chair" belonging to Margaret Junkin Preston. Descended in the family. Mixed woods, 31½ x 16½ x 13¾ inches.*

SIDE CHAIR, *top left, late 1700s. This country version of the Chippendale style has an unadorned back splat and crest rail. Descended in the family of the original owner. Walnut, 38 x 22 x 18½ inches.*

SLAT BACK CHAIR, *top center, late 1800s. Mixed woods, 33 x 18½ x 13¼ inches.*

SIDE CHAIR, *top right, 1825–50. This country version of the Hitchcock chair has a curved seat, turned front legs, and gold decoration. 31½ x 16½ x 15 inches.*

STILE OF ROD-BACK SIDE CHAIR, *top left. This back view of a Sheraton-style Windsor side chair with a shaped crest rail shows how the stiles are pegged into the seat. Descended in the Pendleton-Gadsden family, Lexington. Mized woods.*

SIDE CHAIR, *top right. This chair with turned, splayed legs is typical of Rockbridge County chairs.*

ROCKING CHAIR, *opposite top left, early 1800s. This rod-backed Windsor rocking chair has box stretchers, flat crest rails, and simple turned legs. Descended in a Fairfield area family. Mixed woods, 40½ x 22 x 16½ inches.*

WINDSOR SIDE CHAIR, *opposite top center, early 1800s. This nine-spindle, loop-back chair with traces of green paint is stamped "A. Shields." The only A. Shields listed in county records is Alexander Shields, who owned the Eagle Tavern on Lexington's Main Street in the early nineteenth century and whose 1832 probate inventory listed six "green chairs." Mixed woods, 36 x 16 x 15 inches.*

ARM CHAIR, *opposite top right, 1800–1850. The simple turnings, box stretcher bases, and straight crest rails are common in Rockbridge County chairs. Descended in a Fairfield family. Mixed woods, 33⅛ x 16 x 16½ inches.*

WINDSOR SETTEE, *opposite center, early 1800s. This rod-backed Windsor settee has turned bamboo spindles, stretchers, and legs and a one-board seat supported by eight legs. Descended in a Fairfield area family. Mixed woods, 29½ x 81 x 18¾ inches.*

ARROW-BACK SIDE CHAIR, *opposite bottom left, 1800–1850. The Sheraton style "fancy chair" influence is evident in this side chair, one of a set of six from the Stuarts Draft area. Mixed woods, 31 x 19½ x 17 inches.*

WINDSOR WRITING CHAIR, *opposite bottom center, 1800–1850. This chair came from the two-room schoolhouse at Buffalo Forge. 36 x 22 x 22¾ inches.*

SMALL WINDSOR SIDE CHAIR, *opposite bottom right, 1800–1850. "Inez F." is carved on the bottom of the seat. Descended in the Zachariah Johnston family. 25½ x 19½ x 15 inches.*

CHILD'S WINDSOR-STYLE
ROCKING CHAIR, *top, 1825–50.
This small rocker has descended in
the family of Dr. John McCluer
Alexander (1822–67).*

HIGH CHAIR, *left, by John Miley,
late 1800s. 33½ x 12 inches.*

CHILD'S ARM CHAIR, *above,
c. 1850. The chair's split oak seat
is original. Each arm and front
leg is made from one piece of best
wood. Mixed woods, 20⅛ x 13⅜
x 10 inches.*

STICK CHAIR, *opposite, 1864.
According to one source, this stick
or driftwood chair was made by
an idle Union soldier during
General David Hunter's four-day
occupation of Lexington in June
1864. Such handcrafted chairs,
which Andrew Jackson Downing
promoted for outdoor use in his
magazine* The Horticulturalist,
*were popular in the mid- and late
nineteenth century. Descended in
a Lexington family. Mixed woods,
59½ x 26½ x 20½ inches.*

Tall Clocks

Mority Thurman has been recently repairing and cleaning a clock that was made in 1798 by Thomas Whiteside then of the County of Rockbridge. This clock has been in the possession of one family since 1814 and is now running as regularly as at any previous time in its history.

— LEXINGTON GAZETTE, JANUARY 15, 1875

ost of the towns in the Shenandoah Valley of Virginia, from Winchester to Fincastle, had strong clockmaking traditions. Middletown, a village just south of Winchester, was known at one time as "clocktown," and Winchester gained an early reputation for clocks and other fine furniture.[1] In the southern end of the Valley there appears to have been a close association between the clockmakers of Staunton and Lexington. This study has produced new information on one very productive clockmaking shop in Lexington in the late eighteenth and early nineteenth centuries—that of Thomas Whiteside.

Moses Whiteside, the father of Thomas Whiteside, came from Ireland or England to the Rockbridge County area (then Augusta County) in about 1750 and settled on Borden's Grant, acquiring land first in the Timber Ridge area in 1750.[2] Three years later he was listed as a communicant of Timber Ridge Church.[3] Over the years Moses, who lived in a stone house near South River, accumulated considerable land holdings while working as a gunsmith and silversmith. When he died in 1795, he left tracts of land in the county to his sons, Thomas and Moses II.[4] Earlier, in 1780, Thomas had acquired one of the original half-acre lots in the town of Lexington, on the northwest corner of Nelson and Randolph Streets, where he may have first established his Lexington business and residence.[5]

CLOCK FACE, *opposite, by James Huston, c. 1775. The brass dial is engraved "Jas. Huston/Augusta."*

MOVEMENT, ALEXANDER-ANDERSON CLOCK, *above, by Thomas Whiteside, c. 1810.*

VALLEY
CLOCKMAKERS

The early clockmakers in the Valley often engraved their names on their brass dials, and later they had their names painted on the white dials, but they were not necessarily clock manufacturers. They were rather assemblers and dealers, knowledgeable enough to put together the components of a tall clock, including the movement and the dial, and find cabinetmakers they could count on. Their role was to coordinate the process and manage the marketing, dealing with the local customer who might want a moon dial, some fancy inlay on the case, or an especially tall clock to stand in the front hall of his or her new house. Nonetheless, these dealers had to have a thorough knowledge of how the clock worked, for in many cases they had to assemble the movement from parts from various sources or attach a new dial to an old movement.[6]

Before the American Revolution brass dials and their movements were made in both America and England. As soon as trade with England was resumed in 1783, these were replaced almost entirely by less expensive painted dials and mass-produced movements made in and around Birmingham, England.[7] The new dials were made of iron, painted white, and varnished to simulate enamel. Merchants in England and jobbers on the American East Coast could stock ready-made movements and dials and offer a vast quantity and a large assortment of faces. Not only were the white-painted dials less expensive than brass; their "new and modish neoclassical motifs lent themselves well as decoration for the light, easy-to-read white dials, rapidly making them more fashionable than brass dials, which were associated with the Baroque and Rococo styles."[8]

Probably most of the movements and their white-painted dials came to the Valley from the Birmingham area by way of dealers in Philadelphia and Baltimore. In 1818 one Baltimore clockmaker advertised "Dials in a great variety," including "a large Supply of 12, 13, and 14 inch moon and solid arch Dials."[9] More than likely the dials received their numbering and the paintings in the spandrels and on the moon dials in Birmingham, and the local clockmakers-retailers in this country had their name and sometimes that of their town lettered on the face.

Despite mass production of the parts, a tall case clock represented a considerable investment, so it is not surprising that descendants of the original owners held on to these valuable pieces. This study identified eleven clocks that can be attributed to Thomas Whiteside's business in Lexington from the early 1790s to about 1819.

Whiteside probably began his Lexington clockmaking business around 1790. A 1793 ledger kept by Alphonso Weir, a Lexington blacksmith, notes that he had made a "rod" for Thomas Whiteside. A year later Weir produced something else for Whiteside described in his ledger only as "To clockwork, 0/1/6." The same year Thomas bought from the Lexington store of J. & D. Hoffman & Co. a "ballance of silver" for 35 pounds, 6 pence.[10]

In 1795 a "clock and case"—clearly a tall case clock—was listed in the estate inventory of James Lyle, who would have been a near neighbor of Whiteside's at Timber Ridge. For the next eight years eight estate inventories included "clock and case" or "8 day clock," indicating a considerable number of tall clocks in the county. A number of the owners were communicants of Timber Ridge Church or lived in the Timber Ridge–South River section of the county near the Whiteside family land. All these clocks were probably produced by Thomas Whiteside's shop. At least two appear to be among the clocks found and examined in this survey: the Samuel Lyle clock, found in Texas, and the William Alexander clock, now in Roanoke.

HUSTON-WHITESIDE
GROUP

The clocks attributed to Whiteside in Rockbridge County seem to fall into two groups, divided according to each group's distinctive proportions and architectural characteristics. The earlier group is very similar to a number of clocks made in the Staunton area just north of Lexington and produced by or attributed to James Huston from about 1770 to around 1810. Thomas Whiteside's father, Moses, who served in the same unit with Huston in the French and Indian War,[11] could have been one of Huston's engravers. Also, young Thomas could possibly have served as Huston's apprentice for a while around 1790, before beginning his operation in the Lexington area. Two of Huston's walnut neoclassical clocks that have survived have his name and "Augusta" engraved on their brass dials. Both are of exceptional craftsmanship, with cases by unknown cabinetmakers. Along the trunk and base are fluted quarter columns, and the scrolled pediments, with their delicate dentil work, end in finely carved, six-lobed, incised double rosettes.

The cases of two of Whiteside's Rockbridge County clocks in this group, the Samuel Lyle clock and the Kerrs Creek clock, with their large carved rosettes, fluted quarter columns on the trunk and base, ogee feet, and hollow cornered trunk doors, closely resemble the Huston cases. In both, however, the scrolled pediments appear to rise at a somewhat awkward angle. Perhaps a local cabinetmaker was asked to duplicate the earlier and perhaps more "correct" Huston clock cases but did not have the benefit of a template or pattern. The Samuel Lyle clock has a brass dial (the only one found with a clear Whiteside attribution), and the Kerrs Creek clock has a white dial, which could have replaced an earlier brass one.

BRASS DIAL, *top, by Thomas Whiteside, c. 1795. It is engraved "Thomas Whiteside/Clockmaker/ Lexington" and "Samuel Lyle," probably the owner.*

WHITE DIAL, *above, attributed to James Huston, c. 1795.*

TALL CASE CLOCK, *right, by James Huston, c. 1775. Walnut, 97 x 20½ x 11½ inches.*

GIBSON-LIPSCOMB CLOCK,
by Thomas Whiteside, clockmaker,
and John Smith, cabinetmaker,
c. 1810. All the Whiteside-Smith
clocks illustrated here have a white
dial, diamond-shaped hood
windows, and a chamfered trunk,
and most have French feet.
Walnut, 101 x 19 x 10¼ inches.

ALEXANDER-ANDERSON CLOCK,
by Thomas Whiteside, clockmaker,
and John Smith, cabinetmaker,
c. 1810. "Thomas Whiteside" is
penciled inside the case. Cherry,
101 x 19 x 10¼ inches.

REID-WHITE CLOCK, *by Thomas*
Whiteside, clockmaker, and John
Smith, cabinetmaker, 1815. One of
two clocks signed by cabinetmaker
Smith inside the case, it was
probably made for Andrew Reid
of Mulberry Hill. Cherry, 104 x
18½ x 10¼ inches.

ZACHARIAH JOHNSTON CLOCK,
by Thomas Whiteside, clockmaker,
and John Smith, cabinetmaker,
c. 1810. This is the only clock from
the Whiteside shop with turned
feet. Walnut, 106 x 18½ x 10¼
inches.

WHITESIDE-SMITH GROUP

The second group of Whiteside clock cases is distinctive. It appears that all the cases could have been made by the Lexington cabinetmaker John Smith, for Smith, unlike almost all other casemakers of tall case clocks in the Valley, signed his name several times inside at least two of his clocks. One clock, probably made for Andrew Reid of Mulberry Hill plantation, is signed in pencil "John Smith/Cabinetmaker" and "John Smith/April 4, 1815," and again, "John Smith." Smith signed the Parent-Humphries clock twice in pencil inside the case behind the pendulum.

The two cases signed by Smith are so similar to the other seven that it would appear that Smith or his shop made all the cases in this series for Whiteside. Little is known of Smith's cabinetmaking business in Lexington except that it must have begun in the 1790s and continued until his death in 1819. By 1819 he clearly had a sizable operation, for he advertised in the local paper that he "Wanted Immediately Two Boys of respectable families, From fifteen to 17 years of age, to learn Cabinet Making Business. If immediate application is made, advantageous terms may be expected."[12] The sense of urgency in his notice suggests that Smith may have been ill and anxious to see that his business was ensured a future through his apprentices. He died a few months after placing the notice. What became of his shop is unclear. His estate inventory included, among other things, "1 lot cabinet makers tools $86.00," in addition to a turning lathe, an unfinished secretary, a small poplar desk, a mahogany bureau, a china press, and walnut, cherry, and poplar "planks." The value placed on his cabinetmaking tools, $86.00, would indicate an extensive shop setup. Although he must have produced a great number of pieces of furniture for local consumption, the only piece of Smith furniture, other than his clocks, that is positively identified is an Empire chest of drawers inscribed "John Smith of Lexington" and "made for Robert McClure in 1817."[13]

The two most distinctive characteristics of the seven Whiteside-Smith clocks are the simplicity of the tall, narrow cases and the delicately scrolled pediments ending with small inlay rosettes. The cases are derived from a group of Pennsylvania clocks that show the same verticality and graceful simplicity. A clock in the collection of the Museum of Art at the Carnegie Institute bears a close resemblance to the Lexington-made clocks, except that it is more highly decorated with inlay. The Pittsburgh clock was made by the firm of John Johnston and Samuel Davis, which was active around 1805. Both Johnston and Davis came to Pittsburgh from Ireland. The case was made around 1802 by an unknown Pittsburgh cabinetmaker.[14] Undoubtedly clock patterns were passed from one cabinetmaking shop to another, and the transition of the scrolled ped-

INLAY ROSETTE, GIBSON-LIPSCOMB CLOCK. *This eight-part rosette on the scrolled* *pediment is typical of the Whiteside-Smith clocks.*

iment pattern south from Pennsylvania would not seem unlikely.

In keeping with Smith's penchant for simplicity, only two of his clocks have hood columns, although the hoods were constructed so that columns could be added. And all have pedimented hood tops forming about the same angle. Seven of the nine have diamond hood windows, although the sizes vary considerably; two have the more traditional astragal windows. In every clock in this group the trunk doors have square corners, unlike the two earlier Whiteside clocks and the Augusta County Huston clocks, which have hollow-cornered doors. Consistently Smith chose the simplest route in his construction.

URN MOTIF, ALEXANDER-ANDERSON CLOCK, *right.* *The white painted face and movement were probably produced in Birmingham, England.*

CLOVER MOTIF, PARENT-HUMPHRIES CLOCK, *bottom.* *This painted face, typical of the Whiteside-Smith clocks, is signed inside "John Smith."*

All the Whiteside clock cases are of walnut or cherry; yellow pine was used as a secondary wood. Several have a single-board back, with the top of the board cut to take the pedimented hood. The use of inlay varies considerably and is different on each clock. Several have only a stringing around the hood and the base, while others have various narrow bands on the hood and base. The Mackey-Williams clock has a wide inlay band running vertically in the center of the corner chamfering on the trunk.

Of the clocks that have original white dials the numbering and painted spandrels on the dials appear to have been done in the same style—and presumably by the same person or company—in Birmingham, England. A clover motif is used throughout, but no two dials are painted exactly the same way. The dials themselves are of several designs—some have moon dials, several have sweeping second hands, and some have small second hands. But in every case the painting and numbering seem to have been done by the same artisan.

Thomas Whiteside apparently left his Lexington business around 1816 and moved to Kanawha County, Virginia (later Charleston, West Virginia), where he was counted in the census of 1820. Various members of the Whiteside family also moved on to the South and West, setting up businesses in North Carolina and southwest Virginia and as far away as Missouri. Thomas's brother Moses and his son, Samuel C. A., carried on the Lexington business for several years, but the death of the casemaker John Smith in 1819 apparently ended the Whiteside clockmaking operation.

BONNET, PARENT-HUMPHRIES CLOCK, *left. The pedimented hood is a hallmark of the Whiteside-Smith clocks, but the astragal hood windows are found in only two of the group. Cherry, 101 x 18⅜ x 10¼ inches.*

HOOD INLAY, MACKEY-WILLIAMS CLOCK, *below, by Thomas Whiteside, clockmaker, and John Smith, cabinetmaker. One of the few Whiteside clocks with hood columns, it is also one of the most decorated, with inlay down the chamfered trunk and base. Walnut, 104 x 19¼ x 10¾ inches.*

BASE INLAY, MACKEY-WILLIAMS CLOCK, *left. The inlay continues through the chamfering to the base, where a larger band of alternating light and dark woods runs horizontally across the shaped skirt.*

ELIAS LEWIS—
JACOB BEAR GROUP

By this time Whiteside's son-in-law, Elias Lewis, had a well-established clockmaking shop in Lexington. Where Lewis came from is not known, but in 1820 he reported that he had three sets of clockmaking tools and a capital investment of one thousand dollars, which was considerable for that time. One clock case examined during the study has "Elias Lewis" printed on the white dial. The case has been attributed to Christian Bear, a well-known cabinetmaker in Churchville, a small community north of Lexington in Augusta County.[15] The Lewis-Bear clock case has a much less ornate dial and case than the earlier clocks attributed to Whiteside.

Whether or not Christian Bear made the case for the Elias Lewis clock, it is interesting that Jacob Bear, possibly Christian's brother, began dealing in tall case clocks in Lexington beginning in 1823. Bear announced in the Lexington paper that he had opened a shop "in the West end of Mr. John Sloan's New Brick Building, nearly opposite to the Eagle Tavern where he intends carrying on the Watch Making, and the Gold and Silver Smith business in its various branches."[16] This study identified five clocks that can be attributed to Jacob Bear's business. Bear's casemaker is not known. None of the ledgers of the Lexington cabinetmakers covers the period of his tall case clock production, which was probably from 1823 to about 1835–40. An account book in Augusta County does mention that in 1828 James Rankin, a self-styled carpenter and joiner, had made two clock cases (at $12.00 and $18.00).[17]

Bear's name appears as "J. Bear" or "Jacob Bear, Lexington, Va." on four of his white dial clocks. All the Bear clocks have turned legs and scrolled pediments, but beyond that their cases display few similarities. The legend persists that they were made by Christian Bear, but there seems to be little evidence for this attribution. Perhaps they were done by a variety of Lexington cabinetmakers. The Bear clocks are of walnut and cherry, like the ones by Smith and Whiteside, but they are about twelve inches shorter and make more extensive use of veneer. Some details are reminiscent of the earlier Whiteside clocks—for instance, the inlay

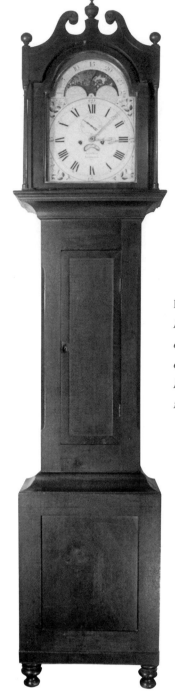

HOPKINS CLOCK, *by Jacob Bear, clockmaker, and unknown cabinetmaker, c. 1823. This is one of six clocks attributed to the Bear shop. Cherry, 97 x 18½ x 10¼ inches.*

rosettes on the Bear-Williamson clock, found in Harrisonburg—which suggests a relationship to the earlier Whiteside-Smith shop.

By the 1830s relatively inexpensive mass-produced shelf clocks made in Connecticut and other northern states became widely available. The days of the tall case clock and its makers came to an end in the Valley and elsewhere. Jacob Bear, like many other clockmakers, carried on his business as a jeweler and silversmith; in 1842 he advertised "Watches and Jewelry" and a "handsome Assortment lately received from Philadelphia." He noted also that he was "repairing clocks and watches as usual."[18]

The tall case clock enjoyed a brief revival during the centennial of the American Revolution. In the 1880s, following the publication of a popular song, it became the "grandfather" clock.

MOON DIAL, *top, c. 1835. The dial includes maps of the Eastern and Western Hemispheres. The case for this clock appears to have been made by the same cabinetmaker who made the Hopkins clock, which is signed by Jacob Bear.*

WHITE DIAL WITH ROMAN NUMERALS, HOPKINS CLOCK, *left. The dial, one of four signed by Bear, is inscribed "Jacob Bear/ Lexington Va."*

Rifles

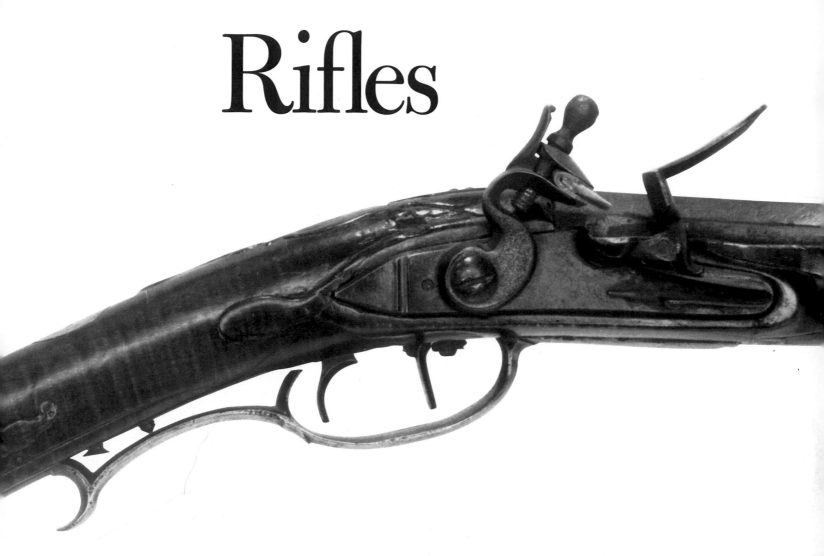

We went to the mountains and got close-grained rock maple—the trees that grow on thin rocky soil are always closer grained and curlier than those that grow in open ground on heavy soil.

—MILTON WARREN, APPRENTICE GUNSMITH TO JOHN M. WHITESIDE[1]

Until the eighteenth century there does not seem to have been any tradition of rifle making in America.[2] Soon after 1700 gunsmiths from southern Germany and Switzerland began arriving in Pennsylvania along with thousands of other emigrants from those countries. They settled mostly west and south of Philadelphia and began turning out the same kinds of rifles they had made for their European customers.

STOCK AND LOCK, DAVIDSON LONG RIFLE, *opposite, by John Davidson, c. 1780s. Davidson's* *initials are engraved on the patch box. Curly maple stock, 45-inch barrel, 44 caliber.*

In small shops a single gunsmith would make the wooden and metal parts himself and fit them together, thus functioning as wood carver, blacksmith, and locksmith. In larger shops three different artisans might work together, one making the lock, another the stock, and the third the barrel—hence the old phrase "lock, stock, and barrel" to mean that everything is taken care of.[3] Each rifle made by the small shops was carefully handcrafted and therefore unique. Each smith had his own style, recognizable then (and to experts now) even if the rifle was unsigned.[4] Fortunately, a number of gunsmiths did engrave their initials or their name, usually in script, on the top of the barrel or on the patch box.

As the enterprising Pennsylvania Germans and their Scotch-Irish neighbors made forays westward into Virginia, Kentucky,

Tennessee, and Ohio, these frontiersmen fast became the best customers of the Pennsylvania gunsmiths. As the woodsmen came back from their travels, they discussed with the gunsmiths what refinements were needed in the rifles. After all, the rifle was the possession most important for ensuring the pioneers' survival as they pushed farther and farther into the new territories.

Soon the rifles made by these first and second generations of gunsmith-settlers took on a special American look—quite different from the stubbier European prototype. The iron barrels became long and slender and usually eight-sided. Most tubes were 36 to 48 inches long; the size was generally related to the client's height and reach.

As a wave of settlers began to follow the first pioneers from Pennsylvania into the Valley of Virginia, so did a number of able gunsmiths. Smiths in Winchester and other Valley towns were soon able to produce enough weapons needed for frontiersmen and the local militia.[5]

Firsthand descriptions of eighteenth-century or early-nineteenth-century long rifle manufacturers in Rockbridge County are not readily available, but John G. W. Dillin's *Kentucky Rifle,* published in 1925, gives a careful account of gunmaking in the south-west Virginia area. Dillin's account of John M. Whiteside's "factory" in King's Mill, near Abington in Washington County, shows strong similarities to the gunmaking process of earlier decades in the Rockbridge area.

John M. Whiteside was born in Rockbridge and was the son of the clockmaker Moses Whiteside II and the grandson of Moses I, an early Rockbridge settler and gun- and silversmith at Timber Ridge. In about 1830 he left Rockbridge to settle in southwest Virginia, where he soon headed a large gunmaking operation. One of his apprentices, Milton Warren, left a detailed description of the barrel- and stock-making processes and every other facet of the Whiteside operation, which Dillin reprinted. For stocking material, Warren recorded,

We went to the mountains and got close-grained rock maple. . . . Sometimes we used walnut, now and then cherry, and occasionally a customer would bring his own stock plank of apple wood. A cherry crotch makes a beautiful stock and apple finishes up very smooth and stays where you put it; it also takes inlaying well, but both apple and cherry depend upon their grain for beauty, while curly maple can be finished with various stains and is just about the prettiest wood in the world.[6]

Warren remembered that at the Whiteside shop "it took about a week to make a good, plain rifle, of which time two days would be spent on the stock." He went on: "While we carried a few guns in stock, they were usually made to specifications as to length of barrel, weight, ornamentation, etc. Not infrequently the order would be to 'make a gun just like' the one used by some famous marksman in the vicinity."[7]

For the barrel "a bar of iron of the right length, width and thickness would be selected." Warren said that the bar was then brought to "welding heat" and turned around a "core rod" that made a bore "somewhat larger than the ultimate bore desired" into half the length of the bar of iron. Then the same process was done to the other end, while the bar itself was worked into an octagonal form.

Warren recalled that "we did not bother much with flatters or shaping devices of any kind—just trusted to hand and eye—yet when the barrels left the anvil they were very straight and regular, requiring but little grinding." As a whimsical footnote to this precise and tedious process, Warren admitted that if a barrel "showed flaws" and did not develop properly "we just threw it away, made some remarks to the mountains, took a drink of spring water and welded another barrel."[8]

Other gunsmiths of the early and mid-nineteenth century would undoubtedly take issue with Warren's descriptions of the accepted processes in Whiteside's Virginia gunmaking shop. But Warren insisted that Whiteside's "guns were all nicely finished; they were symmetrical and pleasing to the eye; they were good in the hand and at the shoulder, and they shot where they were held." He reported that "after the gun was finished the old man [Whiteside] would say, 'Well Milt, she's finished, but she ain't wuth a d—— if she won't shoot straight; let's try her.' He was by all odds the best rifle shot I have ever known and no gun ever suited him unless it was capable of driving a tack three times out of five at fifty yards."[9]

The major period of long-rifle production in the Valley of Virginia was between 1750 and 1830. The earlier guns were fitted with flintlocks, and the stocks generally had elaborately carved relief. Later the stocks received an inlay of silver or brass (or both) and patch boxes, as can be seen in those illustrated here. The percussion cap came into use by the 1820s, and many of the flintlocks were refitted.

James B. Whisker, who examined more than five hundred Virginia rifles for his recent book *Gunsmiths of Virginia*, concluded that in the Shenandoah Valley "guns of artistic significance were still being made well into the percussion period." And he noted that in isolated areas in the Virginia–West Virginia mountains long rifles were still being made almost until the beginning of the twentieth century, as in the case of John Whiteside.[10]

TIMBER RIDGE CHURCH, *opposite, 1755. John Davidson was a member of this church, which was located seven miles north of Lexington on the Valley Pike. Davidson owned property nearby and may have had his shop there.*

IRON LOCKPLATE, FLINTLOCK RIFLE, *above, before 1801. Recent excavation of the ruins of Liberty Hall Academy by the Washington and Lee Laboratory of Anthropology has produced a number of firearms artifacts similar to those documented in this study.*

Walker Long Rifle, by Alexander Walker, c. 1780. The Timber Ridge gunsmith engraved "ALXR Walker" on top of the barrel. Plain maple stock, brass mounts, 44-inch barrel, 50 caliber.

TIMBER RIDGE: THE WALKER AND DAVIDSON SHOPS

There seems to be ample evidence that William Lyle was in the gunmaking business at Timber Ridge in the mid-eighteenth century. Lyle was born at Timber Ridge in approximately 1746, soon after his father, John Lyle, arrived from County Antrim, Ireland, by way of Pennsylvania. William apparently began a gunsmithing operation around 1765. In his estate inventory of August 1782 were listed "gunsmith's tools" and "a forged gun barrel." Nothing more is known of William Lyle, but considerable information is available about his neighbors, the Walker and Davidson families, from contemporary county records and especially listings of tools in wills and estate inventories. For instance, John Davidson's will, recorded in 1835, stipulated that his "Smith tools of every kind [go] to my son John, likewise my clock." Those were perhaps Davidson's most valuable possessions.[11]

The first Walkers settled on Walkers Creek, near Brownsburg, in the early 1700s, but family members a generation later who were involved in blacksmithing and rifle making appear to have lived in the Timber Ridge area. Harold B. Gill's *Gunsmiths of Colonial Virginia* lists two John Walkers who were Rockbridge gunsmiths; one died in 1794, and the other was active in 1796. County land records indicate that there was another John Walker who was a gun stocker.[12] An Alexander Walker was also a gunsmith. It is possible that they all worked together in an active shop. Ample evidence of gunmaking activity is available for all four Walkers, but only one rifle has been found that can be attributed to them; this one is by Alexander Walker.

The 50-caliber rifle by Alexander Walker was probably made about 1780 and has "ALXR Walker" engraved in script on the top of the 44-inch barrel. The stock is plain maple, and the sliding box door appears to be a replacement.[13] All the mounts are brass.

The Augusta County and Rockbridge County records list a number of Alexander Walkers. There are several references to Alexander Walker, a wheelwright, in the Augusta County records in 1767, 1769, and 1771.[14] He could have been the father of the gunsmith Alexander Walker and one of the several John Walkers. This Alexander Walker died around 1850, and at his estate sale John Echard bought "1 sett Blacksmith's tools," for $8.05, and William

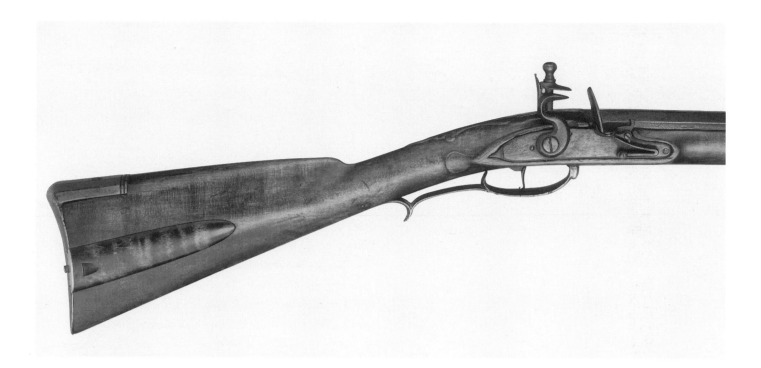

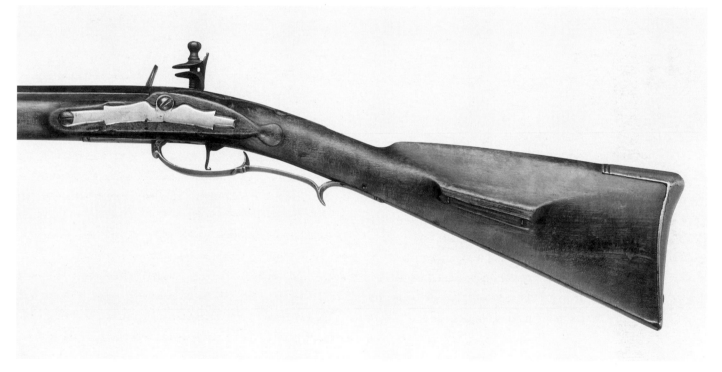

RIFLE STOCK, *top and bottom, by Alexander Walker, c. 1780. This stock is typical of Revolutionary War rifles from the Rockbridge County area. Carvings include* *beaver tails on both sides of the wrist and a floral pattern relief. The stock retains its original wooden slide patchbox cover and iron lock.*

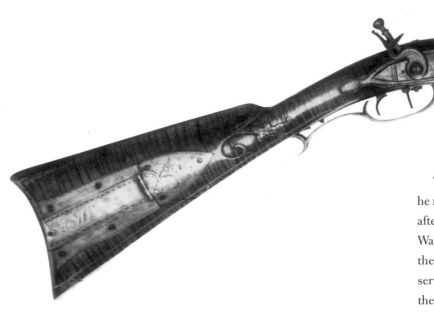

DAVIDSON LONG RIFLE, *by John Davidson, c. 1780s. This is one of four known Davidson rifles.*

Stuart bought "1 rifle gun" for $4.05.[15] The background of the four Walkers associated with the Rockbridge gunmaking business is still unclear.[16] In the county's land books in the 1780s and 1790s, the various John Walkers have a notation beside their names so the tax collector could tell them apart. One gunsmith, John Walker I, died on December 12, 1794, and the appraisal of his estate lists a number of items relating to his smithing business:[17]

One Smith Anvill	5..0..0
One Smiths Vice	2..5..0
Smith Bellices	3..0..0
Iron and Hammers 39 pounds	0.14..7½
Lock Tools 29 pounds	0.10.10½
Handsaw	0..6..0
Riffle Guide	1..0..0
Files	0.12..0
Welding Rods and Boarding Bits	0.12..0
Cutting Knife	0..2..0
Plain for plaining Gun Barrels	0..3..0
Plains and oald Iron Tools	1..0..6
Oald hoes and oald iron	0..4..0

The second John Walker was described as a gunsmith when he received a land grant in Rockbridge County in 1796, two years after the first John Walker died. His land adjoined that of John Walker, the gun stocker in the county records.[18] This is apparently the same gunsmith John Walker whose day book has been preserved in the Wisconsin Historical Society. He was active during the same period as the first John Walker and for at least a year after he died. The entries in the book include:

> March 24, 1791, to Samuel Welch—shears mended—
> ditt gate hanges 1/3/3
>
> Jan. 16, 1792 to James Walker, 1 sett fire Dogs
>
> Jan. 14, 1792 Adam Garnes to a gun barrel
>
> Mar. 10, 1792 John Hays to Branding Iron
>
> July 1792 Alexander Hindman to a Tom hake 2s
>
> 1792 James Elliot plot shield mend and
> iron hook for split
>
> 1793 Walker gunbarrel
>
> 1794 James Walker pr. pot hook
>
> 1794 William Walker broad ax made
>
> 1794 John Geardon a gun barrel, not filed
>
> 1795 William Walker gun forged
>
> 1795 Robert Culton Bowplate Iron
>
> Jan. 1795 Adam Garner gunbarrel not filed

The entries show the variety of iron items he was dealing with. From the number of gun barrels noted in the ledger it seems probable that this John Walker was supplying the gun barrels for the larger Walker shop at Timber Ridge.[19]

John Davidson, probably the best-known Rockbridge gunsmith, was also associated with the Walker gunsmiths, as well as the Whiteside clockmakers, all in the Timber Ridge–South River neighborhood. Davidson was born in 1757 in what was then Augusta (later Rockbridge) County. His period of activity in the Timber Ridge area was from about 1782 to about 1814. In 1808 Davidson applied to the state for a contract to manufacture rifles. A Mr. Grigsby (probably Rueben) of Lexington wrote Governor William Cabell: "I can say from my own knowledge, and information of Others, that Mr. Davidson is Justly entitled to the first order in his profession, and is a man in whom great confidence would be placed by any that have the pleasure of his acquaintance."[20]

No day book of Davidson's gunmaking operation has been located. But the entries in the ledger of Lexington hatmaker John Ruff are useful. Davidson paid his bill to Ruff by repairing two guns on February 14, 1809. On March 6, 1809, Davidson charged Ruff one pound for "straighting cutting making main spring." During the next few years Davidson made "sundry" other gun-related items for Ruff. In 1813 he provided Ruff with "1 pair Bullet Moles" for 50 cents. Later that year he charged Ruff 58 cents for repairing a "pistol lock." And a year later, in January 1814, Davidson charged Ruff $1.34 for "repairing pistol & lock."[21]

Four known John Davidson rifles, which were produced during the period 1770–1810, have been examined. One, collected in Fincastle, is signed in script on the barrel "J. Davidson" and has a 44-caliber bore, a stock of curly maple, and "J.D." engraved on the patch box door.

A second surviving John Davidson rifle was produced about 1800. This one was made for Adam Hickman, a Rockbridge County resident; "A.H." is engraved on the patch box and "Davidson" on the top of the barrel. The carved stock is similar to the other Davidson rifles. Hickman shows up in the county records as a prosperous farmer. He died in 1849, and his estate inventory included eleven slaves, five horses, "lots of cattle," a sixty-gallon still, an "eight day clock," and one rifle gun—presumably the one made for him by John Davidson.[22]

Writers on gunsmithing in Virginia and what is now West Virginia have tended to divide eighteenth and nineteenth-century craftsmen into various schools, such as the Eastern Virginia School, the Berkeley County School, and the James River School. The Walker and Davidson shops fall into the James River group.

JOHN HANNA OF COLLIERS CREEK

Another early gunsmith active in Rockbridge County was the versatile John Hanna. The items in his estate inventory suggest that he was a silversmith, gunsmith, and perhaps a clockmaker. He lived in the Colliers Creek section of the county, near Botetourt County. There is ample evidence that he was active from the mid-1750s until his death in 1781, although no rifles made by him have been located.

The early Augusta County court records indicate that there were more than one—perhaps three—John Hannas in Augusta County before Rockbridge County was formed in 1778. The one whose will is recorded in Rockbridge in 1781 built a mill on Colliers Creek about 1768.[23] That same year John Summers, James Gilmore, and Moses Collier were ordered to "view a road from George Gibson's at House Mountain to John Hanna's Mill."[24] The earliest mention of John Hanna was in 1754, when he agreed to teach "the art and mistery of Black Smith and Gun Smith" to his indentured servant, John Mitchell.[25] The Hanna-Mitchell association apparently prospered, for in 1775 they were both added to the tax books ("added to tithables").[26] In 1780, about a year before he died, Hanna was paid for mending a gun barrel.[27] His estate inventory, recorded in the Rockbridge County will records, included considerable gunsmithing tools and a great many other items used by various artisans. The inventory even included a "leath [lathe] for Clock making, £3."[28] His 1782 estate inventory, only a portion of which is given here, included a wide variety of artisan's tools:

A Sett of Black Smith Tools £20.2 A pair of Large Stilliards 15/ 20.17..0

A pair of Small Stilliards 7/6 two pair of Spoon Mouls & 2 Ladles 36/ 2..3..6

A small Beck Iron and Big Shears 20/ a parcel of Small bench Tools 70/ 4.10..0

A parcel of files and Rasps 3/ 2 Drawing Knives 3/ 0..6..0

A parcel of Small Tools 4/ 2 Boaring Bits and an old Ax 5/ 0..9..0

A pair of Iron vice half made 20/ A Grinding Stone 3/ 1..3..0

A Smooth Boar Gun 7/6 A parcel of old Gun Barrels 6/ 0.13..6

A new forged Gun Barrel & Bored 30/ 106 ½lb Iron 35/6 3..5..6

A Chest and Small Tools in it 65/ A Box & a parcel of tools 10/ 3.15..0

A Saddle Tree & old Saddle 7/6 A parcel of flasks & Sand for Casting Brass 5/ 0.12..6

A parcel of Plains 25 A Small Vice & 2 Augres 22/6 2..7..6

A pair of Wooden Vice 4/ A pair of Small Bellowses 35/ 1.19..0

A Box & Sodering Irons 3/ A Chest & a Candle Stick 10/ 0.13..0

2 Guns & old old hagste 18/ A Brewing Keive 3/ 1..1..0

A Set of Instruments for Cutting Guns 40/ 2..0..0

An old Saw for Cutting Guns 7/ A ew and Two lambs 16/ 1..3..0

Book Accounts £16..8..4 A leath for Clock making £3 19..8..4

CLEMMER AND ZOLLMAN RIFLES

John Clemmer produced rifles at his shop on Walkers Creek around the mid-nineteenth century. Family records indicate he was born in 1799 and died in 1856. Two handsome rifles signed by him were located during this study. Fortunately, Clemmer's estate inventory is preserved in the county records, although the ink has badly faded and only a part of it is legible. The estate sale is dated December 22, 1854, and from the notations in the will books it is clear that Clemmer had a large operation. His estate included the following items:

> H. B. Jones bought a gun shader and a box of caps
>
> James Miller—1 lot of castings
>
> Wm. Stoner—1 pistol lock
>
> Alb. N. Miller—1 lot Bullet moles
>
> W. M. Kinney—1 gun lock
>
> Wm. Reid—1 gun lock
>
> C. Walker—1 lot of gun guards
>
> Jacob Bowman—pistol

Also sold at the estate sale were three augers and a drawing knife. Clemmer's total estate was settled at $2,770.[29]

Another early and apparently very productive Rockbridge County gunsmith was William Zollman. A number of his rifles have survived. Zollman was born in the Locust Bottom community of Rockbridge County but soon moved to the Forks of the James in the Natural Bridge area. Some years after his marriage to Ann Ripley of Fincastle in 1808, he purchased land on Buffalo Creek, at the north end of Short Hill, where he "developed a very fine gunsmith shop, a carding mill, and a distillery."[30] The name "Zollmans Mill" became a place name in the county. Zollman was active as a gunsmith from about 1814 until he died on August 9, 1834. He is buried on his farm. One source says that on William's death, Henry, one of his eleven children, inherited the gunsmithing business and operated it until 1896.[31]

Five rifles signed by or attributed to William Zollman were examined during this study, one of which is shown here. There are striking similarities between the patch boxes on Zollman's rifle and one made by John Sites, a Fincastle gunsmith. One Zollman rifle is signed "W. Zollman" in a silver setting on top of the barrel. Another has a "man-in-the-moon" in silver on the stock.

Zollman's estate appraisal in 1834 listed six slaves and a considerable amount of gunsmithing items, including "1 lot cooper stuff; one set Gun Smith tools ($30.00); 1 set Smith tools ($35.00); 1 lot old iron; 1 shot gun; lot of brass; 5 augers; lot carpenters tools ($5.00)." The estate sale on May 20, 1835, also listed one eight-day clock and case ($40.00).[32]

ZOLLMAN RIFLE DECORATION. *Zollman's engraved silver decoration included the man in the moon, above, on the stock of a c. 1815 gun; his signature "W. Zollman," right top, on the barrel of a c. 1820–25 gun; and a star, right bottom, on the stock of the same gun.*

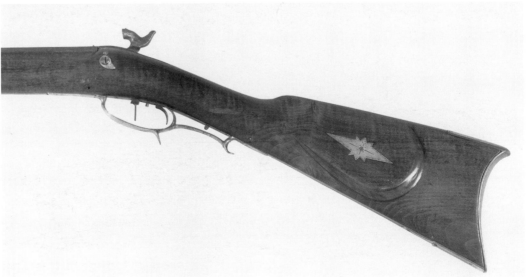

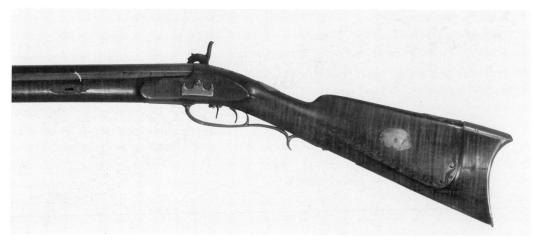

ZOLLMAN LONG RIFLE, *top,*
by William Zollman, c. 1820–25.
The brass stock and patchbox are
engraved with a four-petal, spiral,
flower motif typical of Winchester
rifles. A detail of Zollman's
signature is shown on the opposite
page. Walnut stock, brass mounts,
44¼-inch barrel.

CLEMMER LONG RIFLE, *middle*
and bottom, by John Clemmer,
c. 1825–30. This is one of two rifles
by Clemmer, a Walkers Creek
gunsmith, examined in this study.
The barrel is engraved with
"J. Clemmer" and the stock is deco-
rated with inlay. Curly maple stock,
brass mounts, 41¾-inch barrel.

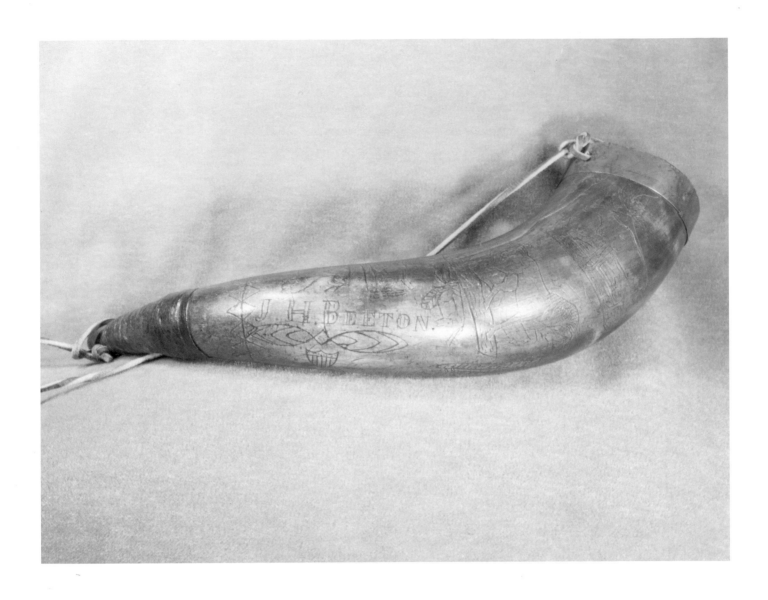

THE BEETON
OPERATION AND VMI

Sometime around 1831 John Beeton moved to Lexington from the Mt. Solon area of Augusta County, near the Mossy Creek iron furnace. Soon after he arrived in Lexington he began a gunmaking operation. Little is known of his early Lexington activity, but when he died in 1848 he left in his estate "a set of gunsmiths tools," valued at $25.00, and 400 feet of "gunstock planks."[33] The Virginia Military Institute museum has in its collection a rifle with "J. Beeton–Lexington" stamped on the barrel. Beeton's son, John Henry Beeton, was born in Middlebrook, Augusta County, in 1831 and followed his father as a Lexington gunsmith. Before the Civil War he joined a militia company in Lexington that later became Company H of the 27th Virginia Infantry of the Stonewall Brigade. After the Battle of First Manassas, he was ordered back to Lexington to serve as an ordnance sergeant at VMI, repairing rifles and other weapons. Several other Lexington members of the Beeton family were engaged in the gunsmithing business after the Civil War.

POWDER HORN, *top, 1853. This horn is engraved "J. H. Beeton—March 29, 1853" and has images of deer, elk, eagle, and George Washington on horseback. 14 inches long.*

ACORN MOTIF, *left, by John Beeton, early 1800s. This motif is engraved in silver on the top of the stock, while Beeton's name and "Lexington, Va." are on the barrel.*

SAMUEL D. ELLIOT AND OTHER LATER RIFLEMAKERS

Little is known about Samuel D. Elliot although he must have had a prominent gunsmithing business in the Collierstown section for a quarter of a century. He is listed in the censuses from 1850 to 1870 as a gunsmith. Two rifles have been found that are attributed to Elliot's shop. One, signed "S. Elliot," is in the Gordon Lohr collection. It is iron mounted, made of curly maple stock, and has an imported British lock and an arrow point shaped patch box with fine engraving. The length of the original rifle is unclear because the butt has been shortened. The rifle was probably made around 1830, but it shows clear relationship to the earlier rifles by John Davidson, such as the high comb stock.[34]

Unfortunately, Elliot left no will, and there is no estate inventory. His eldest son, A. Franklin Elliot, was listed in the 1850 census as a sixteen-year-old gunsmith, but there is no evidence that he pursued this profession. In 1854 Samuel D. was listed as a cabinetmaker, probably while he was working with his cabinetmaker father, Andrew D. L. Elliot, who was active in Lexington.

Research reveals a number of other midcentury gunsmiths, but only a few rifles were found that could be attributed to their shops. George W. Cockrel, who must have run a substantial local operation, advertised in the *Lexington Gazette* on May 5, 1841 as a "Gun and Rifle-maker," and announced that he had begun "business in all its various branches on Front Street, in the shop lately occupied by Mr. Varner, where he will make to order double and single barrel SHOTGUNS, RIFLES, PISTOLS & CANE GUNS on the latest and most improved principles. He will also make MILL and other Brands, Which he will warrent to last for twenty years. Stocking and all kinds of REPAIRING in his line of Business done in the neatest and best styles. N.B. Old gold and silver bought at the highest prices." Less than a year before Cockrel ran this notice, he married Lexington gunsmith John Beeton's daughter Caroline Margaret.[35]

During the period 1850–80 other gunsmiths were listed in various county records, but little is known about their activities. Thomas Ayers listed himself as a gunsmith in county birth records. W. N. Harlow was listed as a gunsmith in Kerrs Creek District in 1870 and Richard Turner in the Walkers Creek District in 1879–80.

Even later, another county blacksmith, probably associated with John Clemmer, was James Franklin Benson, who, according to one source, bought Clemmer's gunsmithing tools at his estate sale. Benson produced rifles for some time in the Walker's Creek area. One of his rifles survives.

The Rockbridge long rifle makers from the early Walkers and Davidsons to the later Elliots and Beetons were an important part of the Valley tradition, which early on provided outstanding rifles for the frontiers of southwest Virginia, Kentucky, and Tennessee. Recent writers have made much of these rifles "deriving their beauty from their severe adherence to functional line and proportion."[36]

These well designed, well executed, and uniquely American tools were cherished objects to their owners, who depended on them for both food and protection. The descendants of the early owners have in many cases held on to these works of art—several of which are significant relics of the history of Rockbridge County.

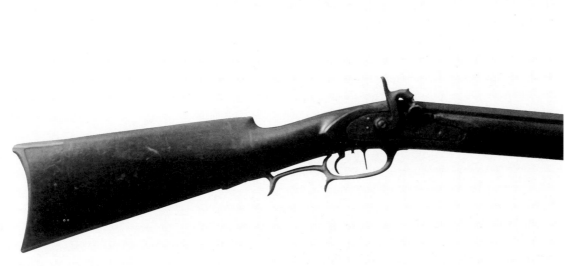

BENSON RIFLE, *by James F. Benson, c. 1855. When the gunsmith John Clemmer died in 1854, Benson bought his gunsmithing tools and continued the riflemaking tradition in that area. Walnut, brass fittings, 45-inch barrel, 40 caliber.*

Ironwork

The new iron fence "adds greatly to the appearance of this town in the neighborhood of the Court House and reflects much credit upon the taste and skill of our enterprising young countrymen, Wm. & E. Leyburn at whose foundry the work was made."

— LEXINGTON GAZETTE, NOVEMBER 10, 1853

Rockbridge County's iron industry began with crude furnaces established on South River during the American Revolution. During the prosperous first half of the nineteenth century, ironworks flourished and fortunes were made. During the Civil War the industry furnished raw iron for Richmond arms manufacturers and, in the form of plow manufacturing, continued through the nineteenth century and into the twentieth—a span of more than 160 years. This survey located a number of utilitarian and decorative pieces produced in the county during this long and productive period.

In the eighteenth century iron ore was plentiful in the Shenandoah Valley, and the Rockbridge County area offered especially rich veins along the Blue Ridge mountain range above South River, where the first ironworks were built.[1] The story of the Rockbridge iron industry features the talent, drive, and ingenuity of the second- and third-generation Virginia Scotch-Irish and the Pennsylvania Germans who entered the industry in the last quarter of the eighteenth century and first half of the nineteenth century. Their entrepreneurism brought a period of prosperity, growth, and change. Despite ups and downs from one decade to the next, no other economic activity had such a far-ranging impact on the area. Among the operations that transformed the county were the Vesuvius Furnace and Foundry, the Rockbridge Foundry, the Bath Iron Works, the furnaces of Buena Vista, Lydia, California, Cotopaxi, Glenwood, and Panther Gap, and the extensive operations at the Buffalo, Gibraltar, and Lebanon forges.

GATE, LEXINGTON CEMETERY, *opposite, by James McDowell Taylor and John McD. Humphries of the Rockbridge Foundry, 1860. This gate is part of the fence around the Alexander family plot. Cast iron, 39½ x 36½ inches.*

STOVEPLATE WITH STORK AND SWALLOW MOTIF, *right, possibly by the Mossy Creek Furnace in Augusta County, early 1800s. This stoveplate was used as a fireback in a Brownsburg house. Cast iron, 28⅜ x 21 inches.*

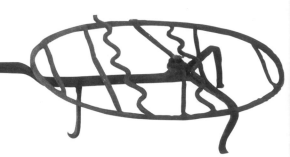

TRIVET, *right, early 1800s. This skilled blacksmith's work was found in the Fairfield area. Wrought iron, 16¾ inches long.*

FROE, *bottom left, c. 1800–1850. Formed with primitive techniques, this early tool was found near Buena Vista. 11¾ x 2¼ inches.*

HATCHET, *bottom right, c. 1800– 1850. This hatchet from the Kerrs Creek area was probably made on a farmer's forge. 8½ x 4¼ inches.*

One of the first efforts in the Valley of Virginia was the Marboro ironworks, established by Lewis Stephens before 1760 at Cedar Creek in Frederick County near Winchester. In 1767 Isaac Zane, Jr. (b. 1743), took over the ownership of Marboro and by the time of the American Revolution had become one of the most important ironmasters in the region. Zane wrote that the ore banks used at his furnace were "excelled in quality by none in America, either for casting or bar iron . . . well known to make choice steel" and that he had nearby sufficient limestone "to flux away the impurities" in the ore.[2]

In Augusta County, north of what is today Rockbridge County, Henry Miller and Mark Bird, who came to the Valley from Berks County, Pennsylvania, bought large tracts of land on Mossy Creek in 1774 and developed an imposing operation consisting of a furnace, a forge, and various mills. This early ironworks produced bar iron for local blacksmiths as well as a range of domestic items, such as firebacks, pots, kettles, and agricultural implements. Unlike Zane at Marboro, who exported "considerable quantities of iron" to centers such as Alexandria, Miller supplied mainly local markets.[3]

Evidence suggests that at least three commercial ironworks were active in the Rockbridge County area during the Revolution: the furnaces or forges of William Daugherty, William Moore, and Halbert McCluer. Probably none at first had the capital to build a full-sized furnace such as the ones built later in the county, but the need for iron products during the Revolution encouraged them to go into business, probably in the early 1780s.[4]

Demand apparently led the early Rockbridge County iron manufacturers to move soon from primitive bloomery forges, which made wrought iron directly from ore, to working furnaces. One account says that Daugherty had a "little three-ton furnace" and that some of the iron he produced "was carried by mountain boats" from the mouth of the South River "to the Colonial ordinance works in Richmond, and there moulded into projectiles and served the batteries of the American army in the siege of Yorktown in 1781."[5]

For early settlers the home forge was a necessity, and the Scotch-Irish and others brought with them a thorough understanding of smelting and blacksmithing. Many of their tools have survived. By the 1790s county furnaces were producing ample pig iron, and local forges were supplying blacksmiths with the bar iron needed for the production of horseshoes and farm implements.[6]

The ledgers of two Lexington blacksmith shops active in the 1790s were examined during this survey. John Walker's ledger, in the collection of the Wisconsin Historical Society, covers the years 1788–95 and shows that he was making gate hinges, fire dogs, broad axes, "plow shields," and "tommy hawks" and mending various household items, as well as producing gun barrels. Adolphus Weir's ledger (1790–1802), in the William and Mary College manuscript collection, reveals that he was making plows, spoons, and parts for Thomas Whiteside's clocks.[7] A wrought-iron trivet from the Fairfield area could have been the product of one of these blacksmith shops.

BLAST FURNACES

The charcoal furnace in full blast was a spectacular sight, belching large volumes of smoke and fire into the sky. It is not surprising that Rockbridge County furnaces were named for famous volcanoes—Vesuvius and Cotopaxi. The stone furnaces were generally built against a hill and near a creek or river. The hill allowed a bridge to be built to the top of the furnace, and the water power from the stream turned a wheel that worked the bellows. The large stone mass that made up the "stack" was tapered inward toward the top, forming a sort of truncated pyramid. The height of the larger ones could reach thirty to forty feet. The inner chamber was bottle shaped and reached its greatest diameter (the bosh) about one-third of its height from the bottom. From the charge hole in the top the furnace was slowly filled with ore, charcoal, and flux (limestone) in layers. In the bottom of the furnace was a crucible into which flowed the molten metal; the slag rose to the top and was skimmed off.

The outside area around the furnace was covered with a roof, and on the ground was poured a deep layer of sand. At regular intervals the furnace was tapped, and molten metal flowed into large gutters shaped in the wet sand, called sows, and into smaller gutters, called pigs.[8] The obvious imagery of this arrangement provided the iron trade with a terminology that was used until the twentieth century.[9] After the molten iron hardened, the pigs were broken off and sold to local foundries and trip-hammer forges or were shipped downstream to Lynchburg and Richmond.

The pig was the principal product of the Rockbridge furnaces. But castings could also be made in the sand straight from the furnace—such objects as stove sides, firebacks, cannonballs, and even hollowware. The success of these direct castings depended on the skill of the resident molder, an occupation mentioned often in early Rockbridge County iron furnace records.

The furnaces ran a good part of the year, though in the summer the heat often made working conditions unbearable. When the furnace was in blast, the life of the worker was one of "drabness and constant labor." There was no time for relaxation, and the chief diversions were gambling and drinking.[10] This problem

MARBORO FURNACE, 1772–96. *This conjectural drawing by W. Stuart Archibald shows the arrangement of functions and work areas.*

was not unique to the Valley or to Rockbridge County. Many years earlier at his works near Williamsburg, Colonel William Byrd had observed that during the summer his iron workers were "obliged to spend no small part of their earnings in strong drink to recruit their spirits."[11]

A large labor force was a necessity, since various specialized trades and a great deal of common labor were required to keep a furnace going. In the ranks of the workers were woodcutters and colliers to supply the charcoal for fuel to maintain the blast, laborers to mine the ore, foundrymen to supervise the casting, pattern makers and potters to provide casting patterns, joiners to make wooden implements such as casting flasks, and hammermen for working the brittle cast-iron pigs into wrought iron at the adjacent forge or chafery.[12]

Some of the Rockbridge County ironworks were extensive. In the 1830s, for example, the Bath Iron Works near Goshen employed some 65 workers, with a total population of about 150. Most of these large operations were practically self-sustaining communities, having flour and grist mills, stores, sawmills, blacksmith shops, leather shops, carpenter shops, post offices, ice houses, stables, dairy barns, slave quarters, kitchens, guest cottages, and usually the owner's or operator's mansion.

GLENWOOD FURNACE, *1847.*
The iron furnace, located in
Arnold's Valley, was built by
Francis T. Anderson and is in good
repair today. 36 x 30 feet.

JOHN JORDAN: HIS CANAL AND HIS ROADS

Transportation was a basic problem for the ironworkers from the beginning. Iron ore and charcoal had to be brought from the mountainside and forest to the furnace, usually a distance of five miles or more. The amount of wood needed was staggering; the rule was that it took an acre of forestland to provide charcoal for one day while the furnace was in full blast.[13] But the main transportation problem was getting the pig iron from the furnaces to the lucrative market centers at Lynchburg, Richmond, and elsewhere.

At first most of the pig iron produced by a furnace could be used by the adjacent forge or sold locally to other forges. But some of the early ironmasters in the Rockbridge area hoped to export their pigs beyond the vicinity. During the late eighteenth century pig iron was shipped by water, down river to Lynchburg, a means of transport that was precarious at best because of the many rapids. By the turn of the century attempts had been made to improve the water route by piling river stones to make wing dams, which allowed smoother navigation. But the trip had to be made at times when the water level was neither too low nor too high. Often during flash floods valuable iron was lost, especially in the James River gorge between Glasgow and Snowden. One story has it that so much pig iron was lost by capsized boats in the gorge that when the water level was very low local residents would collect the pigs and pile them beside the river to await another chance to send them downstream.[14]

The Rockbridge County entrepreneur who did the most to improve navigation was John Jordan. During the 1820s Jordan, along with other hard-working, imaginative, and thoughtful businessmen, prospered and in turn brought prosperity to the county. Historians have written about Jordan's business interests and his part in developing roads, canals, and educational institutions in Rockbridge County. According to one source, Jordan's "dynamic personality quickened the spirit of the community; his enthusiasm for new investments was contagious."[15] In 1802 he married twenty-year-old Lucy Winn of Hanover County, Virginia; soon afterwards, when the iron industry was still in its infancy, the couple came to Rockbridge County. Earlier Jordan had served his apprenticeship as a bricklayer and plasterer, and it appears that he and his two brothers, Samuel and Hezekiah, began a construction business in Rockbridge around 1805. In 1808 Jordan did the brickwork for the Ann Smith Academy building. In 1816 he received the contract to build the Lexington Arsenal, which in 1839 became the first building to house the new Virginia Military Institute. In 1818 he completed his own neoclassical residence, now called Stono, high above the North River. During the 1820s he had

BUENA VISTA FURNACE, *1847. Built by Benjamin and Francis Jordan, sons of John Jordan, the Buena Vista Furnace was active until the Civil War.*

a part in building many of Lexington's finest residences and the early classical buildings of Washington College. In Lexington Jordan's Stono undoubtedly had a strong influence on local architecture,[16] but his role in the iron industry and his consequent interest in improving transportation were undoubtedly his greatest contributions.

Around 1820 Jordan and his partner, John Irvin, decided that there was profit to be made in the iron business and determined to give it a try. William W. Davis and others, including Jordan's sons, Samuel F., Benjamin, and John W., joined him, and over the next three decades they operated ironworks in Rockbridge, Bath, Alleghany, Amherst, and Louisa Counties. Jordan was aware of the lack of dependable transportation from Rockbridge County to the markets beyond the mountains. His answer was first to construct a canal and a series of locks through the James River gorge,

a project that he began in 1825 in conjunction with the James River Company. The new canal made the trip to the Lynchburg market by boat much less difficult and allowed a high percentage of iron shipments to reach their destination.

Jordan also built one of the first roads over the Blue Ridge to Lynchburg, an enterprise that, according to the Rockbridge County historian Harrington Waddell, "others had attempted and failed to complete." The Jordan Road, hailed in its day as a remarkable accomplishment, opened up trade and travel to and from the Piedmont.[17] It is still in existence and still passable. Jordan and Irvin also owned a prosperous furnace in Alleghany County, which they named after their wives: Lucy Selina. They strongly backed a movement to build a road from Collierstown to what is today Longdale across North Mountain. The road, completed in 1826, is still in use as county road 770.[18]

THE McCLUER AND
MOORE FURNACES

Halbert McCluer was representative of the ironmasters who caused the county's South River to be called Iron Valley during the first half of the nineteenth century. At one point he was associated with Moses and Alexander McCluer, apparently his brothers, but Halbert was the key partner. The McCluer operation, begun perhaps as early as the 1780s, was located on the river across from where John Jordan later built his furnace.

Little is known of the early activity of the McCluer furnace—that is, in the 1780s and 1790s—although two firebacks examined during this survey, both stamped "Halbert and Moses McCluer," apparently were made there. Simplified versions of a popular design both carry the motto "Be Liberty Thine," with fifteen stars, indicating that they were made between 1792 and 1796, when the fifteenth and sixteenth states were admitted to the Union. One fireback is at Mulberry Hill, the plantation house just west of Lexington built by Andrew Reid in the 1790s. The other was originally installed in Union Hill, a plantation house in Nelson County, near the James River, completed in 1778.[19] Both firebacks have the initials "W:D" in the casting. These initials were presumably those of the carver or the originator of the mold and suggest the possibility of an association with William Daugherty, whose early ironworks was located near McCluer's operation.

The McCluer furnace and forge must have prospered in the years before 1820. According to one history the McCluer brothers "were esteemed for personal wealth and a fair share of enterprise as the limited opportunities of the times rendered available."[20] By 1820 McCluer had both a furnace and a forge on South River. The furnace, which employed sixteen men, was producing "pig iron and other iron ware." His nearby forge had one water-powered trip-hammer, also employed sixteen men, and was producing bar iron. But the depression of 1819 must have had an impact on the McCluer fortunes, since the 1820 *Census of Manufactures* stated: "Neither [the furnace] nor the forge will be in operation after this year."[21]

Several sources mention William Moore as an early iron manufacturer in Rockbridge County, furnishing "iron and cannon balls for the Continental army." But documentation about his operation is scarce.[22] The Museum of Early Southern Decorative Arts collection has a cast-iron stove side with the names of William and Samuel Moore and the date 1789. The design of the casting incorporates elaborate scrollwork around the sides and a classical urn at the bottom center flanked by the initials "A. B." and "1789." H. E. Comstock suggests that A. B. was Andrew Bear, the father of Augusta County cabinetmaker Christian Bear, who could have been the carver of the original wooden mold.[23]

Patterns were often traded among the furnaces or sold to other ironworks.[24] The Mossy Creek Furnace in Augusta County was using the same pattern during this period for its stove plates. A variation appears in a 1799 fireback in Mauck's Meeting House near Luray, probably made at Redwell Furnace in Page County, Virginia. It carries the initials "A. B.," but the carving is much more elaborate. Perhaps the carver decided to embellish the earlier pattern.

MULBERRY GROVE FIREBACK
opposite, c. 1795. The subtly modeled figure of Fame carries a banner inscribed "Peace & Unity." Cast iron, 13 x 29 inches.

URN STOVEPLATE, *left, by Samuel Miller, 1789. This urn with its classical motif was made at the Mossy Creek Furnace in southern Augusta County. Cast iron, 26⅜ x 32½ inches.*

MULBERRY HILL FIREBACK, *bottom, by Halbert and Moses McCluer, c. 1795. This fireback shows a simplified version of the Fame image carrying two banners. Cast iron, 18 x 25 inches.*

BUFFALO FORGE

During the 1820s Buffalo Forge, located near the confluence of the North River and Buffalo Creek, was employing twenty men and operating two trip-hammers. It turned out mainly bar iron for local use. The 1820 *Census of Manufactures* shows that other small forges and blacksmith shops were turning out axes, augers, hoes, chains, and various household and farming utensils.[25]

Six years earlier, in 1814, a partnership consisting of Thomas Mayburry of Botetourt County and William Weaver of Philadelphia had purchased the forge, then called Union Forge, and renamed it. But because of Mayburry's poor management the forge was not profitable, so in 1823 Weaver came to Rockbridge County to direct the operation. The partnership with Mayburry was dissolved, and under Weaver's sole management Buffalo Forge became a success. In 1850 the forge produced about 100 tons of bar iron for export to Lynchburg and Richmond. Pig iron for the forge came from Weaver's Etna Furnace in Botetourt County. Etna produced some 700 tons of pig iron a year, and the iron not consumed at Buffalo Forge was shipped down the canal for sale by commission merchants in Lynchburg and Richmond.[26]

Buffalo Forge is distinctive in at least two respects: the remarkable volume of business records that have survived and the use of an incentive work system for slave laborers. Weaver, a Pennsylvanian by birth, was uncomfortable, at least at first, with the institution of slavery but found it was essential to a profitable iron business. Soon after he took over Buffalo Forge in the 1820s he set up an arrangement whereby slaves would be paid for their work above a certain production norm.[27]

Extensive studies by the historian Charles R. Dew indicate that Weaver was not alone in his idea of slave management. Other iron-works also had arrangements whereby slaves could accumulate "overwork" in the form of credit in the company store. From Weaver's records for Etna and Buffalo Forge, Dew concluded that blacks working there acquired skills that helped them attain some status as artisans. Dew also concluded that at Weaver's operations slavery functioned "more through accommodation than outright repression." Slaves who were able to produce beyond their weekly quotas and therefore earn cash awards could use the money as they saw fit. Some even used it for vacations. A savings account one of Weaver's slaves kept for a number of years at a Lexington bank was a source of local controversy.[28]

Dew's history includes a detailed account of one slave artisan, Sam Williams. When Williams first came to Buffalo Forge in 1838, he served for at least a year as an apprentice to two of Weaver's slave forgemen, John Baxter and Harry Hunt. Under their guidance Williams learned "to put up and maintain the special refinery fire, heating the pig iron and bringing it 'to nature,' and then pounding the red-hot metal under the huge hammer. . . . "[29] Williams soon became a master refiner. In 1841 his skills were such that he hammered out more than the required one and a half tons of refined iron per week and began earning money. In 1841 he produced more than two tons extra, earning $8.82. In 1844 his overwork pay was $31.00. As a master refiner, he was paid for his overwork at the same rate as a white artisan would have been paid for the same job—$8.00 per ton, with three-fifths of the $8.00 going to the refiner and two-fifths going to his underhand, or assistant. By the early 1850s Williams was making $50.00 per year.[30]

In 1857 Weaver's niece and her husband, Daniel C. E. Brady of Philadelphia, moved to Buffalo Forge at Weaver's behest to help with the operation. Brady kept meticulous records about farm, forge, and slave activity. On a normal day he entered: "Sam at work." Williams had two underworkers, Henry Towler and Jim Garland.[31] Brady's records show that Williams continued to be a very productive worker at Buffalo Forge.

Williams, along with the other slaves at Buffalo Forge and throughout Rockbridge County, was freed by order of the occupying military authorities on Friday, May 26, 1865. The next day Brady wrote in his journal: "All hands quit work as they considered themselves free." On May 29 he wrote: "Commenced work on free labor." The same day Williams and his wife, Nancy, now free citizens of Rockbridge County, signed three-month contracts at Buffalo Forge, he as master refiner at the forge and she as head dairy maid.[32] Williams worked at the forge as master refiner for two more years as a free employee. When severe competition in the iron business beyond the county's boundaries forced the forge to close in 1867, he worked as a sharecropper in the Buffalo Forge area and, as could be expected, prospered.[33]

STRAP HINGE, *opposite top, c. 1840s. From a stable at Buffalo Forge, this hinge terminates in a heart motif. Wrought iron, 24 x 1¾ inches.*

TAILOR'S IRON AND POLISHING IRON, *opposite bottom, mid-nineteenth century. These pressing irons were probably cast at Etna Furnace in Botetourt County but received their wrought-iron handles at Buffalo Forge, where they were found. Tailor's iron, 5½ x 9 x 1¾ inches; polishing iron, 5½ x 6½ x 3¾ inches.*

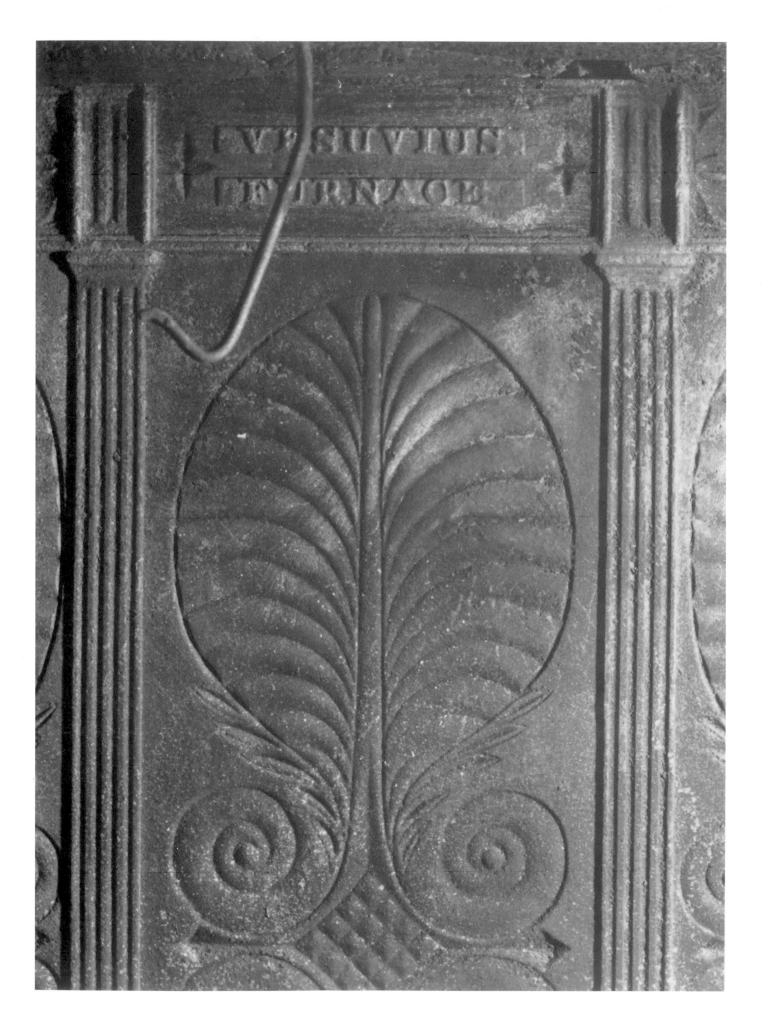

THE VESUVIUS
FOUNDRY AND THE
LIVINGSTON PLOW

Before 1790 farmers in the Valley of Virginia, like their Pennsylvania counterparts, used wood plows—"heavy, cumbersome and very inefficient"—that they made themselves. The wood plow broke the soil with a straight moldboard, which had to be reinforced with strips of iron. The moldboard was often three or more feet long, very shallow, and required three or four men to operate, using four or six oxen. Dirt adhered to the moldboard, and when the plow was in use it had to be cleaned constantly.[34]

In western Virginia after about 1790 the business of making plows passed from the farmer to the blacksmith, and soon each community developed its own plow design. Thomas Jefferson was the first in this country to attempt to standardize the design of plows.[35] He used a spring dynamometer to determine the comparative draft of plows of different designs and reported his findings to the American Philosophical Society together with a design for an improved "moldboard of least resistance." In 1816 Jefferson communicated to the Philadelphia Society of Promoting Agriculture a description of a hillside plow with a shifting moldboard. Afterwards many plows made in quantity incorporated his principles.[36]

In the 1820s John Jordan and other ironmasters in the Rockbridge County area began to cast moldboards at their furnaces. Between 1828 and 1839 Jordan's Lucy Selina Furnace turned out 3,690 cast iron plow blades. Although they proved popular for a while, it was clear that cast iron was brittle and that repairing broken cast moldboard was almost impossible.[37]

Around 1835 two New York state iron manufacturers, Benjamin Avery and Schuyler Bradley, who had a patent on what they called the Livingston County plow, became interested in Rockbridge County, presumably because of the favorable economic climate and the availability of high-quality pig iron. Avery went into business on the South River, where, he advertised, he manufactured "Ward's Livingston County Plows and Snider's Self Sharpening Plows." His foundry used very fine sand in casting and varnished its wood patterns frequently to give its plows a smooth finish. Furthermore, the blades could be reversed and therefore sharpened themselves while in use. John Deere, who developed a plow with these characteristics in New England, was said to have designed a "plow that would scour," meaning that it would break the earth cleanly. The year Avery produced his first Rockbridge County–made plow, the Deere operation, only two years old, made seventy-five.[38]

Avery ran an ambitious operation on the South River; in addition to plows he offered "All kinds of Castings . . . such as . . . andirons, Threshing Machine Castings, Mill Irons, etc. sold at five cents a pound."[39] In 1841 the Livingston County plow received special attention at the New York State Agricultural Fair. Bradley, who represented Avery and the new enterprise for this promotion, soon took up residence in Rockbridge. But in 1842 their operation on Irish Creek washed away in a massive flood.

Avery left the firm for points west, and Bradley acquired a new partner, Matthew Bryan. Together they rebuilt the foundry, this time on Slick Run, between Steeles Tavern and Vesuvius Foundry. Bryan by this time was the sole owner or at least the principal owner of both the furnace and the foundry. The furnace was supplying pig iron to the foundry and casting firebacks. The foundry, according to the Lexington paper, had the "double purpose of making all articles usually executed at foundries" and of manufacturing the Livingston County plow.[40] In 1850 Bryan's Vesuvius Furnace employed thirteen men and was producing a remarkable 675 tons of pig iron per year, while the foundry, with eight employees, was making 300 plows a year and "various castings." That year John Deere, by then in Moline, Illinois, made 1,600 plows.[41]

The James River Canal construction reached the southern end of Rockbridge County in 1850, and each year or two the terminal

VESUVIUS FIREBACK, *opposite, c. 1840. This fireback from a Walkers Creek house is marked "Vesuvius Furnace." Cast iron.*

BEAR, *above, c. 1900. Found at Steeles Tavern, this profile of a bear was probably cast at Vesuvius Furnace. Cast iron, 14 x 9½ inches.*

BEN SALEM LOCK, *built c. 1850s. A key to the success of the local iron industry was safe river navigation via the James River canal system to the Lynchburg and Richmond markets. The Ben Salem lock, constructed of local limestone, is still in good condition.*

moved closer to the mouth of the South River and the county's "Iron Valley." During this period the Vesuvius Furnace shipped large amounts of pig iron down the James to Lynchburg and Richmond. In 1983–85, while construction workers were excavating for a new Richmond office building, twenty-six bars of pig iron, which had evidently been lost overboard while being unloaded, were recovered from the old basin of the James River and Kanawha Canal. Three of the pigs found were marked "Vesuvius," or at least enough of the letters were still legible for certain identification. The pigs varied greatly in size and weight, at 12, 54, and 117 pounds. Probably a number of the other, unmarked pigs had also been shipped from Iron Valley.[42]

After Bryan died in 1854 Bradley offered for sale a large part of the foundry's assets, including "an assortment of Livingston County Plow Flasks and Patterns, of various sizes, both right and left hand. Also the unexpired term of the right to make, use and vend to others to be used, the Livingston County Plow for a large portion of the State of Virginia until the 15th of April 1856 at which time the Patent Right expires." He also offered for sale patterns and flasks for threshing machines and sawmill gearing.[43] In 1863 Bradley sold the foundry to Hugh Franklin Lyle, and the operation, which continued production of the Livingston plow, became known as the Vesuvius Plow Company.

This study located a journal kept by a Vesuvius ironworker that describes work at the foundry in the early 1870s. William S. Humphries became associated with the foundry probably around 1870. On January 1, 1872, twenty-nine-year-old Humphries wrote:

"I have commenced work today with the determination of doing all the work I can this year."[44] The next day he noted that he was "dressing some beams now that [were] sawed out 2 years ago." Two days later, on Thursday, he wrote: "I had only five beams left for today. Finished, then packed away all that I had dressed out. Cleaned out the shop, and I was taken with a violent pain in my back so bad that I had to quit work and go home." The journal paints a picture of hard and repetitive work. Often he noted that he had "wooded 3 plows today" or put handles on the iron blades, seemingly an average day's work for him. On February 8 he wrote that the foundry was "melting new today." Then he "Wooded 3 plows . . . painting a lot of Plows to go away Monday." On March 9 he wrote, "my board shows that I wooded 25 plows, which is a good week's work."

Humphries's journal also includes information about life in Rockbridge County. On March 18, "Just at the middle of the day the alarm was raised that the church was on fire. I went up as soon as I could. Done all that I could. More help came soon, but in spite of what we all could do it burnt down. The first House that I ever saw burn." On April 14 (Sunday) he wrote: "We had Sunday School at Mr. Lyles House. We nearly organized today. I had been Selected as Superintendent, a position that I do not feel worthy to Occupy." He wrote on April 25, "We will not work any more this week." His journal makes it clear that he and his colleagues were more interested in getting corn and other crops in the ground. On April 30 he noted that he had "got all my work done by 2 o'clock. Came home and worked some in the garden."

During the early summer of 1872 Frank Lyle began discussing the possibility of his young worker joining him as a partner. On June 11 Humphries wrote, "Frank and me had a talk about Partnership in the Foundry and I agreed to postpone it until the 1st of January 73, but Mr. Lyle said he would make my year's work amount to 6 hundred & 50 dollars."[45] Humphries became Lyle's partner in 1877. By this time H. F. Lyle and Company had capital of $5,000 and was employing five workers. In 1882 a correspondent to the *Lexington Gazette* wrote: "The manufacture of the Virginia Chilled Plow and of the Lyle Plow is carried on successfully by Mr. Humphries. He reports an active demand for both these plows, many farmers still adhering to the old Livingston plow as the best in the market."[46] A number of miniatures of the plow used for promotion during this period have survived.

Perhaps the writer was a friend of Humphries who was aware of the fierce competition in the plow-making business in Rockbridge County at that time. A Thomas B. Mullen from Pennsylvania began manufacturing at Jordan's Point what he called an "improved Livingston plow." The Lexington paper in 1878 said that Mullen's plow "is highly spoken of. Some persons pronounce it superior to the 'Oliver Chilled which had been patented in Indiana ten years earlier.'" Later in 1878 Mullen won an award at the Rockbridge County Fair for the "Mullen Plow," which he had manufactured and exhibited. His prize was one dollar. In 1879 the Lexington newspaper was still touting Mullen's work: " . . . the Mullen plow cannot be excelled. Its merits are numerous and it is especially valuable in turning under heavy growth of clover." On the other hand, Hugh Lyle argued in the paper's columns: "The shrewed farmer knows that new-fashioned, new-fangled things are seldom improvement, and rarely what they are 'cracked up to be.'"[47] Lyle left the Vesuvius Plow Company in the 1890s, and Humphries's son, William Frank Humphries, joined his father in the business.

The foundry also cast popular items such as iron lions and frogs for doorstops. Mildred S. Goeller, a long-time resident of Steeles Tavern, recalled that when she was in grade school she was taken through the Vesuvius Foundry: "It was exciting to see men working in molten iron. One of the workmen told my brother to put his hand in the big pile of sand and make a print with his fingers spread apart. The workman then brought a big pot of molten iron and poured it into the imprint of his brother's hand. When the iron was cold the iron hand was such a perfect replica that the lines of his hand showed plainly."[48] In the course of the research for this study a similar hand was found, this one made at the Buena Vista Foundry in the early part of the twentieth century.

The Vesuvius Plow Works operated until the 1950s. It was then the "county's oldest industry having been in continuous operation for more than a hundred years."[49]

LION DOORSTOPS, *top c. 1890–1910. The Vesuvius Plow Company and its predecessors cast animal forms—frogs, lions, and so forth—for use as doorstops. Cast iron, each 8½ inches long.*

CAST HAND, *bottom, early 1900s. This casting was found at the Buena Vista Foundry. Cast iron.*

In 1852 William and Edward Leyburn announced they had established the Rockbridge Foundry and Machine Works, located on Irish Creek, where, the Leyburns claimed, "every variety of casting will be executed." They produced hot-air pipes, iron gearing and fixtures for mills, iron railing, "superior agricultural implements, including threshing machines, corn shellers, two-and-three horse plows, hill-side plows."[50] In November 1853 the *Lexington Gazette* praised the new iron fence around the county courthouse saying that it added "greatly to the appearance of the town" and reflected on "the taste and skill" of the Leyburn brothers.[51]

During the summer of 1854 the Rockbridge Foundry was purchased by T. B. Taylor and T. P. McDowell, who announced they would retain the Leyburns' work force and would continue carrying items previously produced, plus "cooking ranges."[52] Less than four years later the foundry changed hands again. This time it was purchased by Dr. J. McDowell Taylor and John McD. Humphries, both of whom had long experience in the county's iron business.[53]

In the Lexington Presbyterian Church cemetery south of the town are three plots dating from 1855 to 1860, with iron fencing and gates with an eagle and lyre motif. One of the gates, for the Alexander plot, has the cast inscription "1860 by Taylor and Humphries." It appears that some of the castings were the work of John McD. Humphries, because he had been referred to earlier as a caster.

Business activity in the county brought improvements to Lexington during the 1850s. Main Street was lowered from Henry Street south to the courthouse and filled north of Henry Street. This gave a gentler grade to North Main but also meant that the street entrances to a number of prominent buildings, such as the Alexander-Withrow House, the Dold Building, the McCampbell Inn, and the Jacob Ruff House, had to be reoriented to accommodate the new street level.[54] During this period a number of Main Street buildings received iron balconies, some of which have survived, such as that on the Main Street side of the Alexander-Withrow Building, with the same eagle and lyre motif found in the cemetery.

THE McCORMICK
CHAPTER

The story of iron manufacture in Rockbridge must include the story of the McCormick family of Walnut Grove. Although Cyrus McCormick (1809–84) was not the only Rockbridge County inventor whose influence went far beyond the county, he was certainly the best known. Actually, Cyrus's father, Robert, although as conservative in most respects

FIRE TONGS, *above, by John McCown, c. 1820. McCown, a South River blacksmith, was associated with both John Jordan and Cyrus McCormick. Wrought iron, 19 inches long.*

ANDIRON WITH HEART MOTIF, *opposite, by John McCown, c. 1830. This andiron, one of a pair, was produced by sand casting at the Vesuvius Furnace. Cast iron, 15 x 8½ inches.*

as were his Scotch-Irish neighbors, was the real innovator of the family and early on developed in his farm workshop in the northern end of the county a hemp break (to separate the lint from the stalk), a thresher, and a blacksmith's tub bellows. He also put together several styles of reapers, "useful mainly as examples of what would not work."[55] As a young boy Cyrus learned blacksmithing on his family farm; he also learned to swing a heavy cradle when reaping wheat by hand. There seems ample evidence that Cyrus, while working with his father, carried his father's innovations several steps further. At the age of twenty-two he produced a mechanized reaper that could cut six acres of wheat in an afternoon, equaling the work of six laborers.[56] The first public exhibition of McCormick's reaper was scheduled for the fall of 1832 on a farm of Lexington's John Ruff. One story has it that after Ruff saw the machine perform he ordered McCormick and his reaper off his rocky and hilly field for fear they would destroy what was left of his grain crop. So the demonstration continued on the nearby fields of William Taylor, where the reaper worked considerably better, much to McCormick's relief and the onlookers' amazement. This first reaper was by no means perfect, but its essential components were workable. McCormick continued to improve the machine, primarily by making it more adaptable to rough ground and differing conditions of the crop.

McCormick had the assistance of a well-established blacksmith, John McCown, who ran his own forge and tilt-hammer shop on South River. In 1820 he was producing sickles, scythes, hoes, axes, augers, and other wrought-iron products.[57] He was also associated with Schuyler Bradley, operator and molder at the nearby Vesuvius Foundry, which made castings such as andirons. When McCormick first demonstrated his reaper, the blade operated very inefficiently because its serrations slanted only in one direction. It cut well enough when moving in one direction, but its return movement was lost motion. Further, it frequently choked and stopped, according to eyewitness accounts. McCown, who had made blades for McCormick's early reapers, solved the knife problem by slanting the serrations in the blade alternately to the right and to the left every few inches along the edge. That simple device made the "knife cut in both directions as it vibrated and thus doubled its efficiency, at the same time reducing its choking tendency."[58]

A number of writers have complained that McCown, as well as Cyrus McCormick's father and perhaps his brother Leander, never received due credit for the parts they played in the development of Rockbridge County's most famous invention. No doubt the reaper was the culmination of several people's ideas and experiments, but Cyrus McCormick's vision of what the reaper could become secured its place in history. He took his manufacturing operation to Chicago, and after the reaper was demon-

strated at the Great Exhibition in London in 1851 it was "hailed as the revolutionary invention it was."[59]

Rockbridge County ironmongers and their molders and foundrymen made a special contribution to the area's, and even the country's, iron industry. This study has traced the story from William Daugherty's early furnace on the South River to Cyrus McCormick's workshop and on until the close of the Vesuvius plow manufactory in the 1950s. Fortunately, monuments to the early days of the iron industry still remain at the South River, Arnold's Valley, and elsewhere.

Early in this century a writer from the *Richmond Times-Dispatch* reported to his readers after a visit to Rockbridge County: "As the tourist rides through the mountains, he will see close to some roaring torrent the ruins of old stone blast furnaces overgrown with ivy and bright with fiery-tinted trumpet flower, gentle and dainty reminders of the ruddy glare of other days, of the sparks and flames from these forgotten shrines of Vulcan."[60]

Pottery

KURT C. RUSS

... Benjamin Darst on his part doth engage to Learn the said Apprentice [Francis Garner] his art or Trade of a Potter & shall find him in Sufficient Meat drink Lodging Washing & apparel & shall teach him or cause him to be taught to Read & Write and also the five Common Rules of arithmetic and when the time is Expired he shall give him a Turning Lathe & five pounds Cash & two Suits of Clothes, one of which shall be new.

—INDENTURE BOND, 1793, RECORDED IN ROCKBRIDGE COUNTY WILL BOOK NO. 1

The first pottery in Virginia was probably established near Jamestown soon after its original settlement in 1607. Throughout the seventeenth century potters in the Jamestown area produced earthenware in the conservative English tradition, providing wares for local consumption.[1] By 1720 William Rogers had established a successful pottery factory in Yorktown that produced a variety of vessel forms in both lead-glazed earthenware and salt-glazed stoneware—the earliest documented stoneware production in Virginia.[2] This comparatively large-scale operation not only supplied local needs but also apparently exported wares to New England, North Carolina, and even to the West Indies.[3]

Despite the success of the Yorktown pottery operation, the Tidewater area was never to develop an extensive ceramic industry. The unavailability of good stoneware clays and the domination of the plantation economy—which depended on an extensive commerce network involving Europe, the northeastern states, and the West Indies—contributed to a continued reliance on imported items. In fact, during the eighteenth century there was limited promotion for traditional craft industries in Virginia. A vast array of items were readily available from Europe and elsewhere, including, in addition to a wide range of ceramic vessels, tin, pewter, and glass containers.

It was not until almost a full century later that the Shenandoah Valley emerged as a center of pottery production in Virginia. The region dominated the industry throughout the nineteenth century. All the prerequisites for the development of successful pottery enterprises existed there: natural resources, including suitable clay

JUG, *opposite, attributed to John Morgan, c. 1830–50. This one-gallon, salt-glazed jug with brushed cobalt decoration and the "Rockbridge" stamp is characteristic of Rockbridge County pottery. 12 x 7 inches.*

STONEWARE CHURNS, *right, by George N. Fulton, c. 1867-80. These three-gallon, salt-glazed pots with cobalt floral decorations were made in Alleghany County. Left churn, 15¼ x 8½ inches; right churn, 15 x 7¾ inches.*

STONEWARE, *by John Heatwole, 1853–69. These five salt-glazed stoneware pieces from Rockingham County are embellished with floral motifs. The decoration of the* *pitcher, second from left, is manganese, while the decoration of the others is cobalt. 7½ x 5¼ inches to 15½ x 8¼ inches.*

deposits; fuel (wood and coal) and water sources; a steadily expanding population with settlements of sufficient size to support potters; and an expanding system of railroads, canals, and river navigation, which provided a ready means for shipping wares and receiving supplies.[4]

By the mid-1700s immigration from southeastern Pennsylvania into and through the Valley provided population centers sufficient for supporting and, in fact, requiring the production of traditional craft items, including pottery. Among the settlers were skilled artisans capable of producing the much-needed items from local raw materials. One of the most important and prominent groups of potters to settle in the northern Shenandoah Valley was the Bell family. Peter Bell, Jr. (b. June 1, 1775), the son of Peter Bell, Sr., the patriarch of this Virginia branch of a German family, started in the pottery business in Hagerstown, Maryland, beginning in 1805 and settled in Winchester, in Frederick County, Virginia, during 1824.[5] Peter's sons, John (b. April 20, 1800), Samuel, and Solomon, participated in the Winchester business. During the 1830s Samuel and Solomon moved "up" the Valley to Strasburg in Shenandoah

County, some eighteen miles south of Winchester and seventy-five miles north of Rockbridge County, where they initiated a pottery tradition that ultimately earned Strasburg the nickname "Pot Town."[6] The earliest manifestation of this largely Germanic pottery tradition in the northern Valley is represented by an enormous variety of both strictly utilitarian and highly decorated earthenwares. The multiglazes of white, brown (iron or manganese dioxide), green (copper oxide), and yellow clay slip used on these earthenware bodies created bold and striking vessels now widely known.

Equally remarkable are the distinctive wares of the early-nineteenth-century earthenware potters located farther "up" the great road, some 125 miles southwest of Rockbridge County, in extreme southwestern Virginia and extending into northeastern Tennessee. The wares produced by these "great road" potters ranged from typically large, ovoid storage jars and jugs with extruded handles, often embellished with splotched or trailed iron or manganese dioxide decorative touches beneath a clear lead overglaze, to small storage vessels with domed lids and polychrome slip decoration, both unquestionably either strongly influenced or produced by a Moravian immigrant into the Virginia area.[7]

Smaller earthenware pottery production centers also developed, although the wares they produced were comparatively unremarkable aesthetically. Most significant is the concentration of earthenware pottery production in the Fincastle area of Botetourt

County, Virginia.[8] Here fewer than a dozen potters produced simple, semiovoid earthenware storage vessels, often embellished with combed and freehand incised decorative treatments. The earthenware tradition in this area appears to have continued for some time after it had been abandoned and replaced by stoneware production in most potteries to the north.

By the end of the first quarter of the nineteenth century the majority of both producers and consumers of Virginia pottery had become aware of the potentially lethal properties of the lead glazes used on earthenware. The northern stoneware pottery tradition was being successfully established by this time, a result of both its success in the north and the diffusion of knowledge regarding stoneware production as artisans trained in this tradition moved into other areas. Stoneware was clearly a superior product for the storage, preservation, preparation, and consumption of foodstuffs and beverages. Because it was fired at a much higher temperature than earthenware and was glazed with salt rather than lead, it was highly durable and vitreous and, most important, was not toxic.

As stoneware supplanted earthenware, the typical European-style kilns of the earthenware tradition were replaced by the characteristic nineteenth-century oval and circular up- and down-draft kilns. Several other changes accompanied this transition, including a significantly larger number and expanded geographical distribution of potters within the state, the use of brushed blue cobalt oxide as the dominant decorative treatment replacing the multicolored clay slips and lead glazes frequently seen on earthenware, and the production of a greater variety of vessel forms.

The salt-glazed stoneware tradition spread across Virginia, with successful manufacturing centers in Alexandria,[9] Richmond,[10] and Petersburg,[11] and throughout the Valley from Frederick County to Washington County in southwest Virginia.[12] The largest concentration of Valley stoneware production was in Strasburg in Shenandoah County.[13] In the second half of the nineteenth century stoneware production flourished in Washington County, where more than thirty-eight potters were producing an enormous quantity of strictly utilitarian wares.[14] Another key pottery center was in Rockingham County, where Andrew Coffman and his sons established three potteries. Eventually more than fifty-three potters were involved in the industry, most either descendants or former employees of Coffman.[15] In Alleghany County, George M. Fulton produced remarkable pottery, sometimes decorated with elaborate trees and floral motifs executed in both cobalt oxide and manganese dioxide.[16] Rockbridge County also developed successful stoneware operations. As will be seen, the manifestation of the tradition there illustrates the way in which early ceramic traditions spread from one part of the country to another.[17]

ROCKBRIDGE POTTERS

Recent documentary and archaeological research indicates that three pottery shops involving at least eleven potters were in operation in Rockbridge County beginning in the late eighteenth and continuing throughout most of the nineteenth century.[18] Benjamin Darst's pottery operation in Lexington, which began in 1785, appears to be one of the earliest in this part of the state. The pottery continued until 1791, and from 1788 on Darst had at least one other person working with him, an apprentice, Francis Garner. Historical information on Darst's pottery activity is sparse, and archaeological evidence is lacking. Nonetheless, there is ample evidence of the key role that he played in the early development of the town of Lexington.

The nine other potters identified in the county during the nineteenth century were working at two related sites: Rockbridge Baths and Bustleburg-Firebaugh. These two pottery kilns were excavated in 1984 and 1988, respectively, by the Washington and Lee Laboratory of Anthropology staff and students as a part of a larger statewide survey of the traditional pottery manufacturing industry in Virginia. As a result of this fieldwork and research, much is now known about the people associated with Rockbridge County's nineteenth-century pottery industry, their methods of production and conducting business, and the earthenware and stoneware they produced.[19]

BENJAMIN DARST'S POTTERY

Benjamin Darst, Sr., was born in 1760 in the Mount Jackson area of Shenandoah (then Frederick) County, Virginia, where he must have learned the pottery business as a young man. His Swiss father, Abraham, who spelled his surname "Derst," had arrived in Philadelphia in 1743 and by the mid-1750s had made his way to the Valley of Virginia. Soon after his father's death in 1772, Benjamin Darst left the Valley, probably to open a business in the Williamsburg area, but for some reason he settled instead in Goochland County, where he set up his operation. In 1781 he married Lucy Woodward of Goochland County and purchased land near Manankintown, a village in the county on the north bank of the James River about twenty miles west of Richmond. During this time Darst owned three slaves, who may have assisted him in the pottery business.[20]

In 1785 Darst returned to the Valley and bought a tract of land adjoining Lexington, where he established his pottery. It is not

POT WITH LID, *by Jesse Hinkle, 1839. This lead-glazed earthenware storage vessel from Botetourt County, signed and dated, is incised with a variety of decortions. It was probably a presentation piece for Hinkle's partner's mother, Mrs. Spigle. 13½ x 6¼ inches.*

surprising that he chose for the location of his pottery a property beside the Valley Road, along which thousands of settlers were traveling in the 1780s on their way to the West and the South. During the 1780s Darst's brother, Samuel, also a potter, moved from Shenandoah County to Franklin County, south of Lexington, where he established a pottery—also on the route of the settlers coming through the Valley.[21]

The tract Benjamin Darst purchased is referred to in the deed as the "Galbraith property," on the east side of Lexington's Main Street between the present Rockbridge County Regional Library at 138 South Main Street and a building housing physicians'

offices and a pharmacy at 146 South Main. The tract of land, 35 feet wide along Main Street, extended approximately 357 feet deep (or eastward) through the recently constructed Raetz and Hawkins office building at 128 South Randolph Street into the area long known as Mudtown.[22] Efforts to learn more about the Darst pottery from official records have been unsuccessful. In the two hundred years since 1791 so much construction has occurred in this section of town that finding the exact location of Darst's kiln now seems unlikely.

Benjamin Darst could have chosen this location for his Lexington operation not only for its proximity to the Valley Road but

CROCK, *far left, by George N. Fulton, 1867–80. This one-gallon, salt-glazed stoneware crock with manganese floral decoration is marked "G. N. Fulton." 10 x 6¾ inches.*

POT, *left, 1840–82. This stoneware storage jar, brushed with cobalt oxide and stamped "Rockbridge," is typical of the pieces produced at the Bustleburg-Firebaugh and Rockbridge Baths potteries. 10¼ x 7¼ inches.*

also because Mudtown, a low-lying area that then had active springs, apparently offered a good source of clay for the new pottery. Winifred Hadsel writes in *The Streets of Lexington* that the area down behind the Darst property "was so poorly drained that it was known as Mudtown" even before any houses were built there. (After the Civil War the town sold lots in this section, and it soon became a portion of Lexington's first black community.) It seems likely that this area was an especially suitable source of Darst's raw materials, and that his pottery activity there could have been reflected in the name Mudtown.[23]

Darst's operation prospered, and in 1788 John Grigsby and David Cloyd, overseers of the poor for Rockbridge County, bound out an apprentice, one Francis Garner, to Darst to learn the pottery "art or Trade." The indenture, dated June 18, 1788, and signed July 1, obligated Darst not only to teach his sixteen-year-old apprentice pottery skills but also to "teach him or cause him to be taught to Read & Write and also the five Common Rules of arthimetic [sic] . . . " and "find him in sufficient Meat, drink, Lodging, Washing & apparel." This remarkable document further ordered that, when "the time is Expired" (1793), Garner must be given "a Turning Lathe & five pounds Cash & two Suits of Clothes, one of which shall be new."[24]

Darst presumably made simple—glazed and unglazed—earthenware similar to several pieces found in the county during this survey. Earthenware was made from red clay with a high mineral content, usually including a large quantity of iron, and could be fired at a much lower temperature than stoneware. It was also not as strong as stoneware. Because it was porous, a clay slip or lead glaze was often used—inside at least—to control seepage. The

fragility of these early earthenware vessels caused one writer to suggest that "ware broken en route from Pennsylvania, New Jersey and elsewhere in the Northeast could be replenished from [Darst's] Lexington factory."[25]

Another reason Darst may have chosen Lexington as his residence was that his brother-in-law, John Woodson, had begun an early brickmaking business there. In the 1790s Darst turned to brick making. Why he gave up the pottery business is not clear, but the transition from potter to brickmaker was an easy one. The raw materials were the same, and he already had a thorough knowledge of running a kiln and a pugmill.[26]

The business success of Darst and Woodson may have influenced John Jordan, the entrepreneur who was also from Goochland County, to move to Rockbridge County.[27] In 1803 Benjamin Darst's son, Samuel, also entered the brickmaking business, probably in association with his father. In the three decades following a devastating fire in Lexington in 1796, the town and the county witnessed the construction of dozens of remarkably fine brick residences, commercial buildings, and school and college structures.

The men who played major roles in the early development of the county and particularly in the construction of the fine row of houses on Lexington's Lee Avenue—Benjamin and Samuel Darst, John Irvin, John Jordan, John Woodson, and John Chandler—were almost all connected by marriage, associated in business at one time or another, or formerly associated in Goochland County. Benjamin Darst, who in 1819 built one of these first residences of the Lee Avenue group, played a special role with his pottery and brickmaking businesses.

BUSTLEBURG-FIREBAUGH POTTERY

Little is known about the pottery industry in Rockbridge County from 1791, when Darst's pottery closed, until the 1830s. It is likely, however, that a few county residents whose primary occupation was farming were engaged in the manufacture of pottery on a part-time basis in small shops supplying needed wares for local use. The next archaeological evidence of pottery manufacture in the county is from recent excavation. In 1984 and 1988 members of the Washington and Lee Laboratory of Anthropology excavated two kiln sites. The earlier of these, although the second excavated, was near the village of Bustleburg, on a farm formerly owned by John Firebaugh. The pottery is situated on the south bank of the Cedar Grove Branch of Cedar Creek at the point where State Route 712 crosses the creek and about 180 yards from the Firebaugh house.

John Firebaugh was born in Harrisburg, Pennsylvania, in 1789 and probably came to Rockbridge County around 1820. Although he was never listed in the census as a potter, there is clear evidence that he was engaged in the business as an owner or manager, if not an artisan. In 1848 Firebaugh granted a tract of land to David Firebaugh (1819–1907) with the exception of "the clay bank called Maple Swamp which said Firebaugh reserves for his own use and purpose and a right of road to and from the same during said John Firebaugh's natural life. . . . " The "clay bank" was clearly an im-

portant part of Firebaugh's pottery business. The deed transferring ownership of the property describes "the Maple Swamp tract" as being located at the confluence of and between the North River and Kerrs Creek.[28]

That Firebaugh was associated with the pottery business is given further credence by the 1867 settlement of his estate, which listed "a set of potter's tools, sold to R. D. Firebaugh (1842–1913) for $0.50, worth $3.00," "2 pitcher molds sold to William Clemmor for $0.70., worth $0.25," a "pipe mold" sold to Ed Wilson for $0.12-½, "turning tools" to Fred Snider for $0.32-½, and several lots of earthen bottles sold to various individuals for between 25 and 70 cents. Also, a map of the United States is listed as sold to J. M. Hinkle for 65 cents.[29] It is likely that this is the same Jesse Hinkle who worked as a potter in Botetourt County.

The pottery produced at the Firebaugh pottery is very similar in form and decoration to pottery produced earlier at the Commeraw pottery at Coerlear's Hook, Manhattan. Specifically, it shows the influence of one person, John D. Morgan, who was trained at the Commeraw pottery and transplanted a strongly Germanic-influenced stoneware tradition to rural Rockbridge County.

Morgan had worked with his father, David, at the Commeraw pottery, which was established by Thomas Commeraw in 1797. From 1795 to 1799 David Morgan was employed by Crolius, a prominent figure in stoneware manufacturing in New York. Subsequently, in 1799 he took over the Commeraw pottery at Coerlear's Hook, which was considered to be in direct competition with the dominant Crolius operation. Several extant stoneware vessels marked "D. Morgan/New York" were apparently made

STONEWARE, *attributed to John Morgan, Bustleburg-Firebaugh pottery, c. 1830–67. These three salt-glazed stoneware jars with lug handles display the blue cobalt decoration that characterizes New York stoneware of the late 1700s and early 1800s. 7 x 4¾ inches to 14¼ x 7¼ inches.*

during the period 1799–1802. By 1802 Commeraw returned to operate the pottery; David Morgan remained associated with the pottery until 1803, when he left the business to become a grocer. John
Morgan, however, continued to be associated with the Commeraw
pottery until 1812. After this time neither he nor any other Morgan appears in documentary records for New York state.[30]

Census records verify John Morgan's presence in Rockbridge
County in 1830. By then he was about sixty-two years old.[31] At
that time Morgan and his wife had a young man, presumably their
son, Henry E. Morgan, living with them, and possibly serving as
an apprentice to Morgan. It seems likely that Morgan arrived
sometime during the 1820s and established residence with or near
John Firebaugh in the Bustleburg area. By the 1830s Morgan had
established a pottery at Bustleburg in association with John Firebaugh. Henry Morgan was probably involved with the operation
as an assistant or apprentice. (By 1840 Henry was living at Rockbridge Baths and may have been involved in establishing the pottery there, most likely with the assistance or perhaps under the su-
pervision of his father.)

Another potter, Robert T. Fulwiler, was living in the Firebaugh
household and was associated with Morgan by 1860. In 1850 and
probably earlier Fulwiler worked as a potter in Botetourt County,
having been involved with the Obenchain pottery operation located along Mill Creek. Nothing else is known of Fulwiler except
that he was born in Virginia.[32] The identification of John Morgan
and Robert Fulwiler as potters in Firebaugh's household in 1850
and 1860, respectively, indicates that the Bustleburg pottery continued to operate into the 1860s. The absence of documentary evidence relating to the operation after this time suggests that the
pottery ceased operation sometime before or coincident with Firebaugh's death in 1867.

The Firebaugh site, like the Rockbridge Baths site, was
identified by the presence of surface shards. Excavation took place
in the spring of 1988. The artifacts recovered at the two sites were
much alike, except that the greater number of earthenware shards
and the increased frequency of incised decorative treatments on
stoneware shards at Firebaugh suggests that it was the earlier pottery, as does the earlier design of its kiln. The Firebaugh kiln was
oval shaped with six heavily glazed brick arches on each side of a
central kiln platform serving to connect the exterior kiln walls with
the platform. It had two fireboxes, situated at opposite ends of the
kiln. The kiln had two basic chambers. The chamber beneath the
arches housed the kiln flues of the firing chamber, which allowed
for the transmission of heat, smoke, and ash, while the area above
the arches was a pot chamber in which vessels were stacked both
on the central kiln platform and on metal bars stretching across
the various flue arches.[33]

EARTHENWARE POT, *late 1700s.*
Benjamin Darst's Lexington
pottery (c. 1785–91) probably pro-
duced similar pieces as well
as plates, bowls, and bean pots.

This piece, found in the
Steeles Tavern area, has a lead-
glazed interior. 12½ x 11½ inches
(including handles).

ROCKBRIDGE BATHS POTTERY

An earlier excavation, in 1984, uncovered another nineteenth-century kiln site, some seven hundred yards southwest of the village of Rockbridge Baths. Local tradition had long associated this pottery with a Rockbridge Baths resident, Isaac D. Lam, and the farm where the pottery was located with the Shewey family. But the exact location of the kiln was unknown until the Washington and Lee archaeologists began their research.

When David Shewey bought the "Shewey Place" from the heirs of Rockbridge Baths ironmaster Isaac Bryan in 1857, the deed mentioned the presence of "the Potter shop" and its location by the county road.[34] The deed transferring ownership of the property from Richard Davis to Bryan in 1843 indicates that Davis retained one-half interest in the potter's house, kiln, and clay source, all located on the south side of the North River within what is referred to as the Lambert Tract.[35] That Davis had in 1843 purchased the land from his brother, Samuel W. Davis, who had himself acquired it in 1839 from one Joseph Lambert[36] explains the Lambert Tract reference, but unfortunately no mention of pottery activity has been noted in official records associated with this transfer of ownership. This would indicate that the Rockbridge Baths pottery was established sometime before 1843. At the time Shewey acquired the land, which consisted of a 138-acre farm that extended for some distance along the North River below Whitmore's (later Mast's) Mill dam, the pottery undoubtedly represented an established business enterprise. To summarize, the records indicate that the pottery was established sometime before 1843 but also show that by the time Shewey acquired the land in 1857 it was an established enterprise.

In 1860 another potter, John D. Campbell, then fifty-six years old, was living at Rockbridge Baths, next door to and probably on the farm of David Shewey.[37] Campbell, born in Virginia, came to Rockbridge County from Albemarle County, Virginia, some time after 1832 and before 1840.[38] But it was not until 1850 that he listed himself as a potter in the census records. That year Campbell's two sons were living with him, James H. and Charles W. Their father must have told the census taker they were "stonepotters," but neither remained to pursue their father's career for very long.[39]

When the pottery at Rockbridge Baths actually began is still not clear. The date of Campbell's arrival in Rockbridge suggests that he may have helped establish the pottery with Morgan in Rockbridge Baths during the period 1839–43, when it was owned by Samuel and, later, Richard Davis. Although John Morgan was not listed in the 1840 census, a Henry Morgan (probably his son), age twenty to thirty, was living at Rockbridge Baths and perhaps was working by that time as a potter. Supporting this early Morgan-Campbell connection with the establishment of the pottery is the fact that a John Campbell, possibly the potter (there were a good number of John Campbells in the 1840 census), was also living nearby.[40] So there is some good evidence that both the Morgans and the Campbells were active at Rockbridge Baths by 1840. The owner of the property from 1843 through 1857, Isaac Bryan, undoubtedly applied his business acumen acquired during his tenure as a prominent ironmaster to the pottery industry, and the Rockbridge Baths establishment began to expand and prosper during this period. Campbell's identification of himself and his sons as potters in 1850 indicates his strong and continued involvement with the operation.

By the 1860s the Shewey farm and pottery was a sizable operation. Shewey listed his real estate at $7,000 and his personal property at $3,500, including presumably the pottery and equipment. Charles D. Campbell was living on the farm and near the pottery,

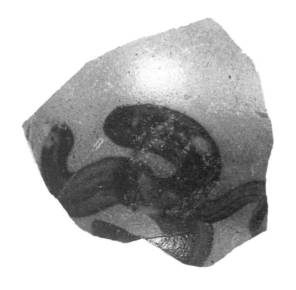

PAINTED SHARDS, *right.*
Excavation of the Rockbridge Baths
pottery unearthed thousands of
shards, a number of which were
painted with blue cobalt decoration.

ROCKBRIDGE BATHS KILN,
bottom. This circular updraft kiln
was excavated in 1984 by the
Washington and Lee University
Laboratory of Anthropology.

STONEWARE PIPE BOWL, 1840–
82. *Excavations at the Rockbridge
Baths pottery site uncovered*
*this salt-glazed pipe bowl depicting
a man's face, which was made from
a two-piece mold.*

What brought these potters from New York and Albemarle and Rockingham Counties and elsewhere to settle at Rockbridge Baths, an area far from the primary traffic routes through the Valley? A combination of factors likely contributed to the pottery industry's establishment and growth in this region. The natural beauty of the area and its natural resources, including abundant cultivable land, the North (Maury) River, mineral (iron) deposits, good clay, and ample timber were of primary importance in the area's development. Beginning in the 1820s, when this section of the county began to prosper, substantial building activity resulted in the construction of several fine brick houses in the 1820s and early 1830s. A number of ironworks, including the Bath Ironworks in Goshen, were established in the area beginning in the mid-1820s. The large work force necessary to support these operations meant an increase in population requiring necessities such as simple storage containers handcrafted from local clay. Contributing also to the area's growth was the emergence during this period of the popular spring resorts and baths: the Rockbridge Baths, the Sprickler (later Wilson's) Springs, Rockbridge Alum Springs, Cold Sulfur Springs, Bath Alum Springs, and others. All were located within a few miles of the pottery. By the 1840s and 1850s these summer institutions were in full swing, and the demand for crockery would have been great as the accompanying hotels expanded and visitors from all over the East began arriving in the area. The expanding transportation systems, involving both North River navigation and the railroad, provided ready means for commercial exchange, ensuring the area's continued growth. Packet boats were able to navigate the North River from Cedar Grove—just below Rockbridge Baths—when conditions allowed. The C&O railroad arrived in Goshen in the 1850s, connecting Washington, Charlottesville, and Richmond with these mountain ironwork complexes and resorts, as well as with the new cities along the Ohio River.

The 1984 Washington and Lee archaeology dig on the Rockbridge Baths or Morgan-Campbell-Lam site uncovered a circular kiln, part of the limestone foundation of a potter's shed,[45] and a clay processing and storage area of about four by eight feet. The kiln was of a circular updraft variety, common during the nineteenth century. It measured twelve and a half feet in diameter and consisted of two opposing fireboxes and a central flue separating two D-shaped pedestals, each surrounded to the exterior by interior flues that connected with the central flue at the point where they joined with the firebox. The very high temperatures (2100° to 2300° Fahrenheit) required to fire stoneware such as the jars and other vessels made at Rockbridge Baths would have called for such an efficient kiln design.

To produce the salt glaze used on stoneware, granulated salt was actually thrown into the firebox or introduced through the kiln's

as was a forty-four-year-old carpenter, Henry Selby. Also living on the Shewey farm was a German-born wagonmaker named John Waggner, whose services could have been useful to the pottery operation.[41] It was during this period that the potter Isaac D. Lam became associated with the Rockbridge Baths operation. Lam (also spelled Lamb), who was born in Rockingham County, Virginia, in 1832,[42] served as an apprentice to Andrew and William Coffman, the Rockingham County potters, during the 1850s and early 1860s at both the East Elkton (Whip-poor-will Springs) and later, Elkton North (Willow Springs) pottery locales.[43] Sometime before February 1864, Lam moved to Rockbridge Baths and began working at the pottery. In 1865, after returning from the Civil War, he married Mary L. Selby, and continued to live at the Baths. Lam's granddaughter recalled that his house was "across the river from the Baths" and near the pottery—which would have placed it on the Shewey farm.[44] Lam is listed as a potter in the Kerrs Creek District of the county in 1870. In 1875 one W. P. Harris, a journeyman or itinerant potter, was working with Lam. Lam continued to live and work in the county until his death on July 22, 1882, when the Rockbridge pottery apparently ceased operation.

chimney during the firing process. "Draw tiles" were used to check the firing temperature of the kiln and the nature of the glaze formed from the combination of the soda (sodium) from the salt and the silica in the clay. In the kiln the pots were stacked on top of each other, usually separated by "kiln furniture," or small, handformed, sandcoated pottery pieces to allow the greatest surface area to be exposed to the heat and to stabilize the stacks of pots, helping to prevent them from sticking together and shifting under heat duress.

The dig produced both salt-glazed stoneware and lead-glazed earthenware shards or damaged portions of churns, jugs, milk pans, bowls, and storage jars, as well as a variety of kiln furniture used to stack and separate vessels during firing. Decorative treatments of the stoneware included incised, brushed, and slipped blue cobalt floral, geometric, and animal motifs. Some redware shards were from forms that are typically thought of as being earlier than mid-nineteenth century—shallow milk pans and bowls with spouts and handles.

Names incised on some of the shards both provide confirmation of those working at the kiln and offer some puzzles. John Campbell's name appears once on a shard, and the name Hugh Marshall was found incised on the bottom of three redware pieces, along with the title "factor." Nothing else has been found about Marshall, but at one point he may have acted as the wholesaler for the Rockbridge Baths operation.[46] One of the most interesting artifacts found in the dig was a lump of fired clay with incised flowers and the name Isaac. This could have been a doorstop or simply a doodle Lam produced for his own amusement. Also found were a large number of mold-made, fluted, reed-stemmed smoking pipes with anthropomorphic relief decoration or faces on the fronts of the bowls.

The stoneware storage jars and jugs produced at this pottery have long been recognized as atypical of those made elsewhere in the Valley. The ovoid shapes and incised decorative treatments with brushed blue cobalt are especially distinctive. It was not possible to trace any of the forms found to Lam's previous association in Rockingham County. Such wares have more in common with examples produced in New Jersey and by Crolius, Commeraw, and David Morgan in New York than with examples from the Valley.[47] Moreover, the Rockbridge Baths stoneware is virtually indistinguishable from pottery produced at the nearby Bustleburg-Firebaugh operation. The "ROCKBRIDGE" mark on shards from both sites provides additional evidence for their association and John Morgan's involvement with both sites. Both Rockbridge potteries produced wares atypical of those manufactured elsewhere in the Valley but similar to forms associated with Manhattan. So John Morgan's presence in Rockbridge provides a probable explanation for the forms and decorations of the wares at both the Campbell-Lam and the Firebaugh potteries.[48]

MILK BOWL, *fragment, top, 1840–82. Hugh Marshall, whose name is incised on the base of this piece, may have been a wholesale merchant who at one time distributed redware and other pieces for the Rockbridge Baths pottery.*

STONEWARE DOORSTOP, *fragment, bottom, 1840–82. This salt-glazed pottery fragment is incised with the name "Isaac," undoubtedly Isaac Lam of the Rockbridge Baths pottery.*

STONEWARE PITCHER WITH
EAGLE, *by John Morgan for the
Bustleburg-Firebaugh pottery,
1838. One of two known pitchers
made by Morgan on the same
day, this one-gallon, salt-glazed
pitcher with an incised blue cobalt
eagle is inscribed "Rockbridge Va.
April the 24th 1838." 11¼ x 6 inches.*

Several extant vessels carry the "ROCKBRIDGE" mark or have been attributed to Rockbridge County on the basis of stylistic attributes that they share with the wasters from the two potteries. Two dated vessels attributed to the Firebaugh pottery provide clues to the beginning of the stoneware industry. An outstanding one-gallon stoneware pitcher with a well-executed incised eagle and inscription was probably made by John Morgan during the first decade of stoneware production in the county. One cylindrical straight-sided jar is dated 1838. Several similar jars have been identified and attributed to the Firebaugh operation as well. The largest of these is decorated with the characteristic brushed blue cobalt loops and dots connected as if to represent a clustering of grapes. Three other vessels of similar form, labeled "Mangos," "Plumbs," and "Peaches," undoubtedly were intended to function as fruit preserve jars. The "Peaches" example has an incised bird on its reverse and unusual coggle decoration below the rim. Although the swag and tassel decoration on the obverse (or front) of the vessel appears to have been stenciled, it is unquestionably related to the dominant brushed "loop" motif observed on many surviving Rockbridge crocks.

The unique incised floral and animal decorative motifs that distinguish Rockbridge pottery from wares produced elsewhere in Virginia appear on several extant vessels. A large-capacity watercooler has incised floral decoration filled with blue cobalt oxide on both its front and back. Jugs with incised floral decoration show variations in the handle attachment and ovid form on pieces made in the county. Similar but less elaborate incising decorates a one-gallon, salt-glazed stoneware pitcher and a half-gallon, salt-glazed stoneware jug with characteristic incised rings around its neck.

Simple, brushed, blue cobalt floral decorations are common on Rockbridge County wares. While the incised and loop- or swag-decorated pieces appear to be relatively early, from the second quarter of the nineteenth century, the simple, splashy floral motifs probably are from the third quarter of the century. Floral embellishments on Rockbridge County examples are decidedly less elaborate than those on other decorated wares from this period.

Other than the frequently observed "ROCKBRIDGE" mark, stamped designs are rare either on pieces in collections or on those found on archaeological sites in the county. No stamps indicating vessel capacity have been found.

Rockbridge pottery provides an example of the transplantation

JAR, *top left, attributed to the Bustleburg-Firebaugh pottery, 1838. 13 x 5 ½ inches.*

TALL STONEWARE CROCK, *top center, 1830–67. 15½ x 7 inches.*

MANGOS CROCK, *top right, 1830–67. This storage jar is stamped "Mangos" and incised "Susan J. Wilson." The overglazed decoration was painted on after manufacture. 14 x 6½ inches.*

"PLUMBS" JAR, *bottom left, 1830–67. 9 x 4¾ inches.*

"PEACHES" JAR, *bottom center and right, attributed to the Bustleburg-Firebaugh pottery,*

1830–67. This tall, salt-glazed stoneware storage jar has a stenciled swag and tassel and the inscription "Peaches." The reverse side is decorated with an incised bird design. 12 x 5¼ inches.

STONEWARE STORAGE JARS,
*c. 1830–82. These seven salt-glazed,
semi-ovoid jars are representative
of the work produced by the
Rockbridge Baths and Bustleburg-
Firebaugh potteries over a
fifty-year period. 3 x 9¼ inches to
15¼ x 9½ inches.*

of the strongly Germanic-influenced stoneware pottery tradition from New York to Virginia.[49] Although the industry began in Rockbridge County with the establishment of the Darst earthenware pottery in Lexington around 1785, the expression of this ceramic tradition is best illustrated by the Rockbridge Baths and Firebaugh potteries. The last quarter of the nineteenth century saw many potteries in the rural areas of Virginia close, as did the Firebaugh operation around 1867 and the Rockbridge Baths pottery around 1882. Increasing industrialization brought competition as well as a myriad of changes to which it was difficult for these traditional potters to adapt. Thus the manufacture of traditional domestic ceramics became economically unfeasible.[50]

WATER COOLER, *top right, attributed to the Bustleburg-Firebaugh pottery, 1830–50. The influence of the Thomas H. Commeraw pottery in New York is seen in this salt-glazed stone-ware piece with strap handles and incised cobalt floral decoration. 15½ x 9¾ inches (including handles).*

THREE-GALLON JUG, *right, 1830–50. The figure-eight stroke is used to incise the rounded flower petals of this semi-ovoid, ring-neck jug. 16½ x 10½ inches.*

Profiles

Rockbridge County Artists & Artisans, 1750–1900

This chapter contains biographical sketches of artists and artisans who were active in the county from the mid-eighteenth century until the end of the nineteenth century. Included are those whose occupation is associated with one of the chapters in the book—generally artists, furniture makers, textile manufacturers, clockmakers, gunsmiths, iron manufacturers, and potters. The exceptions have mostly to do with individuals who are particularly important because of the work they produced or their circumstances. An example is Adolphus Weir, a late-eighteenth–century blacksmith whose shop ledger survives and documents his business relationship with early clockmakers and gunsmiths. While blacksmiths in general are not included, Weir's contribution is well documented and significant. Another example is the Pennsylvania folk painter Edward Hicks, who produced a number of images of Natural Bridge but has not been documented as ever having visited the county.

GEORGE WASHINGTON, *opposite, by Mathew Kahle, 1842–44. Kahle was a cabinetmaker and carpenter who created one of Rockbridge County's most famous icons. His statue of Washington stands atop Center Hall at Washington and Lee University in Lexington. For his woodworking business, Kahle produced a wide range of items and at one point called himself a "Manufacturer of Sideboards, bureaus, and tete a tetes." Painted poplar, 98 inches.*

Information has come from a variety of sources, some well organized and easily accessible to the public, others obscure or in private collections. Names and statistics from the federal population census and the *Census of Manufactures* were our foundation. They were expanded with information obtained from a systematic survey of newspapers and probate appraisals and sales. Other public records—birth, death, marriage, real estate transfers, apprentice bonds, etc.—provided vital statistics as well as established filial and professional relationships. The study greatly benefited from information found in the collections of Washington and Lee University, the Virginia Military Institute, the Rockbridge Historical Society, and the Museum of Early Southern Decorative Arts .

Entries for individuals, partnerships, and manufacturers are alphabetized. Variations in name spellings have been standardized as far as possible. Cross-references are designated "q.v." Following an individual's occupation are birth and death dates and locations. Next are the dates of the individual's period of activity in the county. These dates are based on the earliest and latest documented activity. An attempt has been made to identify the individual's location within the county. This is reflected in the use of local place names—Green Hill, Oak Dale, Bustleburg—as well as established towns. Frequently used sources are listed at the end. A key to those sources follows. Sources cited only once are described in that particular entry. Page numbers are given for primary source materials such as court records and shop ledgers but are not given for published sources with indexes.

KEY TO PROFILE SOURCES

ACDB *Augusta County Deed Book.* Court House, Augusta County, Va.

AHB *Augusta Historical Bulletin.*

BEETON Beeton, John D. *History of the Beeton Family.* Sterling, Va.: Privately printed, 1977.

BIVINS Bivins, John, Jr. "Isaac Zane and the Products of Marboro Furnace." *Journal of Early Southern Decorative Arts* 11, no. 1 (May 1985): 15, 17.

BRADY 1979 Brady, T. T. "The Early Iron Industry in Rockbridge County." *Rockbridge Historical Society Proceedings* 8 (1979): 45–52.

BRADY 1989 Brady, D. E. "Iron Valley Revisited." Paper presented to the Fortnightly Club, Lexington, Va., 1989.

BROCK Brock, Robert A. *Hardesty's Historical and Geographical Encyclopedia (Special Virginia Edition).* New York: H.H. Hardesty, 1884.

BROEHL Broehl, Wayne G., Jr. "John Deere's Shop." *American History Illustrated* 19, no. 9 (January 1985): 16–19.

BRUCE Bruce, Kathleen. *Virginia Iron Manufacturer in the Slave Era.* New York: Century, 1931.

BVA *Buena Vista Advocate.* Buena Vista, Va.

C Population census, followed by year.

CAPRON Capron, Lester J. "Lucy Selina's Charcoal Era." *Virginia Cavalcade,* 7, no. 2 (autumn 1957): 32.

CHALKLEY Chalkley, Lyman. *Chronicles of the Scotch-Irish Settlement in Virginia.* 3 vols. 1912. Reprint. Baltimore: Genealogical Publishing, 1980.

CLARK Clark, Carmen E. *Goodbars I Found.* Lexington, Va.: News Gazette, 1980.

CM *Census of Manufactures,* followed by year.

COULLING Coulling, Mary P. *The Lee Girls.* Winston-Salem, N.C.: John F. Blair, 1987.

COUPER 1939 Couper, William. *100 Years at VMI.* 4 vols. Richmond: Garrett and Massie, 1939.

COUPER 1952 Couper, William. *The History of the Shenandoah Valley.* 3 vols. New York: Lewis Historical Publishing, 1952.

COUPER 1960 Couper, William. *Jackson Memorial Cemetery Survey Complete to 1960.* Lexington, Va., n.d., n.p.

COWDREY Cowdrey, Mary Bartlett. *National Academy, Design Exhibition Record, 1826–1860.* New York: New-York Historical Society, 1943.

CUTTEN Cutten, George Barton. *The Silversmiths of Virginia.* Richmond: Dietz Press, 1952.

DARST Darst, H. Jackson. *The Darsts of Virginia.* Williamsburg, Va.: Privately printed, 1972.

DELMAR Delmar, Dorothy Chittum, John W. Chittum, and Mae Chittum, eds. *Nancy and John: A Chittum Genealogy.* Privately printed, c. 1981.

DEW 1966 Dew, Charles B. *Ironmaker to the Confederacy: Joseph R. Anderson and The Tredegar Iron Works.* New Haven: Yale University Press, 1966.

DEW 1994 Dew, Charles B. *Bond of Iron: Master and Slave at Buffalo Forge.* New York: W.W. Norton, 1994.

DICKENS Dickens, David B. "Frank Buchser in Virginia: A Swiss Artist's Impressions." *Virginia Cavalcade* 38, no. 1 (1988): 4–13.

DIEHL 1971 Diehl, George W. *Old Oxford and Her Families.* Verona, Va.: McClure Press, 1971.

DIEHL 1982 Diehl, George W. *Rockbridge County, Virginia, Notebook.* Compiled by A. Maxim Coppage III. Owensboro, Ky.: McDowell Publishing, 1982.

DILLIN Dillin, John G. W. *The Kentucky Rifle.* Washington, D.C.: National Rifle Association of America, 1924.

DOOLEY Dooley, Edwin L., Jr. "Lexington in the 1860 Census." *Rockbridge Historical Society Proceedings* 9 (1975–79): 189–96.

DOOLEY/KEY Key, Milton H. Cabinetmaker's ledger, 1857–60. Transcribed by Edwin Dooley. Rockbridge County Court House.

DRIVER Driver, Robert J., Jr. From the personal manuscript collection of a Civil War historian, in addition to a dozen published military histories. Brownsburg, Va.

DURAND Durand, John. *The Life and Times of A. B. Durand.* 1894. Reprint. New York.: Kennedy Graphics and Da Capo Press, 1970.

FOTHERGILL Fothergill, Augusta B., and John Mark Naugle. *Virginia Tax Payers 1782–87.* 1940. Reprint. Baltimore: Genealogical Publishing, 1978.

GILL Gill, Harold B., Jr. *The Gunsmith in Colonial Virginia.* Charlottesville, Va.: University Press of Virginia, 1974.

GOELLER Goeller, Mildred S. *The Steeles of Steeles Tavern, Virginia, and Related Families.* n.p., 1974.

GROCE Groce, George C., and David H. Wallace. *The New-York Historical Society's Dictionary of Artists in America, 1564–1860.* New Haven: Yale University Press, 1957.

HADSEL Hadsel, Winifred. *The Streets of Lexington, Virginia.* Lexington, Va.: Rockbridge Historical Society, 1985.

HINTON Hinton, John Howard. *The History and Topography of the United States of North America, Brought Down from the Earliest Period.* 3rd ed. Boston: S. Walker, 1853–54.

HUMPHRIES Humphries, William S. Unpublished diary of one year's activity at Vesuvius Iron Factory, 1872. Private collection.

HUTCHINSON Hutchinson, William T. *Cyrus Hall McCormick.* New York: Century, 1930.

HV *Herald of the Valley.* Fincastle, Va.

KAUFFMAN Kauffman, Henry J. *Early American Ironware.* Rutland, Vt.: Charles E. Tuttle, 1966.

KEGLEY Kegley, Frederick B. *Virginia Frontier.* Roanoke, Va.: Southwest Virginia Historical Society, 1938.

KIRKPATRICK 1888 Kirkpatrick, Dorthie, and Edwin Kirkpatrick. *Rockbridge County Births, 1853–1877.* 2 vols. San Bernardino, Calif.: Bongo Press, 1988.

KIRKPATRICK 1985 Kirkpatrick, Dorthie, and Edwin Kirkpatrick. *Rockbridge County Marriages, 1778–1850.* Athens, Ga.: Iberian Publishing, 1985.

LANE Lane, Mills. *Architecture of the Old South.* New York: Abbeville Press, 1984.

LAWALL Lawall, David Bannar. "Asher Brown Durand: His Art and Art Theory in Relation to His Times." 4 vols. Ph.D. dissertation, Princeton University, 1966.

LEYBURN Leyburn, James G. "The Leyburn Family, 1734–1960." Special collections, Leyburn Library, Washington and Lee University, Lexington, Va.

LI *Lexington Intelligencer.* Lexington, Va.

LG *Lexington Gazette.* Lexington, Va.

LNL *Lexington News-Letter.* Lexington, Va.

LUCK Luck, Barbara. "Lewis Miller's Virginia." *Rockbridge Historical Society Proceedings* 10 (1980–89): 245–72.

LYLE Lyle, Oscar K. *Lyle Family.* New York: Lecouver Press, 1912.

LYLE AND SIMPSON Lyle, Royster, Jr., and Pamela Hemenway Simpson. *The Architecture of Historic Lexington.* Charlottesville, Va.: University Press of Virginia, 1977.

LYONS Lyons, Norbert. *The McCormick Reaper Legend.* New York: Exposition Press, 1955.

MARTIN Martin, Joseph. *A New and Comprehensive Gazetteer of Virginia and the District of Columbia.* Charlottesville, Va.: Joseph Martin Publisher, 1835.

MCCLUNG McClung, William. *The McClung Genealogy.* Pittsburgh: McClung Printing, 1904.

MCCLURE McClure, James Alexander. *The McClure Family.* Petersburg, Va., Privately printed, 1914.

MESDA Museum of Early Southern Decorative Arts, Winston-Salem, N.C.

MITCHELL Mitchell, Robert D. *Commercialism and Frontier: Perspectives on Early Shenandoah Valley*. Charlottesville, Va.: University Press of Virginia, 1977.

MONTGOMERY Montgomery, Charles F. *American Furniture: The Federal Period*. New York: Viking Press, 1966.

MOORE 1963 Moore, John S. "John Jordan: Rockbridge Baptist Layman," *Virginia Baptist Register* 2 (1963): 52–62.

MOORE 1966 Moore, John S. "John Jordan, Baptist Layman." Rockbridge Historical Society Proceedings 6 (1966): 63–71.

MORRESSET Morresset, Marie A. *Abstracts of Rockbridge County, Va., Deed Book A, 1778–1788*. Arcata, La.: Gibson Computers and Publishing, 1987.

MORTON Morton, Oren. *A History of Rockbridge County, Virginia*. Staunton, Va.: McClure Press, 1920.

MYERS Myers, John H. Customer account books for Lexington hardware store. 2 vols. 1837–52. Private collection.

NG *News Gazette*. Lexington, Va.

NIEDERER Niederer, Frances J. *The Town of Fincastle, Virginia*. Charlottesville, Va.: University Press of Virginia, 1965.

ODDFELLOWS International Order of Oddfellows. "The Register of the Rockbridge Lodge No. 158, IOOF," October 29, 1847, until 1900. Private collection.

OTT Ott, Ethelbert Nelson. "William D. Washington, 1833–1870: Artist of the South." Master's thesis, University of Delaware. VMI Archives, 1969.

PAXTON Paxton, W. M. *The Paxtons*. Platte City, Mo.: Landmark Print., 1903.

PERKINS Perkins, Louise M. *Rockbridge County Marriages, 1851–1885*. Signal Mountain, Tenn.: Mountain Press, 1989.

PEYTON Peyton, John L. *History of Augusta County, Virginia*. Staunton, Va.: S. M. Yost and Son, 1882.

RCBR *Rockbridge County Birth Register* 2 (1878–96). Court House, Rockbridge County, Va.

RCDR *Rockbridge County Death Register*. Court House, Rockbridge County, Va.

RCLB *Rockbridge County Land Books*. Court House, Rockbridge County, Va.

RCMR *Rockbridge County Marriage Register*. Court House, Rockbridge County, Va.

RCN *Rockbridge County News*. Lexington, Va.

RCOB *Rockbridge County Order Book*. Court House, Rockbridge County, Va.

RCPB *Rockbridge County Property Book*. Court House, Rockbridge County, Va.

RCWB *Rockbridge County Will Book*. Court House, Rockbridge County, Va.

RHSP *Rockbridge Historical Society Proceedings*. 10 vols.

RR *Rockbridge Repository*. Lexington, Va.

RUFF Ruff, John. Ledger (1809–18). Rockbridge Historical Society collection. Washington and Lee University, Lexington, Va.

RUFFNER Ruffner, William Henry, ed. *Washington and Lee University Historical Papers*. 6 vols. Baltimore: John Murphy, 1890–1904.

RUSS Russ, Kurt C. "The Traditional Pottery Manufacturing Industry in Virginia: Examples from Botetourt and Rockbridge Counties." *Rockbridge Historical Society Proceedings* 10 (1980–89): 453–89.

RUTLAND Rutland, Robert A. "Men in Iron in the Making of Virginia." *Iron Worker* (summer 1976): 15.

SCHNEIDER Schneider, Cary A. "Rockbridge County Gravestones and Their Carvers." *Rockbridge Historical Society Proceedings* 9 (1975–79): 63–76.

SCOTT Scott, Kenneth. *British Aliens in the United States During the War of 1812*. Baltimore: Genealogical Publishing, 1979.

SIMPSON 1977 Simpson, Pamela H. *American Sculpture in Lexington: Selected Examples From Public Collections*. Exhibition Catalogue. Lexington, Va.: Washington and Lee University, 1977.

SIMPSON 1978 Simpson, Pamela H. *Architectural Drawings in Lexington: 1779–1926*. Exhibition catalogue. Lexington, Va.: Washington and Lee University, 1978.

SIMPSON 1980 Simpson, Pamela H., and Mame Warren. *Michael Miley: American Photographer and Pioneer in Color*. Exhibition catalogue. Lexington, Va.: Washington and Lee University, 1980.

SIMPSON 1988 Simpson, Pamela H. *So Beautiful an Arch: Images of the Natural Bridge 1787–1890*. Exhibition catalogue. Lexington, Va.: Washington and Lee University, 1982.

SRS Smith, Samuel R. Cabinetmaker's ledgers. 2 vols. 1831–47 and 1827–59. Private collection.

TOMPKINS Tompkins, Edmund P. *Rockbridge County, Virginia: An Informal History*. Richmond: Whittet and Shepperson, 1952.

TUCKER Tucker, Harry St. George. "A list of white voters with P. office addresses in the 10th District of Virginia, 1889—Alleghany, Appomattox, Augusta, Bath, Cumberland, Fluvanna, Highland, Nelson, Amherst, Buckingham, and Rockbridge—who were the constituents of Congressman Harry St. George Tucker." Ledger, private collection.

TURNER Turner, Charles W. *The Diary of Henry Boswell Jones of Brownsburg: 1842–71*. Verona, Va: McClure Press, 1979.

VARNER Varner, Andrew. Cabinetmaker's ledgers, 1860–64 and 1860–63. Private collection.

VG *Virginia Gazette*. Williamsburg, Va.

VG&GA *Virginia Gazette and General Advocate*. Richmond, Va.

VG&SWA *Virginia Gazette and Staunton Weekly Advertizer*. Staunton, Va.

VHS Manuscript Collection, Virginia Historical Society. Richmond, Va.

VMHB *Virginia Magazine of History and Biography*. Richmond, Va.

VP *Virginia Patriot*. Richmond, Va.

VS *Valley Star*. Lexington, Va.

VT *Virginia Telegraph and Rockbridge Courier*. Lexington, Va.

VMI ALUMNI Virginia Military Institute. Preston Library, VMI archives, alumni files, Lexington, Va.

VMI ARCHIVES Virginia Military Institute. Preston Library, VMI archives, Lexington, Va.

VMI REGISTER *Virginia Military Institute Register, Former Cadets*. Virginia Military Institute, Lexington, Va., 1957.

VMI SUPERINTENDENT Virginia Military Institute. Preston Library, VMI archives, superintendent's files, Lexington, Va.

VMI TREASURER Virginia Military Institute. Preston Library, VMI archives, treasurer's files, Lexington, Va.

WALKER Walker, John. Blacksmith day book, 1788–95. Wisconsin State Historical Society, Madison, Wis.

WB Wilson and Barclay. Store ledger, 1851–54. Special collections, Washington and Lee University, Lexington, Va.

WD *Weaver v. Davis*. Legal transactions among William Weaver, John Jordan, and William W. Davis, 1834–35. Special collections, Leyburn Library, Washington and Lee University, Lexington, Va.

WEIR Weir, Adolphus. Blacksmith ledger, 1790–1806. Swem Library, William and Mary College, Williamsburg, Va.

WL ALUMNI *Washington and Lee University Alumni Catalogue, 1749–1888*. Baltimore: John Murphy, 1888.

WL FRANKLIN SOCIETY Papers relating to a nineteenth-century Lexington literary and debating society. Special collections, Leyburn Library, Washington and Lee University, Lexington, Va.

WL RHS Rockbridge Historical Society collection. Special collections, Leyburn Library, Washington and Lee University, Lexington, Va.

WL SPECIAL COLLECTIONS Manuscript collection, Leyburn Library, Washington and Lee University, Lexington, Va.

WL TRUSTEES' Trustees' papers indexed in the university archival records, Leyburn Library, Washington and Lee University, Lexington, Va.

WL WITHROW Withrow scrapbooks, 2 vols. Special collections, Leyburn Library, Washington and Lee University, Lexington, Va.

WRIGHT Wright, Lewis R. *Artists in Virginia before 1900*. Charlottesville, Va.: University Press of Virginia, 1983.

SIGNATURE, *James Barrett, 1803.*
Found on a bottom drawer of a
neoclassical-style sideboard was the
ink insciption "Made by James
Barrett/Lexington, Sept. 24th
1903." Directly below are the initals
"J. B.," which were incised into the
wood by impressing the edge of a
sharp, pointed metal object such as
a nail.

ADAMS, GEORGE

Cabinetmaker. b. 1825 Rockbridge County, Va. Active 1850–80. Included in the 1850 census household listing of Mathew Kahle (q.v.), for whom he was probably working. Listed again in 1860 and 1880 and in his own household. Made purchases from Myers's hardware store in 1849. C 1850, 1860, 1880; RCMR 1A, 363; Kirkpatrick 1988; Myers; Dooley.

AGNER, JAMES

Cabinetmaker. b. c. 1809. Active 1828–60? Ran away from cabinetmaker Thomas Hopkins (q.v.) in 1828. Could be the James Agnor credited with producing fifty table legs recorded in Milton Key's (q.v.) ledger, 1857–60. C 1860; LI 4/10/1828; Dooley/Key.

AGNOR, FERDINAND OSCAR

Wool manufacturer. b. 1843 Rockbridge County, Va. Active 1865. Listed occupation in marriage records in 1865. RCMR 1A, 115; Kirkpatrick 1988.

AGNOR, THEODORE T.

Cabinetmaker. b. 1856 Virginia. Active 1880–91. Listed as a "cabinetmaker employee" in the 1880 census household of Albert L. Koones (q.v.). When Koones received a certificate at the 1881 county fair for "a suit of really aristocratic Chamber Furniture Manufactured here in our own town," he gave "chief credit . . . to Mr. Theodore T. Agnor." Advertised as a partner of cabinetmaker A. G. Bradley (q.v.) in the Kahle building in 1884. Awarded a certificate at the Rockbridge County Fair, 1884, for a "fine exhibit" of cabinetware. Partner, in 1888, of photographer J.A.A. Miller (q.v.) in "T. T. Agnor & Co." C 1880; Oddfellows; LG 11/21/1881; LG 9/18/1884; LG 12/18/1884; LG 9/23/1888.

ALEXANDER, WILLIAM

Gunsmith. Augusta County, Va.–1797 Lexington, Va. Active 1775–97. Advertised in 1775 for a runaway servant, Thomas Horbert, silversmith. Furnished eight rifles to the Virginia government in January 1776. Gill; VG 2/8/1775; RCWB 2, 14–19.

ALLBRIGHT, FREDERICK

Blacksmith. Active 1819–20. Solicited for the return of an indentured runaway apprentice blacksmith, Willford Downs, in 1816. *Census of Manufactures* for 1820 reports the production of axes, hoes, and chains. LNL 11/27/1819; CM 1820.

ALMOND (ALMAND), JOHN A.

Chairmaker. 1818–60 Walkers Creek, Rockbridge County, Va. Active 1858–60. Letter from Brownsburg, August 31, 1858, offers to sell to Aron Larclay at Goshen "a load of chairs on the same terms as I sold you before, one half money and the other in goods." (Letter in private collection.) Probably related to the other Almond chairmakers. Listed in the county death records as a chairmaker. RCDR, 48.

ALMOND, REUBEN R.

Chairmaker. 1821 Shenandoah County, Va.–1881 Rockbridge County, Va. Active 1870–80. Probably the son of William T. Almond (q.v.). Probate inventory, 1881, listed the items related to his trade. LG 9/15/1881; RCWB 24, 53; C 1870, 1880; Driver.

ALMOND, WILLIAM T.

Chairmaker. 1792 Shenandoah County, Va.–1861 Rockbridge County, Va. Active 1855–60. Listed in the 1860 census as a carpenter, probably the father of Reuben R. Almond (q.v.). Listed as a chairmaker in 1861. Kirkpatrick 1988; RCDR, 48; C 1860.

ANDERSON, FRANCIS T.

Furnace owner. b. Fincastle, Botetourt County, Va. Active 1849–87. Began the Glenwood Furnace, Arnolds Valley, in partnership with D. W. Shanks. Brother of Joseph Anderson, the chief agent and operator of the Tredegar Ironworks Company in Richmond. By 1850 Glenwood Furnace was in full blast, employing sixty-five workers and turning out 700 tons of pig iron. Local paper reports that Anderson "is now the owner of one of the finest principalities in Western Virginia" and owned "valuable Iron Property containing upwards of 30,000 acres" in addition to his own 813-acre estate on the James River. LG 8/6/1857; CM 1850.

ANDY

Blacksmith apprentice (slave). Active 1847–50. Auctioned as part of Gen. C. P. Dorman's estate and described in the *Lexington Gazette* as a "valuable Negro" and "in the service of a Blacksmith, to learn that trade, for the last three years." LG 1/17/1850.

ANNESS, SAMUEL

Artist. Active 1819. Advertised in the local paper in 1819: "Minature Likenesses, TAKEN for Two Dollars and upwards. Also Engraving Done on reasonable terms by Samuel Anness. Specimens can be seen at the *Lexington News-Letter* office." The following month the editor of the *News-Letter*, John N. Snider (q.v.), an-

nounced the sale of a print of Natural Bridge, based on Snider's sketch, which Anness "has had engraved, and now presents it to his readers." LNL 8/17/1819; LNL 9/18/1819; Wright.

ARMSTRONG, JOHN T.

Ironworks manager. 1830–71. Active 1862–64. Served in the 27th Virginia Infantry and was detailed to Jordan Furnace (South River) and to Australia Furnace during the Civil War. Kirkpatrick 1988; Driver.

AVERY, BENJAMIN

Foundryman. New York–Louisville, Ky. Active c. 1835–43. Came to Rockbridge in 1835 from Genessee Valley in New York State to manufacture Livingston County plows, for which he and Schuyler Bradley (q.v.) had a patent. The plow was named for their home county in New York. In 1841 advertised that he was manufacturing at his South River foundry—seven miles northeast of Lexington—"Ward's Livingston County Plows and Snider's Self Sharpening Plows." Several months later the local paper noted that the Livingston County Plow received the "first premium last fall at the Great State Agricultural Fair of New York." LG 2/3/1842; NG 6/9/1842; NG 6/15/1843; WL Withrow, 55; LG 1/29/1920; RHSP 5, 24; BVA 6/26/1899.

AYERS, OBADIAH

Fuller apprentice. b. 1814. Active 1830. Apprenticed to fuller James McFarland (q.v.), from whom he ran away in 1830. LI 9/25/1830.

AYERS (AYRES), THOMAS G.

Gunsmith. 1832 Virginia–1895 Rockbridge County, Va. Active 1850–70. Listed as a gunsmith in birth records for 1854, 1858, and 1861. C 1850, 1870; Kirkpatrick 1988; Driver.

BAKER, CHRISTOPHER

Weaver. Active 1806–19. Advertised weaving of coverlids at his house on Buffalo Creek in 1806. In 1819 announced the sale of "Valuable Lands . . . on the back road leading from Lexington to Pattonsburg, about 10 miles from the former place, on the South Forks of Buffaloe Creek." Property description included a saw and hemp mill. VT 10/18/1806; LNL 8/7/1819.

BARNETT, JOHN

Weaver. Active 1820. Reported in the 1820 *Census of Manufactures* as having one loom, which he worked himself, producing linen, cotton, and woolen cloth and that there "has been & is valuable demand . . . for all made." CM 1820.

BARRETT, JAMES

Cabinetmaker. Active 1803–9? Amherst County wills indicate that in 1797 James became the ward of Hugh Campbell after the death of his father, Thomas (*Amherst County Will Book* 4, 301). Came to Rockbridge around 1803 from Amherst County. Two signed pieces have been documented. One, a neoclassical sideboard signed "Made by James Barrett/Lexington, Sept. 24th, 1803," is now in the collection of the Stonewall Jackson House. There is some evidence that the sideboard could have been commissioned by Andrew Reid, who at the time owned Mulberry Hill, a plantation house just to the west of the town. The Reid family papers at Washington and Lee indicate business exchanges between both James and his brother Charles and the Reid family. A second piece, a bow-front chest also signed by Barrett, is in a private collection in Richmond.

BARTLETT, WILLIAM

Artist. Made four trips to the United States between 1836 and 1852. Six landscape sketches of Virginia, published as engravings in *American Scenery* (1840), included one of Natural Bridge. Simpson 1982; Wright.

BATH IRON WORKS

Iron. Active 1824–35? Bath Iron Works was one of the largest and most complex iron operations in Rockbridge County. Begun in 1824 by William Weaver (q.v.) and John Doyle (q.v.) when they built a furnace at the upper end of Goshen Pass. In about 1827, a forge was added to the operation. Sold in 1835 to Samuel Jordan (q.v.) and William W. Davis (q.v.), both nephews of Weaver. LG 3/4/1836; LG 12/1/1837; Bruce; CM 1850; RHSP 8; Martin.

BAXTER, JOHN

Forgeman (slave). Active c. 1837. Listed along with Phill Eastern (q.v.), Harry Hunt (q.v.), and Billy Hunt, as "skilled slave refinery hands" at Buffalo Forge in the late 1830s. Buffalo Forge Negro Books, 1830–40, 1839–41, Weaver-Brady Records, University of Virginia, as cited in Dew 1994.

BAYLISS, RICHARD H.

Cabinetmaker. 1835 Alexandria, Va.–1896 Alexandria, Va. Active 1870–80. Married Emma Blanche Kahle, daughter of Lexington cabinetmaker Mathew Kahle (q.v.), in 1871. Listed in 1870 and 1880 censuses as a cabinetmaker in Lexington. Advertised in 1877 that he was at "M. Kahle's old Warerooms opposite the Presbyterian Church." Also announced that he would "Manufacture to order furniture of rosewood, walnut, mahogany, or oak." The *Census of Manufactures* of 1880 reports production value at $1,000.

Later moved to Alexandria, Va. and was employed by an undertaker. C 1870, 1880; CM 1880; Tucker, 215; RCMR 1A, 233; LG 1/5/1877; LG 12/23/1880; LG 7/1/1896; LG 7/8/1896; Kirkpatrick 1988.

BEAR, JACOB

Clockmaker, jeweler. c. 1797–1858 Lexington, Va. Active 1823–58. Father, Andrew Bäre (or Bear), came to Rockbridge in the late eighteenth century. The Lexington paper announced in 1823 his "watch and clock" making business in Lexington. The *Rockbridge Intelligencer* noted that "New Clocks" would be warranted to "preform for five years," a notice that seems to refer to the several tall case clocks with Jacob Bear's name painted on the dial that have survived. Advertised in 1839 his return from Philadelphia and published a long list of available goods, consisting of jewelry, watches, and silverware. By 1841 was again touting his "handsome Assortment" of goods "received from Philadelphia." LI 12/6/1823; LB 12/10/1839; LG 12/2/1841; LG 1/6/1842; LG 1/14/1847; LG 12/9/1858; Cutter.

BEARD, SAMUEL

Chairmaker. 1826–56 Brownsburg, Va. Active 1856. Advertised as a chairmaker. VS 7/24/1856.

BEATY, WILLIAM T.

Wool factory worker. 1844 Rockbridge County, Va.–1904 Rockbridge County, Va. Active 1864. Reported occupation in county marriage records. Exempt in 1864 from service in the Confederate army as a "manufacturer of woolen cloth" at the Monmouth Cloth Factory. RCMR 1A, 161; Driver.

BEETON, JOHN

Gunsmith. 1793 Augusta County, Va.–1848 Lexington, Va. Active c. 1831–48. Resided first in the Mt. Solon area of Augusta County, near the Mossy Creek iron furnace. Moved to Lexington sometime after 1831 and began a gunmaking operation. Left in his estate "a set of gunsmiths's tool," valued at $25, and 400 feet of "gun stock plank." The VMI Museum has a signed Beeton rifle. Beeton; Couper 1960.

BEETON, JOHN HENRY

Gunsmith. 1831 Middlebrook, Augusta County, Va.–1904 Lexington, Va. Active 1850–c. 1881. Followed his father, John, as a gunsmith and in 1857 joined a militia company in Lexington that later became Company H of the 27th Virginia Infantry of the Stonewall Brigade. After the Battle of First Manassas, was ordered back to Lexington to serve as an ordnance sergeant at VMI, repairing rifles and other weapons. Residence was 323 North Main Street, near

VMI, a building that survived until 1983. In the back yard was a frame building used as a gunsmith shop, about 30 x 15 feet, with a fireplace and forge. C 1850, 1860, 1870, 1880; Beeton; RCMR 1A, 50; LG 11/18/1857; LG 3/11/1880; NG 19/1/1972; Couper 1960; Driver.

BEETON, ROBERT ELISON

Gunsmith. 1829 Middlebrook, Augusta County, Va.–1907 Roanoke, Va. Active 1850–70. Brother of John Henry. Part of the family's gunmaking operation in Lexington. Served in Company H, 27th Virginia Infantry, during the Civil War and then was transferred to the Ordnance Department, Richmond. Rejoined the family business after the war. In about 1887 moved to Bedford County and stayed there until he moved to Roanoke around 1897. Established a gunsmith shop on Campbell Avenue in Roanoke, where his son succeeded him. C 1850, 1860, 1870; Beeton; Driver.

BEETON, WILLIAM R.

Gunsmith. 1858 Lexington, Va.–1932 Lexington, Va. Active 1885–88. Listed occupation in county marriage records in 1885. Established a laundry operation first in East Lexington and then on North Main Street, c. 1888. Beeton; RCMR 1A, 487; Kirkpatrick 1988; C 1880.

BELL, JOSEPH

Turner. b. 1816? Virginia. Active 1840–41. According to the shop ledgers for the Lexington chairmaker Samuel R. Smith (q.v.), Bell began boarding with him in December 1840. Between January and March of the next year, Bell is credited with turning items for the shop including "3203 peaces rod stretchers, $32.03." Probably the Joseph W. Bell, age thirty-four, born in Virginia, listed in the Augusta County census as a cabinetmaker in 1850. C 1850; SRS.

BELL, THEODORE P.

Cabinetmaker. b. 1853 Virginia. Active 1870. Listed in 1870 as "learning the cabinetmaking business" in the household of James H. Clemmer (q.v.), Fairfield. C 1870.

BENNETT, WILLIAM JAMES

Artist. 1787–1844. An associate member of the National Academy of Design 1827–28 and a member from 1829 to 1844. Lewis P. Clover, Sr., published Bennett's aquatint of Jacob C. Ward's (q.v.) painting of Natural Bridge, which had been exhibited at the American Academy in 1835. Cowdrey; Simpson 1982.

SILVERWARE, *by Jacob Bear, mid-1800s. After opening his shop in 1823, Bear was the principal silversmith, jeweler, and clockmaker in Lexington. These spoons are stamped "J. B." and "J. Bear." Bear molded some of his flat silver and imported some from Philadelphia.*

POWDER HORN, *1853. The horn belonged to John Henry Beeton, who followed his father, John Beeton, as a gunsmith. During the Civil War he served as an ordnance sergeant at the Virginia Military Institute, repairing rifles. Possibly a presentation piece, the horn is incised with the initials "J. H. Beeton," the date 1853, and various images of animals and people.*

BENSON, JAMES FRANKLIN

Gunsmith, blacksmith. 1831 Rockbridge County, Va.–1909 Walkers Creek, Rockbridge County, Va. Active c. 1856–90. In 1856 purchased the tools of the deceased gunsmith John Clemmer. Shop on Walkers Creek burned around 1900. Interview with Irvin Rosen, 2/27/1990; Driver; Kirkpatrick 1985.

BERNARD, JOHN

Reedmaker. b. 1774 Virginia. Active 1850. Listed occupation in 1850. C 1850.

BESSING, AUGUST

Silversmith. b. 1856 Augusta County, Va. Active 1877. Listed occupation in the Oddfellows records, 1877. Oddfellows.

BEYER, EDWARD

Artist. 1840 Germany–1865 Munich, Germany. Studied at the Düsseldorf Academy, Germany. Came to America in 1848. Published *Album of Virginia* in 1858, which included scenes of Natural Bridge and Rockbridge Alum Springs. Simpson 1982; Wright.

BOGGES (BOGAN, BOGUS?), DANIEL

Chairmaker. b. 1816 Virginia. Active 1850–60. Listed occupation in the census. C 1850, 1860.

BOGGES (BOGAN, BOGUS?), ENOCH

Chairmaker. b. 1811 Virginia. Active 1850–73. Listed in the 1850 census. Father of Lorenzo D. (q.v.). C 1850.

BOGGES (BOGAN, BOGUS?), JOHN HENRY

Chairmaker. b. 1843 Virginia. Active 1869–70. Listed occupation in the 1870 census with William F. Bogges (q.v.), who was probably his father. C 1870; Kirkpatrick 1988.

BOGGES (BOGAN, BOGUS?), LORENZO D.

Chairmaker. b. 1852 Rockbridge County, Va. Active 1873. Listed occupation in the Rockbridge County marriage records. Son of Enoch Bogges (q.v.). RCMR 1A, 270.

BOGGES (BOGAN, BOGUS?), WILLIAM F.

Chairmaker. b. 1815 Virginia. Active 1870. Included in the 1870 census listing for William Bogges (q.v.). C 1870.

BOHN, CASIMIR

Artist. Washington, D.C., artist. Visited Lexington in 1856 and made sketches. Returned the next year and set up shop at the Lexington Hotel, selling colored lithographs of Lexington, VMI, and Washington College for $5. Each view bears the inscription "Drawn from nature and printed in color by E. Sache & Co.; Sun Iron Building, Baltimore, Maryland." Also produced a view of Natural Bridge. Lyle and Simpson; LG 6/11/1857.

BOLEN, S.

Silversmith. Active 1826. Mentioned occupation in 1826 advertisement. LI 7/20/1826.

BOOGHER, EDWARD NICHOLAS

Cabinetmaker. 1831 Mt. Pleasant, Md.–1923 Lexington, Va. Active 1850–89. Included in the 1850 census listing for John G. Pole (q.v.). Did carpenter work for VMI, 1850–51. Produced work for Milton H. Key, 1857. Newspaper announcements for 1856–58 indicate involvement in a boot- and shoe-manufacturing business. Exempt from Confederate service as a foundry worker in 1862 and detailed at Vesuvius as a shell maker. *Census of Manufactures* of 1880 reports annual production at $3,000. Completed the carpentry work for the Washington and Lee College library, 1881. C 1850, 1870; CM 1880; Couper 1960, 55; RCWB 41, 350; Driver; Oddfellows 1856; Dooley; Dooley/Key; Kirkpatrick 1988; LG 4/24/1856; LG 10/15/1857; VS 1/21/1858; LG 9/1/1881; LG 7/6/1882; LG 7/13/1882; LG 5/2/1889; Couper 1939.

BOSSERMAN, WILLIAM H.

Cabinetmaker. 1837 August County, Va.–1894. A couple of mid-century pieces have been attributed to Bosserman. Listed occupation in the marriage records. Kirkpatrick 1988.

BOUDE, JOHN CLINTON

Cabinetmaker. 1832 Millwood, Conn.–1896 Lexington, Va. Active 1857–60. Items produced for the Milton H. Key (q.v.) shop, 1857–60, include lounges, tables, presses, and work stands. Census listing in 1860 included Andrew Varner (q.v.), Charles V. Varner (q.v.), and William P. Hartigan (q.v.). Worked for Andrew Varner after Key's death. Varner's ledger records similar items

made for the shop. Lost a leg at Chancellorsville in 1863. Later earned his LL.D. at Washington College in 1870 and served as clerk of Rockbridge Court, 1864–96. C 1860; Driver; LC 52; Oddfellows 1856; Dooley; Dooley/Key; Varner; RCMR 1A, 304; LG 2/16/1882; LG 9/21/1882; LG 9/23/1896; Brock.

BRADLEY, A. G.

Furniture manufacturer. Active 1884. Business partner of Theodore T. Agnor (q.v.), 1884. LG 12/18/1884.

BRADLEY, SCHUYLER

Foundryman, molder. New York State–Rockbridge County, Va. Active 1842–63. Associated with Thomas Mayburry's (q.v.) Vesuvius Furnace and was making Livingston County plows under the management of "Schuyler Bradley, moulder, and Matthew Bryan, owner," an arrangement which went on for more than ten years. In 1863 sold the business to Hugh F. Lyle (q.v.). Later became the Vesuvius Plow Factory. RHSP 5, 25; LG 3/16/1843; LG 7/18/1850; LG 10/12/1854; LG 4/26/1855; LG 3/30/1882; Morresset.

BRADY, CHARLES P. AUGUSTUS

Engineer, furniture carver. 1850 Philadelphia–1911 Rockbridge County, Va. Trained as a civil engineer at VMI, class of 1872. Active in furniture carving while in retirement at his residence at Buffalo Forge. VMI Register, 1957; LG 1/5/1877.

BRADY, DANIEL C. E.

Ironmaster. b. 1821 Pennsylvania. Active 1857–67. A nephew of William Weaver (q.v.), Brady came to Buffalo Forge in 1857 to help with the management of the operation. Under his leadership the firm prospered. The meticulous records he kept have been invaluable and were to a large extent the principal sources for the extremely valuable account of Buffalo Forge by Charles B. Dew published in 1994. Dew 1994.

BROOKE, RICHARD NORRIS

Artist. 1847 Winchester, Va.–1920 Warrenton, Va. Joined the VMI faculty in 1871 and assisted Gen. Thomas H. Williamson (q.v.) with his drawing classes. Originally hired to succeed the late William D. Washington (q.v.) as director of the institute's School of Fine Arts, which failed because of insufficient funding for the project. Later became an instructor in Washington, D.C., and vice principal of the Corcoran School of Art. In 1880 produced a copy of William D. Washington's painting of Chief Justice John Marshall for the Library of Congress in Washington. Couper; Wright.

FIREBACK, *by Schuyler Bradley,*
c. 1840. Bradley, one of the owners
and the principal molder for the
Vesuvius Furnace, probably cast
this fireback along with its
signature plate.

BROWN, FINLEY MOORE

Textile worker. b. 1863 Virginia. Active 1880. Worked for his father, Robert H., in the Rockbridge Woolen Factory. C 1880; Kirkpatrick 1988.

BROWN, JOHN W.

Fuller. Active 1841–59. Advertised fulling and dyeing services in 1841 and that he would "receive and return cloth at the store of S. B. Finley, Lex., Brown and Hutchenson, Brownsburg, and Stevens & Co., Fairfield." May be the John Brown who was mentioned in an 1824 advertisement by William Brown (q.v.) for an apprentice who had run away from the "Fulling and Carding Mill of John Brown, of Augusta County." Probably the J. W. Brown who purchased the Rockbridge Woolen Factory with Robert H. Brown (q.v.) in 1856. LI 8/7/1824; LG 7/29/1841; LG 6/5/1856; LG 6/11/1857; VS 5/20/1858; LG 5/19/1859.

BROWN, PAUL

Artist. In 1881 exhibited in Richmond paintings produced the previous summer of Natural Bridge and nearby Cedar Creek. Wright.

BROWN, ROBERT C.

Textile worker. b. 1861 Virginia. Active 1880. Worked for his father, Robert H. Brown (q.v.), in 1880. C 1880; Kirkpatrick 1988.

BROWN, ROBERT H.

Textile manufacturer. 1819 Pennsylvania–1899 Augusta County, Va. Active 1856–c. 1880. Purchased the Rockbridge Woolen Factory in 1856 with John W. Brown (q.v.). By 1857 it was called the Monmouth Woolen Factory. In 1857 married Mary E. Harper, daughter of J. F. Harper. The 1860 census listed apprentices Samuel and Joseph Welsh (q.v.) as living in Brown's house and in 1880 Belinda Welsh (q.v.) as a "weaver in woolen factory." Real estate property reported at $10,600 in 1870. Assisted by two sons, Robert C. (q.v.) and Finley Moore (q.v.). The factory spun yarn in addition to fulling and dyeing. Awarded premiums at the Rockbridge County Fair in 1880 for the best-fulled cloth, best-fulled factory-made linsey cloth, best factory-made flannel, and best factory-made blankets. C 1860, 1870, 1880; LG 6/5/1856; LG 6/11/1857; VS 1/7/1858; VS 5/20/1858; LG 1/1/1863; RCMR 1A, 51; Kirkpatrick 1988.

BROWN, ROBERT WASHINGTON

Cabinetmaker. 1833 Virginia–1905 Rockbridge County, Va. Active 1857. Listed occupation as cabinetmaker in 1857, carpenter in 1859 and 1860, and farmer in 1870. Kirkpatrick 1988; Driver; C 1860.

BROWN, WILLIAM

Fuller. 1772? Ireland–1877? Rockbridge County, Va. Active 1824. Advertised in 1824 for an apprentice, James Ritchey, who had run away from the "Fulling and Carding Mill of John Brown, of Augusta County." An 1877 obituary for a William Brown reports Brown came to Rockbridge from Pennsylvania after emigrating from Ireland. May be related to other Browns involved in county textile production. LI 8/7/1824; LG 6/22/1877.

BRYAN, HUGH

Forgeman. Active c. 1825–c. 1836. Part owner in Lebanon Forge. Located across the North River from Bethesda Church at Rockbridge Baths, it consisted of "three refining fires, one chafry which draws bar iron, and two forge hammers, weighing from five to six hundred weight each." Forge averaged 150 tons of bar iron annually from about 225 tons of pig iron. At least seventy people were involved in the operation, including "Ten hands . . . in making the iron, 2 in the blacksmith's shop, 1 sawyer, 4 colliers, 8 woodcutters, 1 wagoner, 5 farmers, 1 clerk and manager, and one overseer, the balance being women and children." Martin; LG 1/1/1836.

BRYAN, ISAAC

Iron manufacturer. d. 1850? Active 1850. Business partner of William M. Bryan (q.v.), 1850, probably at the Vesuvius Furnace. *Census of Manufactures* reports twenty-nine employees producing 160 tons of iron and 9,300 pounds of "rolls" per year. Apparently died during 1850, and the executor of his estate, Robert B. Anderson, advertised to sell his slaves, stock, furniture, "harrors, Livingston Plows, Shovel Plows. . . . " LG 12/19/1850; CM 1850.

BRYAN, MATTHEW

Iron manufacturer, furnace and foundry owner. 1805 Rockbridge County, Va.–1854 Midway, Va. Active 1842–49. Built a foundry on the site of the Vesuvius Furnace, which he and Schuyler Bradley (q.v.) operated. The foundry had the "double purpose of making all articles usually executed at foundries, and of manufacturing the Livingston County Plow." In 1850 had working a "melter," Frederick (Ferdinand) G. Keller, and a "moulder," Joseph McCormick. LG 1/20/1842; LG 3/16/1843; CM 1850; LG 10/12/1854; WL RHS, William H. Humphries to E. P. Tompkins, 6/1/1948; Driver.

BRYAN, WILLIAM M.

Iron manufacturer. c. 1820 Rockbridge Baths, Va.–1898 Cedartown, Ga. Active 1850–62. Partner of Isaac Bryan (q.v.). Reported in 1850 an annual production worth $14,000. Continued the operation after Isaac's death. Exempt from Confederate service as a furnace worker in 1862, working at Vesuvius. In 1878 moved to Georgia. CM 1850; LG 6/13/1862; Driver.

BUCHANAN, JAMES W.

Cabinetmaker. b. 1859 Augusta County, Va. Active 1880–81. Listed occupation in the 1880 census and 1881 marriage records. C 1880; RCMR 1A, 419.

BUCHSER, FRANK

Artist. 1828 Feldbrunn, Switzerland–1890 Feldbrunn, Switzerland. Studied in Rome, worked in Paris, and traveled in Europe and Africa. Came to America to record the after-effects of the Civil War. In 1869 painted a portrait of Robert E. Lee in Lexington, one of only three life portraits. Dickens; Wright.

BUENA VISTA CHAIR AND FURNITURE FACTORY

Furniture factory. Active 1878. See also James H. Watts and Charles F. Jordan.

CAMPBELL, CHARLES W.

Potter, carpenter. b. 1832 Albemarle County, Va. Active 1850–66. John D. Campbell (q.v.) told the 1850 census taker that his son was a "stone potter" and living in his house. Soon after that Charles began working with Henry W. Selby as a carpenter's apprentice and house joiner. Recorded as a "runaway" in 1852. In 1861 married Sarah J. Kurtz (b. 1836), the daughter of Frederick Kurtz (q.v.), a Lexington turner. Listed as a carpenter in county marriage records in 1861 and in subsequent county birth records as late as 1866. C 1850; LG 2/29/1852; RCMR 1A, 88; Kirkpatrick 1988.

CAMPBELL, JOHN D.

Potter. b. 1802 Virginia. Active 1835–60. Was in Albemarle County in 1832 and may have moved to Rockbridge soon after that to become one of the early operators of the pottery at Rockbridge Baths. Listed, with his two sons, James H. and Charles W. (q.v.), as stone potters living at Rockbridge Baths, 1850. Reported personal property at $100 in 1850. This same site was later associated with Isaac D. Lam (q.v.). C 1850, 1860; RCMR 1A, 88.

CARRIN, JONATHAN

Chairmaker. b. 1804 Virginia. Active 1850. Listed occupation in the 1850 census. Included in his household was William H. Carrin (q.v.), also a chairmaker. May be related to John Carrin, an Augusta cabinetmaker active in 1772. C 1850; MESDA.

CARRIN, WILLIAM H.

Chairmaker. b. 1834. Active 1850. Listed in the 1850 census in the household of Jonathan Carrin (q.v.). C 1850.

CARTER, PRESTON J.

Blacksmith. b. 1826 Rockbridge County, Va. Active 1866–80. Before the Civil War Carter was probably a free black working as a blacksmith. In 1870 (as a "mulatto") he listed his personal property at $70 and real estate at $100; in 1880 he had his eighteen-year-old son, George, working with him in his shop. C 1870, 1880.

CARUTHERS, ISAAC

Blacksmith. Active 1804–20? Supplied various iron items to Washington Academy during 1804, including "9 Iron fenders," "Making 4 Pare Strap Hinges," "Making 12 Harth Bariers for Perrey," "1 Pare H. Hinges for Chandler and 2 Doz Wood Screws," and "4 Pare H L Hinges." WL Trustees' folder 43, 1804; C 1810, 1820.

CASH, JOHN W.

Foundry molder. 1824 Virginia–1895 Vesuvius, Va. Active 1850–72. Molder at Vesuvius. May have been in business with his brother, Joshua, who was married in Matthew Bryan's (q.v.) house at Vesuvius in 1842. John named his sons Matthew Bryan Cash and Schuyler Bradley Cash. Matthew became a blacksmith and Schuyler was a carpenter at Vesuvius. Worked at the Vesuvius Plow Factory and is mentioned in William S. Humphries's (q.v.) diary in April 1872. A George W. Cash, probably a relative, was active as an iron molder around Vesuvius in the 1871–80 period. C 1850, 1860, 1870, 1880; RCMR 1A, 164, 233; LG 11/4/1880; Driver; Kirkpatrick 1988; LG 11/5/1846; LG 9/26/1889.

CASTLES, R.

Cabinetmaker. Active 1842. In 1842 announced partnership with Mathew Kahle (q.v.). LG 9/15/1842.

CHANDLER, JOHN

Carpenter, builder. Active 1804. Made the following items for Washington Academy in 1804: "2 six pannel Doors, 1 Sircular window in the pediment, 8 Chimney pieces, 6 pediments, 144 feet hat Rail, making 5 Benches, 8 chimney pieces." Also made a table and four benches for the steward's dining room. WL Trustees' 1803–4, Ann Smith Academy Records.

CHAPLIN, JOHN

Textile manufacturer. b. c. 1832 England. Active 1854. Partner in the Rockbridge Woolen Factory in 1854 with William Chaplin (q.v.) and John Coleman (q.v.). LG 1/26/1854; Driver, C 1860, 1870.

CHAPLIN, WILLIAM

Textile manufacturer. 1822 Canterbury, Kent County, England-1900. Active 1854. Partner in the Rockbridge Woolen Factory with John Chaplin (q.v.) and John Coleman (q.v.) in 1854. The 1860 and 1870 censuses record a William Chaplin as a carpenter in the Kerrs Creek area. LG 1/26/1854; LG 9/16/1852; Driver.

CHITTUM, THOMAS G.

Cabinetmaker. 1807 Rockbridge County, Va.–1857 Rockbridge County, Va. Active 1838–55. Hired as manager of James Rockwood's (q.v.) cabinetmaking business in 1838. Later that same year opened his own shop "lately occupied by Mr. J. Dorsly, one door below the Franklin Hall." The following year moved next to Dr. Paine's and opposite John Carr's saddle shop. In 1842 advertised for a runaway apprentice, John Thomas (q.v.). Again in 1843 reminded the public of his offerings in addition to turning. Chairs were added to his line in 1850. VMI purchased, in 1849–53, a variety of items including "two Common Bedsteads" for $8 and "2 Mess Hall Tables" for $12. Probate in 1857 included tools, equipment, and materials, in addition to chair rungs and unfinished bedsteads and "patterns belonging to the shop." C 1850; LG 2/2/1838; LG 10/5/1838; LG 5/18/1839; LG 4/7/1842; LG 5/25/1843; LG 11/19/1846; LG 5/15/1850; VMI Treasurer 1849–53; RCWB 14, 351; Oddfellows 1848; Kirkpatrick 1988; RCDR, 27.

CHURCH, FREDERIC EDWIN

Artist. 1826 Hartford, Conn.–1900 New York City. Member of the National Academy, 1849. In 1851 traveled through Virginia and visited Natural Bridge. Completed a painting of the bridge the following year and exhibited it in 1853 at the National Academy of Design. The exhibit catalogue listed Cyrus Field as owner of the work. Painting is now part of the University of Virginia's collection. Cowdrey; Simpson 1982; Wright.

CLEMMER, FRANCIS J.

Cabinetmaker. 1814 Augusta County, Va.–1889 Fairfield, Va. Active 1850–80. Probably the father of William (q.v.) and James (q.v.), who were in Francis's household in 1860. Jemina Clemmer (q.v.), his wife, was also listed as a cabinetmaker. Cabinetmakers Frederick Clemmer (q.v.), probably his brother, and John J. Rock (q.v.) were included in his 1850 household census listing. The 1850 *Census of Manufactures* reported production value at $1,000. C 1850, 1860, 1870, 1880; CM 1850.

CLEMMER, FREDERICK L.

Cabinetmaker. b. 1809 Virginia. Active 1850. Listed in the 1850 census in the household of Francis Clemmer (q.v.), cabinetmaker, who was probably his brother. C 1850.

CLEMMER, JAMES HARVEY

Cabinetmaker. 1841 Fairfield, Va.–1902 Roanoke, Va. Active 1860–80. Listed occupation in the 1860, 1870, and 1880 censuses. Included in the household of his father, Francis (q.v.) in 1860. The 1870 listing included Theodore P. Bell (q.v.) as "learning cabinetmaking business." Moved to Roanoke in 1887. Probably brother of William Clemmer (q.v.). C 1860, 1870, 1880; Driver; Diehl.

CLEMMER, JEMINA (JENNIE)

Cabinetmaker. b. 1812 Virginia. Active 1860. Listed as a cabinetmaker in the household of Francis Clemmer (q.v.) in 1860. Apparently part of the family cabinetmaking business. C 1860; Diehl.

CLEMMER, JOHN

Gunsmith. 1799–1856 Walkers Creek, Rockbridge County, Va. Active 1850? Produced rifles on Walkers Creek, of which two signed examples are known. Family interviews.

CLEMMER, WILLIAM LEWIS

Cabinetmaker. 1838 Rockbridge County, Va.–1894. Active 1860. Listed in the household of Francis Clemmer (q.v.) in 1860. Brother of James Clemmer (q.v.). C 1860; Driver.

CLINEDINST, BENJAMIN WEST

Artist. 1859 Woodstock, Va.–1931 Pauling, N.Y. Was graduated from VMI in 1860. Studied in Paris. In 1898 was elected to the National Academy of Design. Completed a large panoramic view of the VMI cadets at the 1864 Battle of New Market, which hangs in Jackson Memorial Hall. Also completed a painting of the VMI faculty and staff members who voted, after the war, to contribute one-third of their salaries to help rebuild the institute. The painting was based on an earlier sketch created by William D. Washington (q.v.). Couper; Wright; Lyle and Simpson.

CLOVER, LEWIS P., JR.

Artist. 1819 New York City–1896 New York City. Active 1852–53. Son of New York picture-frame manufacturer and art patron Lewis P. Clover, Sr., and trained as an engraver under Asher B. Durand. Worked as a painter in New York and Baltimore. In 1840 was elected an associate of the National Academy of Design. Studied for the Episcopal priesthood and then served at the Grace (Episcopal) Church in Lexington, 1852–53. While in Lexington painted the *Virginia Seal* for the VMI Society of Cadets. Also produced a painting of George Washington (location unknown) and engraved a masthead for the local newspaper. In July 1853 announced an auction at his residence of "a quantity of household furniture, with several valuable Oil Paintings." Wright; VMI Archives; Oddfellows 1853; LG 3/17/1853; LG 7/4/1853; Lawall.

CLOWES, AMOS K.

Silversmith, watchmaker. b. 1839 Amherst County, Va. Active 1860–61. Listed in Rockbridge census and marriage records. C 1860; RCMR 1A, 87; Dooley.

CLOYD, CYNTHIA

Needleworker. Rockbridge resident who produced a sampler dated 1802.

COCKREL, GEORGE W.

Gunsmith. Active 1841–42. Advertised in 1841 as a "Gun and Riflemaker" and that he had begun "business in all its various branches on Front Street, in the shop lately occupied by Mr. Varner, where he will make to order double and single barrel SHOTGUNS, RIFLES, PISTOLS & CANE GUNS on the latest and most improved principles." Married Lexington gunsmith John Beeton's (q.v.) daughter Caroline Margaret in 1840. LG 5/5/1841; Beeton; LG 5/5/1842.

COLEMAN, JOHN L.

Textile manufacturer. Active 1854–56. Advertised in 1854, along with John and William Chaplin (q.v.), the acquisition of the Rockbridge Woolen Factory. Announced in 1855 that Eli Tutwiler (q.v.) and Coleman had purchased the factory. In January 1856 John Garland (q.v.), probably an investor like Tutwiler, announced the sale of his interest in the factory to Coleman. Appears to have been some trouble when E.J.H. McCampbell, a trustee, announced that "the books and accounts of the Factory are all in my hands" and asked debtors to clear their accounts. Later Coleman announced the sale of the business to settle a chancery suit between himself and John M. Patterson (q.v.). Mill was purchased by Robert H. and John W. Brown that same year. LG 1/26/1854; LG 4/5/1855; LG 1/10/1856; LG 3/13/1856; LG 5/8/1856; LG 6/5/1856; LG 9/16/1851.

CONNER, MARTHA A.

Artist. Active 1883. Produced two painted birth records relating to Collierstown families that were examined during this survey. NG 6/13/1979.

COOPER, J.

Turner. Active 1782. Probate, June 4, 1782, included "1 tenant saw, Sundry tools for making wheels, Sundry tools for turning dishes, 3 plains, one frame saw." RCWB 1,167.

CRAVENS, WILLIAM

Stonemason. b. Rockingham County, Va. Active 1793–94. Contracted by Liberty Hall in 1793 to construct the main building for the school. It was to be "30 by 38 feet, three stories in heights, with a square roof, belfrey, and corner chimneys." Lyle and Simpson.

CRAVER (CRANER?), JOHN S.

Cabinetmaker. 1835–1900. Active 1860. Listed occupation in the 1860 census. C 1860; Driver

CROSS, JOHN A.

Fuller. Active 1840–57. Announced wool carding in 1840 and in 1848 fulling and dyeing. J. A. Cross was listed as a member of the Oddfellows in 1848. In 1857 advertised the sale of his land, mills, and carding machines. May be related to Thomas Cross (q.v.). LG 5/26/1840; LG 9/19/1844; LG 9/30/1848; LG 10/16/1848; LG 2/19/1857.

CROSS, THOMAS

Carder. Active 1825–38. Carding machine and mill burned in 1825. Soon after announced that he had rebuilt the business and was prepared to card wool with two new machines, one of which specialized in Marino wool. The range of services was indicated in the advertisement: "Wool will be taken in once every week until the first of October, at Mr. Isaac Robinson's, Mr. Waskey's Mill, Mr. George Thrasher's, and Capt. Rowland's mill, in Botetourt County; at Mr. William Douglass' Mill, Mr. John Laird's, Mr. John Galbraith's, on the stage road, and on the back road, at Mr. William Zollman's mill, Mr. Eckerly's and Mr. John Leech's mill.

I will haul wool down the river occasionally, as far as Mr. James Greenlee's and Mr. Saling's, and on the north river to Mr. Thomas Beggs's where I will receive wool every week during the carding season, and will receive wool at any house on the road, and return it to the same place in rolls if the wool be prepared for carding. I feel assured I can give general satisfaction to all those that favor me with their custom." Two years later announced the sale of carding machines and cards. In 1838 advertised that carding machines he had built were for sale in addition to a secondhand machine formerly used by Samuel Eliot of Collierstown. Noted location that year as five miles from Natural Bridge and seven below Pattonsburg. May be related to the fuller John Cross (q.v.). LI 6/10/1825; LI 3/22/1827; LG 1/19/1838.

CUMINGS, JOHN P.

Carder. 1818 Rockbridge County, Va.–1867 Rockbridge County, Va. Active 1849–50. Lost his left forearm in an accident while working at a carding machine near Fairfield. Probably the John P. Cummings listed as a carder in the 1850 census. In 1860 was farming and in 1864 was reported as a miller. LG 8/7/1849; C 1850, 1860; Driver.

CUMMINS, ROBERT

Cabinetmaker. b. 1775 Pennsylvania. Active 1850. Listed occupation in the 1850 census. C 1850.

DARST, BENJAMIN

Potter. 1760 Shenandoah County, Va.–1835 Lexington, Va. Active 1785–91. Born in the Mt. Jackson area of Shenandoah County, Va., where he learned the pottery business. About 1780 moved to Goochland County, Va., and established a pottery there. In 1781 married Lucy Woodward and purchased land near "Manankintown," also in Goochland County, where he was active until 1784. In addition to owning land in Goochland County, Benjamin also owned three slaves—Will, Moll, and Jeff—and evidently used them as laborers in his pottery business. In 1785 returned to the Valley and bought a tract of land adjoining Lexington, where he established a pottery—perhaps the first in Rockbridge County. Three years later, in 1788, John Grigsby and David Cloyd, overseers of the poor for Rockbridge County, bound out an apprentice, one Francis Garner, to Darst to learn the pottery "Art and Trade." The document required Darst to give a "Turning Lathe" to his apprentice on his completion of the apprenticeship. The pottery was probably located near South Main Street between the Lauderdale ARP Church and the Stonewall Jackson Cemetery. Russ 1990; RHSP 3, 66–75; Darst; RCWB 1, 319.

DAUGHERTY (DOUGHERTY), WILLIAM

Furnace owner. Active 1782–1801. Owned 100 acres in the county in 1782 and may have been in business with James Daugherty, perhaps his brother, who owned 300 acres. In April 1801 William Daugherty of Augusta County sold to Philemon Towson, a Baltimore merchant, 450 acres on Irish Creek in Rockbridge County, including a furnace, for £200. An early county forgeman, Jacob Leece, married Ann Daugherty, William's sister, in 1802. Morton; RCLB 1 1782–98; Augusta County Deed Book 1A, 349–50; Mitchel; RCLB, 268; Kirkpatrick 1985; RCWB 3, 231.

DAVIDSON, JOHN

Gunsmith. 1757 Augusta County, Va.–1835 Rockbridge County, Va. Active 1782–1834. Son of John and Elizabeth Houston Davidson. Listed occupation in the tax records, 1782. In 1808 applied to the state for a contract to manufacture rifles (Gill,79). In 1809 paid bill to the Lexington hatmaker John Ruff by repairing two guns. In 1813 provided Ruff with "1 pair Bullet Moles" for 50 cents and 58 cents for repairing a "pistol lock." His will was probated July 4, 1835. Gill; Wallace Gusler, "Two Virginia Long Rifles," *Journal of Historical Armsmaking Technology* 2 (June 9, 1987); Morton; Ruff; Diehl; Kegley.

DAVIS, ABRAHAM W.

Iron manufacturer. Active 1835–36. Ironmaster and partner of Samuel F. Jordan (q.v.) and William W. Davis (q.v.) in 1835. Firm of Jordan, Davis and Company, consisting of Samuel Jordan, Abraham W. Davis, and William Davis, was dissolved in 1836 and reorganized under the same name but headed by Samuel Jordan and William Davis. LG 7/17/1835; LG 3/4/1836.

DAVIS, A. J.

Architect. 1803 New York City–1892. Founder of the National Academy of Design in New York and one of the best-known and most prolific American architects in the mid-nineteenth century. In 1845–48 built a Gothic residence for Philip St. George Cocke in Powhatan County near Richmond. During this period Cocke was named to the VMI Board of Visitors. In 1848 VMI Superintendent Francis H. Smith began what was to become a long association with the New York architect. For more than a decade Davis provided drawings for the barracks (begun in 1850), the porter's lodge (1852), the mess hall (1852), two faculty residences (1852), and the superintendent's quarters (1860). Many of the drawings are preserved in VMI's Preston Library. Lyle and Simpson.

DAVIS, JAMES COLE

Iron manufacturer. 1833 Rockbridge County, Va.–1886. Furnace owner. See also William W. Davis.

DAVIS, WILLIAM W.

Iron manufacturer. b. 1806 Pennsylvania. Active 1850–58. Nephew of William Weaver (q.v.). Operated several iron works during the midcentury period. Capital investment at Gibraltar Forge in 1850 was $7,400, with an inventory of 200 tons of metal. Employed fifteen people and estimated production of 130 tons of iron a year, valued at $10,400. In 1858 closed the "North River Iron Works," and advertised to sell "Several No. 1 mules, with their Harnesses; seven or eight Wagons, some two-horse, others four and six horses; about 20 hogs, one blacksmith's bellows and a sett of tools; some Carpenter's and Forgemen's tools; two or three pairs of scales, and many other things too numerous to mention." LG 6/19/1856; VS 11/25/1858; CM 1850; Bruce.

DAY, J. W.

Furniture manufacturer. Active 1888–91. Opened the Point Chair Factory in 1888, "operated by northern capital." Formed a joint stock company in 1891, in which the directors of the Lexington Development Company invested $2,000. Factory was located "on the land of the Development Company near Woods Creek." The *Lexington Gazette* reported in 1891 that "Mr. Day has an order from one firm for five thousand chairs." LG 8/16/1888; LG 4/9/1891; LG 6/11/1891; LG 7/2/1891.

DE TURPIN, BARON

Artist. Visited Virginia in 1782 with the Marquis de Chastellux and produced images of Natural Bridge. Chastellux published three of the images in his *Travels in North America* in 1786. Simpson 1982; Wright.

DEANE, E.

Artist. Worked in Richmond in 1807, where he advertised in the *Richmond Enquirer* May 19 and 22. Executed portrait of Rockbridge resident Juliet Lyle Smith (1794–1820), the granddaughter of Samuel Lyle (q.v.) and the wife of Abram Smith (1781–1852). Abram Smith's parents were John Smith, possibly the Lexington cabinetmaker (q.v.), and Mary Smith. Wright; Lyle.

DECKER, SAMUEL HARVEY

Cabinetmaker. 1816 Virginia–1888 Goshen, Va. Active 1850–70. Listed occupation as a cabinetmaker in 1850, carpenter in 1860, and millwright in the 1870 census. C 1850, 1860, 1870; Kirkpatrick 1988; RCWB 20, 237–39; Driver.

DINSMORE, JOHN

Cabinetmaker apprentice. b. c. 1788. Active 1803. Cabinetmaker Hugh McGuffin (q.v.) advertised for Dinsmore, a runaway apprentice, in September 1803. VT 9/20/1803.

DIXON, JAMES

Chairmaker. Active 1801–10. Announced a partnership with William Keys (q.v.) in 1801, noting that they "have commenced WINDSOR CHAIR MAKING, on the Main [Lexington] street next door to Mr. Samuel Harkins, Hatter." Noted in the 1810 census. An 1860 marriage record for cabinetmaker William A. Dixon (q.v.) reports that he was the son of James Dixon. C 1810; RR 10/12/1801; RCMR 1A, 79.

DIXON, WILLIAM A.

Cabinetmaker. Active 1860. Listed in marriage records. RCMR 1A, 79.

DOYLE, JOHN

Iron manufacturer. b. 1794 Pennsylvania. Active 1850–56. In the 1820s along with William Weaver (q.v.) built the Bath Iron Works near the upper end of Goshen Pass. In 1849 built the Mt. Hope Furnace "situated about 15 miles north of Lexington on Bratton's Run, and 1 1/2 miles from Alum Springs." In 1850 had forty-three employees and was producing 1,000 tons of pig iron a year. In 1854 advertised to sell the furnace, which "is in good order, having only blown some 18 to 20 months. The ore bank is among the most abundant in the United States, within one and one-half miles of the Furnace over a good road. The ore is very easily raised and yields 40 tons per week with cold blast. The North River Canal, which is now being built, will afford great facilities for getting to market. The metal is of first-rate quality both for Forge and Foundry purposes." CM 1850; LG 10/12/1854.

DUDDEN, VALENTINE

Cabinetmaker. Active 1797. Probate listing, June 1797, included tools. RCWB 2, 20, 21.

EASTERN, PHILL

Forgeman (slave). Active c. 1837. Listed along with John Baxter (q.v.), Harry Hunt (q.v.), and Billy Hunt as "skilled slave refinery hands" at Buffalo Forge in the late 1830s. Buffalo Forge Negro Books, 1830–40, 1839–41, Weaver-Brady Records, University of Virginia, as cited by Dew 1994.

EASTMAN, SETH

Artist. 1809 Brunswick, Maine–1875 Washington, D.C. Was graduated from West Point in 1829. From 1833 to 1840 served the Military Academy as a drawing instructor. Honorary member of the National Academy of Design 1839–60. Spent many years in the West and became well known for his paintings of Indians. Work is included in Henry R. Schoolcraft's six-volume series, *Information Respecting the History, Condition, and Prospects of the Indian Tribes of the United States* (Philadelphia, 1851–57). Married to Mary Henderson, sister of Sarah Smith, wife of VMI Superintendent Francis H. Smith. Created two known local sketches—the Lexington Arsenal building, then housing VMI, and a view of Lexington from the Parade Ground in 1849. Both are in the collection of the Peabody Museum, Harvard University. Cowdrey; Lyle and Simpson; Wright; VMI Archives.

EDMUND

Foundryman (slave). b. c. 1818. Active 1858. Recorded as a runaway slave of Samuel Jordan (q.v.) at Buena Vista. VS 6/17/1858.

EDWARDS, FRANCIS M.

Cabinetmaker. Active 1862. Made bedsteads, tables, and a bureau for Andrew Varner (q.v.) in January 1862. Varner.

ELLIOT, ANDREW D. L.

Cabinetmaker. 1832 Virginia–1874. Active 1849–70. Listed occupation in the 1850, 1860, and 1870 censuses. Made purchases from J. H. Myers's hardware store in 1849. Worked for Milton H. Key (q.v.) 1857–60. Services included veneering, varnishing, and making tables, safes, wardrobes, bedsteads, dining tables, tea tables, writing tables and hatracks. Also worked for Andrew Varner (q.v.) and produced similar items. Census listing for 1870 included the "photograph artist" Michael Miley (q.v.), who was apparently rooming at Elliot's house. Record of estate sale in 1874 includes extensive listings of tools and equipment and the individuals who purchased them. C 1850, 1860, 1870; Myers; Dooley/Key; Dooley; Varner; Driver; Kirkpatrick 1988; RCWB 14, 202–205.

ELLIOT, ANDREW FRANKLIN

Gunsmith. b. 1834 Rockbridge County, Va. Active 1850. Son of Samuel D. Elliot (q.v.). Listed in the 1850 census as a gunsmith and in 1860 as a "farmhand." Exempt from service during the Civil War because of "disease of the lungs and general debility." After the war was again listed as a farmhand. C 1850, 1860, 1870; Driver; RCMR 1A, 27.

ELLIOT, JOHN McC.

Gunsmith. 1841 Rockbridge County, Va.–1864. Active 1860. Listed occupation in census. C 1860; Driver.

ELLIOT, SAMUEL D.

Gunsmith. b. 1802 Virginia. Active c. 1840–70. Prominent gunsmith in the Collierstown area for a quarter century. Son, A. Franklin Elliot, age sixteen, was working with him in 1850. In 1854 was listed as a cabinetmaker in county birth records, probably while he was working with his father, Andrew D. L. Elliot (q.v.). The woolcarder Thomas Cross (q.v.) in 1838 advertised a used carding machine for sale that formerly belonged to Samuel Elliot. C 1850, 1860, 1870; LG 1/19/1838; RCN 3/20/1902.

ERHARDT, JOHN

Woolwright and spinning-wheel maker, apprentice. Active c. 1787. Apprenticed to James Lackey (q.v.). WL RHS.

EVANS, W. PRESTON

Blacksmith (slave). b. 1818 Virginia. Active 1841–80. In 1841 was listed as a runaway "Negro boy" apprenticed to the Brownsburg blacksmith James Withrow and belonging to Dr. James McDowell. Apparently became an established blacksmith on his own following the Civil War. In 1880 noted that his fifteen-year-old son, W. Preston Evans, Jr., worked as a blacksmith in his shop. C 1870, 1880; Kirkpatrick 1988; LG 6/10/1841.

EVINS, NATHANIEL

Stonecarver. Active 1774–77. Early settler in the Timber Ridge area and an unlettered stonecarver. Left two coffin-shaped slabstone monuments in the county—one to his wife and another to a friend. The McDowell family graveyard near Fairfield contains the stone marking the grave of his wife:

HERE, LYS, THE,

INTARD BODDY OF

MARY EVINS WHOW

DEPARTED THIS LIFE 1777

THE 83[YE] OF HIR EAG

STAIR BANISTER, THORN HILL, *c. 1792. An unidentified artisan carved this banister at Thorn Hill, Colonel John Bowyer's county house west of Lexington. The same design was carved on both ends of the large stone step at the front entrance.*

Mentioned in a court proceeding in 1749. Listed again in 1770. *(Augusta County Will Book* 4, 308; Chalkley 3, 114). Name appears a number of times in the Augusta County records, both as Nathaniel Evans and Nathaniel Evins. When John Mackey (McKey), one of the early settlers on Timber Ridge, died in 1773, Evins carved his headstone for the Timber Ridge cemetery:

REMAMBER MAN AS YOU PAS BY

AS YOU ARE NOW SO ONCE WAS I

AS I AM NOW YOU SOON WILL BE

THEREFORE THINK ON ETERNIY

NETHANEL EVINS, BUILDER

The headstone carries the date 1774. Evins carved his own name in larger letters than John Mackey's. ACWB 1, 162; Chalkley; ACWB 4, 308; ACDB 6, 256; ACDB 7, 305; ACDB 11, 249; Schneider.

EZEKIEL, MOSES JACOB

Artist. 1844 Richmond, Va.–1917 Rome. An 1866 graduate of VMI. Participated in the Battle of New Market. Later studied at the Medical College of Virginia and the Royal Academy of Art in Berlin. Moved to Rome in 1873 and maintained a studio there for the remainder of his life. Awarded the honorary title of *Cavaliere Ufficiale della Corona d'Italia*, presented by the king of Italy in 1906. Works in Lexington include *Virginia Mourning Her Dead* and *General Thomas Jonathan ("Stonewall") Jackson* (VMI Parade Ground) and a portrait bust of Robert E. Lee at Washington and Lee University. Couper; Simpson 1977; Wright; LG 3/25/1880.

FAGAN, AMBROSE

Stonecutter. b. 1829 Ireland. Active 1850. Listed as a stonecutter in the 1850 census. See also Archibald D. and James Fagan. C 1850.

FAGAN, ARCHIBALD D.

Stonecutter. b. 1830 Ireland. Active 1849?–60. Owner of the Lexington Marble Works. Probably the partner mentioned in an 1849 notice by James Fagan (q.v.) when he announced "Marble Manufacturing. James Fagan and Brother, Sculptors." "Fagan and Bro." advertised again in 1854 that it would provide "Marble Work of plain and ornamental designs, Monuments, Tombs, Mantles, Grave Stones, etc., of the finest Egyptian, Italian, Northern and Virginia Marble." The firm also announced branches in Lynchburg, Liberty, and Salem. C 1860; Dooley; Kirkpatrick 1988; LG 6/12/1849; LG 3/16/1854; VS 3/4/1858.

FAGAN, JAMES

Stonecutter. b. 1825 Ireland. Active 1849–54. Listed as a stonecutter in the 1850 census and marble mason in the Oddfellows records. Fagan "and Brother" were proprietors of a Main Street Marble Manufactory, Lexington, in 1849. See also Archibald D. Fagan. C 1850; Oddfellows 1850; LG 6/12/1849; LG 3/16/1854.

FENN, HARRY

Artist. 1845 Richmond, England–1911 Montclair, N.J. Came to America around 1864 and produced numerous views for *Picturesque America* (New York, 1872–74), a semimonthly serial edited by William Cullen Bryant. Part four, which dealt with Virginia, included four wood engravings of Natural Bridge. Simpson 1982; Wright.

FIREBAUGH, JANE ELIZA McCOWN

Quilter. 1833–97. Documented work has descended in the family.

FIREBAUGH, JOHN

Potter. 1789 Pennsylvania–1867 Bustleburg, Va. Active 1830–67. In 1850 John S. Morgan (q.v.), an eighty-two-year-old potter from New York, was living with John Firebaugh on a farm in Bustleburg, near Rockbridge Baths. Ten years later another potter, Robert T. Fulwiler (q.v.) was listed in the Firebaugh household. These two potters apparently established a sizable operation, beginning perhaps as early as the 1830s, and it clearly had a close relationship with the John Campbell (q.v.) and Isaac D. Lam (q.v.) operation at nearby Rockbridge Baths. An 1848 deed notes that Firebaugh retained "the clay bank called Maple Swamp . . . for his own use." C 1850, 1860; RCLB 22, 135.

FISHER, JOSEPH W.

Wool carder. Active 1871–73. Birth registrations in 1871 and 1873 recorded his occupation. Kirkpatrick 1988.

FORBES (FORBUS, FORBIS), JASPER N.

Chairmaker. b. 1831 Virginia. Active 1860–c. 1910. Worked as a chairmaker in Walkers Creek from 1860 until the end of the century. Census for 1860 noted his occupation as a wheelwright and in 1870 and 1880 as a chairmaker. May have been related to William Forbes, a wheelwright. C 1850, 1860, 1870, 1880; Driver.

FORD, ANDREW D.

Cabinetmaker. b. 1841 Virginia. Active 1860. Listed in the 1860 census. C 1860; Driver.

FORSYTHE, SAMUEL

Forgeworker. Active 1820. Operated a forge on North River by himself in 1820; he would not answer any questions about his operation. The census taker recorded: "I visited the forge once and applied twice to him. . . . " CM 1820.

FORSYTHE, THOMAS

Cabinetmaker. b. 1810. Active 1862–70. Married Frances Kahle, daughter of the Lexington cabinetmaker Mathew Kahle (q.v.) in 1862. Provided items (wardrobes, a safe, cottage bedsteads, dining tables, breakfast tables, a washstand, and a walnut bureau) for the Lexington shop of Andrew Varner (q.v.) in 1862. Listed occupation in 1870 census. Reported his birthplace as Scotland in the 1870 census and England in the 1880 census. Listed as a "pauper" in the 1880 census. C 1870, 1880; RCMR 1A, 93; Varner.

FULLER, NATHAN

Daguerreotypist. Active 1842. Lynchburg daguerreotypist advertised in Lexington in 1842 to "manufacture apparatus similar to his own, for the low price of forty dollars, which would cost at the North $350." LG 7/14/1842; LG 7/21/1842.

FULWILER (FULLWEIDER), ROBERT

Potter. 1825 New York–1908 California. Active 1860–68. Recorded as a potter in 1850 in Botetourt County, possibly associated with the Obenchain pottery. Listed in the 1860 census, as a potter living in the house of John Firebaugh (q.v.) in Bustleburg, near Rockbridge Baths. In 1868 moved to California. C 1850, 1860; Driver; RHSP 10, 471.

GALT, ALEXANDER

Artist. Studied in Florence before opening a studio in Richmond in 1860. His statue of Thomas Jefferson is in the Rotunda of the University of Virginia. While in Europe in 1859 VMI Superintendent Francis H. Smith suggested to Galt that he join the institute as professor of sculpture, but he declined. Smith also solicited Galt's assistance in selecting paintings for one of the cadet societies. Served as an illustrator for Confederate engineers until he died of smallpox in 1863. Bronze copy of his portrait bust of Governor Letcher is in the VMI collection. Couper; Wright.

GARLAND, JOHN

Textile manufacturer. 1820 Virginia–1891 Rockbridge County, Va. Active 1856. Apparently an investor in the Rockbridge Woolen Factory. Sold his interest to John L. Coleman (q.v.) in 1856. LG 1/10/1856; Driver.

GARLAND, WINSTON

Basketmaker. b. 1801 Virginia. Active 1870. Recorded in the 1870 census as a basketmaker and a black. C 1870.

GIBBS, JAMES EDWARD ALLEN

Textile manufacturer. 1829 Raphine, Va.–1902. Active 1850. Son of Richard Gibbs (q.v.), fuller. Worked with his father until he began his own mill in Lexington. Listed in his father's household in 1850 as a woolcarder. Left Rockbridge in the 1850s for Huntersville, where he worked on an improved carding machine. Developed a sewing machine with James Wilcox. In 1889 the *Lexington Gazette* reported, "A patent was issued at Washington to James E. A. Gibbs, of Raphine, assignor to Wilcox & Gibbs Sewing Machine Company for tension apparatus for sewing machines." Morton; C 1850, 1860, 1870; Driver; LG 11/7/1889.

GIBBS, JOHN TRACY

Textile manufacturer. 1819 Brompton, Kent County, England–1887 Lexington, Va. Active 1849. Produced tablecloths, towels, pillow cases, and bedcovers for VMI in 1849. Later served as VMI steward, quartermaster, and treasurer. May be related to James Gibbs (q.v.). VMI Archives; C 1870; Driver.

GIBBS, RICHARD

Carder. 1788 Connecticut–1858 Rockbridge County, Va. Active c. 1819–45. Moved to Fairfax, Va., around 1815, bringing with him a carding machine. Soon afterward moved to Rockbridge and married Isabella G. Poague from Raphine. Operated a fulling mill in Walkers Creek until it burned in 1845. Listed real estate at $1,000 in the 1850 census. Father of James Gibbs (q.v.). Morton; C 1850.

GIGNOUX, REGIS FRANÇOIS

Artist. 1816 Lyons, France–1882 Paris. Came to America in 1841 and maintained a studio in Brooklyn until 1870. Exhibited at the National Academy of Design, 1842–60. Showed a painting of Natural Bridge in 1845. Cowdrey; Wright.

GOODACRE, WILLIAM, JR.

Artist. Created a number of views, including Natural Bridge, for John Howard Hinton's *The History and Topography of the United States* (London and Philadelphia, 1830–32). One of the most popular images of the bridge, it was reprinted in several forms and widely copied in America and Europe. Active in New York

1829–55, where he exhibited at the National Academy of Design in 1830 and again in 1833. Gave his New York address in 1833 as 158 Fulton Street, near Lewis P. Clover, Jr. (q.v.), at 140 Fulton. Cowdrey; Simpson 1982; Wright.

GORDON, NATHANIEL T.

Chairmaker. 1834 Virginia–1863. Active 1860. Listed occupation in 1860. Married Nannie E. Clemmer, daughter of the cabinetmaker Francis J. Clemmer (q.v.), 1860. C 1860; RCMR 1A, 72; Driver.

GRAVES, JOHN L.

Cabinetmaker. b. 1838 Virginia. Active 1860. Listed in the 1860 census. C 1860.

HAIGHT, B. F.

Daguerreotypist. Active 1855. Advertised his "Daguerrean and Photographic Car" at McCown's Hotel, Lexington, in 1855. LG 12/13/1855.

HALL, WILLIAM G.

Chairmaker apprentice. b. 1816. Active 1828. Apprenticed to the Lexington chairmaker Samuel Smith (q.v.) "for the term of Eight years," 1828, and to learn the trade of "windsor chair making." RCWB 6, 248.

HAMILTON, CHARLES F.

Daguerreotypist. b. 1828. Active 1847–48. An 1847 editorial in the *Lexington Gazette* reports, "We have never seen Daguerreotypes that are more perfect. The coloring gives them a life-like appearance, not artificial, but natural, which cannot but recommend them." Advertised that same year that he had "opened a room in Mr. Porter's hotel for a short time only." Announced in February 1848 visits to Buchanan and Fincastle. Later reported his return to Lexington, from New York, and would take "Miniatures in a much improved style." LG 12/9/1847; LG 2/10/1848; LG 11/14/1848; Oddfellows 1848.

HANNA (HANNAH), JOHN

Gunsmith, silversmith. Augusta County, Va.–1781 Rockbridge County, Va. Active 1754–81. Evidence in the early Augusta County court records shows that there were more than one—perhaps three—John Hannas in Augusta before Rockbridge was formed in 1778. The one whose will is recorded in Rockbridge in 1781 built a mill on Colliers Creek about 1768. The earliest mention of John Hanna was in 1754, when he agreed to teach "the art and histery of Black Smith and Gun Smith" to his indentured servant, John

Mitchell. Estate inventory included considerable gunsmithing tools, including a "Lathe for clock making £3." Morresset; ACDB 12, 315; ACDB 4, 324; ACDB 16, 94; Gill; Chalkley.

HARLOW, ANDREW MORTIMER

Textile worker. 1842 Albemarle County, Va.–1880 Rockbridge County, Va. Active 1868–73. Listed as a woolen factory worker in the 1870 census. Reported in 1873 birth records as a "machinist at Brown's factory." See also Robert H. Brown. C 1870; Kirkpatrick 1988.

HARLOW, W. N.

Gunsmith. b. 1829 Virginia. Active 1870. Listed his personal property at $100 in the 1870 census. C 1870.

HARRIS, FREDERICK S.

Cabinetmaker. b. 1808 Virginia. Active 1857–67. Listed as a mason in the 1860 census. Noted in birth records (1857, 1858, 1860, and 1867) as a cabinetmaker. C 1860; Kirkpatrick 1988.

HARTIGAN, WILLIAM PIPER

Cabinetmaker. 1837 Rockbridge County, Va.–1902. Active 1860–65? Included in the 1860 census listing for the Lexington cabinetmaker John Boude (q.v.). Both worked for the cabinetmaker Milton H. Key (q.v.). Married Mathew Kahle's (q.v.) daughter Katherine in 1856. C 1860; Couper 1960; Driver; Oddfellows; Dooley; Dooley/Key; RCMR 1A, 199.

HAYS, ANDREW AND GEORGE

Fuller. Active 1782. Listed, in 1782, in a joint probate for Andrew and George Hays that included "12 yards of Linen seven Hun to W. Hays / 15 yards seven Hundred Linen from Hugh Wilson / 6 yards tow linen." Several members of the Hays family were involved in the fulling business. RCWB 1, 168.

HAYSLETT, SARAH

Quilter. Active c. 1880s. A signed and dated quilt (1882) has descended in the family.

HELMS, SAMUEL McCUNE

Cabinetmaker. 1830 Augusta County, Va.–1911. Active 1860–89. Listed as a cabinetmaker in the 1860 census. C 1860; Tucker, 109; Driver.

HENDERSON, CARRUTHERS LETCHER

Cabinetmaker. 1845 Virginia–1914. Active 1870. Listed as a cabinetmaker in the 1870 census, where he was included in the household of the wagonmaker Hiram Henderson, mayor of Lexington. C 1870; Driver.

HENDRON, SAMUEL

Weaver. b. c. 1757 England. Active 1813. Included as a weaver, age fifty-five, after sixteen years in the United States with a wife and three children, in *British Aliens in the United States during the War of 1812.* Scott.

HERRICK, HENRY W.

Artist. 1824 Hopkinton, N.H.–1906 Manchester, N.H. Studied at the National Academy of Design in 1844. Made several trips to the South during the 1840s and 1850s and produced a painting of Natural Bridge. Wright.

HERZOG, HERMAN

Artist. 1832 Free Hanseatic State of Bremen–1932 Philadelphia, Pa. Studied at the Düsseldorf Academy and came to the United States in 1876. Paintings of America included one of Natural Bridge. Wright.

HICKS, EDWARD

Artist. 1780 Bucks County, Pa.–1849 Newtown, Pa. Minister trained as a coach and sign painter. Created more than sixty religious paintings of the *Peaceable Kingdom,* six of which include Natural Bridge. Toured Virginia in 1829 as an itinerant preacher and may have visited Natural Bridge. Images of the bridge are probably taken from Henry S. Tanner's "Map of North America," illustrated in the *New American Atlas* (Philadelphia, 1818–23). The Natural Bridge paintings, dating from about 1822 to about 1847, are in the collections of the Yale University Art Gallery, New Haven; the Abby Aldrich Rockefeller Folk Art Center, Williamsburg, Va.; Amherst College, Amherst, Mass.; the Reynolda House, Winston-Salem, N.C.; and the Denver Art Museum, Denver, Colo. Simpson 1982; Wright.

HILEMAN, ADAM T.

Marble cutter. b. 1826 Virginia. Active 1849–53. Advertised in 1849 the "manufacture of Monuments, Head and Foot Stones" at his Mill Creek establishment "five miles from Lexington." See also John Joseph Hileman. C 1850, LG 3/6/1849; LG 11/3/1853.

HILEMAN, JOHN JOSEPH

Marble cutter. 1834 Rockbridge County, Va.–1891. Active 1859–80. Listed as a marble cutter in the 1850 and 1880 censuses, a mason in 1860, and a stonemason in 1870. Operated the Rockbridge Marble Works, Main Street, Lexington, below the Exchange Hotel. Advertised in 1859, 1877, 1882, 1889, and 1892. Produced and signed a number of gravestones including that of Gen. Lee's daughter Eleanor Agnes Lee. C 1850, 1860, 1870, 1880; Driver; Brock; Oddfellows; Dooley; LG 3/10/1859; LG 1/5/1877; LG 10/19/1882; LG 12/19/1889; LG 3/26/1891; RHSP 11, 70–76; Coulling.

HILL, JAMES S.

Carder. b. 1814 Virginia. Active 1860. Listed occupation in census records. C 1860.

HINSHELWOOD, ROBERT

Artist. b. 1812 Scotland. Came to America in 1835 and produced landscape engravings for magazines, including *Harper's.* Exhibited at the National Academy of Design, 1837–59. Many of his works are derived from drawings by the engraver James Smellie (q.v.), whose sister he married. Smellie was a member of the New York firm of Rawdon, Wright, Hatch, and Smellie, which was responsible for the engraving of the first VMI diploma. The engraving included Natural Bridge in the design. Cowdrey; Couper; Simpson 1982.

HINTY, THOMAS

Cabinetmaker. 1821 England–1891. Active 1867–80. Listed occupation in county birth records in 1867. Recorded as a cabinetmaker in the 1870 census and a wagonmaker in 1880. C 1870, 1880; Kirkpatrick 1988; Driver.

HINTY, WILLIAM HENRY

Cabinetmaker. 1842 Bath County, Va.–1896. Active 1862–80. Listed as a cabinetmaker in 1864 marriage records and a carpenter in the 1870 and 1880 censuses. Included in the 1870 census listing for Thomas Hinty (q.v.). C 1870, 1880; RCMR 1A, 109; Driver; Kirkpatrick 1988; Couper 1960.

HOLANSWORTH, JOHN

Weaver apprentice. b. c. 1783. Active 1803. Twenty-year-old apprentice to weaver John Spence (q.v.), Lexington. Ran away in 1803. VT 4/26/1803.

HOLT, ANDREW

Blacksmith. b. 1835 Rockbridge County, Va. Active 1859–89. Listed in the 1870 census as a mulatto with personal property of $100. In 1880 listed as black. C 1870, 1880; RCMR 1A, 131; Kirkpatrick 1988.

HOPE, JAMES

Artist. 1818 Drygrange, Scotland–1892 Watkins Glen, N.Y. Worked in Montreal as a portrait artist before opening a studio in New York in 1852. Painted Natural Bridge and other Virginia scenes during the Civil War. Became an associate of the National Academy of Design in 1871. Wright.

HOPKINS, THOMAS

Cabinetmaker. Active 1819–28. Advertised in Lexington in 1825 for runaway apprentice Thomas Robinson (q.v.), alias Thomas Ricketts and in 1828 for James Agner (q.v.). See also John Smith. LI 12/2/1825; LI 4/10/1828; RCWB 5, 14,15.

HUBARD, WILLIAM JAMES

Artist. 1807 Whitchurch, England–1862 Richmond, Va. Trained in England. Came to America in 1824. Exhibited at the National Academy of Design. Moved to Richmond in 1841 and in the 1850s established a foundry for casting in bronze. Between 1853 and 1860 produced six bronze copies of Jean Antoine Houdon's marble statue of George Washington, the original of which stands in the Virginia State Capitol. The first of the six copies was presented to VMI in 1856 and stands today on the parapet facing the barracks. Commissioned by the VMI Society of Alumni in 1853 to create a portrait of Gen. William H. Richardson. Cowdrey; Couper; Simpson 1977; Wright.

HUMPHREYS, JOSHUA

Gunsmith, silversmith, clockmaker. b. 1743 Pennsylvania. Active c. 1775–c. 1781. Bought lot number 12 in Staunton in 1775. Held various official positions in Augusta County during 1778 and 1779 but by 1781 had left the area. In Staunton (principally in 1777) worked with Joshua Perry, Alexander Simpson, and Jacob Gabbott in Augusta County gun manufactory. Listed the same year in an Augusta County tithable list (*Journal of the House of Delegates,* 1777 [Richmond, 1827]; Augusta County Tithables, 1777). Resided in Richmond in 1782 and was listed as a watchmaker, age thirty-nine, together with his wife, Anne, age thirty-six. Property included three slaves, one head of cattle, one horse, and one ordinary license. Three years later, in 1785, opened a shop on Richmond's Main Street, "nearly opposite the Capitol," where he

SIGNATURE PLATE, TAYLOR-HUMPHRIES GATE, *1860. This manufacturer's signature plate, the only one known for James Taylor and John Humphries, is on the fence around the Alexander family* plot in the Stonewall Jackson Cemetery. A number of other balconies and cast-iron fences in Lexington are similar to this one and are probably the work of the Taylor-Humphries Furnace.

"made and repaired clocks and watches." Left Richmond about 1789, but possibly returned to Augusta County for a while that same year. One tall case clock with an engraved brass dial documented with the inscription "Jos. Humphreys, No. 153, Staunton, Virginia." The clock has descended to the Morrison family of Brownsburg. Tall case clocks that Humphreys made while he was living in Richmond between 1782 and 1789 hav been identified. Cutten; Chalkley; Gill; VG 7/9/1785.

HUMPHREYS, SAMUEL

Photographer. Active 1850. Advertised in December 1850 that he had taken a room at Lexington's Porter's Hotel and was "prepared to take Daguerrotype Portraits, under all the late improvements in the art, in all kinds of weather." LG 12/24/1850.

HUMPHRIES, JOHN McD.

Blacksmith, foundryman. 1826 Amherst County, Va.–1870 Rockbridge County, Va. Active 1845–69. Humphries began working as a Rockbridge County blacksmith at nineteen. In September 1845 he made fifteen iron window gratings for VMI and furnished VMI with "iron stove doors" and "2 rods" in 1846. In 1850 he made "1 set of oven irons" and in 1853 "one wrought iron box for the gas stove." The next year he called himself a "gas fitter" (RCMR 1A, 12). In 1858 Humphries formed a partnership with James Taylor to run the Rockbridge Foundry and Machine Works on Irish Creek. Their notice to the public in the *Lexington Gazette* said that "Mr. Humphries, who is a practical mechanic, having been engaged for years in the iron business, will preside at the Foundry on Irish Creek and give his personal and undivided attention to the business and to the inspection of every job before it leaves the shop." The foundry was manufacturing the following articles: "Mill Gearing; Livingston Plows, Hillside Plows; corn crushers; corn shellers; threshing machines made and repaired; Iron Railings for grave and porticos; a variety of patterns, . . . mill spindles; cooking ranges; Hollow-ware and irons; Smoothing irons." The advertisement noted that Humphries "hopes by strict attention to business and prompt execution of work to merit a liberal share of public patronage." In 1864, while exempt from service, he listed himself as a "manufacturer of Iron Utensils." His relationship with William Humphries (q.v.), who was active in the South River–Vesuvius area, 1870–87, is unclear. VMI Superintendent's files; VS 6/10/58; Driver.

HUMPHRIES, WILLIAM SHELTON

Foundryman, plowmaker. 1843 Vesuvius, Va.–1928 Vesuvius, Va. Active 1870–87. Served during the Civil War with the 5th Virginia Infantry, became associated with the Vesuvius Foundry and Hugh

Franklin Lyle (q.v.) shortly after the war. Diary for 1870 survives, giving insights about plow factory operations. His son, William Frank Humphries, later became a partner. In 1919 the partnership was dissolved and a corporation formed. William Humphries remained with the company until his death in 1945, when his son, H. Lyle Humphries, became manager of the corporation. Another son, Harold B. Humphries, was connected with the business until the 1950s. WL RHS Clipping, n.d.; LG 2/14/1887; Driver; Kirkpatrick 1988; RCMR 2, 183.

HUNT, HARRY

Forgeman (slave). b. 1788 Campbell County, Va. Active c. 1837. Born at the Oxford Iron Works in Campbell County, near Lynchburg. His father, a slave owned by the company, had been a limestone miner at Oxford, and Harry and his brother Billy had been trained in the forge at Oxford. Harry Hunt instructed Sam Williams (q.v.) at Buffalo Forge. Dew 1994.

HUTTON, GARDNER PAXTON

Cabinetmaker. 1836 Rockbridge County, Va.–1903 Collierstown, Va. Active 1860–c. 1900. Listed as a Collierstown cabinetmaker and merchant in the 1860 census. Several cupboards and other pieces of furniture are attributed to him. Son of James Cunningham Hutton, a Collierstown millwright. C 1860, 1880; Kirkpatrick 1988; Diehl 1971; Driver; CM 1880; RCN 3/20/1902.

IRELAND, JOHN M.

Cabinetmaker. b. 1802 Virginia. Active 1823–50. Advertised an auction in 1834 at his Fairfield residence to raise money owed to George Ireland. Items offered included "one brace and bits, two work benches, twenty-four planes, two screws, twelve hand screws, twenty chisels, one table, one thousand feet of Plank, in addition to various other articles." Financial problems are reflected again in an 1827 announcement. Advertised his cabinetmaking business in 1848. Listed occupation in the 1850 census. Grandfather of cabinetmaker Charles F. Mays (q.v.). C 1850; LI 8/16/1823; LI 3/15/1827; LG 5/27/1848.

IRVIN, JOHN

Iron manufacturer. d. 1834 Rockbridge County, Va. Business partner of John Winn Jordan (q.v.), 1824–34. LNL 7/31/1829; LNL 9/4/1819; Darst.

IRVINE, WILLIAM S.

Cabinetmaker. c. 1821–c. 1871. Active 1853. Listed occupation in county birth records in 1853. Kirkpatrick; RCWB 20, 255–60, 389–91; Driver.

JOHN

Forgeman (slave). Active 1851. It was reported in the *Lexington Gazette* in 1851 that a slave, John, who previously belonged to "Shanks and children, and worked at their furnaces," had run away from John D. Hobson of Goochland County. See also Shanks and Anderson. LG 8/21/1851.

JOHNSON, DAVID

Artist. 1827 New York, N.Y.–1908 Walden, N.Y. Member of the National Academy of Design. Works include three views of Natural Bridge done in 1860. Two of the paintings are in private collections, the third is at Reynolda House, Winston-Salem, N.C. One view served as a model for an 1860 engraving of Natural Bridge by S. V. Hunt. Simpson 1982; Wright.

JOHNSON, JOHN

Artist. b. c. 1820 Ohio. In 1871 painted a view of Rockbridge County's House Mountain, now in the Governor's Mansion, Richmond. Wright.

JOHNSTON, JAMES T.

Chairmaker. Active 1857. Occupation noted in county birth records, 1857. Kirkpatrick.

JONES, GREEN BERRY

Artist. 1853 Rockingham County, Va.–1932 Richmond, Va. Mural and decorative painter. Itinerant artist who produced a variety of interior decorative works in the Augusta and northern Rockbridge County area. Surviving examples of his work—woodgraining, marbleizing, stenciling, and mural painting—are found in the A. J. Miller House (1892), near Middlebrook; the William Smith House in Greenville; and the William Rimel House (c. 1903–4) in Spring Hill. Also produced paintings for the Salem Lutheran Church and the Oddfellows Hall at Steeles Tavern. Jones conducted camp meetings at Mt. Sidney in 1892, the same year he painted the Miller residence. It was said that he would "preach a little, paint a little, and drink a little." Listed in the 1880 census as a "mechanic." Later moved to Richmond and worked for his son, Mertel, who had established a house-painting business there. No known Richmond works have been documented. Ann McCleary, "Preach a Little, Paint a Little, Drink a Little: The Work of Itinerant Painter Green Berry Jones," AHB 22 (fall 1986): 31–39; interview with Jones's granddaughter, Lillian K. Peters of Staunton, 1991.

JORDAN, CHARLES

Furniture manufacturer. Active 1878. Business partner with James Watts (q.v.) and later J. M. Jordan (q.v.) in the Buena Vista Chair and Furniture Factory. LG 7/12/1878.

JORDAN, EVA

Artist. Active 1889. Awarded a diploma for the best charcoal drawing at the 1889 Rockbridge County Fair. LG 10/1824/89.

JORDAN, IRA F.

Ironmaster. Active 1839. Listed as being in charge of the Lucy Selina Furnace in 1839 in *Weaver v. Jordan, Davis and Company* WD, 58.

JORDAN, J. M.

Furniture manufacturer. Active 1878. Purchased James Watts's (q.v.) share of the Buena Vista Chair and Furniture Factory, making him a business partner of Charles Jordan (q.v.), 1878. LG 7/12/1878.

JORDAN, JOHN WINN
(WILLIAM?)

Furnace owner. c. 1813 Rockbridge County, Va.–1883 Rockbridge County, Va. Active 1850–75. Third son of John Jordan. Built the California Furnace on Brattons Run and operated it from 1850 to 1875. A square iron slab stamped "J.W.J." is located at Stono (VMI). Similar castings were used to line a fireplace in the residence on Route 631 near Kerrs Creek. According to Jean Cameron Agnew (Rockbridge Historical Society files), other iron castings with similar initials are in fireplaces in Goshen and Millboro. Bruce; Morton; Driver.

JORDAN, NANNIE

Artist. Active 1881. Art teacher at the Public Free School, where she produced a drawing of the front of the *Lexington Gazette* building and of Natural Bridge, 1881. LG 1/8/1881; LG 2/24/1881.

JORDAN, SAMUEL
FRANCIS

Iron manufacturer. b. 1805 Rockbridge County, Va. Active 1830–64. Second son of John Jordan (q.v.); followed his father in the iron business. Lived first in Lexington. In business with William Weaver (q.v.) and Abraham W. Davis (q.v.) beginning in 1830. In 1836 announced that he was dissolving the partnership, and the next year announced the sale of the Bath Iron Works. Formed a partnership in 1847 with his brother Benjamin J. (Jordan and Jordan) and announced that they would build Buena

Vista Furnace on South River. Large brick Gothic residence built on the hill overlooking the furnace and river survives today. Also built the furnace superintendent's house, as well as numerous other company structures. By the summer of 1850 were manufacturing cook and parlor stoves and "Horse Powers." In June 1864 the Buena Vista Furnace was destroyed by the forces of Union General Hunter. LG 10/20/1830; LG 3/4/1836; LG 12/1/1837; LG 8/8/1850; WD; Bruce; CM 1850.

KAHLE, JACOB P.

Cabinetmaker. c. 1847 Lexington, Va.–1886 Norfolk, Va. Active 1870. Son of the Lexington cabinetmaker Mathew Kahle (q.v.). Listed occupation in Lexington, in the 1870 census. C 1870; Driver.

KAHLE, MATHEW SALTZER

Cabinetmaker. 1800 Berks County, Pa.–1869 Lexington, Va. Active 1824–69. Advertised in 1824, with the Lexington chairmaker Samuel Smith (q.v.), for "about a thousand feet of curled maple plank and scantling." Next year married Sally Fuller, daughter of Jacob Fuller. Smith was already married to Sally's sister Margaret. Also in 1825 they announced the arrival of a "supply of mahogany of the first quality with which they would manufacture cabinet furniture." They offered "Side-boards, Wardrobes, Secretaries, Book-Cases, Square & Corner Cupboards, Column bureaus, Plain do., Eliptic End, and Square, Pillar and Claw Dining Tables, do., Breakfast do., Work and Toilet do., Book and Candle Stands, high Post, and Acorn Bedsteads of the neatest fashions." In 1826 both Kahle and Smith, in separate notices, listed their Lexington address at the house "one door above the store of Captain Robert White and nearly opposite Mr. Haughawought's tavern." Also solicited for an apprentice. No advertisements appeared between 1826 and 1836. Then in 1836 Kahle announced a "Splendid Hack for Hire." Advertisements from 1838 to 1842 reflected trips to the North and Richmond for materials. In September 1842 R. Castles (q.v.) and Kahle announced their partnership. Sometime between 1842 and 1844 completed the statue of George Washington for the Center Hall at Washington College. For many years built the platform at the Presbyterian Church that was used by both schools for their July commencement exercises. Obituary in 1846 for Kahle's father, Peter, was followed a few months later by an announcement of the sale of a house and lot on Main Street next to Smith and property consisting of "CARPENTER'S & CABINETMAKER'S TOOLS." May have belonged to Peter, also a cabinetmaker. Kahle's mother died a few months later, and her obituary noted that she and her husband had moved to Rockbridge from Berks County, Pa., in 1825, the year following Mathew's arrival. In 1844 presented the Grace Episcopal Church with a wardrobe for the "vestments and

STONEMASON'S MARK, *top.* *Stonemason marks appear on one of the canal locks in Rockbridge County, the massive construction project supervised by John Jordan.*

CAST INITIALS, *above. A number of documented cast-iron pieces marked "J.W.J.," for John Winn Jordan, were probably created as firebacks. 24 x 27 inches.*

S. S. Library." Asked for the return of borrowed tools in 1848 and 1849. Again in 1849 announced his new shop "near the Pump, opposite the Gazette Office" and solicited for an apprentice. Census of 1850 noted $1,000 in personal property and $5,000 of real estate. That same year cabinetmakers Samuel Kahle (q.v.), James McCoy (q.v.), and George Adams (q.v.) were included in Kahle's household listing. An advertisement in 1851 stated that prices for work ranged from $4 to $18. Another article included Kahle as a stockholder in the North River Navigation Company. Advertisements in 1853 report that he had "just finished two of those beautiful 'dressing Bureaus,' made out of crotch elm." Also advertised that his business, located in the "Central Hall Warerooms," could manufacture "Center, Pier, Dining and Breakfast Tables, Plain and Portable Wardrobes." The next year called himself a "Manufacturer of Sideboards, bureaus, and tete a tetes." In August 1855 advertised that his inventory was large and "very superior" and included "Mahogany, Maple, Rosewood, and Walnut, Bureaus of the best finish, Sideboards, Sofas, Ottomans, Tables, Wardrobes, Lounges, Bedsteads, etc." Four months later announced a sale of "all his present stock at cost. . . . All not sold at that time will be disposed of at Public AUCTION on the 22nd of December." In January of the next year, 1856, his sons, Samuel F. and William Henry Harrison (q.v.), announced that they had purchased the stock and fixtures belonging to their father and planned to continue the business. In 1857 Kahle received two twenty-dollar premiums from the State Agricultural Fair for "the best machine for gathering cloverseed . . . the best machine for hulling and cleansing cloverseed; and a premium of $10 for the best scoop or scraper." Was a member of the Franklin Society for many years. Three daughters married local cabinetmakers: Emma Blanche married Richard Bayliss (q.v.) in 1871, Catherine married William P. Hartigan (q.v.) in 1865, and Frances married Thomas Forsyth (q.v.) in 1862. His brother Samuel married Catherine McClain, daughter of the cabinetmaker John McClain (q.v.), in 1841. C 1850, 1860; CM 1860; LI 10/30/1824; LI 3/18/1825; LI 5/27/1825; LI 1/6/1826; LI 7/6/1826; LG 6/10/1836; LG 5/18/1838; LG 5/18/1839; LG 4/15/1841; LG 12/30/1841; LG 3/3/1842; LG 8/18/1842; LG 9/15/1842; R. E. Lee Episcopal Church Property Records 1844/51; LG 8/6/1846; LG 8/6/1846; LG 11/5/1846; LG 3/16/1848; LG 5/1/1849; LG 6/5/1849; LG 6/19/1851; LG 6/30/1853; LG 10/6/1853; LG 2/23/1854; LG 8/9/1855; LG 12/13/1855; LG 1/3/1856; LG 11/5/1857; Couper 1960; Lyle and Simpson; Oddfellows 1849; Dooley; W&L Trustees' 1842; WL Franklin Society; Kirkpatrick 1988; RCDR 94/22; LG 1/13/1841.

KAHLE, SAMUEL F.

Cabinetmaker. b. 1832 Virginia. Active 1850–56. Son of Mathew Kahle (q.v.). In 1856 he and his brother, William (q.v.), purchased their father's Lexington business. The partnership lasted nine months and was "dissolved by mutual consent." Samuel announced that he would continue the business and offered to buy 2,000 feet of "good and well-seasoned Walnut." By the end of the year announced an auction and the closing of the shop. By February 1857 William reported that he had reopened the business. Listed as a cabinetmaker in the 1850 census. C 1850; Oddfellows 1853; LG 11/1/1855; LG 1/3/1856; LG 9/18/1856; LG 12/4/1856; LG 2/19/1857.

KAHLE, WILLIAM
HENRY HARRISON

Cabinetmaker. 1836 Virginia–1863 Pennsylvania. Active 1856–60. Son of Mathew Kahle (q.v.). In 1856 advertised, with his brother Samuel F. (q.v.), the purchase of stock and fixtures of their father's business and that they would continue the trade. The business was dissolved later that year. The following March reopened the business and used his father's old name of Central Hall Warerooms. Advertised in 1858 for the return of "TOOLS, BRACES, SCREW DRIVERS, AND BED WRENCHES" that had been borrowed from him and for customers to settle their debts. Records in the Virginia Historical Society for John H. Lyle's sawmill noted that Kahle purchased 325 feet 4/4 walnut, 200 feet 2/4 walnut, 120 feet 3-inch "skantling," 260 feet 2/4 walnut and 400 feet 4/4 poplar in April 1858 (VHS W. T. Williams Papers). Furniture and coffin-making advertisements continued for a year. In October 1859 announced the sale of "all the Furniture I have on hand at that time." The following month he married Mary Elizabeth Breedlove and may have left town. He was killed in action at Gettysburg in 1863. LG 1/3/1856; 9/18/1856; VS 12/9/1858; VS 1/14/1858; VS 10/14/1858; LG 3/4/1858; VS 10/14/1858; VS 12/9/1858; LG 1/13/1859; LG 1/27/1859; LG 10/27/1859; LG 11/17/1859; RCMR 1A, 70; Driver.

KELLY, G.

Cabinetmaker, carpenter. Active 1780. Received $70 in 1780 for "making a table for the clerk and sundry repairs to the courthouse." Morton.

KELLY, JOSEPH

Photographer, cabinetmaker. 1800 Virginia – 1876 Rockbridge County, Va. Active 1850–69. Listed in the 1850 and 1860 censuses as a cabinetmaker. Following the war produced and distributed General Lee's *carnet de visite* and listed himself as a "photographic artist" on Washington Street in Lexington. C 1850, 1860; Couper 1960.

KELLY, JOSEPH, JR.

Cabinetmaker. b. 1833 Virginia. Active 1850. Listed in the census as a cabinetmaker living in the house of his father, Joseph (q.v.). C 1850.

KELLY, WILLIAM HENRY

Cabinetmaker. 1843 Cedar Grove–1923. Active 1880–96. Probably related to other Kelly cabinetmakers, Joseph (q.v.) and Joseph, Jr. (q.v.). C 1880; Driver; RCMR 2, 141; LG 12/30/1896.

KEY, MILTON H.

Cabinetmaker. 1827 Giles County, Va.–1860 Rockbridge County, Va. Active 1856–60. Married to Andrew Varner's (q.v.) sister Rebecca. An 1852 obituary for his daughter noted his living in Fincastle. Following the death of the Lexington cabinetmaker Leonard S. Palmer (q.v.), originally from Fincastle, Key announced the purchase of Palmer's tools and fixtures and that he would manufacture all kinds of "Cabinet Furniture" from "common to the finest." Shop in 1856 located on Main Street opposite William McCaul's Hotel. Advertised later that same year that he had on hand and would make to order "Bureaus, Bedsteads, Wardrobes, Tables, Sofas, China Presses, Book Cases, Rocking and Parlor Chairs." The identical announcement appeared in the *Virginia Star* two years later. Shop ledger from 1857 to 1860 survives and lists customers and employees in addition to items sold and bartered. Joined the local masonic lodge in 1857 and served as clerk for the Lexington Baptist Church in 1859. Extensive listing of tools, equipment, and supplies recorded in the 1860 probate inventory. *Census of Manufactures* of 1860 reported Rebecca Key operating the cabinetmaking business. In 1862 Varner announced that as "agent for Mrs. Key" he would continue the cabinetmaking business at the old stand "recently occupied by M. H. Key." LG 6/1852; LG 4/10/1856; LG 10/9/1856; VS 8/5/1858; LG 3/24/1859; LG 1/1862; Dooley/Key; CM 1860; RCWB 15, 500–502; Couper 1960; Kirkpatrick 1988; RCDR 40, 10; Lexington Masonic Records.

KEYS, WILLIAM

Chairmaker. Active 1801. Partner with Lexington chairmaker James Dixon (q.v.). Advertised Windsor chair-making and housepainting in 1801. RR 10/23/1801.

KIGER, GEORGE

Carder. Active 1826. Advertised in 1826 the operation of a new carding machine on South River with Cyrus J. Lydick (q.v.). Wool was picked up weekly at "Mr. Robert Caruthers' Fairfield, at Mr. Nataniel Carpenter's about one mile from Edmondson's Mill on the North River and at the machine as above." LI 5/25/1826.

KNICK, JAMES

Turner. Active 1860. Credited with producing 300 table legs for the Lexington cabinetmaker Andrew Varner (q.v.) in 1860.

KNOX, WILLIAM

Weaver. Active 1820. Listed in the 1820 *Census of Manufactures* as having "looms for weaving" and that he produced woolen, linen, and cotton cloths. Reported two looms "all in operation and that he attends to them himself." CM 1820.

KOLLNER, AUGUSTUS

Artist. 1813 Düsseldorf, Germany–1888 Philadelphia, Pa. Came to America in 1839 after studying in Düsseldorf and Frankfurt. In 1845 produced a watercolor of Natural Bridge that is now in the collection of the Valentine Museum, Richmond. This view was included in the 1848–51 Paris publication *Views of American Cities*. Simpson 1982; Wright.

KOONES, ALBERT L.

Cabinetmaker. 1845 Rockbridge County, Va.–1916. Active 1880–95. Household census listing in 1880 included Theodore T. Agnor (q.v.), cabinetmaker, who was probably working for him. Brother and business partner of the Lexington cabinetmaker Charles M. Koones (q.v.), 1884. Provided furnishings for the Buena Vista Hotel in 1889 and was a member of the executive committee of the Point Chair Factory, 1891. C 1880, 1910; LG 8/28/1884; LG 12/20/1888; 6/13/1889; 7/2/1891; LG 1/14/1892; LG 1/24/1895.

KOONES, MRS. ALBERT L.

Artist. Active 1889. Wife of the Lexington cabinetmaker Albert L. Koones (q.v.). Awarded a $2 premium for the best oil painting at the Rockbridge County Fair, 1889. LG 10/24/1889.

KOONES, CHARLES M.

Cabinetmaker. 1835 Virginia–1909. Active 1867–98. Son of the Alexandria cabinetmaker Charles Frederick Koones. Married Mary Elizabeth Kneller in 1860 in Berryville, Va. Advertised in Lexington in 1869 that he was making furniture in addition to selling factory-produced items. An 1869 canal boat ledger in the Rockbridge County Court House records that Koones and Company received

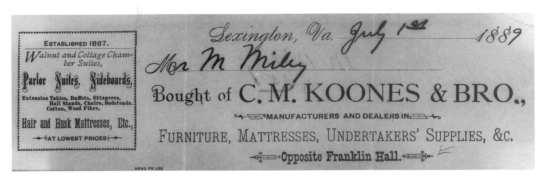

RECEIPTS, 1880 AND 1889. Charles M. Koones was a post-Civil War cabinetmaker in Lexington. Many cabinetmakers made and sold coffins in addition to arranging funerals.

a shipment of "10 Pkgs Bedsteads, 10 Bld slats, 10 Pkgs Bedsteads, 7 Pkgs Rails, 3 Pkgs Do. 12 Pkgs Chairs." Advertisements for 1871 again indicate the arrivals of parlor furniture "direct from manufactures" as well as items made of "seasoned walnut by skillful workmen." Announced in 1871 the addition of machinery that would enable him to produce "all kinds of turning, jig sawing, or making doors, brackets, mantles &c. for builders." Assisted by his brother Albert L. (q.v.). The 1880 *Census of Manufactures* reports production value of $3,000. Employed Theodore T. Agnor (q.v.) in 1884. The business, on the corner of Nelson and Jefferson, burned in 1885. "Koones & Bro" furnished the Buena Vista Hotel with furniture in 1889. Moved to Washington, D.C., where he became treasurer of the Capital Traction Company. C 1870; CM 1880; LG 1/17/1869; VG 7/1871; VG 9/15/1871; LG 12/29/1871; LG 23/24/1877; LG 10/23/1879; LG 7/1/1880; LG 11/21/1881; LG 7/13/1882; LG 10/26/1882; LG 8/28/1884; LG 12/20/1888; LG 6/13/1889; LG 1/14/1892; family correspondence with authors.

KURTZ (KIRTZ), FREDERICK

Turner. b. 1799 Virginia. Active 1850–60. Listed occupation in the 1850 and 1860 censuses. Between 1857 and 1860 produced items (table legs, newell posts, cottage posts, banisters, a music stand, bureau knobs, and 1,375 bedpins) for the Lexington cabinetmaker Milton H. Key (q.v.). Census entry in 1860 includes the turning apprentice Iverson Root (q.v.). After Key's death in 1860, Andrew Varner (q.v.) operated the shop for his sister, Key's widow. Continued to work for the shop and is recorded in Varner's ledger as producing similar items. Probably related to other Kurtzes—the Staunton Windsor-chair maker and turner Jacob Kurtz (c.

1804–7); the cabinetmaker George Kurtz of Winchester (1868–26); and Adam Kurtz, the Winchester cabinetmaker and turner (c. 1806–7). C 1850, 1860; Dooley; Dooley/Key; MESDA; Varner.

KURZ, LOUIS

Artist. c. 1833 Austria–1921 Chicago, Ill. Came to America in 1848. After the Civil War became one of the founding members of the Art Institute of Chicago. Formed a partnership in 1880 with Alexander Allison that produced a lithograph of Natural Bridge. Simpson 1982; Wright.

LACKEY, JAMES

Spinning-wheel maker. Active 1787. John Erhardt Wall (q.v.) was indentured to Lackey as a woolwright and spinning-wheel maker in 1787. A Lacky was listed in the 1820 *Census of Manufactures* as in the wool carding business. WL RHS; CM20.

LAM, ISAAC

Potter. 1832 Rockingham County, Va.–1882 Rockbridge Baths, Va. Active 1854–80. Listed in the 1850 Rockingham County census as a potter. Possibly served as an apprentice to William Coffman, Rockingham potter. In 1854 moved to Rockbridge and probably began working at the Rockbridge Baths pottery with John D. Campbell (q.v.). In 1865 married Mary L. Selby. Lived at the baths until his death in 1882, at which time the Rockbridge Baths pottery apparently ceased operation. Pottery from both the Rockbridge Baths and the Bustleburg kilns was stamped "Rockbridge" rather than with the name of the potters. C 1860, 1870, 1880; Russ 1990; Driver; RCMR 1A, 118; Kirkpatrick 1988; Hardesty; RHSP 10, 471.

LAMB, W. C.

Artist. Active 1881. Awarded a certificate by the 1881 Rockbridge County Fair for a "pencil sketching" entitled *Injured Innocence*. LG 11/21/1881.

LAMBERT, DAVID

Cabinetmaker. Active 1804. Worked with John Chandler (q.v.), providing items to Washington Academy in 1804. WL Trustees' folder 43, 1804.

LAREW, JACOB

Cabinetmaker. 1793 Augusta County, Va.–1875 Rockbridge County, Va. Active 1850–70. Listed in the 1850, 1860, and 1870 censuses as a Brownsburg cabinetmaker. Probably the father of Milton F. Larew (q.v.) and James W. Larew (q.v.), cabinetmakers. C 1850, 1860, 1870; RCWB 21, 308; Kirkpatrick 1988; RCMR 1A, 183.

LAREW, JAMES W.

Cabinetmaker. b. 1826. Active 1854–61. Listed occupation in the 1854 Oddfellows records. Probably son of Jacob Larew (q.v.). Andrew Varner's (q.v.) ledger in 1860 and 1861 lists items and services provided for the Lexington shop. Probably related to other Larew cabinetmakers. Oddfellows 1854; Varner; Kirkpatrick 1988.

LAREW, MILTON F.

Cabinetmaker. 1830 Augusta County, Va.–c. 1863. Active 1850–61. Listed in the 1850 census as a cabinetmaker in the household of Jacob Larew (q.v.), who was probably his father. C 1850; RCMR 1A, 29; Kirkpatrick 1988; RCWB 17, 273–75; Driver.

LAUGHLIN, HUGH

Weaver. c. 1773 England. Active 1812. Included in the *British Aliens in the United States During the War of 1812* as a weaver, age thirty-nine, and as being in Rockbridge County with his wife and three children for seven years and two months. Scott.

LEE, A. F.

Textile worker. b. 1842 Virginia. Active 1869–70. Listed in the 1870 census as a wool factory worker, probably at the Rockbridge Woolen Factory, Kerrs Creek. C 1870; Kirkpatrick 1988.

LEE, L. G.

Photographer. Active 1846. Advertised in March 1846 his ability to take exactly the "form and expression of the human countenance." Solicited customers to his "room" at the Jefferson Hotel, Lexington, where he took "plesure in exhibiting his specimens." Also announced that he used the "GALVANIC process." LG 3/6/1846; LG 3/12/1846.

LEECH, WILLIAM D.

Cabinetmaker. 1833 Virginia–1881. Active 1870–80. Listed as a Natural Bridge millwright in the 1870 census and a cabinetmaker in 1880. C 1870, 1880; Driver.

LEESEE, MR.

Gunsmith. Active 1861. The Lexington paper carried an editorial about Mr. Leesee and his new pistol in August 1861: "We were shown today a large seven shooter every part of which was made at the Rockbridge Foundry, on Irish creek by Mr. Leesee." LG 8/8/1861.

LEWIS, ELIAS

Clockmaker. Active 1820. In 1820 reported using "brass, copper and iron sheets" in his business, in which he was the only employee. Had three sets of clockmaking tools, although only one set was used. Capital investment was $1,000. One clock with Lewis's name painted on the dial was documented in Lexington. Married the daughter of the Lexington clockmaker Thomas Whiteside (q.v.). No known record after 1820. The relationship is unclear between Elias Lewis and C. C. Lewis, a clockmaker and watchmaker in Staunton (1844–47). Cutten; C 1820; CM 1820.

LEYBURN, EDWARD JENNER

Foundryman, contractor. 1829 Rockbridge County, Va.–1900 McDonogh, Md. Active 1852–85. Educated at Rev. James Morrison's school in Brownsburg, Washington College (1846–47), and studied mechanical engineering at Lowell Technical Institute in Massachusetts. In 1852 established the Rockbridge Foundry and Machine Works "on Irish Creek, nine miles east of Lexington and six miles from Fairfield," where "every variety of castings, however intricate, will be executed." Brother William Leyburn (q.v.) was partner. Product line and capabilities included hot air pipes, iron railings, and agricultural implements—threshing machines, corn shellers, two- and three-horse plows, and hillside plows. In 1853 advertised holloware, fireplace jams, and back plates. Lexington paper in 1853 praised their new iron fence around the county courthouse. Foundry was purchased in 1854 by Thomas Taylor (q.v.) and Thomas McDowell (q.v.). Became a prominent builder in Lexington following the Civil War, constructing numerous private residences and public buildings, including the R. E. Lee Memorial Episcopal Church, Lee Mausoleum attached to Washington and Lee University's Lee Chapel, and 1885 law offices on the courthouse yard. LG 8/5/1852; LG 5/5/1853; 7/14/1843; LG 11/10/1853; LG 8/31/1854; LG 12/20/1878; LG 4/13/1882; LG 6/22/1882; Leyburn; Lyle and Simpson.

LEYBURN, MARY

Artist. Active 1884. Winner of diploma for the best crayon drawing, fine arts division, Rockbridge County Fair, 1884. LG 9/18/1884.

LEYBURN, WILLIAM CARUTHERS

Foundryman. 1827 Rockbridge County, Va.–1882 California. Active 1852–54. Studied mechanics at VMI in 1846. Established the Rockbridge Foundry and Machine Works. Brother Edward Leyburn (q.v.) was partner. Sold the foundry in 1854 to Thomas Taylor (q.v.) and Thomas McDowell. Moved in 1854 to Washington, D.C. Became associated with the Cyrus McCormick (q.v.) operation and moved about 1859 to Galesburg, Ill., where the reaper factory was established. Moved to California in 1879. Leyburn; LG 6/8/1854; LG 8/31/1854; VMI Alumni.

LOVEJOY, NATHANIEL F.

Artist. Active 1819. Advertised in 1819 that "The subscriber intends doing PAINTINGS OF ALL DESCRIPTIONS. In Augusta, Rockbridge, and the adjoining Counties in the neatest and most elegant stile, also on the lowest terms: specimens of my Painting may be seen in Staunton and the Co. around." LNL 9/18/1819.

LUDWIG, EDWARD ALBERT

Artist. c. 1813 Switzerland–1865. Active 1858. Included in the 1858 schedule of classes for Lexington's Ann Smith Academy as professor of music and drawing. Tuition for drawing class was $7.50. Professor of modern languages at Washington College from 1857 to 1860. C 1860; WL Alumni; VS 7/15/1858; Driver.

LYDICK, CYRUS J.

Carder. Active 1826. Operated a carding machine on the South River with George Kiger (q.v.). LI 5/25/1826.

LYLE, DANIEL

Stonemason. Larne, County Antrim, Ireland–1781. Active 1755–56. Credited with doing the stonework on Timber Ridge Presbyterian Church. Ruffner; Lyle.

LYLE, HUGH FRANKLIN

Foundryman. 1834 Rockbridge County, Va.–1902 Staunton, Va. Active 1863–91. Bought the Vesuvius Foundry from Schuyler Bradley (q.v.) in 1863. In 1864 announced that the manufacture of "Lyle's Original Livingston Plow" and other castings "will be carried on, as heretofore, at the old stand. . . ." Also noted that the plows "will be kept for sale at Antrim & Lafferty and H. H. Myers in Lexington, [and] A. Alexander at the Point." In 1878 offered several reasons why "you should buy the Livingston," including:

The shrewd farmer knows that new-fashioned, new-fangled things are seldom improvements, and rarely what they are 'cracked up to be.'

He knows that our works are a fixed institution in this country, and that he will be, at all times, able to get these plows and the repairs readily, cheaply, and no trouble about it.

He knows that in patronizing us, he is encouraging home enterprise, and building up home interests, which is the right thing to do.

William S. Humphries (q.v.) became a partner in the firm sometime during the 1870s and eventually became the sole owner. The firm operated until after World War II. LG 1/5/1877; LG 2/22/1875; LG 1/14/1887; Lyle; Morresset.

LYLE, SAMUEL

Carpenter. c. 1725 County Antrim, Ireland–1796 Timber Ridge, Va. Active 1755. Came to Virginia about 1745 from Ulster. In 1751 purchased 235 acres from Benjamin Borden, near the farm of his uncle, Daniel Lyle (q.v.), on Timber Ridge. That year married Sarah McClung. Worked as a carpenter before becoming a farmer, merchant, "a magistrate in the first court held in the new county of Rockbridge," and an early trustee of Liberty Hall Academy. Daniel Lyle is credited with building the Timber Ridge stone church in 1755, and Samuel constructed the communion table, which is still used today. Ruffner; Lyle.

LYLE, WILLIAM

Gunsmith. c. 1746 Timber Ridge, Va.–c. 1778. Active c. 1765–c. 1778. Son of John Lyle, who was born in County Antrim, Ireland, c. 1720. In 1746 Benjamin Borden's estate conveyed to John Lyle 746 acres on Mill Creek at Timber Ridge. William, the younger of two sons, was born shortly after the family arrived at Timber Ridge. Apparently began a gunsmithing operation around 1765. Married Nancy Agnes Gilmore around 1770. One source says Lyle died in 1778. The estate inventory, recorded four years later in August 1782, included a rifle, gunsmith's tools, and "a forged gun barrel." Gilmore could have been the daughter of John Gilmore, who worked with Staunton gunsmith Joshua Humphreys (q.v.) around 1777. Gill; RCWB 1, 169; Lyle.

MATHENEY, JAMES F.

Cabinetmaker. b. 1830 Virginia. Active 1850. Included as a cabinetmaker in the 1850 census household listing of the Lexington cabinetmaker Leonard S. Palmer (q.v.). C 1850.

MAYBURRY (MAYBERRY), THOMAS

Ironmaster. b. Pennsylvania–1850 Louisa County, Va. Active 1820–42. Came to the Valley from Pennsylvania and erected the Vesuvius Furnace. Sold the furnace to Matthew Bryan (q.v.) around 1842 for "twelve to thirteen thousand dollars." Partner in 1820 with William Weaver (q.v.) at Buffalo Forge, where they employed twenty men and had two trip-hammers and made bar iron. Operated for six years (c. 1830–36) what was known as Mayburry's Iron Works or Gibraltar Forge, located between Rockbridge Baths and Cedar Grove. According to Joseph Martin's *Gazetteer* (1835), the operation was equal in size to the rather extensive Lebanon Forge located only one mile upstream. WD, 241, 498, 507; Martin; BVA 6/26/1891; CM 1820; LI 2/11/1825.

MAYS, CHARLES F.

Cabinetmaker. b. 1856 Virginia. Active 1877–82. Listed in the 1880 census, Oddfellows membership, and marriage records as a cabinetmaker in Lexington. Grandson of the cabinetmaker John M. Ireland (q.v.). Established a "new furniture house" on Main Street in 1881. Awarded a certificate for a suite of parlor furniture at the Rockbridge County Fair, 1881. C 1880; RCMR 14, 312; LG 3/24/1881; LG 4/21/1881; LG 10/27/1881; LG 11/21/1881; LG 4/6/1882; Oddfellows 1877.

MAYS, JAMES A.

Cabinetmaker. Active 1856. In 1856 married Sarah W. Ireland, daughter of the Fairfield cabinetmaker John M. Ireland (q.v.). Father of the cabinetmaker Charles F. Mays (q.v.). Kirkpatrick 1988.

McCAFFREY, J. H.

Foundryman. Active 1886. Announced in 1886 that he had "leased the OLD Mullen Foundry for a term of years" and that he would repair and construct "machinery in all its branches," as he "had a life-time experience at the business." LG 4/1/1886.

McCAUL, JOHN R.

Cabinetmaker. 1844 Amherst County, Va.–1917. Active 1880. Listed as "works at cabinetmaking" in the 1880 household of his brother-in-law, the Lexington cabinetmaker Andrew Varner (q.v.). C 1880; Couper 1960; Driver.

McCLAIN, JOHN

Cabinetmaker. Active 1820. Listed occupation in the 1820 *Census of Manufactures.* Reported that he "makes use of walnut, pine, and poplar plank, employs one man and no boys, with one set of tools

to make 'Bureaus, Tables, Cupboards &c.'" Daughter Catherine married Samuel Kahle, brother of Mathew Kahle (q.v.) in 1841. LG 1/13/1841; CM 1820.

McCLUER (McCLURE), HALBERT

Furnanceman, forgeman. c. 1750 Rockbridge County, Va.–c. 1830 Rockbridge County, Va. Active c. 1780–1820. The Rockbridge Historical Society collection contains an undated paper by Elsie C. Strickler stating: "Three of the McClurers, Herbert, Moses, and Alexander, built a small bank furnace with a two or three ton daily capacity which was located on the west side of the river from the present Jordan stack. This was between 1778 and 1780. Later they erected a furnace [there] and a forge with a small foundry attached one mile below, the remains of which were seen as late as 1889." In 1786 Halbert bought 249 acres of land in Rockbridge, perhaps associated with the family's iron business. Two firebacks that bear the stamp "Halbert and Moses McClure" were most likely made between 1780 and 1790. Halbert and Alexander were mentioned in David Daugherty's estate inventory in 1809 as having an outstanding debt to Daugherty. But by 1820 the operation appeared to be winding down. The forge, which still employed sixteen men, was producing primarily bar iron, but only one of its two tilt hammers was in use. The census noted that the furnace was "now nearly in ruins." The adjacent furnace was still making "pig metal and Ironware," with 468 tons of iron ore in inventory. The census taken noted that "none of the machinery is in operation." Also noted that "McClure does not know the amount of capital either in the forge or the furnace . . . the furnace is new but going to decay. Neither it nor the forge will be in operation after this year." A year earlier Halbert placed a notice in the local paper warning readers not to trade with fellow ironman Samuel Mc-Crory (q.v.). He contended that "McCrory is considerably indebted to me, and refuses to settle and adjust the said account." WL RHS; RCWB 3, 231; McClure; BVA 6/1/1891; CM 1820; LNL 5/29/1819; CM 1820.

McCLUNG, WILLIAM HENRY

Cabinetmaker. 1773 Timber Ridge, Va.–1846 Staunton, Va.. Active 1802–30. Received $6 for "making bookcase," "9 Square Tables," "2 Bedsteads, Turned post," and "5 Plain bedsteads," from Washington Academy in 1803. Between 1808 and 1811 purchased hats from the Lexington hatmaker John Ruff and paid his bill by making furniture—a bookcase, four bureaus, a walnut cupboard, and a candlestand. Apparently the same McClung who lived on "Poorhouse Farm" near Timber Ridge, served as a captain from

Rockbridge during the War of 1812, and was a trustee of Washington College from 1812 until 1830, when he moved to Staunton. WL Trustees,' 1803, 1804; Ruff, 26; Ruffner; McClung.

McCORKLE, HENRY

Cabinetmaker. Active c. 1830. Collierstown cabinetmaker and postmaster. RCN 3/20/1902.

McCORKLE (McCORCLE), JOHN

Carder. Active 1820. Listed in the 1820 *Census of Manufactures* as having a carding machine, one set of cards, and a picker. CM 1820.

McCORKLE, REBECCA McNUT

Needleworker. Active 1789. Wife of John McCorkle, Collierstown. Produced a signed and dated whitework coverlet.

McCORMICK, CYRUS HALL

Blacksmith, inventor, manufacturer. 1809 Rockbridge County, Va.–1884 Chicago, Ill. Born at Walnut Grove farm, near what is today Steeles Tavern. Son of Robert McCormick (q.v.). In 1831 at the age of twenty-two he took out a patent for a hillside plow. Inventor of the McCormick reaper. Hutchinson; Lyons.

McCORMICK, ROBERT

Furnace manager. Active 1835. In 1835 built with his son Cyrus McCormick (q.v.) a furnace four miles north of Vesuvius that they named Cotopaxi, after the volcano in Ecuador. Lyons.

McCOWN, JAMES LARUE

Photographer. 1845 Virginia–1922. Active 1870–80. Listed in the 1870 and 1880 censuses as a photographer in Lexington. C 1870, 1880; Driver.

McCOWN, JOHN

Blacksmith. 1785–1873 South River, Rockbridge County, Va. Active 1807–73. Was in business on the South River with his brother James (q.v.), 1807–8. Also produced iron. In 1820 reported that the forge on the South River had one tilt hammer "3 finer and 3 bellour" all going by water wheel, and was producing sickles, scythes, hoes, axes, and augers. Employed four men, including himself. When the McCormick reaper was first demonstrated, a number of defects contributed to its poor performance. According to local and family traditions, McCown was producing blades for McCormick's (q.v.) reapers and was responsible for solving a critical technical problem that resulted in the successful operation of the reaper. Ruff; CM 1820; BVA 6/26/1891; Lyons; C 1850, 1860, 1870.

McCOWN, SAMUEL

Weaver. 1764 Ireland–1853 Rockbridge County, Va. Active 1850. Listed in the 1850 census as a weaver living in the home of his son-in-law Seaborn Charlton, a Lexington house painter. C 1850; Couper 1960; LG 1/5/1854; RCDR 1, 2.

McCOY, JAMES M.

Cabinetmaker. b. 1823 Virginia. Active 1850. Included in the 1850 census listing of the Lexington cabinetmaker Mathew Kahle (q.v.). C 1850.

McCRORY, SAMUEL

Iron manufacturer. Active c. 1810–19? The *Buena Vista Advocate* reported in 1891 that "two or more brothers named McCrory" had an early furnace on Marl Run across the South River from the present ruin of Jordan's Buena Vista Furnace. Their location was said to have been "higher up the stream" from the site of Halbert McClure's (q.v.) furnace and forge. The furnace was known as the "Beverley," and attached to it was a foundry where "stoves and hollow ware were made." LNL 5/29/1819; BVA 6/26/1891.

McDOWELL, THOMAS PRESTON

Foundryman. 1810 Lexington–1867 Lexington? Active 1854–56. Ran the Rockbridge Foundry Works on Irish Creek in 1854 with Thomas Taylor (q.v.). Formerly operated by Edward Leyburn (q.v.) and William Leyburn (q.v.), the foundry manufactured "Cardwell's Horse-Powers and Threshers hill-side plows, iron axle-trees, cooking ranges," and other items. LG 8/31/1854; Morton; LG 9/28/1854.

McFARLAND, JAMES

Fuller. d. 1849. Active 1808–30. Advertised in the Fincastle *Herald of the Valley* in 1821 that he would attend "on the first day of every Court, at Mr. Neices in Fincastle, and at Mr. Issac Robinson's between that place and Pattonsburg, where I will receive and deliver cloth dressed according to the directions left with it. . . ." In 1825 offered a reward for information leading to the recovery of cloth taken from his fulling machine. The advertisement listed the following stolen items: fulled black cloth; black linsey; light drab cloth; yellow brown cloth; coarse dark drab cloth; home made plaid, colors red, blue, and green; London brown flannel for women's wear; London brown flannel tolerably coarse; snuff brown cloth; light drab cloth; and pale blue linsey. The 1820 *Census of Manufactures* reports that McFarland had a wool carding machine and fulling mill. Announced in 1830 that Obadiah Ayers (q.v.), an apprentice, had run away from the fulling business. Estate inventory in 1849 listed "1 Sett Wool Carding machine $400 in 1849." HV 10/15/1821; 10/15/1821; LI 12/16/1825; LI 9/25/1830; Darst; CM 1820; Morresset.

McGILVARY

Cabinetmaker. b. 1832 Virginia. Active 1857–60. Listed occupation in 1860. C 1860; Kirkpatrick 1988; Driver.

McGUFFIN, HUGH

Cabinetmaker. Active 1803–20. Advertised in 1803 for John Dinsmore (q.v.), an "indented apprentice to the Cabinet-Making business." VT 9/20/1803.

McMANNUS, GEORGE

Chairmaker. Active 1834. Noted in the shop ledger for the Lexington chairmaker Samuel Smith (q.v.) as boarding with Smith from May to July 1834. Credited with "framing 5 doz. Mortis back chairs," "1 settee," "1 doz. slat back chairs," "plaining & bending bows," and "framing rocking chair." SRS.

MERCER, GIDEON

Dyer. d. 1814. Active 1806–14. Advertised in 1806 that his mill, formerly occupied by James Davis, near Brownsburg, would dye cloth. VT 9/7/1806; RCWB 4, 68.

MILBERT, JACQUES GERARD

Artist. 1776 Paris, France–1840 Paris, France. Beginning in 1815, spent eight years in America documenting his travels for the Paris Museum. His account of the trip, *Itineraire Pittoresque* (2 vols. and portfolio, Paris, 1828–29), includes a description of Natural Bridge. An engraving of the bridge was published separately in 1828 and reprinted in 1837. Simpson 1982; Wright.

MILEY, HENRY

Photographer. b. Lexington, Va.–d. Lexington, Va. Son of the photographer Michael Miley (q.v.). Assisted his father in the operation of the Lexington studio. Simpson 1980; LG 12/9/1852.

MILEY, JOHN W.

Cabinetmaker. 1844 Rockingham County, Va.–1924. Active 1880–1910. Brother of the Lexington photographer Michael Miley (q.v.). Listed occupation in the 1910 census as an undertaker. Several furniture pieces, tools, and a work bench have descended in the family. C 1880, 1910; Driver; family interview; Kirkpatrick 1988.

JOHN McCOWN ANDIRON, *c. 1830. This andiron, found at Steeles Tavern, appears to be the mold used in making the sand imprint for the cast at one of the nearby furnaces, probably Vesuvius. 15 x 8½ inches.*

CHILD'S RATTLE, *by John Miley, late 1800s. Carved from a single piece of wood, this rattle shows the cabinetmaker's versatility. Walnut, 8 inches.*

MILEY, MICHAEL

Photographer. 1841 Rockingham County, Va.–1918 Lexington, Va. Active 1866–1918. Moved from Rockingham to the Fairfield area of Rockbridge as a youth, and during the Civil War served in Jackson's Stonewall Brigade. Began his photographic career with a Mr. Burdett in Staunton. Later worked for Andrew Plecker, a Lynchburg photographer. Opened a Lexington studio in 1866. Produced, with his son Henry, thousands of negatives from the late nineteenth century through the early decades of the twentieth century. Also recorded General Lee's last years in Lexington, in addition to copying the Washington, Custis, and Lee family pictures that were available. Photographed the Lee and Jackson statues and related memorial exercises. Known as "General Lee's photographer." Works are in the collections of VMI, Washington and Lee, the Rockbridge Historical Society, and the Virginia Historical Society. Numerous advertisements and announcements appear in the *Lexington Gazette* from 1874 to 1896. Simpson 1980.

MILLER, J.A.A.

Photographer. b. 1856 Rockbridge County, Va. Active 1889. Partner of Theodore Agnor (q.v.) in 1888. Announced the opening of his "first class gallery" in the Barkley Building, Lexington. LG 9/23/1888; LG 3/14/1889; Kirkpatrick 1985.

MILLER, LEWIS

Artist. 1796 York, Pa.–1882 Christiansburg, Va. Trained as a carpenter but produced more than 2,000 scenes of eastern America and Europe. Sketches made during visits to Virginia between 1846 and 1871 include nine scenes of Rockbridge County, now found in the Abby Aldrich Rockefeller Folk Art Center, Williamsburg, Va. Simpson 1982; Wright; Luck.

MITCHELL, JAMES

Carder. Active 1819. Announced in 1819 his "Carding Machine, at the Boat-Yard Mills, on the mouth of Buffaloe Creek." Requested that customers put less grease on their wool because "one pound of soft grease to every ten or twelve pounds of Wool is sufficient." LNL 6/19/1819.

MOORE, MARTHA

Needleworker. 1791–1851. Known as "Patsy." Produced a sampler dated 1804. Married William Moore Lusk in 1814 and lived in Rockbridge.

MOORE, SAMUEL

Furnace owner, forgeman. South River, Va.–Kentucky. Active c. 1785–1804. Apparently the brother of William Moore (q.v.) and in the furnace and forge business with him until 1804, when he sold his share of the business to Joseph Dilworth or Joseph Budd, his father-in-law, including "a forge, etc.," on Marys Creek. Chalkley; Diehl 1982.

MOORE, WILLIAM

Furnace owner, forgeman. 1758 South River, Va.–1841 Lexington, Va. Active 1784–1823. One of the earliest and most important iron men in Rockbridge. Appears to have begun in the early 1780s. One source says that he "furnished iron and cannon balls for the Continental army." Another source reports that he served in the Revolutionary army as a captain and participated in the Battle of Point Pleasant. Brother of Lexington's Gen. Andrew Moore and David Moore. In 1779 married Nancy McClung, the sister of David's wife. After the war became a merchant in Lexington but soon returned to South River to begin his iron business. For a period the operation was known as Nancy Furnace. In 1799 offered to sell all or half of his furnace and went out of the iron business temporarily around 1810. There is an 1806 reference to a 31-acre tract Moore was selling "adjoining the forge tract." In 1823 John Irvin, a trustee, advertised in the *Lexington Intelligencer* to sell the bulk of Moore's real estate, apparently to pay his debts. This included 1,000 acres at his residence near Fairfield; a 160-acre tract "adjoining the same and Matthew Shaw's land;" and the "Furnace tract on South River, containing 900 or 1,000 acres, about 150 of which are cleared." Among the personal property that was sold was "One still, a sett of blacksmith's tools, . . . and a number of patterns and flasks at the furnace." Two cast-iron firebacks, stamped "William and Samuel Moore" and dated 1789, have been documented. Kirkpatrick; Kiehl; LI 9/13/1806; LI 11/8/1823; LI 12/27/1823; LI 1/10/1824; BVA 6/26/1891; RHSP 5, 25; Bruce.

MORAN, JOHN

Artist. b. c. 1831 England. Came to the United States in 1844 with his brothers, Edward and Peter. All became known as painters and engravers. Visited Virginia in 1855 and produced a painting of Natural Bridge that is now in the collection of the Virginia Governor's Mansion in Richmond. Simpson 1982; Wright.

MORGAN, ALEXANDER P.

Cabinetmaker. Active 1853. Listed occupation in the 1853 county birth records. May be related to Morgan and Pippitt, early-nineteenth-century Staunton cabinetmakers, and to Gideon Morgan, also from Staunton. Kirkpatrick; MESDA.

MORGAN, HENRY E.

Potter. Active c. 1830–c. 1840s. Probably served as an apprentice to his father, John D. Morgan (q.v.), during the 1830s at Bustleburg, thereafter moving to help establish the Rockbridge Baths pottery about 1840. Russ 1990.

MORGAN, JOHN D. (OR S.)

Potter. b. 1768 New York. Active c. 1830–50. Involved in the New York pottery industry during the first decade of the nineteenth century. Moved to Rockbridge around 1830 and resided with John Firebaugh (q.v.) at Bustleburg, where he started a pottery. Probably assisted his son Henry E. Morgan (q.v.) in establishing Rockbridge Baths pottery around 1840. Russ 1900.

MORRIS, MINNIE

Artist. Active 1881. Won a certificate and premiums at the Rockbridge County Fair for oil paintings, watercolors, and crayon work in 1881 and 1882. Reported in 1884 as an art student at the Cooper Institute in New York. LG 1/9/1882; LG 11/24/1881; LG 10/26/1882; LG 3/13/1884; LG 10/16/1884.

MOSER, JAMES HENRY

Artist. 1854 Whitby, Ontario–1913 Washington, D.C. Came to the United States in 1865 and studied in New York and Washington. Exhibited a painting of Natural Bridge at the National Academy of Design in 1881. Wright.

MULLEN, THOMAS BRADLEY

Iron molder. 1839 Franklin County, Pa.–1885 Lexington, Va. Active 1847–84. The Lexington newspaper noted in 1878 the making of a new plow. Won an award at the Rockbridge County Fair for the "Mullen Plow." In 1880 reported that his shop employed three men and produced seventy-five plows that year in addition to various types of iron castings. In 1881 the local paper noted that Mullen "has repaired the iron fence around the Court House Square and it now presents a much better appearance than it has for some months past. Mr. Mullen did all the work at his foundry.

The castings look even better than those bought from the North." LG 6/7/1878; LG 11/1/1878; LG 7/17/1879; LG 7/28/1881; LG 7/27/1879; LG 10/23/1884; Couper 1960; Brock; CM 1880; C 1880.

MULLON, GORDON P.

Cabinetmaker. b. 1836 Virginia. Active 1880. Listed occupation in the 1880 census, Buffalo. C 1880.

NEAL, PATRICK

Weaver. Active 1801. Advertised for a "Journeyman Stocking-Weaver" in 1801 and that he was located on a "plantation near said town [Lexington]. . . . " RR 10/23/1801.

NEWKIRK, C. W.

Ironmaster. Active 1844. Assumed sole management of the Bath Iron Works in 1844. Previously was a business partner of William Weaver (q.v.). LG 11/28/1844.

NORRIS, JOHN

Blacksmith. 1817–92 Riverside, Va. Active 1831–92. A slave of John Jordan, was employed in the iron business on the South River as early as 1831. "Learned the blacksmith trade under the late John McCown" beginning in 1831. "He was industrious and a good workman, had built himself a nice little home, adorned it with fruits and flowers." BVA 1/5/1892.

PALMER, LEONARD S.

Cabinetmaker. 1815 Pennsylvania–1856 Lexington, Va. Active 1844–56. Living in Fincastle in 1841, married Mary Jane Wallace, daughter of James Wallace of Rockbridge. Announced the opening of his Lexington shop, a frame building behind the courthouse, in 1844. Later mentioned the addition of a "new and elegant Hearse" for his coffin-making business. In 1845 purchased a house and lot on Main Street formerly occupied by John T. Figgat, opposite Samuel Smith's (q.v.) chair factory. Provided VMI with thirty-six tables, thirty-two washstands, racket sticks, twenty-four rules, twenty-four triangles, and four blackboards in 1848. Purchased items related to his trade from the Lexington firm of Wilson and Barclay in 1844. Lexington merchant J. H. Myers's account book records Palmer's purchases in 1849: 1 dozen 2-inch butts, 1 desk lock, 4 dozen knobs, 1 turning chisel, 1/4 gross escutcheons, 1/2 gross plated screws, 1 super brace, 6 lbs nails, 4 dozen knobs, 1 tooth plane, 1 pair strap hinges. Cabinetmakers James F. Matheney (q.v.) and Harvey Patterson (q.v.) were included in his 1850 census listing. Personal property that year was reported at $2,800. Made a bookcase for the Franklin Society in 1855. In 1852–53 purchased from Wilson and Barclay a folding two-foot rule, a press lock, three wardrobe locks, three dozen till

Incised Bird Motif, c. 1830–50, attributed to John Morgan of the Bustleburg-Firebaugh pottery. This decoration is on the opposite side of the jar marked "Peaches."

locks, one dozen wardrobe hooks, three chisels, and a tack hammer. Obituary appeared in the *Lexington Gazette* in May 1856. The next month an announcement was made that the business was to continue "under the direction of an experienced workman." In October of that same year Milton H. Key (q.v.), also from Fincastle, advertised the purchase of Palmer's tools and fixtures. Probate listing included fifteen shares of stock in the Lexington Building Fund Association, valued at $405, and five shares in the Lexington Savings Institute, $140. Estate appraisers were D. L. Hopkins, Samuel Smith (q.v.), chairmaker, and John G. Pole, carpenter. C 1850; LG 11/25/1841; LG 2/22/1844; LG 11/14/1844; LG 1/23/1845; VMI Treasurer; LG 1/17/1856; LG 2/7/1856; LG 4/10/1856; LG 1/29/1857; WL RHS, Wilson and Barclay ledger; RCWB 14, 82–86; Myers; RCWB 14, 50–54; WL Franklin Society; Couper 1960; Kirkpatrick 1988.

PANTHER GAP FURNACE

Iron. Active 1878. In 1878 the *Lexington Gazette* mentioned that Panther Gap Furnace would soon go into blast under the management of Jordan, Echols and Company. Two years later the local paper reported that the "Central Iron Company will commence work shortly at the Panther Gap furnace." The paper also noted, "All through Virginia there seems to be an awakening to the importance of developing her resources, and the large amount of Northern capital being invested here will stimulate all business interests." LG 4/26/1878; LG 1/22/1880.

PARENT (PERENT?), ELY H.

Chairmaker. Active 1835–38. Listed in the shop ledger for the Lexington chairmaker Samuel Smith (q.v.), where he was credited for turning, painting chairs, and "framing" chairs and a settee. Probably related to Jacob Parent (q.v.), who also worked for Smith in 1844. Both might be related to the Augusta County cabinetmaker John Perent, who, according to the 1850 census, was thirty years old and born in Virginia. C 1850; SRS.

PARENT (PERENT?), JACOB

Turner. Active 1844. Shop ledger for the Lexington chairmaker Samuel Smith (q.v.) notes, "February 12, 1844 Jacob Parent commenced turning." During the next two months he is credited with turning 4,244 legs, "common elbow," "stretchers X," "stump elbows," "cane elbows," and "215 fancy legs." Probably related to Ely Parent (q.v.), who worked for Smith from 1835 to 1838, and John Perent, an Augusta County cabinetmaker listed in the 1850 census. C 1850; SRS.

PATTERSON, HARVEY

Cabinetmaker. 1830 Rockbridge County, Va. Active 1850–71. Included as a cabinetmaker in Leonard S. Palmer's (q.v.) 1850 census listing. Appears to have moved to Collierstown and established his own business. C 1850, 1860; RCMR 1A, 29; Kirkwood 1988; LG 12/13/1855.

PATTERSON, J. F., JR.

Cabinetmaker. b. 1830. Active 1851. Listed his occupation in the 1851 Lexington Oddfellows records. Oddfellows 1851.

PATTERSON, JOHN M.

Textile manufacturer. Active 1852–56. Advertised in 1852 for a boy to learn the wool manufacturing business. Mentioned in an 1856 advertisement by John L. Coleman (q.v.) for the sale of the Rockbridge Woolen Factory. *Census of Manufactures* of 1850 listed J. M. Patterson, who employed two male hands and produced 9,300 rolls of wool. A photograph by Michael Miley includes S.W. Haughawaute, Wm. Wallace ("Bigfoot"), and J. M. Patterson. LG 2/5/1852; LG 3/13/1856; LG 5/8/1856; CM 1850; Simpson 1980.

PATTERSON, SAMUEL

Carder. b. 1797 Virginia. Active 1847. Advertised in 1847 that his Brownsburg mill and carding machine had burned recently and that the machine was full of both carded and uncarded wool. Census listing for 1860 reports $25,000 real estate and $4,814 personal property. LG 7/22/1847; C 1860.

PATTON, BESSIE ANDERSON

Artist. 1870 Fairfield, Va.–1942 Fairfield, Va. Produced a number of paintings of local scenes.

PAXTON, JOHN W.

Clockmaker, jeweler. 1776 Lexington, Va.–1865 Danville, Va. Active 1815? Worked with Moses Whiteside (q.v.), the Lexington clockmaker and jeweler, for several years in Lexington before he married Sarah C. Price of Pittsylvania County, Va., in 1815 and moved to Danville to establish a jewelry business. VHS, Clayborne file; Paxton.

PAXTON, MADGE

Artist. Active 1894. Winner of the following awards at the 1884 Rockbridge County Fair, division of fine arts: diploma for best oil painting; $2 premium for "best specimen [of] lady handicraft;" and $5 premium for the "best exhibit of household manufacture utility and adornment considered." LG 9/18/1884.

PECK, S.

Cabinetmaker. Active 1823. John Ruff purchased one mahogany bureau and one set of circular dining tables from Peck for $52.40 in 1823. Ruff; Morresset.

PETTIGREW, ADA BOOZE

Quilter. Documented quilter from Rockbridge.

PETTIGREW, SAMUEL G.

Photographer. 1828 Virginia–1868 Lexington, Va. Announced his business in 1854 by inviting the public to the "Sky-Light Rooms" of his gallery. Asked, "What is more pleasant than a promenade around a Daguerrean Gallery where you can again look upon the faces of those who are now far distant and perhaps almost forgotten?" In 1856 advertised "Ambrotype or Vitrotype and Photographic Gallery." In 1857 was prepared to take pictures on "PATENT LEATHER." Executed a daguerreotype of Maj. Thomas J. (later "Stonewall") Jackson while he was a resident of Lexington. Listed in the 1860 census as a daguerreotypist with personal property valued at $3,000. C 1860; Driver; LG 3/2/1854; LG 1/3/1856; LG 11/26/1857; VS 7/3/1856; VS 3/4/1858; Couper 1960; Dooley; Kirkwood 1988.

PICKARD, J. D.

Photographer. Active 1847. Advertised "Daguerrotype Drawing" at his gallery in the Lexington Hotel, 1847. LG 11/25/1847.

PLATT, R.

Photographer. Active 1849. Advertised in 1849 that his daguerreotypes were "very superior to those taken by any former Artist in Lexington, and possess a lifelike beauty and brilliancy which cannot be excelled by any Artist in the Union. LG 10/16/1849.

PLECKER, ANDREW H.

Photographer. 1840 Rockingham County, Va.–1923 Richmond, Va. Came to Lynchburg from Botetourt County after the Civil War and practiced photography there until retirement in 1926. Operated Plecker's Mammoth Photograph Gallery in Salem, Va., and traveled with the Lexington photographer Michael Miley (q.v.). Sometimes credited with the famous photograph of Gen. Robert E. Lee mounted on his horse, Traveller, at Rockbridge Baths in 1866. Simpson 1980; Driver.

POINT CHAIR FACTORY

Chair manufacturer. Active 1888–91. Chair factory established in 1888 with J. W. Day (q.v.) as manager. See also Albert L. Koones.

POOL, D. L.

Ornamental painter. Active 1856. Business partner of G. A. Fisher. Advertised plain and ornamental painting in 1856. *Lexington Gazette* reported in 1884 that "Mr. D. L. Pool is painting a handsome drop curtain for the Deaver Opera House, Lexington. See also Pool and Fisher. LG 7/17/1856; LG 12/11/1884.

POOL AND FISHER

Ornamental painters. Active 1856. Pool and Fisher advertised in the *Valley Star* and *Lexington Gazette* in 1856 that one partner of the firm had served an apprenticeship at both plain and ornamental painting. See also D. L. Pool. VS 6/3/1856; LG 7/17/1856.

PORTER, VERLINDA ALEXANDER

Needleworker. 1793–1846. Married Reuben Grigsby (1780–1863) and moved from Orange County, Va., to Hickory Hill in Rockbridge. Documented whitework bedcover is in the collection of the Abby Aldrich Rockefeller Folk Art Center, Williamsburg, Va.

POTTER, DAVID

Chairmaker. b. 1800 Virginia. Active 1880. Listed as a Walkers Creek chairmaker in the 1880 census. C 1880.

RANKIN, R. J.

Photographer. Active 1850. Philadelphia daguerreotypist. Announced his services in Lexington in 1850 and advertised that his work would "far excel the finest PAINTING" yet was "equally as durable. The plates on which they are taken are of the finest FRENCH MANUFACTURE." Sittings for singles or groups were held at William Jordan's Hotel. LG 5/15/1850.

ROBERTS, WILLIAM

Artist. Came to Virginia about 1805 and created a view of Natural Bridge that was engraved in London in 1808 and later by others. May be the same William Roberts who presented paintings of Natural Bridge and Harpers Ferry to Thomas Jefferson. Simpson 1982; Wright.

ROBINSON, THOMAS (THOMAS RICKETTS)

Cabinetmaker apprentice. Active 1825. Ran away from the Lexington cabinetmaker Thomas Hopkins (q.v.) in 1825. LI 12/2/1825.

ROCK, JOHN J.

Cabinetmaker. b. 1832 Maryland. Active 1850. Listed in the 1850 household census for Francis J. Clemmer (q.v.), Walkers Creek area. C 1850.

ROCKWOOD, JAMES

Cabinetmaker. Active 1829–39. Newspaper reports damage to his Lexington shop in an 1829 fire. Advertised the next year to exchange cabinetwork for the services of a "Negro Man or Boy." Also noted his location as one door above the Eagle Tavern and that he would do turning for carpenters and others and called for two journeymen—"none need apply but good workmen." Provided Washington College in 1834 with a "Black board for Grammer School . . . 6 feet long and 4 wide" and in 1835 one "Large walnut Table with 2 drawers and 6 Legs" for $10. Expanded business activities in 1837 with the purchase of a Lexington blacksmith stand. Poor health caused him to hire a shop manager, the cabinetmaker Thomas G. Chittum (q.v.), in February 1838. Advertised in August for a journeyman cabinetmaker. In October Chittum announced the opening of his own shop. LI 3/26/1829; LI 8/28/1830; LI 12/11/1830; LG 5/26/1837; LG 2/2/1838; LG 8/10/1838; LG 7/20/1839.

RODENHIZER, JOHN

Foundryman. Active c. 1832–39. According to the *Buena Vista Advocate* of June 26, 1891, was Cyrus McCormick's (q.v.) foundryman at Cotopaxi Furnace, where they produced "castings for the successful reaper." BVA 6/26/1891.

ROOT, IVERSON J. L.

Cabinetmaker. b. 1845 Nelson County, Va. Active 1860–72. Listed in the 1850 census as a turning apprentice in the household of Frederick Kurtz (q.v.), a Lexington turner. Paid by Andrew Varner (q.v.) in 1860 and 1861 for turning items—100 bedpins, 160 bedpins, 200 bedpins, and sets of table legs. Occupation listed in 1870 census and 1871 Oddfellows records. C 1860, 1870; RCMR 1A, 67; Kirkwood 1988; Varner; Driver; Oddfellows 1871.

ROSEN, THOMAS MARTIN

Cabinetmaker, carpenter. 1845 Rockbridge County, Va.–1931 Augusta County, Va. Active 1860–1910. Walkers Creek carpenter, son of Jacob Rosen. C 1850, 1860, 1880, 1910; Driver; RCMR 1A, 235; Kirkwood 1988.

RUSK, G. W.

Cabinetmaker. b. 1801 Virginia. Active 1870. Occupation listed in the 1870 census, Walkers Creek. C 1870.

SEARIGHT, ALEX

Fuller. d. 1791 Rockbridge County, Va. Probate inventory (1791) lists tools related to the fulling trade. RCWB 1.

SECHRIST, J.

Cabinetmaker. b. 1849. Active 1871. Listed occupation in the Lexington Oddfellows records in 1871. Oddfellows 1871.

SEHORN, SARAH MILDRED WILLSON

Quilter. b. 1834. Married Lafayette Sehorn of Collierstown in 1865. Quilt pieces have descended in the family.

SENSENEY, AMOS ARCHIBALD

Cabinetmaker. b. 1829 Middletown, Frederick County, Va. Active 1857–91. Recorded in the Milton H. Key (q.v.) ledger as providing a variety of furniture pieces. From 1860 to 1862 he provided Andrew Varner (q.v.) with tables, bureaus, chairs, wardrobes, desk safes, cribs, and coffins. Also did turning for the shop, much of which was for VMI—rammers and sabots—as well as the usual banisters, newell posts, and table legs. Purchased "1 carving tool" at Andrew Elliot's (q.v.) estate sale in 1876. Listed occupation in the 1860–80 census records. C 1860, 1870, 1880; RCMR 1A, 48; Kirkwood 1988; RCWB 14, 202–205; Driver; LG 6/20/1889; LG 3/5/1891; Dooley; Dooley/Key; Varner.

SENSENEY, JAMES MADISON

Blacksmith. 1831 Middletown, Frederick County, Va.–1915 Lexington, Va. Active 1852–1910. Opened a blacksmith business in Lexington at "Middleton's old stand in 1852, Served as Justice of the Peace, harrier for General Lee's horse Traveller, and was known as the 'Singing Blacksmith.'" In 1867 was in partnership with another Lexington blacksmith, Andrew J. Brown (q.v.), and did business with Washington College. LG 4/34/1879; C 1860, 1880, 1910; LC; RCMR 2, 299; Driver; Oddfellows; Dooley; Hadsel; LG 7/22/1852; WL Withrow; WL Treasurer; LG 10/25/1878.

SHANKS AND ANDERSON

Iron. Active 1850. Operated by D. W. Shanks and Francis Anderson (q.v.). *Census of Manufactures* reports production of 700 tons in 1850, sixty-five employees, and property valued at $26,000. CM 1850; C 1850.

SHAW, DANIEL W.

Chairmaker. b. 1818 Virginia. Active 1854–80. Listed in the 1850 census as a miller, a millwright in 1860, and a chairmaker in 1880. Other records report him as a carpenter in 1854 and 1857, possibly in the Natural Bridge area. C 1850, 1860, 1880; Kirkpatrick 1988.

SHAW, LORENZO

Furnace owner. Active 1854. Following the death of partner Matthew Bryan (q.v.), advertised to sell "Valuable Iron Property and Farming lands in the Counties of Rockbridge and Augusta." Properties for sale included the Vesuvius Furnace. LG 10/12/1854.

SHELLY, SAMUEL

Chairmaker. Active 1835–37. Began boarding with the Lexington chairmaker Samuel Smith (q.v.) in December 1835 and assisted in the shop for the next year and a half. SRS.

SHERRARD, S.

Iron manufacturer. Active 1849–50. *Lexington Gazette* announced the sale of "all the remaining property formerly of S. Sherrard at Bath Iron Works" in 1849 and 1850. Items to be sold included two complete sets of blacksmith tools and a complete set of furnace tools, as well as "a large stock of Patterns and Flasks (many of them Iron), a number of castings, consisting of Hollow-ware, Stoves, Saw-Mill Irons. . . . " in addition to a "machine for washing ore. . . ." See also S.A.F. Sherrard. LG 11/20/1849; LG 1/24/1850.

SHERRARD, S.A.F.

Artist. Active 1851–55. Advertised in the *Lexington Gazette* in 1850 and 1851 as an oil portrait painter. Lexington newspaper reported in 1850 that an "opportunity is now afforded to the public to have portraits and landscape sketches taken, of a most superior quality, by Mrs. S. A. F. Sherrard, artist, at the Washington Hotel." In 1855 Sherrard, the wife of S. Sherrard (q.v.), received a prize for a painting at the Mechanics Institute fair in Richmond. LG 11/21/1850; LG 2/20/1851; Wright.

SIMMS, SAMUEL R.

Textile manufacturer. Active 1824. Advertised in 1824 that "A situation is wanted," either in Augusta, Rockbridge, or Botetourt County to establish a wool factory. Asked for a set of operating carding machines in a thriving neighborhood and promised to add a "SPINNING APPARATUS." Winchester address given. LI 7/18/1824.

SKEENS, ROBERT

Forgeman. Active 1820. Ran a tilt-hammer operation on Buffalo Creek. CM 1820; Ruff.

SLAGLE, SUSAN J.

Artist. Active 1857. Trained in Paris, and later while residing in Lynchburg advertised in the *Lexington Gazette* (1857) that she would teach drawing and painting. Classes, $10 for ten lessons, would be from nine to twelve o'clock for "Ladies" and three to six o'clock for "Gentlemen." The announcement closed with an endorsement from Adolphus Ernett that was "to certify that Miss Susan J. Slagle was my pupil" and "has attained remarkable proficiency in the art of drawing and painting by my process." LG 7/9/1857; LG 7/16/1857; Wright.

SLOSS, ROBERT

Dyer. Active 1803. Advertised in 1803 that he would dye wool, cotton, and linen deep blue or half blue. RR 12/29/1803.

SMELLIE, JAMES

Artist. b. 1807 Edinburgh, Scotland–d. 1885 Poughkeepsie, N.Y. Associate member of the National Academy of Design, 1832–52, and member, 1853–85. Member of the New York engraving firm of Rawdon, Wright, Hatch, and Smellie, which produced the first VMI diploma in 1842. In 1836 published an engraving of West Point based on a painting by Robert Walker Weir (1803–89), professor of drawing at West Point. Francis H. Smith was a pupil of Weir's, and later, as VMI superintendent, asked Weir to design the institute's first diploma. Smellie's sister married the artist Robert Hinshelwood (q.v.), who produced a print of Natural Bridge. Also did banknote engravings and became well known for his steel engravings; the most famous was Thomas Cole's *Voyage of Life* series. Couper; Cowdrey; Simpson 1982.

SMILEY, T. H.

Photographer. Active 1844. Trained in New York and resided in Staunton, made several trips to Lexington in 1843–44 to produce "Photographic Miniature Portraits," which he displayed at the courthouse. LG 11/16/1843; LG 11/23/1843; LG 1/4/1844.

SMITH, JOHN

Cabinetmaker, clockcase maker. d. c. 1819 Lexington, Va. Active c. 1790–1819. Advertised for two boys "from 15 to 17 years of age, to learn the Cabinet Making Business" in May 1819. Obituary that same year referred to an illness of two months, his "young and amiable wife," and his military associations. Probate listed "1 lot cabinet makers tools—$86.00" in addition to a turning lathe, an unfinished secretary, a small poplar desk, sets of bedpost, four work benches and various types of wood, such as walnut, poplar, and cherry. One entry noted items—screws and chisels—as being the "property of T. Hopkins" (q.v.), another Lexington cabinetmaker. LNL 5/8/1819; LNL 8/28/1819; RCWB 5, 14, 15.

SMITH, HANSFORD BERNARD

Molder. 1883 Spottswood, Augusta County, Va.–1931 Charlottesville, Va. Active c. 1900. Worked under William S. Humphries (q.v.); molded cast-iron lions and frogs. Interview with Smith's daughter, Mrs. James W. Crawford of Vesuvius, 1990.

SMITH, SAMUEL RUNKLE

Chairmaker. 1788 Pendleton County, Va. (now W. Va.)–1869 Greensboro, N.C. Active 1819–60. Son of Heinrich Schmidt, who was born in Germany in 1755 and came to America in 1778. Family records note Henry took an oath to the new government in Lancaster, Pa., in 1783. His father died in 1796, and the children were raised by the mother in Augusta County. Served in the army during the War of 1812. Purchased a lot in Lexington from the saddler Jacob Fuller. In 1878 married Fuller's daughter Margaret, a greatgranddaughter of the Rockbridge settler John Peter Salling. Son Alphonso was editor of the *Lexington Gazette,* and Jacob Henry was president of Washington College. Announced a public auction of chairs in 1819. Later was in partnership with Mathew Kahle (q.v.). Smith and Kahle offered to buy "a thousand feet of curled maple plank and scantlings" in 1824. Also advertised furniture offered by the firm plus a "supply of mahogany of the first quality with which they would manufacture cabinet furniture." Advertised his own business "one door above Mr. Haughawought's Tavern" in 1826. Announced the sale of chairs and settees and a few pieces of "elegant CABINET WORK." Kahle, in a separate notice, gave the same address but with no mention of the partnership. Apprenticed William G. Hall (q.v.) in 1828. Provided Washington College with a half dozen chairs for $7 and "1 Writing chair" for $5 in 1835. Offered fancy Windsor chairs, cane chairs, and Grecian and slat-back cane settees and to "repaint and ornament every kind of work in his line of business" in 1836. Referred to his business as the "Chair Factory" in 1838. Reminded the public in 1844 and 1847 that he would also paint, varnish, and repair chairs. Presented the Episcopal church with four chairs for the vestry room in 1844. Purchases are recorded in Myers's hardware store in 1849. Advertisements for the early 1850s indicated importation of northern chairs plus "Common and Windsor chairs of his own manufacture." Offerings in 1853 included rosewood chairs of square and round fronts, maple O.G., cane, stained light maple, harp, cane-back, walnut O.G., stained walnut ,and roll-top rush-bottom chairs. Reminded the public in 1853 that he was below the Central Hotel and the next year that he was located in the house "immediately below the Capital Hotel." Reminded the public that he still continued the "Manufacture of Chairs at his old and well-known stand" in 1855. Announcements for 1855, 1857, and 1858 included mentions of "city work" in addition to his own, and in 1859 the addition of bedsteads. Census for 1850 notes Smith's personal property at $1,800 and in 1860 his real estate at $1,200. C 1850, 1860; Dooley; LNL 10/9/1819; LI 5/22/1824; LI 10/30/1824; LI 5/27/1825; LI 1/6/1826; LI 3/2/1826; RCWB 6, 248; WL Trustees' 1835; LG 6/10/1836; LG 4/29/1838; LG 4/18/1844; R. E. Lee Episcopal Church Property Records 1844/51; Myers; LG 5/9/1850; LG 7/4/1850; LG 10/6/1853; LG 7/13/1854; LG 11/8/1855; LG 3/26/1857; VS 5/27/1858; LG 11/17/1857; family interview.

SNIDER, JOHN NELSON

Artist. Active 1819. Editor of the *Lexington News-Letter.* Announced in September 1819 that he had "visited the *Natural Bridge,* and took a sketch of it, which he has had engraved, and now presents it to his readers, accompanied with a description, that has been pronounced, by all who have ever seen this grand natural curiosity, to be strictly correct." Snider's sketch may have been engraved by the artist Samuel Anness (q.v.). LNL 8/17/1819; LNL 9/18/1819.

SNYDER, W. P.

Artist. Engraving of Natural Bridge was published in *Harper's Weekly* on September 8, 1888. Simpson 1982; Wright.

SPEAR (SPEER), JOHN

Stonemason. Active 1797. References to John Spear (or Speer) appear in the Augusta County court records in the 1740s and 1750s. Probably the same Spear who was responsible for the stonework of Zachariah (or Zechariah) Johnston's 1797 Rockbridge residence. Carved his name and "1797" into a large stone in the gable end of the house. Johnston came to the Lexington area from around Staunton and could have brought the stonemason Spear with him. Could also be the same John Spear who married Mary Hashbarger, February 21, 1792, at New Providence Church, with John Brown officiating. Spear is also mentioned in an 1801 "surety bond" in Augusta County. Chalkley; Kirkpatrick 1985; Lyle and Simpson.

SPENCE, JOHN

Weaver. Active 1803. Advertised in 1803 for a runaway apprentice, John Holansworth (q.v.). VT 4/26/1803.

STONE SIGNATURE, *John Spear,*
1797. Stonemason Spear carved
his imprimatur in a large, shaped
stone located in the gable of the
Zachariah (variously Zechariah)
Johnston house near Lexington.

STRATTON, RICHARD H.

Iron manufacturer. Active 1852–56. Advertised in 1852 that "the best plough now made in this country" was manufactured at the Lexington Foundry at Jordan's Point. Advertised the sale of property at Jordan's Point belonging to the firm of Jordan and Stratton in 1856. LG 8/26/1852; LG 10/6/1853; LG 1/24/1856.

STRICKLAND, WILLIAM

Artist. English artist. Toured the United States in 1795 and included sketches of Natural Bridge in his *Journal of a Tour in the United States of America* (London, 1796). Wright.

**SVININ, PAVEL
PETROVITCH**

Artist. Russian artist. Studied at the Academy of Fine Arts in St. Petersburg. Later, as secretary to the Russian consul-general in America, traveled to Virginia and painted Natural Bridge. On returning to Russia, published *A Picturesque Voyage in North America.* Simpson 1982; Wright.

SWEET, JAMES J.

Cabinetmaker. b. 1848 Rockbridge County, Va. Active 1868. Occupation listed in 1868 marriage records. RCMR 1A, 183.

SWINK, JAMES

Photographer. b. 1836 Augusta County, Va. Active 1860. Listed occupation in the 1860 census. Later moved to Missouri. C 1860; Driver.

SWINK, JOHN H.

Textile manufacturer. b. 1840 Rockbridge County, Va. Active 1864–70. Exempt from service in 1864 because he was manufacturing wool cloth on Whistle Creek. Reported in 1865 marriage records as a woolen manufacturer and 1870 birth records as "factory boss." Listed in the 1870 census as a woolen factory worker. C 1870; RCMR 1A, 122; Kirkpatrick 1988; Driver.

TANNER, N. S.

Photographer. Active 1850. Advertised his Lexington "DAGURREAN GALLERY" and "Dagurrean Rooms" twice in 1850. Claimed that his work was "as good as can be taken in the Eastern cities" and that it "will NEVER FADE." Also offered "Portraits of deceased persons copied accurately." LG 9/26/1850; LG 10/10/1850.

**TATE, DRUSILLA
DE LA FAYETTE**

Needleworker. Produced a needlework picture dated 1802. Lived in both Augusta and Rockbridge Counties.

TAYLOR, JAMES McDOWELL

Foundry owner. 1813 Rockbridge County, Va.–1888 Lexington, Va. Active 1858–60. Attended Washington College, 1835–36, and was a member of the Virginia legislature, 1853–55 and 1865–67. Formed a partnership in 1858 with John McD. Humphries (q.v.) to run the Rockbridge Foundry and Machine Works on Irish Creek. A cast-iron gate on the enclosed Alexander plot in the Lexington cemetery has a plaque marked "Taylor & Humphries, 1860." LG 6/10/1858; WL Alumni; Driver.

TAYLOR, THOMAS BENTON

Foundry worker. Active 1854–56. Member of the Washington College class of 1853–54. Operated the Rockbridge Foundry with Thomas McDowell (q.v.), 1854 to 1856, on the south side of Irish Creek, about a half mile above the confluence with the South River. Business partner briefly with his brother James Taylor (q.v.). By 1870 he was practicing law in Lexington and later became commonwealth's attorney. Eventually lived in St. Louis and Fulton, Mo. Morton; LG 9/28/1854, LG 11/29/1855, LG 7/10/1856; Driver.

TEAFORD, GEORGE C.

Photographer. 1840 Augusta County, Va.–1921 Augusta County, Va. Active 1876. Listed occupation in 1876 birth records. Kirkpatrick 1988; C 1870; Driver.

TEDFORD, ALEXANDER

Gunsmith, gunstocker. d. 1781. Active c. 1781. Rockbridge County resident killed during the Battle of Guilford Court House, N.C. Estate appraisal in 1781 included "1 Coopers adze 17/10, 1 Hammer and Pinchers 14/, 1 Cutting Knife and Steel 10/, The whole of the Gun Stocking Tools 110/, 1 Bible and sermon book 31/, 1 Drawing knife 7/10, 1 Saw 20/." Gill; RCWB 1, 119.

TERRILL, HENRY L.

Cabinetmaker. 1834 Augusta County, Va.–1895 Brownsburg, Va. Active 1861–95. Listed as working in Staunton in 1860 and Brownsburg in 1870. C 1860, 1870; Kirkpatrick 1988; Driver.

THOMAS, JOHN

Cabinetmaker apprentice. b. c. 1826. Active 1842. Ran away from Thomas Chittum (q.v.) of Lexington, in 1842. LG 4/7/1842.

TRAINER, BARNER

Cabinetmaker. b. 1834 Virginia. Active 1850. Included as a cabinetmaker in the 1850 census household listing of the Lexington saddler George W. Adams. C 1850.

TURNER, RICHARD

Gunsmith. b. 1830. Active 1879–80. Listed in the Walkers Creek area in the 1880 census. C 1880; RCMR 1A, 375.

TUTWILER, ELI SHORER

Textile manufacturer. 1826 Fluvanna County, Va.–1891 Lexington, Va. Active 1855. Advertised in 1855 as business partner of the woolen manufacturer John L. Coleman (q.v.) at Rockbridge Woolen Factory, Whistle Creek. LG 4/5/1855/ Driver.

VALENTINE, EDWARD VIRGINIUS

Artist. 1838 Richmond, Va.–1930 Richmond, Va. Studied anatomy at the Medical College of Virginia and drawing with William Hubard (q.v.). From 1859 to 1865 studied in London, Paris, and Italy, and with August Kiss in Berlin. Returned to Richmond after the Civil War and opened a studio. Lexington works include the recumbent statue of Gen. Robert E. Lee in Lee Chapel and the Jackson statue in the town's cemetery. Also produced the bronze statue of Jefferson Davis atop the Davis monument on Monument Avenue, Richmond. Simpson 1977, Wright; LG 4/4/1879; LG 4/13/1882; 8/17/1882; LG 11/23/1882; LG 2/7/1880; LG 7/11/1889.

VARNER, ANDREW WALLACE

Cabinetmaker. 1831 Lexington, Va.–1910 Lexington, Va. Active 1850–85. Brother of Charles Van Buren Varner (q.v.) and son of Charles Varner (q.v.), a Lexington hatmaker. Listed in 1850 as a carpenter in the household of John G. Pole, a Lexington carpenter with whom he later formed a partnership. In 1860 also listed as a carpenter but in the household of John Boude (q.v.). His brother-in-law, John McCaul (q.v.), who "works at cabinetmaking," was listed in Varner's household in 1880. Lost an arm in the Civil War but returned to Lexington and continued the furniture-making business. Shop ledgers survive and document activities 1860–61 and 1887–89. Ledgers indicate the following individuals employed: William Charlton (q.v.), James Larew, Andrew D. L. Elliot (q.v.), Amos Senseney (q.v.), Frederick Kurtz (q.v.), John Boude (q.v.), James Knick (q.v.), and Iverson Root (q.v.). Activities recorded in the ledger reflected current community events.

For instance, in July 1864 Varner was hired by the city of Lexington for a coffin for a "Yankee Soldier" who had presumably died during General Hunter's raid on Lexington that same month. Also hired by Nathan G. Moore to remove "sons body from battlefield. . . . Four days going and coming . . . $20.00." Several pieces attributed to the Varner shop, including a table owned by Robert E. Lee, have been documented. Both Washington College and VMI ordered furniture from Varner. Lee ordered ten tables for the school in 1867. Listed as a member of the Oddfellows in 1864. Sister Rebecca married the cabinetmaker Milton H. Key (q.v.). After Key's death in 1860 Varner advertised in 1862 that he was operating as "agent for Mrs. Key." Member of the Franklin Society and postmaster in 1885. House and shop are next to the current Trinity Methodist Church. C 1850, 1860, 1870, 1880; RCMR 1A, 181; Kirkpatrick 1988; LG 9/14/1882; Couper 1960; Driver; Dooley; WL Special collections, Lee papers 11/16/1867; Oddfellows 1864; WL Franklin Society.

VARNER, CHARLES

Hatmaker. b. 1796 Virginia. Active 1830–50. Operated a hatmaking business in Lexington. Father of the Lexington cabinetmakers Charles Van Buren Varner (q.v.) and Andrew Varner (q.v.). LI 10/23/1830; C 1850; RCWB 7, 80; Driver; Oddfellows 1860; Dooley; Kirkwood 1988.

VARNER, CHARLES VAN BUREN

Cabinetmaker. 1838 Lexington, Va.–1907. Active 1860–80. Brother of Andrew Varner (q.v.) and son of the Lexington hatter Charles Varner (q.v.). Listed in the census as a Lexington carpenter in 1860, a cabinetmaker in 1870, and a carpenter again in 1880. Included in the listing of cabinetmaker John Boude (q.v.) in 1860. Credited for work in the 1857–69 ledger of cabinetmaker Milton H. Key (q.v.). C 1860, 1870, 1880; Couper 1960; RCMR 1A, 87; Kirkpatrick 1988; Driver; Dooley; Oddfellows 1864; Dooley/Key.

VOLCK, ADALBERT JOHANN

Artist. 1828 Augsburg, Bavaria–1912 Baltimore, Md. Dentist and chemistry instructor from Baltimore who produced political cartoons in support of the Southern cause during the Civil War. Painting of Robert E. Lee, executed in Lee's office at Washington College, is in the collection of the Valentine Museum, Richmond. Brother of Frederick Volck (q.v.). Wright.

VOLCK, FREDERICK

Artist. 1822 Bavaria–1891. Brother of the artist Adalbert Volck (q.v.). During the Civil War worked in naval ordinance under Capt. John Mercer Brooke, who became a VMI professor after the war and was probably instrumental in arranging for Volck to make a life mask of Robert E. Lee. In 1866 Volck visited Lexington and made the mask and bust. The bust, cast in bronze in 1895, is in the collections of Washington and Lee University. Also created an equestrian statuette of Lee given to VMI. Commissioned in 1863 to execute a bronze equestrian statue of Stonewall Jackson for the VMI campus. Abandoned the project after two years work because of the institute's postwar financial straits. Made the death mask of Stonewall Jackson while the body lay in state in Richmond during May 1863. Used the mask to make two busts of Jackson—one in the Virginia State Library and another in the Confederate Museum, Richmond. Created the statue of Jackson in Lexington's Stonewall Jackson Cemetery in 1888–89. Also planned to create another equestrian statue of Jackson, but the project failed and he sold the mask to the Richmond sculptor Edward Valentine (q.v.). Wright; Couper 1939; Simpson 1977.

WALKER, JOHN

Gunsmith (gunstocker). Active 1796. This John Walker had land that adjoined the property of the gunsmith John Walker (1). Gill.

WALKER, JOHN (1)

Gunsmith. Active 1796. Described as a gunsmith when he received a land grant in Rockbridge County in 1796. Land adjoined that of another John Walker designated as a gunstocker. Gill.

WALKER, JOHN (2)

Gunsmith. d. 1794 Rockbridge County, Va. Active c. 1794. Estate inventory, December 12, 1794, included "One Smith Anvill," "One smith's Vice," "riffle Guide," and a "Plain for plaining Gun Barels." Gill; RCWB 1, 470–71.

WALKER, JOHN (3)

Gunsmith, blacksmith. Active 1788–95. He may have been a fourth John Walker, a Rockbridge gunsmith whose day book (1788–95) has been preserved in the Wisconsin State Historical Society. Active a year after John Walker (2) died.

WALL, J.

Spinning-wheel maker apprentice. Active 1787. Indentured as a woolwright and spinning-wheel maker to James Lackey (q.v.), December 27, 1787. WL RHS Misc. papers.

WALL, WILLIAM GUY

Artist. 1792 Dublin, Ireland–after 1864 Dublin. Visited America in 1818 and again in 1856–62. Produced a painting of Natural Bridge. Cowdrey; Wright.

WALLACE, ANDERSON

Cabinetmaker. d. c. 1829. Active before 1829. Occupation listed in court records. RCWB 6, 271.

WALLACE, SAMUEL

Carpenter. Active 1780. Paid by the county in 1780 for two days' work for "making benches for the use of the county." Also built a county prison. RBOB 1, 82, 177.

WARD, JACOB C.

Artist. 1801 Bloomfield, N.J.–1891 Bloomfield, N.J. Worked mainly in New York and New Jersey. Lewis P. Clover, Sr., lent Ward's painting of Natural Bridge to the American Academy of Design in 1835. Clover also published William Bennett's (q.v.) engraving of Ward's painting. See also Lewis P. Clover, Jr. Cowdrey; Simpson 1982; Wright.

WARD, M. HOUSTON

Artist. b. 1863. Active 1887. Oddfellows records for 1887 record Ward as an artist. Oddfellows 1887.

WASH, MARTHA

Textile worker. b. 1840 Virginia. Active 1880. Listed along with her brother Thomas Wash (q.v.) as working in a "woolen factory" in Kerrs Creek for the 1880 census. C 1880.

WASH, THOMAS HENRY

Textile manufacturer. 1836 Rockbridge County, Va.–1891 Rockbridge County, Va. Active 1880. Overseer for the canal in 1860. Listed as a "woolen factory" worker in the 1880 census. C 1880.

WASHINGTON, GEORGE

Blacksmith. b. 1837 Virginia. Active 1870–78. Listed as a mulatto in the 1870 census. Possibly the same George Washington who won a premium for horseshoes and nails at the Rockbridge County Fair in the fall of 1878. LG 2/22/1878.

WASHINGTON, WILLIAM D.

Artist. 1833 Clarke County, Va.–1870 Lexington, Va. Active 1869–70. Studied in Philadelphia and Düsseldorf and worked in Washington, D.C., from 1855 to 1860. Appointed professor of fine arts at VMI in 1869. Produced at least twenty paintings, principally portraits and landscapes of VMI and the Lexington countryside. Best-known painting is *The Burial of Latané*, which was subse-

quently engraved by John Gadsby Chapman (1808–89) and widely circulated. Wright; Couper 1939; Driver; Couper 1960; RCDR 100, 42.

WATTS, JAMES H.

Furniture manufacturer. Active 1878. Business partner of Charles Jordan (q.v.) in the Buena Vista Chair and Furniture Factory. Sold his share in the business to J. M. Jordan (q.v.) in 1878. LG 4/26/1878; LG 7/12/1878.

WEAVER, WILLIAM

Iron manufacturer. 1781 Pennsylvania–1863 Rockbridge County, Va. Active 1820–63. Financial partner in the Buffalo Forge operation run by Thomas Mayburry (q.v.). *Census of Manufactures* reports that in 1820 they ran a forge with twenty employees and two trip-hammers and their principal product was bar iron. Came to Virginia in 1823 and took over the direction of the forge operation and dissolved the partnership with Mayburry. Acquired additional iron properties including the Retreat furnaces in Botetourt County and the Bath Iron Works at the upper end of Goshen Pass. At Buffalo Forge, in addition to the farm and the forge buildings, there were two mills, a harness shop, blacksmith shop, carpenter shop, ice house, office building, dairy, carriage house, company store, saw mill, and one thousand acres of land. CM 1820; Brady 1979, 1989; RHSP 8, 55; NG 5/6/1852.

WEIR, ADOLPHUS

Blacksmith. Active 1790–1806. Shop ledger survives and notes that he made a "plough shovel" for John Davidson (q.v.) in 1791 and for the clockmaker Thomas Whiteside (q.v.) a "laying Spoon punch" and "mending square" in 1793. Adolphus Weir's ledger (1790–1806), Swem Library, William and Mary College.

WELCH, BELINDA, JOSEPH, AND SAMUEL

Textiles workers. Active 1880. Worked in Robert Brown's (q.v.) Rockbridge Woolen Factory. C 1880.

WELD, ISAAC

Artist. 1774 Dublin, Ireland–1856 Ravenswell, Ireland. Traveled in the United States and Canada for approximately three years starting in 1795. Drawing of Natural Bridge was published in 1798 in *Travels through the State of North America* (London, 1799). Simpson 1982; Wright.

WELSH, NANCY CHRISTIAN

Needleworker. Active 1818. Produced two whitework embroidery pieces that are in the collection of the National Museum of American History, Smithsonian Institution.

WHITE, AGNES

Artist. Active 1882–84. Commended at the 1882 Rockbridge County Fair for "two lovely Oil paintings. . . . " LG 10/26/1882; LG 9/18/1884.

WHITE, ISAAC N.

Photographer. b. 1832 Virginia. Active 1867–70. Listed as a Lexington photographer in the 1867 Oddfellows records and the 1870 census. Oddfellows 1867; C 1870.

WHITESIDE, JOHN M.

Gunsmith, axmaker. b. Rockbridge County, Va–d. Washington County, Va. *The Kentucky Rifle* (1925), by John G. W. Dillin, gives a lengthy account of John M. Whiteside's "factory" in King's Mill, near Abington in Washington County. Married Hannah Karlin of Rockbridge in 1830. Probably left about that time to settle in southwestern Virginia, where he soon headed a substantial rifle-making production. Apprentice Milton Warren left a detailed description of the barrel- and stock-making processes and every other facet of the operation. Dillon.

WHITESIDE, MOSES I

Gunsmith, silversmith. 1725 Pennsylvania?–1795 Rockbridge County, Va. Active c. 1795. One of the early settlers on Borden's Grant, acquiring property about 1750. Father of Thomas Whiteside (q.v.) and Moses Whiteside II. A number of references to Moses Whiteside's early land ownership in the Rockbridge area are available. ACDB 6, 222; Chalkley.

WHITESIDE, SAMUEL C.

Clockmaker. Active 1815–c. 1833. Probably the son of the Staunton clockmaker Samuel Whiteside. Active in Lexington from about 1815 to 1833, apparently working in the family's shop. Later, probably in the late 1830s, moved to Fincastle and by 1845 had established himself there in the silversmith and jewelry business. Probably the nephew of Thomas Whiteside (q.v.) and Moses Whiteside (q.v.). Cutten; Niederer; Ruff, 287.

WHITESIDE, THOMAS

Clockmaker. c. 1760 Timber Ridge, Va.–after 1820 Kanahwa County, Va. (later W. Va.) Active c. 1790–c. 1819. Probably opened his Lexington shop before 1790. Bought one of the original lots in 1780. A 1793 reference in the Mackey family papers records Whiteside helping appraise a watch belonging to Mary Mackey. Also listed in a 1794 Lexington store ledger of J. and D. Hoffman and Company (Swem Library, William and Mary College). Whiteside's name and "Lexington clockmaker" appear on the brass dial of a clock he made for Samuel Lyle (q.v.), a neighbor on Timber Ridge. This is apparently the same clock that is listed in Samuel Lyle's estate inventory in 1796. Only known clockmaking operation active in Rockbridge in the 1790s. Advertised in the *Virginia Telegraph* in 1803: "Apprentices Wanted. Two lads, from 12 to 16 years of age, will be taken, if offered immediately, as apprentices to the clock, Watch, and Silver-smith business. Good encouragement will be given. Thomas Whiteside." Gave his address in this notice as "Red House," which was a prominent county residence on the Valley Road several miles north of the Timber Ridge community and near the newly established village of Fairfield. By 1820 had moved to Kanahwa County, Va. C 1820; VT 7/9/1803.

WILLIAMS, SAM ("ETNA")

Iron forgeman (slave). b. 1820. Active 1837–67. William Weaver (q.v.) bought Williams when he took possession of Etna Furnace in Botetourt County in 1837. Williams worked his way up to become a master forgeman at Weaver's Buffalo Forge through the Civil War and until the forge shut down in 1867. Dew 1994.

WILLIAMSON, THOMAS HOOMES

Architect, artist. 1813–88 Lexington, Va. Active 1841–87. Hired in 1841 to serve as professor of engineering, architecture, and drawing at VMI. Also listed as a part-time professor of engineering and drawing at Washington College in 1842. Advertisement by the Ann Smith Academy, 1843, offered "Drawing and Painting, including sketching from Nature," to be taught by Williamson. Advertised in 1844 to "furnish plans for buildings of all descriptions, private dwellings, churches and other public edifices, as well as bridges, and such other constructions as come under the head of Civil Engineer." Credited with the design of Lee Chapel and the tower on Washington and Lee University's Main Hall, which supports Mathew Kahle's (q.v.) statue of George Washington. Couper 1939; Wright; Lyle and Simpson; LG 9/23/1841; LG 7/7/1842; LG 7/28/1842; LG 6/22/1843; LG 3/21/1844; LG 4/24/1844; LG 10/23/1879; Couper 1960.

WHITEWORK TABLE COVER, *by Nancy Christian Welsh, 1818. This cover is one of two extant pieces by Welsh. 28 x 44 inches.*

WILSON, DAVID STEELE

Chairmaker. b. 1807 Virginia. Active 1850–55. Listed occupation in the 1850 census. C 1850; Kirkpatrick 1988.

WILSON, JAMES

Chairmaker. Active 1825. Listed occupation in the county property books. RCPB 1825, 251.

WILSON, JAMES P.

Chairmaker. b. 1802 Virginia. Active 1850. Listed in the 1850 census as a chairmaker and in 1860 as a mechanic. May be related to David Wilson (q.v.), another chairmaker. C 1850, 1860.

WILSON, WILLIAM

Furnaceman, forgeman. d. c. 1823. Active 1806–14. Established Union Forge near the mouth of Buffalo Creek around 1811. May have had an earlier operation in the same area. Sold his operation to Thomas Mayburry (q.v.) and William Weaver (q.v.) They later changed the name to Buffalo Forge. VT 9/13/1806; LNL 7/31/1819; RHSP 8, 53; Dew 1994; Brady 1979, 1989.

WRIGHT, BLANCHE GILKERSON

Quilter. Active c. 1890s. A number of her quilts were documented for this study and remain in her family.

YARNELL, WILLIAM

Photographer. Active 1851. Advertised his partnership with N. S. Tanner (q.v.) in Lexington, 1851. LG 11/6/1851.

YOUNG, GEORGE A.

Artist. Active 1847. In 1847 advertised his "new and beautiful system of monochromatic painting" to the "Ladies and Gentlemen of Lexington." Offered to teach a few "general principles" in a few lessons as well as to "go into the fields with crayon and paper, and delineate the beautiful views he sees around him." Boarded at "Mr. Norgrove's Boarding House." LG 9/2/1847.

ZOLLMAN, WILLIAM

Gunsmith. c. 1785 Rockbridge County, Va.–1834 Rockbridge County, Va. Active c. 1814–c. 1834. Married Ann Ripley of Fincastle in 1808. Purchased land on Buffalo Creek at the north end of Short Hill, where he "developed a very fine gunsmith shop, a carding mill, and a distillery" (George W. Diehl, *The Zollmans and Their Kin*, 1968). "Zollmans Mill" became a place name in the county. His son Henry Zollman inherited the gunsmithing business. Five rifles signed or attributed to William Zollman have been documented. WL Withrow 1, 2; Kirkpatrick 1988.

Notes

INTRODUCTION

1. Oren Morton, *History of Rockbridge County, Virginia* (Staunton, Va.: McClure Press, 1920).

2. Laura Moore Stearns, "First Years and First Families: Rockbridge County, 1734–1745," *Rockbridge Historical Society Proceedings* 10 (1980–89): 117–18. Stearns's paper gives an in-depth and well-documented account of the settling of the Rockbridge area in the early eighteenth century.

3. Thomas Jefferson, *Notes on the State of Virginia* (Chapel Hill, N.C.: University of North Carolina Press, 1955), 24, 25. Jefferson's *Notes on the State of Virginia* is his only published full-length book and is recognized as the best example of his varied interest and a broad statement of his principles.

4. Herman Melville, *Moby Dick* (New York: W. W. Norton, 1967), 448.

5. Marquis de Chastellux, *Travels in North America,* 2 vols. (London: G.G.J. and Robinson, 1787).

6. Winifred Hadsel, "Who's Who in the Streets of Lexington," *Rockbridge Historical Society Proceedings* 10 (1980–89): 365.

7. Royster Lyle, Jr., and Pamela Hemenway Simpson, *The Architecture of Historic Lexington* (Charlottesville, Va.: University Press of Virginia), 11.

8. *State Gazette of North Carolina,* May 19, 1796.

9. Stearns, 131.

10. William Darby, *Universal Gazetteer* (Philadelphia: Bennett and Walton, 1827), 391.

11. James G. Leyburn, *The Scotch-Irish: A Social History* (Chapel Hill, N.C.: University of North Carolina Press, 1962), 200.

12. John S. Wise, *End of an Era* (Boston: Houghton Mifflin, 1899), 240.

FINE ARTS

1. *Lexington Gazette,* June 2, 1840.

2. Andrew Jackson Downing, *The Architecture of Country Houses* (1850; reprint, New York: Dover Publications, 1969), 32.

3. *Rockbridge County Will Book,* 1809–74, 68, and *Rockbridge County Will Book,* no. 16, 26.

4. *Rockbridge County Will Book,* no. 9, 8.

5. Royster Lyle, Jr., "John Blair Lyle of Lexington and His Automatic Bookstore," *Virginia Cavalcade* 21 (August 1972): 20.

6. The union, begun as the Apollo Association in 1839, created a market for American art by offering engravings of paintings to its members in addition to a chance in an annual raffle of paintings in New York. The lottery was declared illegal in 1852, and the remaining pieces were auctioned the following year. Joshua C. Taylor, *The Fine Arts in America* (Chicago: University Press of Chicago, 1979), 79–81.

7. John C. Bingham's *The Jolly Flatboatman* was engraved in 1847 for distribution to union members. In 1848 Thomas Cole's *Voyage of Life,* engraved by James Smellie, was offered to members. Taylor, 81, 86; *Lexington Gazette,* April 17, 1843; July 2, 1849; May 11, 1854.

8. *Lexington Gazette,* January 4, 1855; November 22, 1855; December 4, 1856; December 8, 1859.

9. Royster Lyle, Jr., and Pamela Hemenway Simpson, *The Architecture of Historic Lexington* (Charlottesville, Va.: University Press of Virginia), 2; *Lexington Gazette,* June 11, 1857; and William Couper, *100 Years at VMI* (Richmond: Garrett and Massie, 1939), 1: 320.

10. William W. Pusey III, *Elusive Aspirations: The History of the Female Academy in Lexington, Virginia* (Lexington: Washington and Lee University, 1983), 10, 15, 16.

11. *Lexington Gazette,* June 22, 1843.

12. Ibid., August 14, 1849.

13. *Lexington News-Letter,* August 7, 1819.

14. Ibid., September 18, 1819.

15. *Lexington Gazette,* September 2, 1847.

16. Ibid., November 21, 1850; March 20, 1851.

17. Ibid., July 9, 1857.

18. Elizabeth Preston Allen, *The Life and Letters of Margaret Junkin Preston* (Boston and New York: Houghton Mifflin/Riverside Press, 1903), 38, 105.

19. Burnet's book went through several editions with different illustrators and editors. The 1853 volume is the only one with which Clover was involved.

20. In an 1854 report on the school's two literary and debating societies, the Society of Cadets, formed in 1839, and the Virginia Dialectic Society, formed in 1848, Superintendent Francis H. Smith noted that the Society of Cadets "fitted [the room] up with great taste and comfort, at an expense of $1,200. It is handsomely carpeted; it is provided with cushioned seats, and is lighted with gas from a handsome suspended chandelier. Their library contains 600 volumes, and their hall is ornamented with the portraits of two members of a former board of visitors, and one of the professors, and with a painting of the coat of arms of Virginia."

21. For information on political imagery of the period see Elinor Lander Horwitz, *The Bird, the Banner, and Uncle Sam: Images of America in Folk and Popular Art* (Philadelphia: J. B. Lippincott, 1976), 78.

22. *Lexington Gazette,* March 17, 1853. Clover's other artistic contributions in Lexington include a painting of George Washington for VMI, possibly a mate for the painting of Liberty, and a masthead for the *Lexington Gazette.* The location of the Washington painting is unknown at this time. In a 1909 letter to the VMI librarian Nellie Gibbs, Robert A. Marr, dean of the engineering department at VMI, wrote, "The Sic Semper Tyrannis Seal of Virginia was painted by the Episcopal minister—a Mr. Clover. I was shipmates with his son in Alaska and always intended asking that I be allowed to send

the copy of Washington painted by him while he was in Lexington as minister to this son who had nothing of his Fathers and was anxious to have a bit of his work. This copy of Washington had several holes in the canvas and was simply stored in the 4th story. If Gen. Nichols does not care to have it framed and doctored I would like to send it to this old shipmate." No further correspondence has been located.

23. Robert P. Turner, ed., *Lewis Miller, Sketches and Chronicles: The Reflections of a Nineteenth Century Pennsylvania Folk Artist* (York, Pa.: Historical Society of York County, 1966), xvi.

24. Ibid., xvii, xviii.

25. The wet-plate process, introduced by Frederick Scott Archer in 1851, soon replaced the daguerreotype. Robert Taft, *Photography and the American Scene: A Social History, 1839–1889* (New York: Dover Publications, 1964), 118–19.

26. Pamela Simpson and Mame Warren, *Michael Miley: American Photographer and Pioneer in Color* (exhibition catalogue, Lexington, Va.: Washington and Lee University, 1980), 3.

27. Ibid. Prints in the VMI archives that are stamped "Boude and McClelland" indicate that Boude also entered into an arrangement with another photographer.

28. "The Loss at Miley's," *Rockbridge County News,* October 17, 1907 (report on a fire in Miley's studio).

29. Henry Miley, oral recollections, 1941, transcript, special collections, Washington and Lee University, Lexington, Va., as quoted in Simpson and Warren, 3.

30. Ibid.

31. Ibid., 9.

32. Ibid., 4.

33. Simpson and Warren, 42, includes the complete text of the citation describing the color process.

34. The Franklin Society, a local literary and debating club, was established at the beginning of the nineteenth century to " . . . improve our mind, cultivate friendship, and promote the public good." In addition to a library of more than six hundred volumes, the society sponsored a lecture series and weekly debates. For more information on the society see Ellen Eslinger, "The Social Organization of an Antebellum Town in Virginia," Historic Lexington Foundation, and Philip Williams, Jr., "The Franklin Society: A Study of the Debates, 1850–1861," master's thesis, Washington and Lee University, Lexington, Va., 1941. Additional information can be found in Lauren L. Butler, "'Splendid Failures:' The Meaning of the James River and Kanawha Canal and the North River Navigation in Nineteenth Century Rockbridge," Historic Lexington Foundation, 1985.

35. During the war Kahle served as hospital steward for VMI. The 1863 superintendent's report records that "On the 11th of January Mr. M. S. Kahle was detailed from the army on temporary duty in this hospital, and, up to the present time, has continued to discharge the duties of 'hospital steward,' with assiduous attention and efficiency. It is earnestly recommended that his detail be made permanent, and that he be placed in all respects, as regards pay, clothing and rations, upon an equal footing with the hospital stewards of the army." VMI superintendent's report, June 15, 1863, 29.

36. Lyle and Simpson, 156.

37. William Henry Ruffner, ed., *Washington and Lee University Historical Papers* (Baltimore: John Murphy, 1890–1904), 2: 67.

38. Thomas H. Williamson, *An Elementary Course of Architecture and Civil Engineering, Compiled from the Most Approved Authors for the Use of the Cadets of the Virginia Military Institute* (Lexington, Va.: Samuel Gillock, 1850), 7; see Couper, *100 Years at VMI,* 1: 211.

39. For additional discussion see Lyle and Simpson.

40. *Rockbridge County News,* September 21, 1899.

41. Ruffner, 6: 67.

42. Washington and Lee Records of Board of Trustees, March 4, 1820, and October 2, 1844.

43. *Lexington Gazette,* May 30, 1844. The March 13 entry may reflect that the building committee had been working on the idea before that meeting and that they knew the statue would be wooden.

44. *Valley Star,* December 21, 1843.

45. *Rockbridge County News,* September 21, 1899. In the 1840s the $100 Kahle was paid would have been a handsome salary for two months' work. VMI's Colonel Williamson, who worked with Kahle on the project, was paid only $500 per annum, or $41 per month, when he was hired in 1841. Couper, *100 Years at VMI,* 1:113.

46. *Lexington Gazette,* May 30, 1844.

47. *Valley Star,* May 30, 1844.

48. *Lexington Gazette,* May 1839 and April 1841. It was typical for local merchants to run the same advertisement for several weeks or even months at a time and not unusual for the same notice to be used all year.

49. William Rush, *American Sculptor* (exhibition catalogue, Philadelphia: Pennsylvania Academy of Fine Arts, 1982), 68.

50. Henry Marceau, *William Rush, 1756–1833: The First Native American Sculptor* (Philadelphia: Pennsylvania Museum of Art, 1937), 47.

51. Pamela H. Simpson, *American Sculpture in Lexington: Selected Examples from Public Collections* (exhibition catalogue, Lexington, Va.: Washington and Lee University, 1977), 9; Thomas W. Davis, ed., *A Crowd of Honorable Youths: Historical Essays on the First 150 Years of the Virginia Military Institute* (Lexington, Va.: VMI Alumni Association, 1988).

52. "Old George Comes Down," *W & L: The Alumni Magazine of Washington and Lee* 65 (July 1990): 2–3.

53. Washington completed the painting, a romanticized representation of the burial of Capt. William Latané, in 1864. It was engraved in 1868 by A. G. Campbell and published in the 1870s, for $10 a copy, by the firm of Pate and Company. *Southern Magazine* gave reproductions of the print to subscribers to the magazine. The picture quickly became for southerners a popular image of the "Lost Cause."

54. The Washington Art Association was closely affiliated with the National Academy of Design in New York. The first exhibition of the association included the work of W. D. Washington, Asher B. Durand, Eastman Johnson, Henry Inman, Thomas Moran, William Hart, and Robert W. Weir. For additional information on Washington see Ethelbert Nelson Ott, "William D. Washington 1833–1870: Artist of the South," master's thesis, University of Delaware, 1969.

55. VMI had a number of portraits on campus relating to the school. The Cadet Society had portraits of Colonel Crozet, General Peyton, and Colonel Smith in its meeting hall. Smith reports that during Hunter's raid of 1864, his "private library was rifled of many of its most valuable and portable volumes, and the portraits of Ex-Governors McDowell, Wise, and Letcher, which occupied prominent positions in it, were removed." (Couper, *100 Years at VMI,* 1:191; 3:38). From its beginning the institute established its

preference for the work of professional, often northern artists. The official portrait paintings and sculpture associated with VMI and Washington and Lee are well documented and are not discussed at length here.

56. For additional discussion see Couper, *100 Years at VMI.*

57. Elizabeth Gray Valentine, *Dawn to Twilight: Work of Edward V. Valentine* (Richmond: William Byrd Press, 1929), 108.

58. Ibid., 109, 110.

59. Lyle and Simpson, 167.

60. Margaret Junkin Preston, "Edward Virginius Valentine," *American Art Review* 1 (1880): 277–82, special collections, Washington and Lee University, Lexington, Va.

61. Joseph Gutman and Stanley F. Chyet, eds., *Moses Jacob Ezekiel: Memoirs from the Baths of Diocletian* (Detroit: Wayne State University Press, 1975), 124.

62. Couper, *100 Years at VMI,*4:91.

63. Ibid., 92.

64. Gutman and Chyet, 112, 113.

TEXTILES

1. Edwin Morris Betts and James Adam Bear, Jr., eds., *The Family Letters of Thomas Jefferson* (Columbia, Mo.: University of Missouri Press, 1986), 35.

2. Matthew Pope of Yorktown to John Jacob of London, August 25, 1775, in Victor Clark, *History of Manufacturers in the United States* (New York: 1929), 1:223. Quoted in Dorothy Foster McCombs, "Virginia Cloth," master's thesis, Virginia Polytechnic Institute, 1970, 32. Osnaburg, or osnabrig, was named for Osnabrück, Germany, where it originated, but was also called country cloth or Virginia cloth. It was usually a blend of several fibers, cotton mixed with wool or linen to make a rough, utilitarian cloth used for servants' or work clothing. George White, a former Lynchburg slave, remembered osnaburg clothing as being "jus' like needles when it was new. Never did have to scratch our back. Jus' wiggle yo' shoulders an' yo' back was scratched." Writers Program of the Works Progress Administration in the State of Virginia, *The Negro in Virginia* (New York, 1940), 71; quoted in McCombs, 25.

3. McCombs, 49. McCombs used Tench Coxe, "Digest of Manufactures," *American State Papers, Finance,* vol. 2 (Washington, D.C., 1832).

4. Percy S. Flippin, "William Gooch: Successful Royal Governor of Virginia," *William and Mary Quarterly,* 2d ser., 5 (1925): 240, as quoted in Robert D. Mitchell, *Commercialism and Frontier: Perspectives on the Early Shenandoah Valley* (Charlottesville, Va.: University Press of Virginia, 1977), 146.

5. Flax had been the major fiber crop for the valley prior to the 1760s. Mitchell, 138, 222. See Mitchell for further discussion of the hemp industry in the Valley.

6. Ibid., 201, 222, 223, 225.

7. Oren Morton, *History of Rockbridge County, Virginia* (Staunton, Va.: McClure Press, 1920), 104. Morton also noted two other early accounts related to textiles. In 1778 Christopher Meath and his wife, Hanna, were acquitted of stealing some linen cloth while the "other parties" were given "thirty lashes on the bare back" (p.83). In a reference to old Augusta County wills Morton mentioned one widow's provisions: in addition to a "minimum of garden space, firewood, flour, corn, bacon, etc." she was allowed "a stated area of flax" (p. 41).

8. Ibid., 106.

9. Mitchell, 213. Morton reported that the "goods for the merchants of Lexington came by the Tennessee road wagon, a huge vehicle drawn by six horses in gay toppings. The cover was sometimes bearskin instead of canvas. The wagoner was somewhat like the boatman of the Western rivers. He was a hardy, swaggering personage, but the stage driver would not tolerate the idea of lodging in the same tavern with him" (p. 106).

10. One explanation for the large number of spinning wheels, besides the variety needed for different yarns, is that spinning was a labor-intensive activity and probably as many hands as possible helped. Spinning also required less training and skill than weaving. In his 1843 diary James B. Dorman of Lexington commented on a visit to Gloucester County when he remembered that "In speaking of slaves being a burden rather than a benefit to their master, he [Dorman's host] cited the case of neighbour John Tobb, Esq. who has been accustomed to raise and spin his own cotton. By an apparently fair calculation, he proved that the Negro women employed in spinning could not earn more than 10 cents per week or $5.50; per annum for food, clothing and besides the trouble and vexation of this maintenance she must cost him $20.00 and too the odium which he incurred with them proves their belief that they were tasked hard to make money for him. And yet these men will not liberate their slaves." James B. Dorman Diary, November 1843, Rockbridge Historical Society General Papers, Washington and Lee archives, Lexington, Va.

11. Morton reported that the "loom-house was an adjunct of the prospering farm. Elsewhere, the loom was a feature of the living-room or the kitchen. Girls who learned to weave were able to make some money by going from house to house" (p. 108). Another account, an anecdote from the Robert Alexander family from Rockbridge, reflects weaving activities between different households. In the early 1760s or 1770s Robert's son was sent to a neighbor's house to inquire about a fabric order for the Alexander children's winter clothes. The child was instructed to announce, "Winter is almost upon us and all the children are naked." To present the message honestly the child removed and hid his clothing before delivering it. The dramatic effect caused the woman to dash to the loom and weave the fabric. Robert Enoch Withers, *Autobiography of an Octogenarian* (Roanoke, Va.: Stone Printing and Manufacturing Company Press, 1907), 14, as quoted in McCombs, 131.

12. Tench Coxe, in his *A View of the United States of America, in Series of Papers Written at Various Times, in the Years Between 1787 and 1794,* listed eight or nine weavers and two spinning-wheel makers in Staunton. According to the files of the Museum of Early Southern Decorative Arts, the following people were operating as weavers in Augusta before 1800: Matthew Armstrong, James Baggs, Charles Bagly, Samuel Bean, Andrew Bird, Patrick Campbell, Thomas Chambers, John Christian, Patrick Christian, Thomas Gordon, Nathaniel Hunter, James Laird, James McLackey, Christian Painter, John Pogue, John Preston, William Preston, Smith Thompson, and Conrad Tutch. Several of these men also had apprentices working with them.

13. McCombs, 83.

14. Washington and Lee University papers, Lexington, Va., 4:79–91.

15. *Rockbridge County Will Book,* no. 1.

16. The procedure for preparing flax and hemp is described in detail by both Mitchell and Morton. According to Mitchell, "Western frontier settlers used a winter-rotting process to separate fiber from stalk: the harvested plants were spread out in the fields to allow the fall and winter rains and

ground frost to leach out the gum substance binding the lint to the main stalk, a process which could take up to three months. After the hemp had been winter-rotted, further processing necessitated much additional labor. The outer bark and other woody parts had to be reduced to small pieces and separated from the bark, resulting in a minimally processed 'gross' hemp. An additional procedure, involving the scraping of the hemp so that only the fiber remained (scutching), resulted in a more finely processed 'neat' hemp. Although it had not gone through the final procedure of hackling, whereby the fibers were individually separated, neat hemp was suitable for sail and tent cloth and a variety of coarse materials for clothing. During the pioneer period it was incorporated into osnaburg for everyday clothes, and it was sometimes used as warp along with a wool weft to produce linsey-woolsey. . . . " (pp. 163–64). In Morton's description, "The flax patch was seldom of more than one acre. The stalks were pulled when the seeds were fully ripe, and were laid out in gavels, the stem-ends forming a line. After a while the bundles were set up, and when dry were put into the barn. In the winter season the stalks were broken to loosen the fiber. This was done by laying them against slats and giving a few blows with a wooden knife. Scutching was the next step, and was performed by holding the broken stems against a upright board and striking them obliquely with the same knife. Them came in succession the spinning, the weaving, and the bleaching. The unbleached cloth was of the color of flaxen hair. The homemade linen was of two grades, one for fine and one for corse cloth. Six yards a day was about the utmost the weaver could accomplish, if the weaving were to be tight enough" (p. 107).

17. Sarah may have been related to Thomas Beggs, who appears to have operated a mill in the county. He was mentioned in an 1825 advertisement by Thomas Cross, who operated a carding machine. *Lexington Intelligencer,* June 10, 1825.

18. *Rockbridge County Will Book,* no. 1.

19. *Rockbridge County Will Book,* no. 1 and no. 2.

20. Hays also built a grist mill in the same area. *Augusta County Order Book,* no. 2, 297; *Augusta County Deed Book,* no. 4, 392–99.

21. Morton, 56.

22. U.S. Treasury Department [Tench Coxe], *A Statement of the Arts and Manufactures of the United States of America, for the Year 1810* (New York: Luther M. Cornwall, n.d.; photographic facsimile, Philadelphia: A. Corman, Jr., 1814).

23. *Rockbridge County Will Book,* no. 1.

24. Ibid.

25. *Virginia Telegraph,* September 7, 1806.

26. *The Rockbridge Repository,* December 29, 1803.

27. *Lexington News-Letter,* June 19, 1819.

28. *Lexington Gazette,* January 19, 1838.

29. Ibid., September 19, 1844. Some years later Cross announced the sale of land, mills and carding machines because he was moving to the southwest. Ibid., February 19, 1857.

30. The degree of fineness of the fabric was controlled by the reed size. The higher the number of the reed the more closely spaced the reed openings and consequently the warp threads. A 1200 reed was suitable for fine linen or cotton. A 900 reed would produce medium fabric and a 450 was appropriate for coarse fabric or carpeting.

31. *The Virginia Telegraph and Rockbridge Courier,* April 26, 1803.

32. Indenture bond, Rockbridge Historical Society collection, Washington and Lee University, Lexington, Va.

33. Jefferson to Thaddeus Kosciuszko, June 28, 1812, quoted in McCombs, 57; Edwin Morris Betts, *Thomas Jefferson's Farm Book* (Princeton: 1953), 477.

34. Preston also served in the Virginia legislature and the U.S. Army. His son, John Thomas Preston, was one of the founders of VMI.

35. Virginia Historical Society collection, manuscript 2R5903a1.

36. Morton, 169.

37. *Lexington Gazette,* September 18, 1849.

38. Ibid., October 9, 1849.

39. Ibid., February 13, 1851. Other articles supporting local industry appear in the *Lexington Gazette,* November 13 and 27, 1849.

40. *Virginia Telegraph,* April 25, 1807.

41. For additional discussion on the Rockbridge Agricultural Society see Charles W. Turner, "Agricultural Expositions and Fairs in Rockbridge County, 1828–1891," *Rockbridge Historical Society Proceedings* 10 (1980–89): 387–409.

42. *Lexington Gazette,* January 26, 1854, and April 5, 1855.

43. Ibid., May 8, 1856.

44. Ibid., July 29, 1841. In the advertisement Brown thanked his customers for their patronage and announced that he would "receive and return cloth at the store of S. B. Finley, Lex; Brown and Hutchenson, Brownsburg; and Stevens & Co., Fairfield." Robert H. Brown, from Pennsylvania, who was thirty-six at the time of the sale, could have been the son of John W. Brown.

45. Ibid., June 11, 1857.

46. *Rockbridge County Will Book,* no. 4, 13.

47. Helen Comstock, ed., *The Concise Encyclopedia of American Antiques* (New York: Hawthorn Books, 1958), 339.

48. *Virginia Telegraph,* October 18, 1806.

49. Ibid., April 25, 1803.

50. Even simpler is the two-harness loom, which could produce plain-weave fabrics in plaid designs for clothing, sheeting, sacking, and blanketing.

51. Marguerite Ickis, quoting her great-grandmother, in Mirra Bank, *Anonymous Was a Woman* (New York: St. Martin's Press, 1979), 94.

52. The 1854 inventory for Matthew Bryan is one of the few in the county that indicate some of the names applied to the quilts at that time. His appraisal includes "1 peona quilt," "1 compas quilt," and "1 fancy quilt" valued at five dollars each in addition to "1 Buenavesta quilt," and "1 Dahlia quilt" each at eight dollars.

53. Catharine Ester Beecher, *A Treatise on Domestic Economy for the Use of Young Ladies at Home and at School,* rev. ed. (Boston: T. H. Webb, 1843).

54. William W. Pusey III, *Elusive Aspirations: The History of the Female Academy in Lexington, Virginia* (Lexington, Va.: Washington and Lee University, 1983), 10. Thomas Jefferson made a $25 donation in 1809. His contact with the academy was probably through William C. Ruthers, an academy trustee. Ruthers also served as agent for Jefferson's Natural Bridge property (p. 14).

55. Ibid., 15, 16.

56. Ibid., 34.

57. Charles W. Turner, *Virginia's Green Revolution* (Virginia: C. W. Turner, 1986), 64, 65.

58. Ibid., 65. In 1833 the following were awarded premiums: "Mrs. James Greenlee—Figure Table cloth Linen, Miss Agnes Paxton—Piece of

Cassinet, Mrs. Reuben Grigsby—Piece of Flannel, Mrs. Hanna Greenlee—Pair of blankets, Mrs. John Laird—All wool carpeting, and Miss Frances Grigsby—Dozen skeins of sewing silk" (ibid., 66–67).

59. *Lexington Gazette,* July 22, 1836.

60. Ibid., June 16, 1842.

61. Ibid., June 23 and July 7, 1842.

62. Ibid., July 7, 1842.

63. Ibid., October 26, 1843.

64. Rockbridge Historical Society collection, box 77, no. 7, Washington and Lee University, Lexington, Va.

65. *Virginia Gazette,* May 12, 1871.

FURNITURE

1. Edwin L. Dooley, Jr., "Lexington Ledgers: A Source for Social History," *Rockbridge Historical Society Proceedings* 10 (1980–89): 2.

2. *Lexington Gazette,* December 6, 1865.

3. Helen Comstock, ed., *The Concise Encyclopedia of American Antiques* (New York: Hawthorn Books, 1958), 23.

4. Charles Hummel, *With Hammer in Hand: The Dominy Craftsmen of East Hampton, New York* (Winterthur, Del.: Winterthur Museum, 1968).

5. Andrew Jackson Downing, *The Architecture of Country Houses* (1850; reprint, New York: Dover Publications, 1969), 387–88.

6. Ibid., 441.

7. Washington and Lee University treasurer's records, file no. 29, bound volume 1774–1803, April 20, 1785, Lexington, Va., 50–52.

8. The fire received wide attention, and it was reported that "by the combined exertions of the students and the inhabitants, the library, apparatus, and the furniture were all preserved to a mere trifle, not exceeding in value 100 dollars." *Charleston Courier,* January 29, 1803.

9. Royster Lyle, Jr., and Pamela Hemenway Simpson, *The Architecture of Historic Lexington* (Charlottesville, Va.: University Press of Virginia, 1977), 145–51.

10. The trustees' specifications for the steward's house indicate the workmanship expected of Chandler in addition to the materials to be used. The contract calls for the "outside door frames to be of yellow poplar scantling with locust sills single Architrave wrought out in the solid. The doors to be quarter round and raised panels inch and a quarter thick. Ionic Cornice with a dental bed mould in front." H. Jackson Darst, *The Darsts of Virginia* (Williamsburg, Va.: 1972), 46.

11. Washington and Lee University trustees' records, 1803, 1804, Lexington, Va.

12. This tradition continued into the twentieth century. In 1936 Washington and Lee built a new law school, Tucker Hall, which was to reflect the classical style of the existing Colonnade. The building committee decided to furnish the new structure with reproductions appropriate to its period style. The committee studied "furniture encyclopaedias" and "visited Williamsburg and other centers of early Virginia architecture" in its search for models. The alumni magazine reported that as a result there is "scarcely a piece of furniture in the Law School the original of which could not have been found there had the building really been erected before 1800." In addition to looking for models in published sources and historic sites in Virginia, the committee used at least one local example, for the library chairs, "old fashioned Hitchcock Windsors," which were copied from an original found in a Rockbridge County farmhouse and was reported to have been made by an "old cabinetmaker who lived here in the county before 1800." Most of the furniture for the building was produced in the college workshop or by Lexington artisans. Charles R. McDowell, "Furnishings of the Law Building," *The Alumni Magazine,* Washington and Lee University (spring 1936): 7, 8, 15.

13. Washington and Lee University trustees' records, 1835.

14. Ibid., 1867.

15. Capt. Robert E. Lee, *Recollections of General Lee* (Garden City, N.Y.: Garden City Publishing, 1924), 203. For additional information on Mrs. Cocke see Mary P. Coulling, *The Lee Girls* (Winston-Salem, N.C.: John F. Blair, 1987), 152.

16. *Lexington Gazette,* December 6, 1865.

17. That year Lee also received furniture shipments by canal. Company ledger entries report Lee was billed for "4 stands, 3 pkgs bedsteads, 1 bureau, boxes furniture, boxes marble, bales bedding, 4 boxes furniture." Canal ledger, Rockbridge County Court House, Lexington, Va.

18. A. J. Davis, Daybook, Davis collection, New York Public Library, 425, as cited in Mills Lane, *Architecture of the Old South* (New York: Abbeville Press, 1984), 238.

19. VMI treasurer's files, VT4 and VT6, Lexington, Va.

20. In 1853 Mathew Kahle advertised "beautiful 'dressing bureaus,' made out of crotch elm," an unusual use of that wood.

21. *Rockbridge County Will Book,* no. 5, 14–15. Scantling is a small beam or timber.

22. *Lexington Gazette,* February 22, 1844. Also see the Wilson-Barclay ledger, Rockbridge Historical Society collection, Washington and Lee University, Lexington, Va. Hugh L. Wilson, of Wilson and Barclay, made semiannual trips to Philadelphia to purchase stock for his establishment. In 1846 he stayed at the Merchant's Hotel. Several Lexington artisans purchased tools and supplies from his Lexington firm.

23. *Rockbridge County Will Book,* no. 21, 497.

24. Two ledgers belonged to Samuel Smith and are in private collections. The first dates from 1831 to 1847 and the second from 1827 to 1859. The three Varner ledgers, also in a private collection, cover the years 1860–63, 1860–64, and 1865–66. For additional information on Milton H. Key's ledger see Dooley, "Lexington Ledgers." The Key ledger was in storage in the Rockbridge County Court House, and Dooley transcribed the complete manuscript before it was sent to Richmond to be microfilmed. All information for this study came from Dooley's copy. The ledger contains business records for the period from January 1857 to June 1860.

25. Kurtz was probably the Staunton chairmaker Jacob Kurtz. It is interesting to note that the artist and cabinetmaker Lewis Miller, who made frequent trips to Rockbridge County and recorded it in sketches, was also from York.

26. On July 19, 1808, McClung purchased from Ruff a "wool hat per Smith" ($1.25). Two years later a similar entry appeared. Jacob Ruff ledger (1809–18), Rockbridge Historical Society collection, Washington and Lee University, Lexington, Va.

27. *Rockbridge County Deed Book* A, 1819, 308, described the house and lot as on "Main Street bounded on the S.W. by a lot of Zachariah Johnston and on the south east and north east by lots of Jacob Hanghawont. 42½ feet in front and 90 feet deep."

28. *Lexington News-Letter,* October 9, 1819.

29. *Lexington Intelligencer,* July 31, 1824.

30. Ibid., October 30, 1824.

31. *Rockbridge County Will Book*, no. 6, 249. According to the rule of three, the "product of the means of a proportion equals the product of the extremes. . . . This rule enables one to find any one of the number of a proportion if the other three are given." Glenn James and Robert C. James, *Mathematics Dictionary* (New York: Van Nostrand, 1960).

32. Some of the purchases noted in the institute's treasurer's records are:

8/29/40   3 doz. chairs for the use of cadets of the VMI $38.00

2/17/45   3 doz. stools for drawing academy

          6 chairs for section room $28.50

7/17/45   46 chairs and repairing 24 charge cadet society $87.00

12/31/45 repairing 1 large easy chair (hospital)

33. *Lexington Gazette*, June 10, 1836.

34. Ibid., April 29, 1838.

35. A sabot, traditionally meaning a wooden shoe, was also a military term referring to the turned wooden disk that fit over the projectile used in a muzzle-loading cannon. Many of Varner's pieces have feet that resemble sabots.

36. See Mary Anna Jackson, *Memoirs of Stonewall Jackson by His Widow* (Louisville, Ky.: Prentice Press, 1895), 115.

37. Canal ledger, Rockbridge County Court House, Lexington, Va.

38. *Virginia Gazette*, July 1871.

39. *Rockbridge County Will Book*, no. 2, 278, and no. 1, 191.

40. Ibid. no. 3, 157.

41. Ibid. no. 4, 270.

42. Ibid. no. 9, 8. Caruthers's inventory included the following seating forms:

Parlor furniture

1 doz green windsor chairs 15.00

1 piano windsor chair 1.25

1 spring seat sofa 15.00

Back room upstairs

4 black chairs 1.50

Dining Room

1 doz green windsor chairs 9.00

Chamber furniture

1 doz yellow chairs 10.00

2 small green chairs .75

2 infants green chairs .37½

1 large rocking chair 1.00

1 rocking chair .75

43. Samuel Kercheval, *A History of the Valley of Virginia*, 4th ed. (Strasburg, Va.: Shenandoah Publishing House, 1925), 264–65.

44. *Rockbridge County Will Book*, no. 5, 150–53.

45. The 1795 estate listing for John Paul of Rockbridge reflects the variety of items stored in a cupboard of that period. His held twenty-one pewter plates, seven quart basons [sic], nineteen spoons, four white dishes, ten white plates, six flowered plates, and six small bowls. *Rockbridge County Will Book*, no. 1, 504.

46. Howard Paine, *The Heritage of Country Furniture: A Study in the Survival of Formal and Vernacular Styles from the United States, Britain, and Europe Found in Upper Canada, 1780–1900* (New York: Van Nostrand Reinhold, 1978), 46.

47. The 1818 probate for James Scott included the cherry cupboard for $20 in addition to one poplar cupboard at $4. *Rockbridge County Will Book*, no. 4, 362.

48. Paine, 44.

49. *Rockbridge County Will Book*, no. 13, 83.

50. Ibid., no. 5, 14, 15.

51. Ibid., no. 14, 50–54.

52. Ibid., 1809–74, 8.

53. Ibid., no. 3, 50.

54. Ibid., no. 2, 177; no. 2, 20, 21; no. 3, 471.

55. Oren Morton, *A History of Rockbridge County, Virginia* (Staunton, Va.: McClure Press, 1920), 84.

56. *Rockbridge County Will Book*, no. 3, 23.

57. Ibid., 243.

58. Ibid., no. 6, 112, 129.

59. Ibid., 46.

60. Ibid., no. 1, 138.

61. Ibid., 195.

62. Ibid., no. 13, 32.

63. Downing, 442.

64. *Rockbridge County Order Book*, 1778–83, 177.

65. *Rockbridge County Will Book*, no. 2, 129.

66. The American Windsor chair, which was introduced into the colonies about 1725, has its roots in European styles. In England, where it originated, it was commonly used as garden or porch furniture, but in eighteenth- and nineteenth-century America the Windsor came into almost universal use in all areas of the house.

67. *The Rockbridge Repository*, October 23, 1801.

68. *Rockbridge County Will Book*, no. 5, 70, 71, 72.

TALL CLOCKS

1. Philip Whitney, *The Clocks of the Shenandoah* (Stevens City, Va.: Commercial Press, 1983), 11. Whitney contends that "more fine clocks were made by more Virginia craftsmen in the Valley than in any other Virginia community."

2. Moses Whiteside's 1750 tract shows on the plat of Borden's Grant (original in the Rockbridge County Court House). Also see Whiteside family file, Rockbridge Historical Society collection, Washington and Lee University, Lexington, Va.

3. Oren Morton, *A History of Rockbridge County* (Staunton, Va.: McClure Press, 1920), 459. Moses paid taxes in 1782 on seven horses and twenty head of cattle.

4. *Rockbridge County Will Book*, no. 1, 489–91.

5. *Rockbridge County Deed Book* A, 243; Thomas sold the lot six years later. *Rockbridge County Deed Book* A, 589.

6. See Jane Webb Smith, "A Large and Elegant Assortment: A Group of Baltimore Tall Clocks, 1795–1815," *Journal of Early Southern Decorative Arts* 8 (November 1987): 35. Early clockmakers often referred to themselves as silversmiths.

7. In 1772 the Birmingham *Gazette* carried an advertisement for Osborne and Wilson, manufacturers of "White Clock Dials in Imitation of Enamel, in a Manner entirely new" (ibid., 48). Also see Brian Loomes, *White Dial Clocks* (North Pomfret, Vt.: David and Charles, 1981), 33. Japan varnish was less expensive than genuine enamel, which required vitrification in a kiln.

8. Smith, 49.

9. Ibid., 51.

10. Adolphus Weir's ledger, Swem Library, William and Mary College, Williamsburg, Va. Also see Hoffman ledger, special collections, Washington and Lee University, Lexington, Va.

11. Lloyd DeWitt Bockstruck, *Virginia's Colonial Soldiers* (Baltimore: Genealogical Publishing, 1988), 206.

12. *Lexington News-Letter,* May 8, 1819.

13. See Helen Comstock, "Furniture of Virginia, North Carolina, Georgia, and Kentucky," *The Magazine Antiques* 61 (January 1952): 58–99.

14. Carnegie Institute Museum of Art, *Collection Handbook* (Pittsburgh, Pa.: Carnegie Institute, 1985), 166, 167. The face of the clock is signed "Johnston and Davis, Pittsburgh," and inscribed "For Gelix Negley." The white dial is signed (incised) on the back of the moon dial "W. H. Price/Birm'm." According to the catalogue description, "The overall shape of the case soars vertically upwards, uninterrupted by its horizonal division into three sections. The inlay, which consists of linear stringing, is geometric in its arrangements."

15. There is evidence that Christian Bear made other clock cases. The Elias Lewis clock is owned by the great-great-granddaughter of Christian Bear.

16. *Lexington Intelligencer,* December 6, 1823.

17. Ann McCleary, "A Study of the Account Book of James Rankin," *Augusta Historical Bulletin* 19, no. 1 (1983): 30

18. *Lexington Gazette,* January 6, 1842.

RIFLES

1. John G. W. Dillin, *The Kentucky Rifle* (National Rifle Association of America, 1924), 29.

2. Robert Lageman and Albert C. Manucy, *The Long Rifle* (Eastern Acorn Press, 1980), 7. Gill records that there were early gunsmiths among the colonists in Tidewater. For instance, a William Hunt of Charles City County had an indentured gunsmith who was "a very good workman" at his own smith's shop, which was "well furnished with good bellows . . . and all manner of gunsmith tools." But most of the activity of these colonial smiths had to do with keeping the firearms from England in good condition. Harold B. Gill, Jr., *The Gunsmith in Colonial Virginia* (Charlottesville, Va.: University of Virginia Press, 1974), 15.

3. Lageman and Manucy, 7.

4. Wallace Gusler, "Virginia Frontier Rifles," *Virginia Cavalcade* 17, no. 1 (summer 1967): 21.

5. Gusler, 21.

6. Dillin, 29.

7. Ibid., 30.

8. Ibid.

9. Ibid., 33.

10. James B. Whisker, *Gunsmiths of Virginia* (Bedford, Pa.: Old Bedford Village Press, 1992), 1.

11. *Rockbridge County Will Book,* no. 7, 363.

12. Gill, 105.

13. Interview with Gusler, May 20, 1991.

14. Lyman Chalkley, *Chronicles of the Scotch-Irish Settlement in Virginia,* vol. 2 (1912; reprint, Baltimore: Genealogical Publishing, 1980), 403, 406, 407.

15. *Rockbridge County Will Book,* no. 11, 445.

16. Emma Siggins White's *Genealogy of the Descendants of John Walker* (1902) mentions only two Walker gunmakers and does not give their birth dates or periods of activity, only that the John Walkers were uncle and nephew. They were "distinguished as 'Gun-maker' John and 'Gun-stocker John' . . . Gunmaker John Walker made the locks and barrels of the rifles on the anvil of his shop, and Gunstocker John made the woodwork," 169, 170.

White also contends that "the gallant uncle and nephew took up lands on both sides of the rapid stream which still bears their names, flowing parallel to the mountain range some two miles distant." Other records do not support this location.

17. Walker's estate appraisal was dated January 6, 1775. Gill published most of the inventory on pages 61 and 62. See *Rockbridge County Will Book,* no. 1, 470–71.

18. Virginia Land Office, Grant Book, 33: 618, Virginia State Library, as quoted in Gill.

19. John Walker Day Book, Cyrus McCormick collection, University of Wisconsin, Madison, Wis.

20. Letter, March 4, 1808, executive papers, Virginia State Library, as quoted in Gill, 79.

21. Jacob Ruff ledger, Rockbridge Historical Society collection, Washington and Lee University, Lexington, Va.

22. *Rockbridge County Will Book,* no. 11, 223.

23. *Rockbridge County Will Book,* no. 1, 145; *Augusta County Order Book,* no. 12, 315; Chalkley, 1:150.

24. *Augusta County Order Book,* no. 12, 495; Chalkley, 1:153. See also Gill, 18.

25. *Augusta County Order Book,* no. 4, 323; Chalkley, 1:65. See also Gill, 18.

26. *Augusta County Order Book,* no. 16, 94; Chalkley, 1:186.

27. E. W. Hubard Papers, University of North Carolina, as cited in Gill, 86.

28. *Rockbridge County Will Book,* no. 1, 169. Gill published Hanna's entire estate inventory, which was recorded on January 1, 1782, on pages 90–93.

29. *Rockbridge County Will Book,* no. 14, 419. Will dated December 22, 1854.

30. George W. Diehl, *The Zollmans and Their Kin* (Privately printed, 1986). See also *Rockbridge County Will Book,* no. 7, 271. Will dated September 9, 1834.

31. Withrow scrapbook 1, n.p., Rockbridge Historical Society collection, Washington and Lee University, Lexington, Va. Also see *Rockbridge County Birth Register,* no. 2, 709.

32. *Rockbridge County Will Book,* no. 7, 271.

33. John D. Beeton, *History of the Beeton Family* (Sterling, Va.: Privately printed, 1977), 65; *Rockbridge County Will Book,* no. 11, 44.

34. Interview with Wallace Gusler, May 25, 1991.

35. Beeton, 16.

36. Merrill Lindsay, *The Kentucky Rifle* (York County, Pa.: Arma Press, 1972), 1.

IRONWORK

1. John Carmichael's 1884 map of Rockbridge County clearly delineates the iron ore deposits throughout the county. Several originals of the map are on display in Lexington, Va., at the VMI Museum, Stonewall Jackson House, and Rockbridge County Court House.

2. John Bivins, Jr., "Isaac Zane and the Products of Marboro Furnace," *Journal of Early Southern Decorative Arts* 11 (May 1985): 15, 17.

3. Kathleen Bruce, *Virginia Iron Manufacture in the Slave Era* (New York: Century, 1931), 132. Henry Miller subsequently bought out his partner and operated Mossy Creek Iron Works until his death in 1796. The Miller works stayed in the family until 1834, when it was bought out by John Keneagy, "a newcomer from Pennsylvania." Also see Robert D. Mitchell, *Commercialism and Frontier: Perspectives on Early Shenandoah Valley* (Charlottesville, Va.: University Press of Virginia, 1977), 205.

4. Mitchell, 205. "The demands of the army during the Revolution and the growing demands for iron manufacturers after the war encouraged the de-

velopment of other iron interests in the Valley. During the 1780s two furnaces were opened in the Southwestern Shenandoah County and an ironworks was erected near Lexington. Between 1790 and 1804 at least two successful and one abortive attempts were made to establish ironworks near Staunton and Lexington." Mitchell cites *Augusta County Order Book*, no. 21, 474; no. 2, 242; and no. 23, 337; *Rockbridge County Order Book*, no. 3, 422; and the *Virginia Gazette*, November 26, 1799. In 1782 William Daugherty owned 100 acres valued at 30 pounds, and his brother, James Daugherty, owned 300 acres assessed at 55 pounds. Perhaps the Daughertys were just beginning to develop their iron operation. In 1786 Halbert McCluer bought 249 acres from Nathaniel Dryden valued at 65 pounds, possibly in connection with his iron business. By 1797 William and Samuel Moore had increased their collective land holdings in the county to 1,053 acres. It is not possible from the land books to determine the location of these properties, although it is assumed that they were all in the South River vicinity. *Rockbridge County Land Book*, no. 1, n.p.

5. A bloomery forge was not unlike a blacksmith's forge; it required special skill in heating and hammering and the output was limited. Also see *Buena Vista Advocate*, June 26, 1891, and Oren Morton, *A History of Rockbridge County, Virginia* (Staunton, Va.: McClure Press, 1920), 170. This story could have some validity, although it was written 110 years after the fact. The trip from the South River to Richmond in the Revolutionary period was at best precarious but possible. The "three-ton furnace" reference is from an 1896 clipping in the Withrow scrapbook.

6. Lester J. Capron, "Lucy Selina's Charcoal Era," *Virginia Cavalcade* 8 (autumn 1957): 32.

7. Adolphus Weir's ledger (1790–1806), Swem Library, William and Mary College, Williamsburg, Va.

8. Henry J. Kauffman, *Early American Ironware* (Rutland, Vt.: Charles E. Tuttle Company, 1967), 24.

9. Bivins, 25.

10. Ibid., 26.

11. Robert A. Rutland, "Men in Iron in the Making of Virginia," *Iron Worker* (summer 1976), 8.

12. Bivins, 23.

13. Rutland, 6. Charcoal was made at the "coaling grounds" in the forest and then hauled to the furnace.

14. Morton, 165; William E. Trout III, personal manuscript collection, Richmond, Va.

15. Capron, 33. Jordan was a difficult fellow. When a census taker requested information about his production for the 1820 *Census of Manufactures*, Jordan refused to give it, even though a response was required by law.

16. Royster Lyle, Jr., and Pamela Hemenway Simpson, *The Architecture of Historic Lexington* (Charlottesville, Va.: University of Virginia Press, 1977), 18.

17. John S. Moore, "John Jordan: Rockbridge Baptist Layman," *Virginia Baptist Register* 2 (1963): 56; Harrington Waddell, paper presented to the Fortnightly Club, published in *Rockbridge County News*, April 14, 1938. Waddell described the road as "a remarkable piece of engineering and grading through some of the most beautiful scenery in this section of the Valley of Virginia."

18. Moore, 56. Apparently there was a third road over the Blue Ridge, built in 1820 in conjunction with the James River Canal, which ran from the mouth of the North River (Glasgow today) to Snowden, approximately the present route of highway 501.

19. In 1980 Union Hill was moved to Goochland County. It is still in the Cabell family. The present owners are Mr. and Mrs. Royal E. Cabell, Jr. Goochland County Court House, Va.

20. *Buena Vista Advocate*, June 26, 1891.

21. *Census of Manufactures*, 1820.

22. The 1782–83 land tax books record that Capt. William Moore owned 440 acres assessed at 220 pounds and that Samuel Moore, presumably his brother, owned 115 acres assessed at 70 pounds. This per-acre value was considerably greater than other comparable county land at the time, giving some indication of a furnace on the property. T. T. Brady and D. E. Brady found slag at what they think is the Moore furnace site between Vesuvius and Steeles Tavern but could find no evidence of the furnace stonework. T. T. Brady and D. E. Brady, interview with Royster Lyle, Jr., Lexington, Va., January 10, 1985.

23. H. E. Comstock, "The Redwell Ironworks," *Journal of Early Southern Decorative Arts* 7, no. 1 (May 1981): 73.

24. Donald A. Crownover, *Manufacturing and Marketing of Iron Stoves at Hopewell Furnace, 1835–1844* (Washington, D.C.: National Park Service, 1970), 108, as cited in Ian M. G. Quimby and Polly Anne Earle, "Technological Innovation and Decorative Arts," *Winterthur Conference Report, 1973* (Charlottesville, Va.: University Press of Virginia, 1974), 158.

25. *Census of Manufactures*, 1820.

26. Charles B. Dew, "Disciplining Slave Ironworkers in the Antebellum South: Coercion, Conciliation, and Accommodation," *American Historical Review* 79 (April 1974): 396.

27. D. E. Brady, Jr., "Iron Valley Revisited" (paper presented to the Fortnightly Club, November 15, 1989). Also see T. T. Brady, "The Early Iron Industry in Rockbridge County," *Rockbridge Historical Society Proceedings* 8 (1979), 57, 58.

28. Charles B. Dew, *Bond of Iron* (New York: W. W. Norton, 1994), 171, 184.

29. Ibid., 172.

30. Ibid.

31. Ibid., 103.

32. Ibid., 185.

33. Ibid., 186

34. A. Fletcher, review of *The Agrarian History of England and Wales*, by Joan Thirsk, *History* 71, no. 236 (1987): 92.

35. Ibid.

36. Thomas Jefferson, in *American Philosophical Society, Transactions* 4 (1799) and *Philadelphia Society for Promoting Agriculture, Memoirs* 4 (1818): 16–17, as quoted in Fletcher, 92.

37. Kathleen Bruce, *Virginia Iron Manufacture in the Slave Era* (New York: Century, 1931), 135.

38. Wayne G. Broehl, Jr., "The Plow That Broke the Prairies," *American History Illustrated* 19 (January 1985): 16.

39. *Lexington Gazette*, February 3, 1847.

40. *Lexington Gazette*, March 16, 1843.

41. *Census of Manufactures*, 1850, 50; Broehl, 16.

42. The twenty-six pigs from the Richmond canal basin were excavated by members of the Virginia Canal and Navigation Society and the Archeological Society of Virginia. The range in size indicates that they could have been shipped to Richmond any time between 1800 and 1880.

43. *Lexington Gazette*, April 27, 1854.

44. Humphries served in the Civil War with the 5th Virginia Infantry. Quotations are from his journal for January–December 1872 (private collection, unpaginated).

45. Humphries journal; *Census of Manufactures,* 1820; *Lexington Gazette,* May 4, 1882.

46. *Census of Manufactures,* 1880; *Lexington Gazette,* May 4, 1882.

47. *Lexington Gazette,* June 7, 1878, November 1, 1878, July 17, 1879; *Census of Manufactures,* 1880. In 1880 Mullen produced seventy-five plows. The Oliver Chilled plow was named for James Oliver of South Bend, Ind., who in 1868 secured a patent for hardening ("chilling") cast-iron moldboards that would wear and scour better. See Fletcher, 57.

48. Mildred S. Goeller, *The Steeles of Steeles Tavern, Virginia and Related Families* (privately printed, 1974), 5.

49. Newspaper clipping, n.d., Rockbridge Historical Society files, Washington and Lee University, Lexington, Va.

50. *Lexington Gazette,* May 5, 1852.

51. *Lexington Gazette,* November 10, 1853.

52. *Lexington Gazette,* August 31, 1854.

53. *Lexington Gazette,* June 10, 1858.

54. For a description of the lowering of Lexington's Main Street in the 1850s, see Lyle and Simpson, 33, 34.

55. Louise K. Dooley, "Cyrus McCormick, Rockbridge Inventor," *Main Street* 1 (March 1974): 7.

56. Cyrus McCormick's role in the invention of the reaper he later so successfully marketed throughout the country and the world is dealt with in Norbert Lyons, *The McCormick Reaper Legend* (New York: Exposition Press, 1955).

57. *Census of Manufactures,* 1820, 20.

58. Lyons, 143.

59. William H. McClure, "A Cyrus McCormick Story," *Rockbridge Historical Society Proceedings* 8 (1979), 83.

60. Morton, 171.

POTTERY

1. See Jeffrey P. Blomster and Kurt C. Russ, "Early Pottery Production in Eastern Virginia: An Examination of Its Extent and Development," (paper presented at the annual meeting of the Society for Historical Archaeology, Richmond, Va., January 1991): 12–13.

2. In addition to Rogers's pottery, as many as seven other seventeenth- and eighteenth-century endeavors have been identified in the Tidewater area of Virginia; see Blomster and Russ, 12–13.

3. Beth A. Bower, "The Pottery-Making Trade in Colonial Philadelphia: The Growth of an Early Urban Industry," *Domestic Pottery of the Northeastern United States, 1625–1850* (New York: Academic Press, 1985), 276; Norman F. Barka and Chris Sheridan, "The Yorktown Pottery Industry, Yorktown, Virginia," *Northeast Historical Archaeology* 6 (1977): 21.

4. Kurt C. Russ, "The Traditional Pottery Manufacturing Industry in Virginia: Examples from Botetourt and Rockbridge Counties," *Rockbridge Historical Society Proceedings* 10 (1980–89), 455–56.

5. H. E. Comstock, introduction to *Folk Pottery of the Shenandoah Valley* (New York: E. P. Dutton, 1975), 19. This Winchester pottery was in operation 1824–45. Peter Bell did not begin manufacturing stoneware until 1832.

6. Samuel was the first to move to Strasburg in 1833, when he purchased the old Beyer pottery. He continued to be actively engaged in the business un-

til 1853. Solomon did not participate in his brother's pottery until 1837. He soon dominated the pottery production end of the business, which he continued to be involved with until his death in 1882. Solomon's sons, Richard Franklin (Polk) Bell and Charles Forrest Bell, continued the Bell family pottery until 1908.

7. See Roderick J. Moore, "Earthenware Potters along the Great Road in Virginia and Tennessee," *The Magazine Antiques* 124 (1983): 528–37.

8. Kurt C. Russ, "The Fincastle Pottery (44BO304): Salvage Excavations at a Nineteenth-Century Earthenware Kiln in Botetourt County, Virginia," *Occasional Papers in Anthropology,* no. 28 (Lexington, Va.: Laboratory of Anthropology, Washington and Lee University, May 1989); Russ, "The Traditional Pottery Manufacturing Industry in Virginia;" Russ, "The Nineteenth Century Traditional Pottery Manufacturing Industry in Botetourt County, Virginia" (paper presented to the Roanoke Historical Society, Roanoke, Va., March 27, 1990).

9. Dennis Pogue, "An Analysis of Wares Salvaged from the Swan-Smith-Milburn Pottery Site (44AX29), Alexandria, Virginia," *Quarterly Bulletin of the Archaeological Society of Virginia* 34 (1980): 149–60; Barbara Magid, "The Potter Hath Power over His Clay: From Earthenware to Stoneware in Alexandria, Virginia" (paper presented to the Society for Historical Archaeology, Richmond, Va., 1991).

10. B. L. Rauschenberg, "B. Duval and G. Richmond: A Newly Discovered Pottery," *Pottery Collections Newsletter* 8, no. 4 (1978): 8–9.

11. The Henri Lowndes pottery manufacturing concern was prominent in Petersburg, Virginia, c. 1840. The typically semi-ovid, one- to five-gallon salt-glazed stoneware vessels are often embellished with elaborate blue cobalt floral motifs including the signature "Henri Lowndes, Manufacturer, Petersburg, Virginia."

12. See Russ, "The Traditional Pottery Manufacturing Industry in Virginia," 455–57, 474–86. The statewide survey of potters shows a concentration and lineal distribution of potters in the Ridge and Valley area. Of 294 potters identified as working in the state, eighty-one percent were located in this region.

13. A. H. Rice and John Baer Stoudt, *The Shenandoah Pottery* (Strasburg, Va.: Shenandoah Publishing, 1929). More than thirty-five potters have been identified as working in Strasburg from about 1820 through 1908.

14. Russ, "The Traditional Pottery Manufacturing Industry in Virginia," 484–85; Klell Bayne Napps, "Traditional Pottery in Washington County, Virginia and Sullivan County, Tennessee," *The Historic Society of Washington County, Virginia,* 2d ser., no. 10 (1972): 3–16.

15. See Paul R. Mullins, "Historic Pottery Making in Rockingham County, Virginia" (paper presented at the Archaeological Society of Virginia symposium Ceramics in Virginia, Virginia Piedmont Community College, Charlottesville, Va., 1988) and "The Boundaries of Change: Negotiating Industrialization in the Domestic Pottery Trade" (paper presented at the annual meeting of the Society for Historical Archaeology, Richmond, Va., 1991); Stanley A. Kaufman, *Heatwole and Suter Pottery* (Harrisonburg, Va.: Good Printers, 1978).

16. Kurt C. Russ and Tom Langheim, "The Alleghany County Pottery Manufacturing Industry" (paper presented to the Virginia Social Science Association, Sweet Briar College, Sweet Briar, Va., April 1988); Russ, "The Traditional Pottery Manufacturing Industry in Virginia," 457–61; Kurt C. Russ and John McDaniel, "Understanding Virginia's Traditional Pottery Manufacturing Industry: An Interim Report on the Statewide Survey" (pa-

per presented at the Archaeological Society of Virginia symposium Ceramics in Virginia, Virginia Piedmont Community College, Charlottesville, Va., April 16, 1991): 24–28, 31, 34.

17. Kurt C. Russ and John M. McDaniel, "Understanding the Historic Pottery Manufacturing Industry in Rockbridge County, Virginia: Archaeological Excavation at the Firebaugh Pottery (44RB290)," *Journal of Middle Atlantic Archaeology* 7 (1991): 155–68.

18. See Russ, "The Traditional Pottery Manufacturing Industry in Virginia," 464–73; Russ and McDaniel, "Understanding Virginia's Traditional Pottery Manufacturing Industry," 38–44.

19. Ibid.

20. H. Jackson Darst, *The Darsts of Virginia* (Williamsburg: privately printed, 1972), 25; *Goochland County Deed Book,* no. 14, 79–81.

21. Burt Long and Vaughan Webb, "Early Potters of Franklin County," *Blue Ridge Institute Newsletter* 5, no. 1 (1982): 7.

22. *Rockbridge County Deed Book* A, 517, 518; Darst, 64, 413.

23. Winifred Hadsel, *The Streets of Lexington* (Lexington, Va.: Rockbridge Historical Society, 1985), 141.

24. *Rockbridge County Will Book,* no. 1, 319. "Turning lathe" was the contemporary name for a foot-operated potter's wheel, which Darst himself was using.

25. H. Jackson Darst, "Benjamin Darst Sr. Architect-Builder of Lexington," *Rockbridge Historical Society Proceedings* 8 (1974): 61–76.

26. A pugmill was a horse- or mule-powered grinding operation to prepare the mud or clay for use.

27. L. Moody Sims, "John Jordan: Builder and Entrepreneur," *Virginia Cavalcade* 23 (summer 1973): 20.

28. *Rockbridge County Deed Book,* no. 22, 135. There was another Maple Swamp in the county, located at the intersection of Maple Swamp Road (Va. 622) and Turkey Hill Road (Va. 624). See Winifred Hadsel, *Roads of Rockbridge County* (Lexington, Va.: Rockbridge Historical Society, 1993), 51. Several local residents had heard that this Maple Swamp was a source of the clay for the potteries, as it was fairly close to both operations.

29. *Rockbridge County Will Book,* no. 18, 662.

30. D. B. Webster, *Decorated Stoneware Pottery of North America* (Rutland, Vt.: Charles E. Tuttle, 1971), 160; William C. Ketchum, Jr., *Early Potters and Potteries of New York State* (New York: Funk and Wagnalls, 1970); Russ and McDaniel, "Understanding the Historic Pottery Manufacturing Industry in Rockbridge County, Virginia," 158–59, 167, and "Understanding Virginia's Traditional Pottery Manufacturing Industry," 39, 41, 43–44; William C. Ketchum, Jr., personal communication, 1987.

31. The 1830 census lists a John Morgan between the ages of sixty and seventy. The alphabetical order of the census does not provide for determining in which section of the county Morgan was residing. It is also not clear why Morgan does not appear again until the 1850 census, when he is listed, at the age of eighty-two, as living in the residence of John Firebaugh at Bustleburg.

32. *Rockbridge County Census Report,* 1860; Russ, "The Traditional Pottery Manufacturing Industry in Virginia," 470, and "The Nineteenth Century Traditional Pottery Manufacturing Industry in Botetourt County, Virginia," (paper presented to Historic Fincastle, Fincastle, Va., April 1991): 3.

33. Russ and McDaniel, "Understanding the Historic Pottery Manufacturing Industry in Rockbridge County, Virginia," 161–64, and "Understanding Virginia's Traditional Pottery Manufacturing Industry," 42–43.

34. *Rockbridge County Deed Book* FF, 324.

35. Ibid., W, 406.

36. Ibid., W, 361; V, 165.

37. *Rockbridge County Census Report,* 1840, 1850.

38. The 1860 census household number for Campbell was 2275, next to Shewey, 2276.

39. By 1860 James had left the county and Charles W. had become a carpenter.

40. By 1840 potter John Morgan would have been seventy-two, and perhaps he was not active as a potter, had moved away from the county temporarily, or was missed by census takers. In 1850 John was back in the Rockbridge Baths area or, more precisely, Bustleburg, and Henry appears to have left. In 1852, however, a $200 bond was issued on behalf of Henry E. Morgan and John B. Connery; apparently this bond related to Henry's administration of John Morgan's estate. *Rockbridge County Will Book,* no. 12, 287.

41. *Rockbridge County Census Report,* 1860.

42. Robert A. Brock, *Hardesty's Historical and Geographical Encyclopedia Illustrated* (Special Virginia Edition) (New York: H. H. Hardesty, 1884), 418.

43. See Mullins, "Historic Pottery Making in Rockingham County, Virginia," 1–4, 14–15; Russ and McDaniel, "Understanding Virginia's Traditional Pottery Manufacturing Industry," 11–15.

44. Brock, 418. Lam apparently rented a house from Shewey, as he did not list any real estate value in the censuses. Also, interview with Mrs. Calvin E. Allen of Bustleburg, January 18, 1984, indicates that her father, Charles N. Lam, born in 1870, was eighteen years old when his father, Isaac, died.

45. The shed was perhaps the one William A. Wilson remembered seeing as a boy. William A. Wilson, interview by Royster Lyle, Jr., October 1, 1983. The clay processing and storage area was about thirty-seven feet from the kiln to the northeast, and the pottery shed was about thirty feet to the south.

46. An H. Marshall, whose son James was residing in Rockbridge in 1871, may have been procuring "milk bowls" and other vessels for use at the spring resorts such as Hot Springs, Warm Springs, and Bath Alum Springs, which were operating in the area. Royster Lyle, personal communication, February 9, 1991.

47. Russ and McDaniel, "Archaeological Excavations at the Rockbridge Pottery (44RB84)" (paper presented at the annual meeting of the Archaeological Society of Virginia, Blacksburg, Va., 1985): 4; Russ and McDaniel, "Archaeological Excavations at the Rockbridge Pottery (44RB84): A Preliminary Report," *Quarterly Bulletin of the Archaeological Society of Virginia* 41, no. 2 (1986): 73–86.

48. *Rockbridge County Census Records,* 1850; Russ, "The Traditional Pottery Manufacturing Industry in Virginia," 5; Georgeanna Greer, personal communication, 1987.

49. This New York–trained potter's coming to Rockbridge and producing unique vessels is reminiscent of the mysterious "Bird and Fish Potter" of Fayetteville, N.C., and later Randolph County. The creators of this anomalous ware were found to have been two or three brothers from the Webster family of potters who migrated from Hartford, Conn., to North Carolina about 1820 (Scarborough, 1984). The wares produced by Morgan and the Webster potters are indicative of the transplantation of an early New York and New England decorative stoneware tradition characterized by decorative incising, which continued in the rural Mid-Atlantic and South for many years after it was abandoned in the North.

50. See Mullins, "The Boundaries of Change," 24–26, 28–30.

Bibliography

BOOKS

Allen, Elizabeth Preston. *The Life and Letters of Margaret Junkin Preston.* Boston and New York: Houghton Mifflin/Riverside Press, 1903.

Anderson, Margo J. *The American Census: A Social History.* New Haven: Yale University Press, 1988.

Arnold, Thomas Jackson. *Early Life and Letters of Thomas J. Jackson.* New York: Fleming H. Revell, 1916.

Bailey, Chris H. *Two Hundred Years of American Clocks and Watches.* Englewood Cliffs, N.J.: Prentice Hall, 1975.

Bank, Mirra. *Anonymous Was a Woman.* New York: St. Martin's Press, 1979.

Beecher, Catharine Ester. *A Treatise on Domestic Economy for the Use of Young Ladies at Home, and at School.* Rev. ed. Boston: T. H. Webb, 1843.

Beeton, John D. *History of the Beeton Family.* Sterling, Va.: Privately printed, 1977.

Betts, Edwin Morris, and James Adam Bears, Jr., eds. *The Family Letters of Thomas Jefferson.* Columbia, Mo.: University of Missouri Press, 1966.

Bockstruck, Lloyd DeWitt. *Virginia's Colonial Soldiers.* Baltimore: Genealogical Publishing, 1988

Boley, Henry. *Lexington in Old Virginia.* Richmond: Garrett and Massie, 1936.

Boney, F. Nash. *John Letcher of Virginia.* University, Ala.: University of Alabama Press, 1966.

Bower, William S. *Gunsmiths of Pen-Mar-Va: 1790–1840.* Mercersburg, Pa.: Irwinton Publishers, 1979.

Brock, Robert A. *Hardesty's Historical and Geographical Encyclopedia Illustrated.* Special Virginia edition. New York: H. H. Hardesty, 1884.

Brooke, George M., Jr. *General Lee's Church.* Lexington, Va.: News Gazette, 1984.

Brown, James Moore, and Robert B. Woodsworth. *The Captives of Abbs Valley.* Staunton, Va.: McClure Press, 1942

Brown, M. L. *Firearms in Colonial America.* Washington, D.C.: Smithsonian Institution Press, 1980.

Bruce, Kathleen. *Virginia Iron Manufacture in the Slave Era.* New York: Century, 1931.

Bruce, Philip A. *History of Virginia.* 6 vols. Chicago: American Historical Society, 1924.

Caldwell, Benjamin Hubbard, Jr. *Tennessee Silversmiths.* Winston-Salem, N.C.: Museum of Early Southern Decorative Arts, 1988.

Cappon, Lester J. *Virginia Newspapers 1821–1935: A Bibliography with Historical Introduction and Notes.* New York: D. Appleton-Century, 1936.

Chalkley, Lyman. *Chronicles of the Scotch-Irish Settlement in Virginia.* 3 vols. 1912. Reprint. Baltimore: Genealogical Publishing, 1980.

Chambers, S. Allen. *Lynchburg: An Architectural History.* Charlottesville, Va.: University Press of Virginia, 1981.

Clark, Carmen E. *Goodbars I Found.* Lexington, Va.: News Gazette, 1980.

Clark, Victor Selden. *History of Manufactures in the United States.* 3 vols. Published for the Carnegie Institution of Washington. New York: McGraw-Hill, 1929.

Collection Handbook. Pittsburgh: Carnegie Institute, Museum of Art, 1985.

Comstock, H. E. Introduction to *Folk Pottery of the Shenandoah Valley.* New York: E. P. Dutton, 1975.

_____. *The Pottery of the Shenandoah Valley Region.* Winston-Salem, N.C.: Museum of Early Southern Decorative Arts, 1994.

Comstock, Helen, ed. *The Concise Encyclopedia of American Antiques.* New York: Hawthorn Books, 1958.

Coulling, Mary P. *The Lee Girls.* Winston-Salem, N.C.: John F. Blair, 1987.

Couper, William. *The History of the Shenandoah Valley.* 3 vols. New York: Lewis Historical Publishing, 1952.

_____. *100 Years at VMI.* 4 vols. Richmond: Garrett and Massie, 1939.

_____. *The VMI New Market Cadets.* Charlottesville, Va.: Michie, 1933

Cowdrey, Mary Bartlett. *National Academy, Design Exhibition Record, 1826–1860.* New York: New-York Historical Society, 1943.

Coxe, Tench. *A View of the United States of America, in a Series of Papers Written at Various Times, in the Years Between 1787 and 1794.* New York: A. M. Kelley, 1965.

Crawford, Barbara L., and Royster Lyle, Jr., eds. *Stonewall Jackson and the Virginia Military Institute.* Lexington, Va.: Garland Grey Research Center, Stonewall Jackson House, 1982.

Crenshaw, Ollinger. *General Lee's College.* New York: Random House, 1969.

Cutten, George Barton. *The Silversmiths of Virginia.* Richmond: Dietz Press, 1952.

Darby, William. *Universal Gazetteer: A Dictionary Geographical, Historical, and Statistical of the Various Kingdoms, States, Provinces, Seas, Mountains, etc in the World.* 4th ed. Philadelphia: Grigg and Elliott, 1837.

Darst, H. Jackson. *The Darsts of Virginia.* Williamsburg, Va.: Privately printed, 1972.

Davis, Thomas W., ed. *A Crowd of Honorable Youths: Historical Essays on the First 150 Years of the Virginia Military Institute.* Lexington, Va.: VMI Alumni Association, 1988.

Delmar, Dorothy Chittum, John W. Chittum, and Mae Chittum, eds. *Nancy and John: A Chittum Genealogy.* Privately printed, c. 1981.

Dew, Charles B. *Bond of Iron: Master and Slave at Buffalo Forge.* New York: W. W. Norton, 1994.

_____. *Ironmaker to the Confederacy: Joseph R. Anderson and the Tredegar Iron Works.* New Haven: Yale University Press, 1966.

Diehl, George W. *The Brick Church on Timber Ridge.* Verona, Va.: McClure Press, 1975

_____. *Old Oxford and Her Families.* Verona, Va.: McClure Press, 1971.

_____. *Rockbridge County, Virginia, Notebook.* Compiled by A. Maxim Coppage III. Owensboro, Ky.: McDowell Publishing, 1982.

_____. *The Zollmans and Their Kin.* Privately printed, 1986.

Dillin, John G. W. *The Kentucky Rifle.* Washington, D.C.: National Rifle Association of America, 1924.

Distin, William H. and Robert Bishop. *The American Clock.* New York: E. P. Dutton, 1976.

Downing, Andrew Jackson. *The Architecture of Country Houses.* 1850. Reprint. New York: Dover Publications, 1969.

Driver, Robert J., Jr. *58th Virginia Infantry.* Lynchburg, Va.: H. E. Howard, 1990.

_____. *14th Virginia Cavalry.* Lynchburg, Va.: H. E. Howard, 1988.

_____. *Lexington and Rockbridge in the Civil War.* Lynchburg, Va.: H. E. Howard, 1989.

_____. *Staunton Artillery and McClanahan's Battery.* Lynchburg, Va.: H. E. Howard, 1988

Durand, John. *The Life and Times of A. B. Durand.* 1894. Reprint. New York: Kennedy Graphics and Da Capo Press, 1970.

Ezekiel, Moses Jacob. *Memoirs from the Baths of Diocletian.* Edited by Joseph Gutman and Stanley F. Chyet. Detroit: Wayne State University Press, 1975.

Ford, Alice. *Edward Hicks: His Life and Art.* New York: Abbeville Press, 1985.

Fothergill, Augusta B., and John Mark Naugle. *Virginia Tax Payers 1782–87.* 1940. Reprint. Baltimore: Genealogical Publishing, 1978.

Gibbs, James W. *Dixie Clockmaker.* Gretna, La.: Pelican Publishing, 1979

Gill, Harold B., Jr. *The Gunsmith in Colonial Virginia.* Charlottesville, Va.: University Press of Virginia, 1974.

Gloag, John. *A Social History of Furniture Design from 1300 B.C. to 1960 A.D.* New York: Bonanza Books, 1966.

Goeller, Mildred S. *The Steeles of Steeles Tavern, Virginia, and Related Families.* n.p., 1974.

Groce, George C., and David H. Wallace. *The New-York Historical Society's Dictionary of Artists in America, 1564–1860.* New Haven: Yale University Press, 1957.

Gusler, Wallace B. *Furniture of Williamsburg and Eastern Virginia.* Richmond: Virginia Museum of Fine Arts, 1979.

Hadsel, Winifred. *The Streets of Lexington, Virginia.* Lexington, Va.: Rockbridge Historical Society, 1985.

Hinton, John Howard. *The History and Topography of the United States of North America, Brought Down from the Earliest Period.* 3rd ed. Boston: S. Walker, 1853–54.

Horwitz, Elinor Lander. *The Bird, The Banner, and Uncle Sam: Images of America in Folk and Popular Art.* Philadelphia: J. B. Lippincott, 1976.

Howe, Henry. *Historical Collections of Virginia.* Charleston, S.C.: Babcock and Company, 1845.

Hummel, Charles. *With Hammer in Hand: The Dominy Craftsmen of East Hampton, New York.* Winterthur, Del.: Winterthur Museum, 1968.

Hutchinson, William T. *Cyrus Hall McCormick.* New York: Century, 1930.

Joyner, Peggy Shomo. *Henry Roosen-Rosen: To Pennsylvania 1765.* Norfolk, Va.: Liskey Lithograph, 1980.

Kauffman, Henry J. *Early American Ironware.* Rutland, Vt.: Charles E. Tuttle, 1966.

Kaufman, Stanley A. *Heatwole and Suter Pottery.* Exhibition catalogue, Eastern Mennonite College. Harrisonburg, Va.: Good Printers, 1978.

Kegley, Frederick B. *Virginia Frontier.* Roanoke, Va.: Southwest Virginia Historical Society, 1938.

Ketchum, William C., Jr. *Early Potters and Potteries of New York State.* New York: Funk and Wagnalls, 1970.

Kirkpatrick, Dorthie, and Edwin Kirkpatrick. *Rockbridge County Births, 1853–1877.* 2 vols. San Bernardino, Calif.: Bongo Press, 1988.

_____. *Rockbridge County Marriages, 1778–1850.* Athens, Ga.: Iberian Publishing, 1985.

Lageman, Robert, and Albert C. Manucy. *The Long Rifle.* New York: Eastern National Park and Monument Association, 1980.

Lanansky, Jeannette. *Made of Mud: Stoneware Potteries in Central Pennsylvania: 1831–1929.* University Park, Pa.: Pennsylvania State University Press, 1979.

Lane, Mills. *Architecture of the Old South.* New York: Abbeville Press, 1984.

Lee, Capt. Robert E. *Recollections of General Lee.* Garden City, N.J.: Garden City Publishing, 1924.

Leyburn, James G. *The Scotch-Irish: A Social History.* Chapel Hill, N.C.: University of North Carolina Press, 1962.

Lindsay, Merrill. *The Kentucky Rifle.* New York: Arma Press, 1972.

Loomes, Brian. *White Dial Clocks.* North Pomfret, Vt.: David and Charles, 1981.

Lore, Adelaide, Eugenia Morrison, and Lt. Col. Robert Hall Morrison. *The Morrison Family of the Rocky River Settlement of North Carolina.* Charlotte, N.C.: Observer Printing House, 1950.

Lyle, Oscar K. *Lyle Family.* New York: Lecouver Press, 1912.

Lyle, Royster, Jr., and Pamela Hemenway Simpson. *The Architecture of Historic Lexington.* Charlottesville, Va.: University Press of Virginia, 1977.

Lynch, Earnest Carlyle. *Furniture Antiques Found in Virginia.* New York: Bonanza Books, 1954.

Lyons, Norbert. *The McCormick Reaper Legend.* New York: Exposition Press, 1955.

Martin, Joseph. *A New and Comprehensive Gazetteer of Virginia and the District of Columbia.* Charlottesville, Va.: Joseph Martin Publisher, 1835.

Mather, Eleanore Price, and Dorothy Canning Miller. *Edward Hicks: His Peaceable Kingdoms and Other Paintings.* Newark, Del.: University of Delaware Press, 1983.

McClung, William. *The McClung Genealogy.* Pittsburgh: McClung Printing, 1904.

McClure, James Alexander. *The McClure Family.* Petersburg, Va.: Privately printed, 1914.

Mitchell, Robert D. *Commercialism and Frontier: Perspectives on the Early Shenandoah Valley.* Charlottesville, Va.: University Press of Virginia, 1977.

Montgomery, Charles F. *American Furniture: The Federal Period.* New York: Viking Press, 1966.

Morresset, Marie A. *Abstracts of Rockbridge County, Va., Deed Book A, 1778–1788.* Arcata, La.: Gibson Computers and Publishing, 1987.

Morton, Oren. *A History of Rockbridge County, Virginia.* Staunton, Va.: McClure Press, 1920.

Niederer, Frances J. *The Town of Fincastle, Virginia.* Charlottesville, Va.: University Press of Virginia, 1965.

Paine, Howard. *The Heritage of Country Furniture: A Study in the Survival of Formal and Vernacular Styles from the United States, Britain, and Europe Found in Upper Canada, 1780–1900.* New York: Van Nostrand Reinhold, 1978.

Paxton, W. M. *The Paxtons.* Platte City, Mo.: Landmark Print, 1903.

Perkins, Louise M. *Rockbridge County Marriages, 1851–1885.* Signal Mountain, Tenn.: Mountain Press, 1989.

Peyton, John L. *History of Augusta County, Virginia.* Staunton, Va.: S. M. Yost and Son, 1882.

Piorkowski, Patricia A. *Piedmont Virginia Furniture: A Product of Provincial Cabinetmakers.* Exhibition catalogue. Lynchburg, Va.: Lynchburg Museum System, 1982.

Pusey, William W., III. *Elusive Aspirations: The History of the Female Academy in Lexington, Virginia.* Lexington, Va.: Washington and Lee University, 1983.

Ramsay, John. *American Potters and Pottery.* Clinton, Mass.: Hale, Cushman and Flint, 1939.

Rawson, Marion N. *Candleday Art.* New York: E. P. Dutton, 1938.

Rice, A. H., and John Baer Stoudt. *The Shenandoah Pottery.* 1929. Facsimile reprint. Berryville, Va.: Virginia Book Company, 1974.

Rubin, Cynthia Elyce, ed. *Southern Folic Art.* Birmingham, Ala.: Oxmoor House, 1985.

Ruffner, William Henry, ed. *Washington and Lee University Historical Papers.* 6 vols. Baltimore: John Murphy, 1890–1904.

Schiffer, Margaret. *Arts and Crafts of Chester County, Pennsylvania.* Exton, Pa.: Schiffer Publishing, 1980.

Scott, Kenneth. *British Aliens in the United States During the War of 1812.* Baltimore: Genealogical Publishing, 1979.

Simpson, Pamela H. *American Sculpture in Lexington: Selected Examples from Public Collections.* Exhibition catalogue. Lexington, Va.: Washington and Lee University, 1977.

———. *Architectural Drawings in Lexington: 1779–1926.* Exhibition catalogue. Lexington, Va.: Washington and Lee University, 1978.

———. *So Beautiful an Arch: Images of the Natural Bridge 1787–1890.* Exhibition catalogue. Lexington, Va.: Washington and Lee University, 1982.

Simpson, Pamela H., and Mame Warren. *Michael Miley: American Photographer and Pioneer in Color.* Exhibition catalogue. Lexington, Va.: Washington and Lee University, 1980.

Smith, Elmer L. *Household Tools and Tasks.* Lebanon, Pa.: Applied Arts Publishers, 1979.

———. *Pottery: A Utilitarian Folk Craft.* Lebanon, Pa.: Applied Arts Publishers, 1972.

Sparks, Jarred. *Life of Washington.* Russel, Odironc, Metcalf, and Hilliard, Gray, and Company, 1834.

Taft, Robert. *Photography and the American Scene: A Social History, 1839–1889.* New York: Dover Publications, 1964.

Taylor, Joshua C. *The Fine Arts in America.* Chicago: University Press of Chicago, 1979.

Tompkins, Edmund P. *Rockbridge County, Virginia: An Informal History.* Richmond: Whittet and Shepperson, 1952.

Turner, Charles W. *The Diary of Henry Boswell Jones of Brownsburg: 1842–71.* Verona, Va: McClure Press, 1979.

———. *Virginia's Green Revolution.* Waynesboro, Va.: Humphries Press, 1986.

Turner, Herbert S. *Bethel and Her Minister: 1746–1974.* Verona, Va.: McClure Press, 1974.

Turner, Robert P., ed. *Lewis Miller, Sketches and Chronicles: The Reflections of a Nineteenth Century Pennsylvania Folk Artist.* York, Pa.: Historical Society of York County, 1966.

U.S. Congress. [Coxe, Tench]. "Digest of Manufactures," 1810. *American State Papers* 2 (1832). Washington, D.C.: Gales and Seaton, 1832.

U.S. Treasury Department [Coxe, Tench]. *A Statement of the Arts and Manufactures of the United States of America for the Year 1810.* Photographic facsimile. Philadelphia: A Cornman, Jr., 1814.

Valentine, Elizabeth Gray. *Dawn to Twilight: Work of Edward V. Valentine.* Richmond: William Byrd Press, 1929.

Virginia Military Institute. *Virginia Military Institute Register, Former Cadets.* Lexington, Va.: Virginia Military Institute, 1957.

Waddell, J. A. *Annals of Augusta County, Virginia from 1726 to 1871.* Harrisonburg, Va.: C. J. Carrier, 1902.

Washington and Lee University Alumni Catalogue, 1749–1888. Baltimore: John Murphy, 1888.

Webster, D. B. *Decorated Stoneware Pottery of North America.* Rutland, Vt.: Charles E. Tuttle, 1971.

Whisker, James Biser. *Gunsmiths of Virginia.* Bedford, Pa.: Old Bedford Village Press, 1992.

Whitney, Philip. *The Clocks of the Shenandoah.* Stevens City, Va.: Commercial Press, 1983.

Willett, E. Henry, and Joey Brackner. *The Traditional Pottery of Alabama.* Montgomery, Ala.: Montgomery Museum of Fine Arts, 1983.

William Rush, American Sculptor. Exhibition catalogue. Philadelphia: Pennsylvania Academy of Fine Arts, 1982.

Williamson, Thomas H. *An Elementary Course of Architecture and Civil Engineering, Compiled from the Most Approved Authors for the Use of the Cadets of the Virginia Military Institute.* Lexington, Va.: Samuel Gillock, 1850.

Wilson, Howard McK. *The Tinkling Springs: Headwater of Freedom.* Fisherville, Va.: Tinkling Spring and Hermitage Presbyterian Churches, 1954.

Wiltshire, William E. *Folk Pottery of the Shenandoah Valley.* New York: E. P. Dutton, 1975.

Wright, Lewis R. *Artists in Virginia before 1900.* Charlottesville, Va.: University Press of Virginia, 1983.

Wurst, Klaus. *Folk Art in Stone: Southwest Virginia.* Edinburg, Va.: Shenandoah History, 1970.

Zug, Charles G. *Turners and Burners: The Folk Potters of North Carolina.* Chapel Hill, N.C.: University of North Carolina Press, 1986.

ARTICLES

Arthur, Ralph. "Back Country Potters along the Valley of Virginia." *The Antique Market Tabloid* 3, no. 9 (1983): 18–21.

Barka, Norman F. "The Kiln and Ceramics of the 'Poor Potter' of Yorktown: A Preliminary Report." *Ceramics in America* (1972): 291–318. Edited by Ian M. G. Quimby.

Barka, Norman F., and Chris Sheridan. "The Yorktown Pottery Industry, Yorktown, Virginia." *Northeast Historical Archaeology* 6, nos. 1–2 (1977): 21–32.

Beckerdite, Luke. "A Virginia Cabinetmaker: The Eventon Shop and Related Work." *Journal of Early Southern Decorative Arts* 10, no. 2 (November 1983): 21–42.

Bivins, John, Jr. "Isaac Zane and the Products of Marboro Furnace." *Journal of Early Southern Decorative Arts* 11, no. 1 (May 1985): 15, 17.

Bower, Beth A. "The Pottery-Making Trade in Colonial Philadelphia: The Growth of an Early Urban Industry." *Domestic Pottery of the Northeastern United States, 1625–1850* (1985): 265–84. Edited by S. P. Turnbaugh.

Brady, T. T. "The Early Iron Industry in Rockbridge County." *Rockbridge Historical Society Proceedings* 8 (1979): 45–52.

Broehl, Wayne G., Jr. "John Deere's Shop." *American History Illustrated* 19, no. 9 (January 1985): 16–19.

———. "The Plow That Broke the Prairies." *American History Illustrated* 19, no. 9 (January 1985): 16–19, 47.

Capron, Lester J. "Lucy Selina's Charcoal Era." *Virginia Cavalcade* 7, no. 2 (autumn 1957): 32.

Comstock, Helen. "Furniture of Virginia, North Carolina, Georgia and Kentucky." *Antiques,* no. 61 (January 1952): 58–99.

Coulling, Anne, ed. "Old George Comes Down." *W&L: The Alumni Magazine of Washington and Lee* 65 (July 1990): 2–3.

Darst, H. Jackson, "Benjamin Darst, Sr.: Architect–Builder of Lexington," *Rockbridge Historical Society Proceedings* 8 (1979): 61–76.

Dickens, David B. "Frank Buchser in Virginia: A Swiss Artist's Impressions." *Virginia Cavalcade* 38, no. 1 (1988): 4–13.

Dooley, Edwin L., Jr. "Lexington in the 1860 Census." *Rockbridge Historical Society Proceedings* 9 (1975–79): 189–96.

———. "Lexington Ledgers: A Source for Social History." *Rockbridge Historical Society Proceedings* 10 (1980–89): 236–44.

Dooley, Louise K. "Cyrus McCormick, Rockbridge Inventory." *Main Street* 1, no. 1 (March 1974): 7–8.

Earle, Polly Anne, and Ian M. G. Quimby. "Technological Innovation and Decorative Arts." *Winterthur Conference Report, 1973.* Charlottesville, Va.: University Press of Virginia, 1974.

Fletcher, A. Review of *The Agrarian History of England and Wales,* by Joan Thirsk. *History* 72, no. 236 (1987): 523–25.

Gusler, Wallace. "Queen Anne Style Desks from the Virginia Piedmont." *The Magazine Antiques* 104 (July–December 1973): 665–73.

———. "Two Virginia Longrifles." *Journal of Historical Armsmaking Technology* 2 (June 1987): 4.

———. "Virginia Frontier Rifles." *Virginia Cavalcade* 17, no. 1 (summer 1967): 20–26.

Hanger, Jim. "Pots, Potteries, and Potting in Augusta County, 1800–1870." *Augusta Historical Journal* 9, no. 1 (spring 1973): 4–15.

Long, Burt, and Vaughan Webb. "Early Potters of Franklin County." *Blue Ridge Institute Newsletter* 5, no. 1 (1982): 7.

Luck, Barbara. "Lewis Miller's Virginia." *Rockbridge Historical Society Proceedings* 10 (1980–89): 245–72.

Lyle, Royster, Jr. "John Blair Lyle of Lexington and His Automatic Bookstore." *Virginia Cavalcade* 21, no. 2 (autumn 1972): 20–27.

McCleary, Ann. "A Study of the Account Book of James Rankin." *Augusta Historical Bulletin* 19, no. 1 (1983): 22–34.

McClure, William H. "A Cyrus McCormick Story." *Rockbridge Historical Society Proceedings* 8 (1970–74): 77–84.

McDowell, Charles R. "Furnishings of the Law Building." *The Alumni Magazine, Washington and Lee University* (spring 1936): 7, 8, 15.

Moore, J. Roderick. "Earthenware Potters along the Great Road in Virginia and Tennessee." *The Magazine Antiques* 124, no. 3 (1983): 428–537.

———. "Painted Chests from Wythe County, Virginia." *The Magazine Antiques* 122 (September 1982): 516–21.

Moore, John S. "John Jordan, Baptist Layman." *Rockbridge Historical Society Proceedings* 6 (1966): 63–71.

———. "John Jordan: Rockbridge Baptist Layman." *Virginia Baptist Register* 2 (1963): 52–62.

Myers, Susan H. "A Survey of Traditional Pottery Manufacture in the Mid-Atlantic and Northeastern United States." *Northeast Historical Archaeology* 6, nos. 1–2 (1977): 1–13.

Napps, Klell Bayne. "Traditional Pottery in Washington County, Virginia and Sullivan County, Tennessee." *The Historical Society of Washington County Virginia,* 2d ser., no. 10 (1972): 3–16.

Pogue, Dennis. "An Analysis of Wares Salvaged from the Swan-Smith-Milburn Pottery Site (44AX29), Alexandria, Virginia." *Quarterly Bulletin of the Archaeological Society of Virginia* 34 (1980): 149–60.

Preston, Margaret Junkin. "Edward Virginius Valentine." *American Art Review* 1 (1880): 277–82.

Prown, Jon. "A Cultural Analysis of Furniture-making in Petersburg, Virginia, 1760–1820." *Museum of Early Southern Decorative Arts Journal* 18, no. 1 (May 1992): 1–173.

Rauschenberg, Bradford. "L. B. Duval and Co., Richmond: A Newly Discovered Pottery." *Pottery Collectors Newsletter* 8, no. 4 (1978): 26–38.

Russ, Kurt C. "The Traditional Pottery Manufacturing Industry in Virginia: Examples from Botetourt and Rockbridge Counties." *Rockbridge Historical Society Proceedings* 10 (1980–89): 453–89.

Russ, Kurt C., and John M. McDaniel. "Archaeological Excavations at the Rockbridge Pottery (44RB84): A Preliminary Report." *Quarterly Bulletin of the Archeological Society of Virginia* 42 (1986): 72–88.

———. "Understanding the Historic Pottery Manufacturing Industry in Rockbridge County, Virginia: Archaeological Excavations at the Firebaugh Pottery (44RB290)." *Journal of Middle Atlantic Archaeology* 7 (1991): 155–68.

Rutland, Robert A. "Men in Iron in the Making of Virginia." *Iron Worker* (summer 1976).

Scarborough, Quincy. "Connecticut Influence on North Carolina Stoneware—The Webster School of Potters." *Journal of Early Southern Decorative Arts* 10 (1984): 14–74.

Schneider, Cary A. "Rockbridge County Gravestones and Their Carvers." *Rockbridge Historical Society Proceedings* 9 (1975–79): 63–76.

Sims, L. Moody. "John Jordan Builder and Entrepreneur." *Virginia Cavalcade* 23, no. 1 (summer 1973): 19–30.

Smith, Jane Webb. "A Large and Elegant Assortment: A Group of Baltimore Tall Clocks, 1795–1815." *Journal of Early Southern Decorative Arts* 8, no. 2 (November 1987): 33–103.

NEWSPAPERS

Buena Vista Advocate. Buena Vista, Va.

Herald of the Valley. Fincastle, Va.

Lexington Gazette. Lexington, Va.

Lexington Intelligencer. Lexington, Va.

Lexington News-Letter. Renamed *Lexington Weekly.* Lexington, Va.

Rockbridge County News. Lexington, Va.

Valley Star. Lexington, Va.

Virginia Gazette. Williamsburg, Va.

Virginia Gazette and General Advocate. Richmond, Va.

Virginia Patriot. Richmond and Fincastle, Va.

Virginia Telegraph and Rockbridge Courier. Lexington, Va.

PUBLIC RECORDS

Augusta County Deed Book. Court House, Augusta County, Va.

Augusta County Order Book. Court House, Augusta County, Va.

Goochland County Deed Book. Court House, Goochland County, Va.

Queen, Katherine J. Index of 1860 census, Rockbridge County, Va. Columbus, Ohio: K. J. Queen, 1986. Washington and Lee University, Lexington, Va.

Rockbridge County Death Register. Court House, Rockbridge County, Va.

Rockbridge County Land Book. Court House, Rockbridge County, Va.

Rockbridge County Order Book. Court House, Rockbridge County, Va.

Rockbridge County Property Book. Court House, Rockbridge County, Va.

Rockbridge County Will Book. Court House, Rockbridge County, Va.

U.S. Bureau of Census. Rockbridge County, Va., 1820, 1850, 1870, 1880. Archives, Virginia State Library, Richmond.

U.S. Bureau of Census. Rockbridge County, Va., 1860. Duke University, Chapel Hill, N.C.

U.S. Census of Manufactures. Rockbridge County, Va., 1820, 1850, and 1860. Microfilm Division, National Archives, Washington, D.C.

U.S. Census Office. Rockbridge County, Va., 1810, 1829, 1840, 1850, 1860, 1870, 1880, and 1890. National Archives Microfilm. Washington and Lee University, Lexington, Va.

UNPUBLISHED WORKS

Blomster, Jeffrey P., and Kurt C. Russ. "Early Pottery Production in Eastern Virginia: An Examination of Its Extent and Development." Paper presented at the annual meeting of the Society for Historical Archaeology, Richmond, January 1991.

Bogley, Beverly A. "Virginia's First Potters: Why Did They Fail?" Paper, Virginia Research Center for Archaeology, Yorktown, Va., 1984.

Brady, D. E. "Iron Valley Revisited." Paper presented to the Fortnightly Club, Lexington, Va., 1989.

Canal Boat Ledger. Rockbridge County Court House.

Couper, William. *Jackson Memorial Cemetery Survey Complete to 1960.* Lexington, Va., n.d.

Crenshaw, Ollinger, "General Lee's College." 2 vols. Special collections, Leyburn Library, Washington and Lee University, Lexington, Va., 1969.

Davis, A. J. Daybook. Davis collection. New York Public Library. 1828–53.

Driver, Robert J., Jr. Personal manuscript collection. Brownsburg, Va.

Fortson, Elizabeth. "Arming the Confederacy: The Valley of Virginia Iron Furnaces in the Civil War," Paper, Stonewall Jackson House collection, Lexington, Va., September 1988.

Franklin Society records. Special collections, Washington and Lee University, Lexington, Va.

Hoffman, J. D. Shop ledger for Lexington merchant, c. 1790s. Special collections, Washington and Lee University, Lexington, Va.

Humphries, William S. Diary of one year's activity at Vesuvius Plow Factory, 1872. Private collection.

Index of Early Southern Artists and Artisans. Museum of Early Southern Decorative Arts, Winston-Salem, N.C.

International Order of Oddfellows. "The Register of the Rockbridge Lodge No. 158, IOOF," October 29, 1847–1900. Private collection.

Key, Milton. Cabinetmaker's ledger, 1857–60. Transcribed by Edwin Dooley. Rockbridge County Court House.

Lawall, David Bannar. "Asher Brown Durand: His Art and Art Theory in Relation to His Times." 4 vols. Ph.D. dissertation, Princeton University, 1966.

Leyburn, James G. "The Leyburn Family, 1734–1960." Special collections, Leyburn Library, Washington and Lee University, Lexington, Va.

McDaniel, John M., and Kurt C. Russ. "Rockbridge Origins: An Anthropological Perspective." Paper presented at the symposium A Search for Early Rockbridge County Artisans, Southern Seminary Junior College, Buena Vista, Va., 1985.

Mullins, Paul R. "The Boundaries of Change: Negotiating Industrialization in the Domestic Pottery Trade." Paper presented at the annual meeting of the Society for Historical Archaeology, Richmond, Va., 1991.

——. "Historic Pottery Making in Rockingham County, Virginia." Paper presented at the Archaeological Society of Virginia symposium Ceramics in Virginia, Virginia Piedmont Community College, Charlottesville, Va., 1988.

Myers, John H. Customer account books for Lexington hardware store. 2 vols. 1837–52. Private collection.

Ott, Ethelbert Nelson. "William D. Washington, 1833–1870: Artist of the South." Master's thesis, University of Delaware. VMI archives, 1969.

Ruff, John. Ledger (1809–18). Rockbridge Historical Society collection. Washington and Lee University, Lexington, Va.

Russ, Kurt C., and Tom Langheim. "The Alleghany County Pottery Manufacturing Industry." Paper presented at the meeting of the Virginia Social Science Association, Sweet Briar College, Sweet Briar, Va., April 1988.

Russ, Kurt C., and John M. McDaniel. "The Historic Pottery Manufacturing Industry in Rockbridge County, Virginia—1785–1882." Laboratory of Anthropology, Washington and Lee University, Lexington, Va., 1986.

——. "Understanding Virginia's Traditional Pottery Manufacturing Industry: An Interim Report on the Statewide Survey." Paper presented at the annual meeting of the Society for Historical Archaeology, Richmond, Va., January 1991.

Smith, Samuel R. Shop ledgers. 2 vols. 1831–47 and 1827–59. Private collection.

Taylor, Warren T. "A Study of Nineteenth-Century Rockbridge Account Books." Laboratory of Archaeology, special collections. Washington and Lee University, Lexington, Va., 1984.

Trout, William E., III. Personal manuscript collection. Richmond, Va.

Tucker, Harry St. George. "A list of white voters with P. office addresses in the 10th District of Virginia, 1889—Alleghany, Appomattox, Augusta, Bath, Cumberland, Fluvanna, Highland, Nelson, Amherst, Buckingham, and Rockbridge—who were the constituents of Congressman Harry St. George Tucker." Ledger, private collection.

Varner, Andrew. Lexington cabinetmaker ledgers, 1860–64 and 1860–63. Private collection.

Virginia Military Institute. Preston Library, VMI archives, alumni files, Lexington, Va.

Virginia Military Institute. Preston Library, VMI archives, superintendent's files, Lexington, Va.

Virginia Military Institute. Preston Library, VMI archives, treasurer's files, Lexington, Va.

Walker, John. Blacksmith day book, 1788–95. Wisconsin State Historical Society, Madison, Wis.

Weaver v. Davis. Legal transactions among William Weaver, John Jordan, and William W. Davis, 1834–35. Special collections, Washington and Lee University, Lexington, Va.

Weir, Adolphus. Blacksmith ledger, 1790–1806. Swem Library, William and Mary College, Williamsburg, Va.

Wilson and Barclay. Store ledger. Special collections, Washington and Lee University, Lexington, Va.

Withrow scrapbooks, 2 vols. Special collections, Leyburn Library, Washington and Lee University, Lexington, Va.

Illustration Credits

Unless otherwise noted, all photographs are by the authors and the objects are in private collections.

Abby Aldrich Rockefeller Folk Art Center, Williamsburg, Va.: 6–7, 32, 36, 46 bottom left, 56

Mr. and Mrs. Richard G. Anderson collection, Brownsburg, Va.: 121 left, 124 top right

Andre Studio, Lexington, Va.: 68, 69 top left, 71 top left, 72 top right (photographs by Michael D. Collingwood)

Ransom Averitt, Tobaccoville, N.C.: 90 left

Jane Burns collection: 42–43 (Michael Miley photograph printed from the original glass plate by Sally Mann)

Bernard Caperton: 2–3

Colonial Williamsburg Foundation, Williamsburg, Va.: 31 top, 74 right

H. E. Comstock, Winchester, Va.: 178

Edith Humphries Crissman collection, Roanoke, Va.: 135 left

Jim Goodridge, P and J Residential Enterprises, Guilford, Conn.: 28 top and bottom

Wallace Gusler, Williamsburg, Va.: 142, 143

Historic American Buildings Survey: 84 right

Historical Society of York, Pa.: 44 top

Stephanie Huebinger, photographer, Austin, Tex.: front jacket, 131 top

Illinois State Historical Society Library, Old State Capitol, Springfield, Ill.: 40 bottom

Independence National Historical Park collection, Philadelphia: 51 bottom right

The Library of Virginia, Richmond, Va.: 51 bottom left

B. Alexander and Mary S. Lipscomb collection, Raphine, Va.: 82 bottom left and right, 132 far left, 133, 156

Sally Mann, photographer, Lexington, Va.: 224

Mint-Spring Antiques, Mint Spring, Va.: 126 center

J. Roderick Moore collection, Ferrum, Va.: 148 top, 190

Museum of Early Southern Decorative Arts, Winston-Salem, N.C.: 20, 40 top, 74 bottom, 75, 77, 78, 80 right, 98, 105, 108 both, 110, 111 right, 112 top, 114 right, 119 top right, 123, 128, 131 right, 132 center right, 146 top right and bottom right, 147 top, 151, 153, 157 left; MESDA collection: 80 left, 123 left and center, 153, 170

National Gallery of Art, Washington, D.C.: 58–59

National Museum of American History, Smithsonian Institution, Washington, D.C.: 66, 67 left, 229

National Trust for Historic Preservation, Lyndhurst, Tarrytown, N.Y.: 87 bottom

Todd D. Prickett of C. L. Prickett, Yardley, Pa.: 128, 131 right

R. E. Lee Episcopal Church collection, Lexington, Va.: 94, 102 right, 115 bottom, 118 bottom left and bottom right

Rockbridge Historical Society collection, Lexington, Va.: 44 bottom right, 71 top right, 91, 116 bottom, 120, 121 center, 181 top right

Linda and Kurt Russ collection, Lexington, Va.: 27 right and bottom; 68; 69 top left; 71 top left; 72 top left; 97; 106 top left; 117 bottom; 119 top left; 121 top; 166; 167; 168; 171 far left and left; 172; 179 top left, bottom left, bottom center, and right; 180–81; 181 bottom right; 218

Nancy Spencer, photographer: 69 bottom left, bottom right, and top right; 70; 71 left; 72 right; 73

Stonewall Jackson House, Lexington, Va.: 26 (photograph by H. K. Barnett, Wexford, Pa.); 46 right; 86, 186 (photographs by Museum of Early Southern Decorative Arts, Winston-Salem, N.C.)

Timber Ridge Presbyterian Church collection, Lexington, Va.: 79 right

University of Virginia Art Museum: 17

Valentine Museum, Richmond, Va.: 49 top

Virginia Military Institute, Lexington, Va., Archives: 55 left, 87 top, 90 right; Museum collection: 21, 41, 53, 54, 88, 107, 122 right, 148 left; Office of Alumni Publications: 22 far right, 23, 46 bottom right, 47, 55 right (photographs by Kathryn A. Wise)

Washington and Lee University, Lexington, Va., James G. Leyburn Library, special collections: 1, 10, 24, 45, 48, 57, 210; Laboratory of Anthropology: 141, 174–75, 175 right, 176, 177 both; Office of Public Relations: 22 right and bottom, 49 left, 50, 51 top, 182

James Biser Whisker, Bedford, Pa.: 138–39, 144–45

Woodrow Wilson Birthplace Foundation, Staunton, Va.: 131 bottom left

Acknowledgments

Over the decade spent developing this research project, numerous institutions and organizations and countless people have provided invaluable support. From the beginning the Virginia Foundation for the Humanities and Public Policy, Rob Vaughn, director; and Southern Virginia College (formerly Southern Seminary College), Presidents Joyce Davis and John Ripley, have underwritten and endorsed the project. Dr. Davis was responsible for gaining special funding for the book. Additional support for research assistance came from the Rockbridge Historical Society. The Richard Gwalthmey and Caroline T. Gwalthmey Foundation made a generous contribution toward the publication.

Of great importance was assistance and encouragement from various museums and institutions. Frank Horton and Brad Raushenberg at the Museum of Early Southern Decorative Arts have been influential in determining the nature and direction of our research. Our consultants brought breadth and insight to the endeavor. Consultants Barbara Luck, Abby Aldrich Rockefeller Folk Art Center; Swannee Bennett, Arkansas Territorial Restoration; Wallace Gusler, Colonial Williamsburg Foundation; Bill Moore, Greensboro Historical Museum; Roddy Moore, Blue Ridge Institute; and Kurt C. Russ, Department of Sociology and Anthropology Washington and Lee University, and the services provided by their institutions were critical to our success. Another consultant, Gene Comstock, a long-time supporter, provided early guidance.

Local institutions and their staffs furnished a wealth of information and unflagging assistance. These include Joe Malloy, Von Canon Library, Southern Virginia College; Lisa McCown, Barbara Brown, Betty Kondayan, and Vaughan Stanley, Special Collections, Washington and Lee University; Diane Jacob and Sis Davis, Preston Library, Virginia Military Institute; Keith Gibson and June Cunningham, VMI Museum; Michael Lynn and Joanna Smith, Stonewall Jackson House; Larry Bland, George C. Marshall Library; Bruce Patterson, Rockbridge County Court House; and Mac Gilliam, Rockbridge Historical Society. The news offices at both the Virginia Military Institute and Washington and Lee University generously provided answers and illustrations.

Individuals at other institutions offered research assistance, answering endless questions and requests. These include Kip Campbell, Virginia State Library; Linda Baumgarten, Colonial Williamsburg Foundation; Doris Bowman, Smithsonian Institution; Susan Klaffky, Woodrow Wilson Birthplace; Calder Loth, Virginia Landmarks Commission; Laura Lyon, Reynolda House Museum of American Art; Stanley Sherman, Nelson Atins Museum of Art; Sandra Stark, Library, Illinois State Historical Society; and Jon Prown, Colonial Williamsburg Foundation.

Other historians and scholars who provided information and critical observations include Pam Simpson, Katherine Brown, Ann McCleary, Mary Coulling, Robert Driver, Charles Turner, Sarah Watts, Bill Rasmussen, Sue Stevenson, Ann McCleary, Ellen Eslinger, John McDaniel and Katherine Bushman, Jane Webb Smith, Ken Koones, Linda Hyatt, Louise Dooley, and Ed Dooley.

Professional services were provided by Jim Dedrick at the *News Gazette* and Norma Stotz at Southern Virginia College. Photographic assistance and advice came from Patrick Hinley, Fay and Tom Bradshaw, Mike Collingwood, Sally Mann, Jeremy Leadbetter, Nancy Spencer, and Nick Mathis. Over the years a number of Southern Virginia College students helped with research. Special contributions were made by Suzanne Gardner, Rebecca Stevens, and Melissa Whitten. Through a special grant Jackson House scholar Lynn Pearson extended her stay in Lexington to complete the exhaustive task of indexing local newspapers.

In 1991 Southern Virginia College sponsored an exhibition, Valley of Virginia Folk Art. The exhibit featured pieces from the collection of Linda and Kurt Russ and was sponsored by Cora B. Womeldorf and Florence S. Womeldorf. The exhibition catalogue was sponsored by Grant H. Griswold. The exhibit and those who made it possible are a reminder of how strongly the community feels about its history and material culture. The heart and soul of the research was provided by hundreds of people who opened their houses to us and shared their love of the county, its history, and its material culture with us. Many of these are descendants of early artists and artisans and have retained pieces made by them or information relating to our research. Each allowed us to invade—and often dismantle—their houses to photograph various pieces. They often led us through attics and basements, were patient when we blew fuses, took extra time to answer our questions, and were always supportive. Others were admirers and collectors of county material culture and assisted us in various ways. Without them, this book would not have been possible. While not all can be listed, we are deeply indebted to Mr. and Mrs. Tate Alexander, Mrs. Calvin E. Allen, Mr. and Mrs. Richard G. Anderson, Mr. and Mrs. Ranson Averitt, Gordon Barlow, W. Arthur Beeton, Senora Bogert, Mr. and Mrs. D. E. Brady, Jr., Manly Brown, Mr. and Mrs. Thomas Cabe, Mr. and Mrs. Royal Cabell, Mr. and Mrs. Herbert Chermside, Mr. and Mrs. Dan Chrisman, Carmen E. Clark, Mrs. Houston Close, David Coffey, Mrs. Jay D. Cook, Jr., Rev. and Mrs. David Cox, Mr. and Mrs. Hugh Crawford, Louise Crawford, Mr. and Mrs. Claude A. Crissman, Mrs. Lloyd M. Cummins, Mr. and Mrs. Jim Davis, Carter Drake, Orval Drawbond, Edna Driver, Jean Dunbar, Mr. and Mrs. Halstead Dunlap, Mr. and Mrs. Gerald Eggleston, Bennie Fauber, Mr. and Mrs. Burton W. Folsom, Mr. and Mrs. Gary Gearhart, Mr. and Mrs. Thomas B. Gentry, Mr. and Mrs. B. McClure Gilliam, Cris Gladden, Mrs. John J. Gravatt, Mr. and Mrs. Grant H. Griswold, Peggy Hays, Mrs. W. W. Heffelfinger, Mrs. G. Effinger Herring, William L. Hess, Mr. and Mrs. B. P. Knight, Jr., Johnsey Leef, Ruby W. Leighton, Mrs. B. A. Lipscomb, Patti

Loughridge, Dr. and Mrs. Todd Lowry, Dan Malcolm, Larry Mann, Mrs. Robert E. Mason, Bill Mauck, Mr. and Mrs. James A. McAleer, Mr. and Mrs. "Mac" McKenney, Tom McNemar, Gertrude Neff, Sarah Francis O'Hare, Mrs. William W. Old, R. O. Paxton and Sarah Plimpton, Mrs. W. M. Paxton, Sr., Mr. and Mrs. W. M. Paxton, Jr., Mr. and Mrs. Charles Potter, Todd D. Prickett, Mrs. Taylor Reveley, Jack Roberson, Irvin Rosen, Kurt and Linda Russ, Mrs. J.J.B. Sebastian, Sally and Ted Seder, Henry Simpson, Mr. and Mrs. Daniel R. Snider, Tommy Spencer, Mr. and Mrs. Richard Sessoms, Laura Stearns, Frederick Stone, Mr. and Mrs. Blair Tolley, William E. Trout, Susan Coe Tucker, Mrs. Edward F. Turner, Mrs. Gillie Tutwiler, Mr. and Mrs. Lewis Tyree, A. B. Varner, Jr., Robert Walker, Mr. and Mrs. Earl Watts, Cora B. and Florence Womeldorf, Mr. and Mrs. Richard Whipple, James B. Whisker, James White, James Whitehead, Mr. and Mrs. John L. Whitesell, George Whiting, and Charles D. Williams.

A number of people who keenly understood the importance and richness of the county's past have passed from us before we finished. Our gratitude to them is too great to leave them unlisted. They include Mrs. Lewis Adams, Mr. and Mrs. William H. Agnor, Louise Alexander, Virginia Bird, T. T. Brady, Mrs. E. J. Deaver, Margaret M. Lackey, Gen. John S. Letcher, Mrs. J.M.B. Lewis, Jr., Carlyle Lynch, Mrs. F.M.P. Pearse, Carl L. Varner, Mrs. Andrew B. Varner, and Thomas M. Williams.

Finally we thank Janet Cummings, who typed the manuscript in its many stages numerous times and remained remarkably calm when dealing with our notes, charts, and requests for changes and rewrites, all the while maintaining the most incredible rose garden in Lexington! To Frances Lyle and Claire Lyons, our special thanks for their inspiration.

And to Katie and Mario, we give our thanks for their constant support and encouragement.

Index

Hill, James S., 203

Hinkle, Jesse, 172

    pottery by, *170*

Hinshelwood, Robert, 203

Hinty, Thomas, 203

Hinty, William Henry, 203

Holansworth, John, 203

Holt, Andrew, 204

Hope, James, 204

Hopkins, Thomas, 109, 204

Hopkins House, Lexington, Va.

    furniture from, *114*

    mantel of, 51, *83*

Houdon, Jean Antoine, statue by, *51,*
    52

House Mountain, Rockbridge
    County, *2–3, 10*

Hubard, William James, 52, 54, 204

Humphreys, Joshua, 204

Humphreys, Samuel, 45, 205

Humphries, John McD., 164, 205

    ironwork by, *151, 204*

Humphries, William Shelton,
    162–63, 205

Hunt, Harry, 158, 205

Hunter, David, 95, 126

Huston, James, 130, 133

    clocks by, *128, 131*

Hutton, Gardner Paxton, 205

I

Ireland, John M., 205

Irish Creek, ironworks in, 161, 164

Irish linen weavers, 59

Iron Valley (South River),
    Rockbridge County, 156,
    161, 162

Ironwork, 151–65, *192, 204, 215*

Irvin, John, 155, 171, 205

Irvine, William S., 205

J

Jackson, Thomas Jonathan
    ("Stonewall"), 35, 45, 79,
    88, 95, 96, 97

    depictions of, *22, 46, 47,* 54, 55

    grave of, *22*

    home of, 12, *26*

Jacquard weaving, 63, *64*

James River, Rockbridge County

    canals and locks of, *20,* 155, 161,
    162, 207

    iron transport on, 154, 155, 162

James River School of gunsmithing,
    145

Jamestown, Va., pottery in, 167

Jefferson, Thomas, 8, 34, 57, 61, 161

John (forgeman), 206

Johnson, David, 206

Johnson, John, 34, 206

    painting by, frontispiece

Johnston, James T., 206

Jones, Green Berry, 206

Jordan, Charles, 206

Jordan, Eva, 206

Jordan, Ira F., 206

Jordan, J. M., 206

Jordan, James Winn, 155, 206

    initials of, *207*

Jordan, John, 35, 81, 154–55, 161, 171

    home of, *see* Stono

Jordan, Nannie, 206

Jordan, Samuel Francis, 155, 206

Jordan Road, 155

Jordan's Point, East Lexington, Va.,
    44

    ironworks at, 163

    mill at, 61

K

Kahle, Jacob P., 207

Kahle, Mathew Saltzer, 88, 90, 99,
    109, 207

    furniture by, *28, 83, 116*

    statue by, *22, 50, 51,* 51–52, *182*

Kahle, Samuel F., 208

Kahle, William Henry Harrison, 208

Kelly, G., 114, 208

Kelly, Joseph, 208

Kelly, Joseph, Jr., 209

Kelly, William Henry, 209

Key, Milton H., 13, 84, 86, 89, 90,
    95–96, 99, 104, 109, 115, 120,
    123, 209

Keys, William, 122, 209

Kiger, George, 209

Knick, James, 95, 209

Knox, William, 209

Kollner, Augustus, 209

Koones, Albert L., 209

Koones, Mrs. Albert L., 209

Koones, Charles M., 90, 96, 209

    receipt from, *210*

Kurtz, Frederick, 95, 210

Kurz, Louis, 210

L

Lackey, James, 60, 61, 210

Laird, David, 45

    residence of, *32*

Lam, Isaac, 174, 176, 177, 210

Lamb, W. C., 211

Lambert, David, 211

Landscapes

    paintings, *2–3, 17, 18–19, 54*

    photographs, *42–43*

Larew, Jacob, 211

Larew, James W., 95, 211

Larew, Milton F., 211

Laughlin, Hugh, 211

Lee, A. F., 211

Lee, L. G., 211

Lee, Robert E., 35, 53, 55, 86–87

    depictions of, *22, 45, 48, 48, 49,*
    53–54

Lee Avenue, Lexington, Va., 171

Leech, William D., 211

Leesee, Mr., 211

Lewis, Elias, 136, 211

Lexington, Va., *32*

    architecture and construction of,
    34, 81, 85, 114, 155, 164, 171

    cemetery in, *22, 150,* 164

    Civil War occupation of, 95, 126

    founding of, 34

Lexington Gazette (newspaper),
    accounts of artisans in, 38,
    39, 40, 52, 76, 86, 129, 151,
    163, 164

Lexington Military School (Miller),
    46

Leyburn, Edward Jenner, 151, 164,
    211

Leyburn, Mary, 212

Leyburn, William Caruthers, 151,
    164, 212

Liberty Hall Academy, Lexington,
    Va., 12, 34, 80, 85, 141

Linen production, 59, 60

Lithographs, nineteenth-century
    popularity of, 38, 39

Lovejoy, Nathaniel F., 39, 212

Lucy Selina Furnace, Alleghany
    County, Va., 155, 161

Ludwig, Edward Albert, 212

Lydick, Cyrus J., 212

Lyle, Daniel, 80, 212

Lyle, Hugh Franklin, 162–63, 212

Lyle, John Blair, 38

Lyle, Juliet, portrait of, *37*

Lyle, Samuel, 79–80, 114, 115, 212

    furniture by, *79*

Lyle, William, 142, 212

Lynchburg, Va., market for
    Rockbridge County iron in,
    153–55, 158, 162

M

Mantels, *82, 83*

Marlboro ironworks, Frederick
    County, Va., 152, *153*

Marshall, Hugh, 177

Matheney, James F., 212

Mayburry, Thomas, 158, 213

Mays, Charles F., 213

Mays, James A., 213

McCaffrey, J. H., 213

McCaul, John R., 213

McClain, John, 99, 104, 213

McCluer, Halbert, 152, 156, 213

    ironwork by, *157*

McClung, William Henry, 85, 213

McCorkle, Henry, 214

McCorkle, John, 214

McCorkle, Rebecca McNut, 214

    whitework by, *67*

McCormick, Cyrus Hall, 35, 164–65,
    214

McCormick, Robert, 164–65, 214

McCown, James Larue, 214

McCown, John, 164, 165, 214

    ironwork by, *164, 165, 215*

McCown, Samuel, 214

McCoy, James M., 214

McCrory, Samuel, 214

McDowell, James, 34

McDowell, John, 33

McDowell, Thomas Preston, 164,
    214

McFarland, James, 214

McGilvary (cabinetmaker), 215

McGuffin, Hugh, 215

McMannus, George, 92, 215

Melville, Herman, 34

Mercer, Gideon, 60, 215

Middletown, Va., clockmaking in, 129

Milbert, Jacques Gerard, 215

Miley, Henry, 45, 48, 215

Miley, John W., 215

    sign by, *89*

    woodwork by, *126, 216*

Miley, Michael, 12, 45, *45,* 48, 216

    advertisement for, *1*

    photographs by, *10, 42–43, 48*

COLOPHON

This book was composed in Monotype Bulmer, based on the types cut by the Englishman William Martin and used by the printer William Bulmer (c. 1790). Martin, then working for George Nicol, bookseller to George III, joined Bulmer in 1790 at the Shakespeare Printing Office, established under the firm of W. Bulmer and Company. Together Bulmer and Martin produced fine editions that raised the standards of typography and printing in England. Their work included the nine-volume set of Boedell's *Shakespeare* (1792–1802), *The Poems of Goldsmith and Parnell* (1795), and *The Chase* by William Somerville (1796).

Martin's font combines beauty with functionality and anticipates the modern style of Bodoni while retaining qualities from the transitional style of Baskerville. This digital version of Bulmer, orginally released in 1994, was redrawn in the Monotype Drawing Office by Ron Carpenter. This font is largely based on a private version of Bulmer that Monotype cut in England for the Nonesuch Press in the early 1930s.